Lecture Notes in Computer Science   13977

Founding Editors

Gerhard Goos
Juris Hartmanis

The series Lecture Notes in Computer Science (LNCS), including its subseries Lecture Notes in Artificial Intelligence (LNAI) and Lecture Notes in Bioinformatics (LNBI), has established itself as a medium for the publication of new developments in computer science and information technology research, teaching, and education.

LNCS enjoys close cooperation with the computer science R & D community, the series counts many renowned academics among its volume editors and paper authors, and collaborates with prestigious societies. Its mission is to serve this international community by providing an invaluable service, mainly focused on the publication of conference and workshop proceedings and postproceedings. LNCS commenced publication in 1973.

Muhammad Younas · Irfan Awan ·
Tor-Morten Grønli

Editors

Mobile Web and Intelligent Information Systems

19th International Conference, MobiWIS 2023
Marrakech, Morocco, August 14–16, 2023
Proceedings

 Springer

Editors
Muhammad Younas
Oxford Brookes University
Oxford, UK

Irfan Awan
University of Bradford
Bradford, UK

Tor-Morten Grønli 🆔
Kristiania University College
Oslo, Norway

ISSN 0302-9743   ISSN 1611-3349 (electronic)
Lecture Notes in Computer Science
ISBN 978-3-031-39763-9   ISBN 978-3-031-39764-6 (eBook)
https://doi.org/10.1007/978-3-031-39764-6

This Springer imprint is published by the registered company Springer Nature Switzerland AG
The registered company address is: Gewerbestrasse 11, 6330 Cham, Switzerland

Preface

It was a great privilege to present to the authors and delegates the proceedings of the 19th International Conference on Mobile Web and Intelligent Information Systems (MobiWis 2023). The conference was held during 14—16 August 2023, in a hybrid mode. We were pleased that in addition to online presentations, the conference was held onsite in the historic city of Marrakech, Morocco. Marrakech, a former imperial city in Morocco, is one of the main economic centres and home to mosques, palaces and gardens. Marrakech attracts a large number of international visitors each year.

MobiWis 2023 provided an exciting forum for researchers, developers and practitioners for sharing ideas and discussing recent developments in areas of mobile web and intelligent information systems. The conference brought together academic and industry researchers, engineers and practitioners from different countries across the world in order to exchange ideas, experiences and research results and discuss future challenges in mobile web and intelligent information systems. The use of mobile devices is continuously increasing with more and more services moving towards mobile (network) services and handheld (mobile) devices. Though mobile networks and devices offer significant ease and flexibility in service provisioning and consumption, they pose complex research challenges, for instance: storing and managing data, maintaining security and privacy, performance and reliability of networks and communication media, user interfaces and interaction, designing and developing software applications for mobile devices and so on.

The conference program committee put together an exciting technical program which included papers on recent and emerging topics such as mobile augmented reality, deep learning in intelligent transportation, blockchain in environmental services, healthcare applications, IoT, SDN, edge and network modelling, user interaction and interfaces and other advanced applications such as urban data platforms, safety-critical systems, cash-on-delivery systems, career advisor systems and security aspects. Papers accepted for the conference came from academic research institutes and industry research.

This year the conference received a good number of quality submissions from authors from different countries across the world. Submitted papers were reviewed by multiple members of the technical program committee. A total of 18 papers were accepted for the conference, which represents a 33% acceptance rate of the submissions.

The success of this conference is truly attributed to the organizing and technical committee members who made serious efforts for the smooth running of the conference. We greatly appreciate all the committee members who have contributed their time and efforts to organize the conference. We were sincerely grateful to the Program Committee members who provided timely, constructive and balanced feedback to the authors. We were also thankful to the authors for their contributions to the conference.

We sincerely thank Stephan Böhm and Jamal Bentahar (General Co-Chairs), Filipe Portela (Workshop Coordinator), Irfan Awan (Publication Chair), Tan Saw Chin (Publicity Chair), Natalia Kryvinska (Special Issue Coordinator) and Abdeslam En-Nouaary, Youssef Iraqi and Ahmed Ratnani for their help and support.

We greatly appreciate the Springer LNCS team for their valuable support in the production of the conference proceedings.

August 2023   Muhammad Younas
Tor-Morten Grønli

Organization

General Co-chairs

Stephan Böhm — RheinMain University of Applied Sciences, Germany

Jamal Bentahar — Concordia University, Canada & Khalifa University, UAE

Program Co-chairs

Tor-Morten Grønli — Kristiania University College, Norway

Muhammad Younas — Oxford Brookes University, UK

Publication Chair

Irfan Awan — University of Bradford, UK

Local Organising Co-chairs

Abdeslam En-Nouaary — INPT, Morocco

Youssef Iraqi — UM6P, Morocco

Ahmed Ratnani — UM6P, Morocco

Journal Special Issue Coordinator

Natalia Kryvinska — Comenius University in Bratislava, Slovakia

Workshop Coordinator

Filipe Portela — University of Minho, Portugal

Publicity Chair

Tan Saw Chin   Multimedia University, Malaysia

Program Committee

Abdel Lisser	Université Paris Sud, France
Agnis Stibe	EM Normandie Business School, France
Anthony Wasserman	Carnegie Mellon University, USA
Apostolos Papadopoulos	Aristotle University of Thessaloniki, Greece
Christophe Feltus	Luxembourg Institute of Science and Technology, Luxembourg
Dan Johansson	Umeå University, Sweden
Dragan Stojanovic	University of Niš, Serbia
Fatma Abdennadher	National Engineering School of Sfax, Tunisia
Florence Sedes	Université Paul Sabatier, France
Inmaculada Medina Bulo	Universidad de Cádiz, Spain
Ismail Berrada	UM6P, Morocco
Ivan Demydov	Lviv Polytechnic National University, Ukraine
Jung-Chun Liu	Tunghai University, Taiwan
Katty Rohoden Jaramillo	Universidad Técnica Particular de Loja, Ecuador
Lalit Garg	University of Malta, Malta
Lech Madeyski	Wroclaw University of Technology, Poland
Lidia Ogiela	AGH University of Science and Technology, Poland
Loubna Mekouar	UM6P, Morocco
Ludger Martin	RheinMain University of Applied Sciences, Germany
Marek R. Ogiela	AGH University of Science and Technology, Poland
Maria Luisa Damiani	Universita degli Studi di Milano, Italy
Masahiro Sasabe	Nara Institute of Science and Technology, Japan
Mikko Rissanen	I2 Network LLC, USA
Mohamed Ben Aouicha	ENIS, Tunisia
Norazlina Khamis	Universiti Malaysia Sabah, Malaysia
Novia Admodisastro	Universiti Putra Malaysia, Malaysia
Ondrej Krejcar	University of Hradec Kralove, Czech Republic
Pablo Adasme	University of Santiago de Chile, Chile
Perin Unal	Middle East Technical University, Turkey
Philippe Roose	IUT de Bayonne, France
Pınar Kirci	Istanbul University, Turkey

Rabeb Mizouni	Khalifa University of Science and Technology, UAE
Rachida Dssouli	Concordia University, Canada
Raquel Trillo	University of Zaragoza, Spain
Riccardo Martoglia	University of Modena and Reggio Emilia, Italy
Sergio Ilarri	University of Zaragoza, Spain
Shinsaku Kiyomoto	KDDI R&D Laboratories Inc., Japan
Tacha Serif	Yeditepe University, Turkey
Thomas Barton	University of Applied Sciences, Worms, Germany
Vikram Bodicherla	Meta Labs, USA
Youssef Iraqi	UM6P, Morocco

Contents

Mobile Interfaces and Interactivity

Machine Learning and Stochastic Methods

Advanced Mobile Applications

Smart and Intelligent Systems

Factors Affecting Mobile Augmented Reality Acceptance: A Study on Traveler Information in Public Transport

Stefan Graser[1]([⊠]) [iD], Stephan Böhm[1] [iD], Daria Gütlich[2], and Melissa Bodtländer[3]

[1] CAEBUS Center of Advanced E-Business Studies, RheinMain University of Applied Sciences, Hesse, 65195 Wiesbaden, Germany
{stefan.graser, stephan.boehm}@hs-rm.de
[2] RheinMain University of Applied Sciences, Hesse, 65195 Wiesbaden, Germany
[3] DB Systel GmbH, Hesse, 60329 Frankfurt/Main, Germany
melissa.bodtlaender@deutschebahn.com

Abstract. Technological advances in mobile devices such as smartphones facilitate the development of innovative Mobile Augmented Reality (MAR) applications. Thus, investigating technology acceptance is a continuing concern in implementing new products for users. While little research in this field was carried out, no previous study has investigated the technology acceptance using MAR for traveler information in public transport. This article provides insights into the factors influencing the acceptance of MAR in this field. Therefore, a quantitative study was conducted in cooperation with *DB Systel*, the digital partner and IT subsidiary of the largest German railway operator *Deutsche Bahn*. The study applied a modified Technology Acceptance Model (TAM) referring to MAR technology. The data includes a total of 204 respondents. Overall, the empirical validity of the basic TAM was proven for the MAR studied. Among the four MAR-specific factors added to the model, the Perceived Value of Entertainment and Quality of Information showed the strongest significant influences on Perceived Usefulness. The hypothesis that the Subjective Smartphone Experience influences the Perceived Ease of Use of MAR was also statistically confirmed. However, the assumption that Perceived Visual Attractiveness positively affects the usefulness of the MAR and that Technology Affinity impacts Intention to Use were rejected.

Keywords: Technology Acceptance · Technology Acceptance Model (TAM) · Mobile Augmented Reality (MAR) · Public Transport

1 Introduction

Over the last decades, Augmented Reality (AR) as an emerging technology has spread to mass markets. AR gives users an impression of their natural environment, augmented with computer-generated digital content [1]. As mobile devices have evolved from mobile phones to small, high-performance multimedia computers with many sensors, most modern smartphones support AR applications [2]. In the following, Mobile Augmented Reality (MAR) is an AR application that can be used on a mobile device, typically

M. Younas et al. (Eds.): MobiWIS 2023, LNCS 13977, pp. 3–19, 2023.
https://doi.org/10.1007/978-3-031-39764-6_1

a smartphone or tablet connected to a mobile network [3]. Given the widespread use of smartphones and their always-on and ubiquitous use, MAR can be deployed in a wide range of application fields, such as public transport [4]. For example, MAR can support travelers in obtaining location-relevant information quickly and easily. The case study analyzed in our study is the orientation at train stations and finding the carriage of a seat reservation when at the platform. In addition to navigation at the station, this app could replace or supplement conventional displays. Moreover, it could provide other travel information or content related to the travelers' location at the station.

The company *DBSystel GmbH* is located in Germany and developed an app concept for MAR-based traveler information at the train platform. *DB Systel GmbH* is a subsidiary of *Deutsche Bahn (DB) AG*, the largest railway operator in Germany and the digital solution partner of the whole *DB* group [5]. As a primary field of activity, *DB Systel GmbH* develops and implements innovative technologies to support travelers. The MAR app was available in the first functional prototype for test users. While the prototype can be further developed in terms of usability and user experience based on the derived user feedback, the overriding question is whether such an app will be accepted by users and, in particular, what factors drive an intention to use it.

Technology acceptance research has developed to answer such questions concerning technical innovations. However, technology acceptance models for MAR rarely exist in the scientific literature. Furthermore, models analyzing acceptance factors of MAR apps for traveler information were not known to the authors when writing this study. Against this background, the present study attempts to answer two research questions:

- *RQ1: To what extent can technology acceptance research models explain acceptance factors of MAR apps for travelers?*
- *RQ2: Which MAR-specific factors are to be added to these models to reflect the particularities of the acceptance of the MAR app investigated?*

The paper is structured as follows: Section two describes the theoretical foundation regarding technology acceptance research. Furthermore, current research in the field of technology acceptance referring to MAR is determined in section three. Section four describes this study's methodological approach, including the research model and its empirical validation. The fifth section presents the results and a discussion. Finally, the paper closes with the conclusion and limitation in section six.

2 Theoretical Foundation

In general, the concept of acceptance describes the users' intention to use the object of acceptance in the designed way [6]. In the last three decades, various models have been developed to explain acceptance factors of innovative technologies and their relationships [7]. These include, for example, the Technology Acceptance Model (TAM) [8] with its extensions as well as the Unified Theory of Acceptance and Use of Technology UTAUT [9]. The TAM developed by Davis has been the most widely adopted acceptance model over the last decades [6, 8–11]. It is based on the Theories of Planned Behavior (TPB) [12] and Reasoned Action (TRA) [13] as the most important theoretical foundation. A basic TAM is shown in Fig. 1.

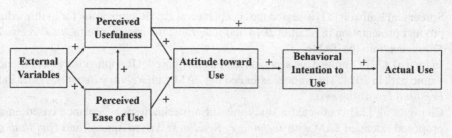

Fig. 1. The Technology Acceptance Model by Davis [8].

The fundamental assumption of the model is that the *Actual Use of a System* depends on the *Behavioral Intention*, which in turn is influenced by the *Attitude Toward Using* and *Perceived Usefulness*. The TAM consists of two core variables: *Perceived Usefulness*, which is "...*the degree to which a person believes that using a particular system would enhance his or her job performance*", and *Perceived Ease of Use*, which is defined as "...*the degree to which a person believes that using a particular system would be free of effort*" [8]. Both core variables affect the *Attitudes Toward Using* positively. In addition, *Perceived Ease of Use* influences *Perceived Usefulness*, whereas *Perceived Usefulness* impacts *Behavioral Intention to Use*. At least, the *External Variables* influence the core variables [8, 14]. The TAM has proven to be a robust and powerful scientific model [7, 10]. Parallel with its frequent use, the TAM was extended with additional variables resulting in TAM2 and TAM3 [15, 16].

3   Related Work

Several acceptance models have been applied to AR in recent years. Nevertheless, a rather rudimentary state of technology acceptance research on AR can be pointed out. For example, Graser and Böhm [17] identified 204 articles about AR acceptance research. Forty-five of these articles specified research models for measuring technology acceptance. The TAM was the most widely used acceptance model here. In addition, the authors identified 33 model extensions and, in total, 34 consolidated AR-specific variables. Concerning the application fields, most articles referred to training and education [17]. Within the identified AR papers, there were even fewer contributions addressing the acceptability of AR in mobile contexts. More precisely, only eleven studies referred to the TAM and its extensions related to MAR. These papers and, thus, the status quo on MAR acceptance research are described in the following:

- Haugstvedt and Krogstie [18] developed and evaluated a MAR application with historical photographs and information in 2012. The TAM was extended with the variable *Perceived Enjoyment*.
- Rese et al. conducted an acceptance study on the IKEA mobile catalog app in 2014 [19] and examined two marker-based and two markerless AR apps in 2017 [20]. Within these two studies, the TAM was extended with *Perceived Enjoyment* and *Perceived Informativeness*.

- Spreer and Kallweit [21] assessed the acceptance of an AR application for multimedia product presentation in retail in 2014 and integrated the acceptance factor *Perceived Enjoyment* into the TAM.
- Jung et al. [22] examined the acceptance of a GPS-based AR application at a touristic theme park in 2014. The authors extended the TAM with *Relative Benefits*, *Trust*, and *Personal Innovativeness*.
- Chung et al. [23] conducted a study measuring technology acceptance based on a proposed extended TAM with *Technology Readiness*, *Visual Appeal*, and *Facilitating Conditions* in 2015.
- Tom Dieck and Jung [24] presented an AR technology acceptance model for tourism in 2018. The TAM was extended with seven variables identified by a qualitative approach: *Information Quality*, *System Quality*, *Costs of Use*, *Recommendation*, *Personal Innovativeness*, *Risk*, and *Facilitating Conditions*.
- Schreiber [25] conducted another study on the IKEA place app. For this, the author 2020 designed and validated an extended research model using *Perceived Quality of Information*, *Perceived Value of Entertainment*, *Perceived Visual Attractiveness*, *Affinity of Technology*, and *Subjective Smartphone Experience*.
- Alvarez-Martín et al. [26] designed a MAR app for students' assistance in electrical engineering in 2021. They extended the TAM with *Subjective Norm*, *Technology Innovativeness*, and *Technology Optimism*.
- Koutromanos and Mikropoulos [27] developed a proposed Mobile Augmented Reality Acceptance Model applied in teaching and education. Their MARAM research model from 2021 contains the variables *Perceived Enjoyment*, *Facilitating Conditions*, *Perceived Relative Advantage*, and *Mobile Self-Efficacy*. The underlying model is again the TAM.
- Zheleva et al. [28] investigated the consumer's acceptance of an AR app whose purpose was to place 3D objects into a room. In their research model from 2021, *Perceived Enjoyment*, *Perceived Informativeness*, and *Product Type* extended a modified TAM.

The eleven articles can be categorized into three application fields: Five studies refer to trade and retail, four to cultural heritage and tourism, and two studies can be assigned to education. All of the MAR studies extended the TAM. In total, the MAR-specific model extensions can be consolidated into 23 variables. However, no MAR technology acceptance study could be found in the literature for the application field of public transport. Against this background, our study seeks to fill this research gap and investigate acceptance factors of a MAR app in public transportation.

4   Methodological Approach

4.1   Research Design and Data Collection

This study investigates acceptance factors on a MAR app concept for traveler information. The prototype provides the user with digital information within a train station and at the platform. *DBSystel* has already developed a functional prototype for orientation at a single train station in Germany. The app can navigate travelers within the train station and to the platforms. Moreover, the app can indicate where specific train sections and seats can be found once the train arrives, as well as information about the journey is displayed to the traveler. This app function can supplement and replace the conventional displays at the station. In later phases, this app could be integrated into the *DBNavigator* app, which is widespread in Germany and offers rail travelers a wide range of functions, including ticket purchasing.

Due to the current development stage, practical testing of the MAR app in a larger group of study participants was not an option. Therefore, we conducted the study as an online survey using a demo video explaining the MAR prototype. Parts of the video are illustrated in Fig. 2. The lack of user experience with the app prototype could be a study limitation. However, this limitation is not critical, as our study is yet to be concerned with the concrete implementation and its usability or user experience. Instead, our study intends to investigate more fundamental aspects of app acceptance within a larger group of potential users. For this purpose, the demo video provides a sufficient overview of the supported use cases.

Fig. 2. Demo video of the MAR application.

The sample is adapted to the specific research design. In particular, we conducted a convenience sample. The participants' age ranges from 14 to 65 years. This age group reflects groups with high smartphone use, which means they typically meet the technical requirements for using a MAR app for platform orientation. The study was accessible from 16.12.2022 until 09.01.2023 for three weeks. As DB Systel developed the app for the German market and the prototype was implemented in German, this study addresses a German-speaking target group. Participants were acquired starting from RhineMain University of Applied Sciences students, using DB Systel and social media channels. The study is, therefore, a convenience sample and not representative.

4.2 Research Model and Hypotheses

The existing research models on MAR in the literature were first reviewed to select an appropriate research model. We chose a modified version of Schreiber's extended and empirically validated TAM [25] from 2020. The model was chosen because, on the one hand, it represents specific factors for MAR that are important for public transportation but is not over-specified or overly focused on a particular use case.

The model consists of the core variables *Perceived Usefulness (PU)*, *Perceived Ease of Use (PEOU)*, *Attitude Toward Using (A)*, and *Behavioral Intention (BI)*. In addition, the original TAM provides the variable *Actual System Use*. However, since the acceptance object in the present study has yet to be available on the market, the actual use of the app cannot be measured. Thus, the acceptance in this study is reflected by the variable *Intention to Use*.

Furthermore, the original TAM is extended with five additional variables *Perceived Quality of Information*, *Perceived Value of Entertainment*, *Perceived Visual Attractiveness*, *Subjective Smartphone Experience*, and *Affinity for Technology* [25]. The model is illustrated in Fig. 3.

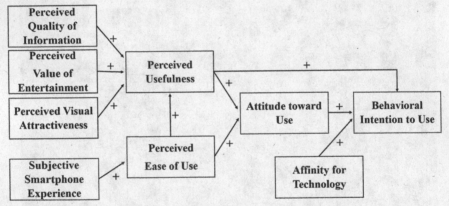

Fig. 3. Research model of this study based on Schreiber [25].

The variables of the model by Schreiber [25] extending the TAM and their relevance in the present study are explained below:

- *Perceived Quality of Information* can be traced back to the Information System Success Model by DeLone and McLean [29]. Here, high qualitative information is one of the success factors of information systems. The influence on technology acceptance was confirmed for the AR technology by Olsson et al. [30] and thus integrated into the MAR acceptance model by Schreiber [25]. In this study, the variable can be seen as the extent to which accurate, complete, and on-time traveler information is displayed via the MAR application.
- *Perceived Value of Entertainment* was first introduced in acceptance research by Davis et al. [31] and is described as the degree to which the technology is enjoyable or fun for the user. Previous research observed that this variable relates to MAR, especially

in unknown environments [25, 30, 32]. Hence, MAR can improve the orientation at a train station through entertainment value.

- *Perceived Visual Attractiveness* refers to the layout and visual graphics of the interface of a system, which is an essential component of the technology MAR [25, 33].
- *Subjective Smartphone Experience* is the previous knowledge and experience concerning the technology. Previous research has proven the influence of this factor on various technologies [16, 25, 34–36].
- *Affinity for Technology* is the last variable used in our model. It describes the type of personal innovativeness and the extent to which a person tends to apply a new technology earlier than others [37–40]. Rauschnabel and Ro confirmed this variable regarding AR [41].

The variable *Brand Loyalty* of the Schreiber [25] model was excluded from our research model. The first reason is that the app under investigation is a prototype yet to be competitively available on the market. In addition, there is limited competition in passenger rail transport in Germany, so specific brand loyalty is not relevant to the acceptance of the app in this use case.

The research model in Fig. 3 shows the variables considered and the relationships assumed and empirically validated by Schreiber [25]. Each link between two variables represents a hypothesis about an effect relationship and direction. The items were based on a seven-point Likert scale from 1 (strongly agree) to 7 (strongly disagree). All questions were taken from the questionnaires of the original models and adapted to the research design. An overview of all model variables and the associated hypotheses is compiled in Table 1. Moreover, this overview references the sources from which Schreiber [29] derived the corresponding variables and associated measurement items.

Table 1. Overview of the hypotheses.

Variable	Hypothesis	Source
Attitude Toward Use	H1: The Attitude Toward Use has a positive influence on the Intention to Use	[8]
Perceived Usefulness	H2a: The Perceived Usefulness has a positive influence on the Attitude Towards Use H2b: The Perceived Usefulness has a positive influence on the Intention to Use	[8]

(continued)

Table 1. (*continued*)

Variable	Hypothesis	Source
Perceived Ease of Use	H3a: The Perceived Ease of Use has a positive influence on the Perçeived Usefulness H3b: The Perceived Ease of Use has a positive influence on the Attitude Toward Use	[8]
Perceived Quality of Information	H4: The Perceived Quality of Information has a positive influence on the Perceived Usefulness	[29]
Perceived Value of Entertainment	H5: The Perceived Value of Entertainment has a positive influence on the Perceived Usefulness	[30–32]
Perceived Visual Attractiveness	H6: The Perceived Visual Attractiveness has a positive influence on the Perceived Usefulness	[25]
Subjective Smartphone Experience	H7: The Subjective Smartphone Experience has a positive influence on the Perceived Ease of Use	[25, 35, 36]
Affinity for Technology	H8: The Affinity for technology has a positive influence on the Intention to Use	[38–40]

5 Data Analysis and Results

A questionnaire was designed for empirical validation of the acceptance model. The questionnaire contained sections on the participants' demographics and general questions about rail travel, smartphone, and AR use. The core part of the questionnaire was based on the questions for the proposed acceptance model derived from the literature.

5.1 Demographics and Sample Characteristics

The survey was started 283 times and completed by 216 participants. This results in a completion rate of over 76%. In the next step, participants outside the defined age group or those who stated they did not own a smartphone were excluded from the sample. This resulted in an adjusted sample size of $N = 204$. The majority of 56% of the participants were male, whereas 41% were female. One participant stated to be diverse, and four respondents did not specify their gender. The participants were classified into age categories based on the following generation constructs: (1) Generation Z at the age of 14 to 27, (2) Generation Y at the age of 28 to 42, (3) Generation X at the age of 43 to 57, and (4) Babyboomer at the age of 58 to 65. Generation Z had the largest proportion, with 41%, followed by Generation Z, with 26%. The third largest proportion, with 20%, belonged to Generation Y, whereas the group Babyboomers only accounts for 13% in our study. The study thus predominantly reflects the situation in Generation Z. This fact can be attributed to how participants are recruited for the study—primarily via students at the university. However, the age group of Generation Z is well suited to the study, as their members are typically familiar with digital technologies and open to corresponding innovations.

In addition, some insights into the usage of MAR and applications for traveler information were derived. Ninety-two percent of those who travel via public transport indicated using mobile apps for traveler information; of these, 83% use the *DBNavigator* app of the *DB* group. Concerning MAR, 70% of the respondents have already used the technology, and 29% do not. Only one percent stated that they were not sure about this. Regarding the future use of MAR, only less than half, 49%, would use this technology. Twenty-six percent of the respondents do not tend to use MAR, whereas 25% are not sure about their future usage.

5.2 Empirical Validation of the Research Model

Partial least square structural equation modeling (PLS-SEM) was applied to validate the acceptance model empirically. The measurement and structural model were analyzed using the software SmartPLS 4.0 following the process of data analysis as proposed by Hair et al. [42].

Measurement Model Results Evaluation
We used the results provided by SmartPLS 4.0 to evaluate the measurement model based on the sample data to confirm the validity and reliability. In the following, the composite reliability (rho_a and rho_c) and Cronbach's Alpha for internal consistency reliability, AVE for the convergent validity, and the Fornell-Larcker criterion, as well as the cross-loadings for the discriminant validity, are examined. The following procedure was taken from Hair et al. [42] as recommended for (reflective) measurement model evaluation.

For convergent validity, it must be examined if all indicator loadings of the measurement items are above the critical value of 0.708. High loadings indicate a high item similarity whereas a low value indicates that the item does not suit the construct very well. This criterion is satisfied for our model for all items except AFT4, which represents the question: *"With regard to cell phone and computer technology I am very often asked for advice"*. Nevertheless, the ATF4 loading of 0.667 is in the recommended range above 0.4 and close to 0.7. Thus, deletion of the indicator is not necessary but can be considered if, for example, the composite reliability can be improved. After the deletion of AFT4, the value of rho_c increased from 0.923 to 0.948. Additionally, Cronbach's Alpha increased from 0.895 to 0.919. This shows that the deletion of AFT4 increases the internal consistency of the variable Affinity for Technology. Thus, AFT4 was deleted for further measurement.

Cronbach's Alpha measures internal consistency reliability. All values are greater than 0.7 and can be considered satisfactory. However, it must be stated that Cronbach's Alpha values of the variables BI, ATU, PEOU, PVE, and PVA are above 0.9, which indicates a similarity of the questions. However, the values are below 0.95 and thus not desirable but acceptable.

Next, the average variance extracted (AVE) was examined to verify the convergent validity. All values are greater than 0.5 and thus indicate convergent validity. The discussed results of the tests are summarized in Table 2.

Table 2. Convergent validity and internal consistency reliability of the measurement model.

Variable	Indicator	Loadings	AVE	Composite Reliability (rho_a)	Composite Reliability (rho_c)	Cronbach's Alpha
BI	BI1	0.924	0.808	0.946	0.955	0.940
	BI2	0.858				
	BI3	0.880				
	BI4	0.911				
	BI5	0.919				
ATU	ATU1	0.903	0.800	0.939	0.952	0.937
	ATU2	0.891				
	ATU3	0.907				
	ATU4	0.932				
	ATU5	0.835				
PU	PU1	0.885	0.766	0.855	0.907	0.846
	PU2	0.914				
	PU3	0.824				
PEOU	PEOU1	0.886	0.776	0.904	0.933	0.903
	PEOU2	0.890				
	PEOU3	0.896				
	PEOU4	0.850				
PQI	PQI1	0.861	0.757	0.843	0.904	0.840
	PQI2	0.897				
	PQI3	0.853				
PVE	PVE1	0.864	0.789	0.915	0.937	0.911
	PVE2	0.900				
	PVE3	0.901				
	PVE4	0.887				
PVA	PVA1	0.932	0.811	0.923	0.945	0.922
	PVA2	0.902				
	PVA3	0.884				

(continued)

Table 2. (*continued*)

Variable	Indicator	Loadings	AVE	Composite Reliability (rho_a)	Composite Reliability (rho_c)	Cronbach's Alpha
	PVA4	0.885				
AFT	AFT1	0.924	0.860	0.932	0.948	0.919
	AFT2	0.939				
	AFT3	0.918				
SSE	SSE1	0.873	0.705	0.808	0.878	0.793
	SSE2	0.833				
	SSE3	0.813				

For discriminant validity assessment, we analyzed two measures. First, the outer loadings were taken into account in relation to their cross-loadings. The outer loadings of a construct should be greater than their cross-loadings. This criterion could be confirmed (the cross-loadings are not shown due to space limitations). Second, the Fornell-Lacker criterion was performed. According to this criterion, the AVE of a construct should exceed the correlation to all other constructs. Table 3 shows that this criterion is also fulfilled.

Table 3. Fornell-Larcker criterion analysis.

	BI	ATU	PU	PEOU	PQI	PVE	PVA	AFT	SSE
BI	**0.899**								
ATU	0.841	**0.894**							
PU	0.774	0.864	**0.875**						
PEOU	0.545	0.633	0.632	**0.881**					
PQI	0.524	0.646	0.666	0.609	**0.870**				
PVE	0.748	0.807	0.737	0.630	0.600	**0.888**			
PVA	0.603	0.694	0.639	0.624	0.650	0.743	**0.901**		
AFT	0.312	0.345	0.301	0.230	0.234	0.208	0.234	**0.868**	
SSE	0.497	0.273	0.253	0.339	0.304	0.217	0.281	0.497	**0.840**

The discriminant validity of the measurement model can be confirmed by the two criteria. In summary, the reliability and validity of our research model can be confirmed.

Structural Model Results Evaluation

In the second step, we assessed the key criteria of the structural model. In particular, we calculated the VIF to measure the collinearity. All values are in the required range between 0.2 and 5 predicting a moderate multi-collinearity between the independent variables and high model accuracy. We applied bootstrapping to examine the t-value and p-value for the significance of the path coefficients. The two-tailed test was performed with a recommended total of 5,000 bootstrap samples and a significance level of 5% [42]. As shown in Table 4, all relationships are considered significant except for two. Perceived Visual Attractiveness (PVA) does not show a significant relationship with Perceived Usefulness (PU). This also refers to the relationship between Affinity for Technology (AFT) and Behavioral Intention to Use (BI). All values including the path coefficients are illustrated in Table 4.

Table 4. Significance testing results.

Interdependencies	path coefficients	VIF	t-value	p-value	Significance (p < 0.05 = * p < 0.01 = **)
Perceived Quality of Information → Perceived Usefulness	0.286	1.999	3.817	0.000	Yes**
Perceived Value of Entertainment → Perceived Usefulness	0.451	2.529	5.819	0.000	Yes**
Perceived Visual Attractiveness → Perceived Usefulness	0.015	2.705	0.172	0.864	No
Subjective Smartphone Experience → Perceived Ease of Use	0.339	1.000	4.681	0.000	Yes**
Perceived Ease of Use  Perceived Usefulness	0.164	1.991	2.556	0.011	Yes*
Perceived Usefulness → Attitude Toward Use	0.773	1.664	18.828	0.000	Yes**
Perceived Ease of Use → Attitude Toward Use	0.144	1.664	2.752	0.006	Yes**
Perceived Usefulness → Behavioral Intention to Use	0.184	3.957	2.166	0.030	Yes*
Attitude Toward Use → Behavioral Intention to Use	0.670	4.082	8.360	0.000	Yes**
Affinity for Technology → Behavioral Intention to Use	0.032	1.140	0.802	0.423	No

To sum up, the external variables Perceived Quality of Information and Perceived Value of Entertainment show a significant positive influence on Perceived Usefulness. Subjective Smartphone Experience influences Perceived Ease of Use significantly. In contrast, Perceived Visual Attractiveness and Affinity for Technology did not indicate an important impact on them. Moreover, both Perceived Usefulness and Perceived Ease of Use indicate to lead to an increased behavioral Intention to use MAR technology. In Fig. 4, the structural model with the different path coefficients is illustrated.

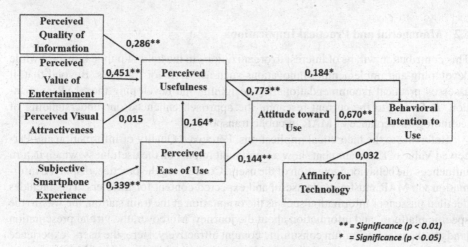

** = Significance (p < 0.01)
* = Significance (p < 0.05)

Fig. 4. Applied Structural model.

6   Conclusion and Limitation

The main goal of the current study was to determine the technology acceptance of MAR applications for traveler information in public transport. Therefore, this research is among the first study to examine the technology acceptance of MAR in this application field. A quantitative study assigning a modified research model based on the TAM referring to MAR technology was applied. The core variables of the TAM were extended with five independent variables. This study considers important implications for theory and practice referring to MAR technology.

6.1   Theoretical Implications

PLS-SEM analysis was applied to find the relation between influencing factors and the usage of MAR technology in public transport. Against this background, the research questions could be answered. Results revealed that the applied research model relying on a modified TAM by Schreiber [25] is a valid measurement model for the technology acceptance of MAR. The research model was extended with five external variables. Three of five external variables significantly influence technology acceptance.

Perceived Quality of Information, Perceived Value of Entertainment, and Subjective Smartphone Experience indicate to be positively influencing external factors whereas Perceived Visual Attractiveness and Affinity for Technology do not have a significant impact. This study also confirms previous research, as Perceived Usefulness and Perceived Ease of Use are important for technology acceptance [29, 30, 32]. In summary, eight out of ten hypotheses could be confirmed. This study contributes to the theoretical understanding of influencing factors of technology acceptance of MAR applications in the specific field of public transport.

6.2   Managerial and Practical Implications

This contribution will be of interest to organizations in the field of public transport while developing and implementing innovations such as MAR for travelers. Beyond that, it assesses practical recommendations for designing and developing the MAR application. Referring to the current research, the approach enhanced our understanding of technology acceptance of MAR in public transport.

Referring to the theoretical implications, Perceived Quality of Information and Perceived Value of Entertainment show a significant impact on the usefulness, which in turn influences the behavioral intention of the users. Concerning the practice, displayed information via MAR must provide useful and expected content for travelers. This includes detailed passenger information such as the orientation at the train station, the way to the specific platform, and information about the journey. Moreover, the virtual presentation leads to the user having fun consuming content attractively. Here, the users' experience with the smartphone facilitates the use. Nevertheless, the introduction of MAR to travelers is important. Travelers must recognize the benefit of using MAR. These results must be taken into account during development.

However, in relation to the second research question, the study also shows, that only about half of all users would use the MAR application at present. Previous research revealed, that the usage of MAR apps is often still driven by curiosity [43]. This indicates that the benefit of the MAR application must be pointed out to encourage travelers to use it. In particular, the added value of MAR must be addressed.

6.3   Limitations and Future Research

In interpreting the results, some limitations must be considered. One study limitation is the sample size. Even though a total sample size of 204 was conducted, most of the respondents refer to generation Z between the age between 14 and 27. Moreover, this can be traced back to the fact that the survey was distributed via Social Media. Especially Social Media channels are most likely to represent this group. By implication, a follow-up study with a larger sample could be performed. Furthermore, the lack of user experience concerning the prototype must be mentioned. A demo video describing the prototype lacks practical experience. The actual use can only be assumed by the sample. Hence, users' perception is limited. For further studies, practical testing should be ensured. In addition, the applied acceptance model was developed for MAR, but for the field of retail and trade. Other influencing factors must be taken into account to assess whether they are more suitable for this specific application field or not.

However, technology acceptance research concerning MAR as well as the application of the technology in this specific application field still lacks research. Considerably we recommend doing more work on both aspects to gather further insights about users' perceptions. This helps to develop and design user-centered applications, which in turn is necessary for the introduction and adoption of new technologies.

References

1. Azuma, R.T.: A survey of augmented reality. Presence: Teleop. Virtual Environ. **6**(4), 355–385 (1997)
2. Irshad, S., Rambli, D.R.A.: Advances in mobile augmented reality from user experience perspective: a review of studies. In: Zaman, H.B., et al. (eds.) IVIC 2017. LNCS, vol. 10645, pp. 466–477. Springer, Cham (2017). https://doi.org/10.1007/978-3-319-70010-6_43
3. Dirin, A., Laine, T.H.: User experience in mobile augmented reality: emotions, challenges, opportunities and best practices. Computers **7**(2), 33 (2018). pp. 1–18
4. Chatzopoulos, D., Bermejo, C., Huang, Z., Hui, P.: Mobile augmented reality survey: from where we are to where we go. IEEE Access **5**, 6917–6950 (2017)
5. DB Systel: Strong rail needs a strong digital partner (2023). https://www.dbsystel.de/dbsystel-en/about-us/profile-3714990. Accessed March 2023
6. Legris, P., Ingham, J., Collerette, P.: Why do people use information technology? A critical review of the technology acceptance model. Inf. Manage. **40**(3), 191–204 (2003)
7. Taherdoost, H.: A review of technology acceptance and adoption models and theories. Procedia Manuf. **22**, 960–967 (2018)
8. Davis, F.D.: A technology acceptance model for empirically testing new end-user information systems: theory and results (1986)
9. Venkatesh, V., Morris, M.G., Davis, G.B., Davis, F.D.: User acceptance of information technology: toward a unified view. MIS Q. **27**(3), 425–478 (2003)
10. Yousafzai, S.Y., Foxall, G.R., Pallister, J.G.: Technology acceptance: a meta-analysis of the TAM: part 1. J. Modell. Manage. **2**(3), 251–280 (2007)
11. Marangunić, N., Granić, A.: Technology acceptance model: a literature review from 1986 to 2013. Univ. Access Inf. Soc. **14**(1), 81–95 (2014). https://doi.org/10.1007/s10209-014-0348-1
12. Ajzen, I.: From intentions to actions: a theory of planned behavior. In: Kuhl, J., Beckmann J. (eds.) Action Control. SSSP Springer Series in Social Psychology, pp. 11–39. Springer, New York (1985). https://doi.org/10.1007/978-3-642-69746-3_2
13. Fishbein, M., Ajzen, I.: Belief, Attitude, Intention and Behavior: An Introduction to Theory and Research. Addison-Wesley, MA (1975)
14. Davis, F.D.: Perceived usefulness, perceived ease of use, and user acceptance of information technology. MIS Q. **13**(3), 319–340 (1989)
15. Venkatesh, V., Davis, F.D.: A Theoretical extension of the technology acceptance model: four longitudinal field studies. Manage. Sci. **46**(2), 186–204 (2000)
16. Venkatesh, V., Bala, H.: Technology acceptance model 3 and a research agenda on interventions. Decis. Sci. **39**(2), 273–315 (2008)
17. Graser, S., Böhm, S.: A systematic literature review on technology acceptance research on augmented reality in the field of training and education. In: Centric 2022, The Fifteenth International Conference on Advances in Human-Oriented and Personalized Mechanisms, Technologies, and Services, Lisbon, Portugal, vol. 12, pp. 20–28 (2022)
18. Haugstvedt, A., Krogstie, J.: Mobile augmented reality for cultural heritage: a technology acceptance study. In: IEEE International Symposium on Mixed and Augmented Reality (ISMAR), pp. 247–255 (2012)

19. Rese, A., Schreiber, S., Baier, D.: Technology acceptance modeling of augmented reality at the point of sale: can surveys be replaced by an analysis of online reviews? J. Retail. Consum. Serv. **21**, 869–876 (2014)
20. Rese, A., Baier, D., Geyer-Schulz, A., Schreiber, S.: How augmented reality apps are accepted by consumers: a comparative analysis using scales and opinions. Technol. Forecast. Soc. Chang. **124**, 306–319 (2017)
21. Spreer, P., Kallweit, K.: Augmented reality in retail: assessing the acceptance and potential for multimedia product presentation at the PoS (2014)
22. Jung, T.H., Kim, M., Dieck, M.C.: Acceptance of GPS-based augmented reality tourism applications (2014)
23. Chung, N., Han, H., Joun, Y.: Tourists' intention to visit a destination: the role of augmented reality (AR) application for a heritage site. Comput. Hum. Behav. **50**, 588–599 (2015)
24. tom Dieck, M.C., Jung, T.H.: A theoretical model of mobile augmented reality acceptance in urban heritage tourism. Curr. Issues Tour. **21**, 154–174 (2018)
25. Schreiber, S.: Augmented-reality-anwendungen im handel. In: Schreiber, S. (ed.) Die Akzeptanz von Augmented-Reality-Anwendungen im Handel. Forschungsgruppe Konsum und Verhalten, pp. 11–57. Springer Gabler, Wiesbaden. (2020). https://doi.org/10.1007/978-3-658-29163-1_2
26. Álvarez-Marín, A., Velázquez-Iturbide, J.Á., Castillo-Vergara, M.: Technology acceptance of an interactive augmented reality app on resistive circuits for engineering students. Electronics **10**(11), 1286 (2021)
27. Koutromanos, G., Mikropoulos, T.: Mobile augmented reality applications in teaching: a proposed technology acceptance model. In: 2021 7th International Conference of the Immersive Learning Research Network (iLRN), pp. 1–8 (2021)
28. Zheleva, A., Smink, A.R., Vettehen, P.H., Ketelaar, P.: Modifying the technology acceptance model to investigate behavioural intention to use augmented reality. In: tom Dieck, M.C., Jung, T.H., Loureiro, S.M.C. (eds.) Augmented Reality and Virtual Reality. PI, pp. 125–137. Springer, Cham (2021). https://doi.org/10.1007/978-3-030-68086-2_10
29. Delone, W.H., McLean, E.R.: Information systems success: the quest for the dependent variable. J. Manage. Inf. Syst. **3**, 60–95 (1992)
30. Olsson, T., Kärkkäinen, T., Lagerstam, E., Ventä-Olkkonen, L.: User evaluation of mobile augmented reality scenarios. J. Ambient Intell. Smart Environ. **4**(1), 29–47 (2012)
31. Davis, F.D., Bagozzi, R.P., Warshaw, P.R.: Extrinsic and intrinsic motivation to use computers in the workplace1. J. Appl. Soc. Psychol. **22**(14), 1111–1132 (1992)
32. Olsson, T., Lagerstam, E., Kärkkäinen, T., Väänänen-Vainio-Mattila, K.: Expected user experience of mobile augmented reality services: a user study in the context of shopping centres. Pers. Ubiquit. Comput. **17**(2), 287–304 (2013)
33. Parboteeah, D.V., Valacich, J.S., Wells, J.D.: The influence of website characteristics on a consumer's urge to buy impulsively. Inf. Syst. Res. **20**(1), 60–78 (2008)
34. Kim, D.-Y., Park, J., Morrison, A.M.: A model of traveller acceptance of mobile technology. Int. J. Tour. Res. **10**(5), 393–407 (2008)
35. Karahanna, E., Straub, D.W., Chervany, N.L.: Information technology adoption across time: a cross-sectional comparison of pre-adoption and post-adoption beliefs. MIS Q. **23**, 183–213 (1999)
36. Venkatesh, V., Morris, M.G.: Why don't men ever stop to ask for directions? gender, social influence, and their role in technology acceptance and usage behavior. WGSRN: Gender Equality (2000)
37. Parasuraman, A.: Technology readiness index (Tri). J. Serv. Res. **2**(4), 307–320 (2000)
38. Agarwal, R., Prasad, J.: The role of innovation characteristics and perceived voluntariness in the acceptance of information technologies. Decis. Sci. **28**, 557–582 (1997)

39. Agarwal, R., Prasad, J.: The antecedents and consequents of user perceptions in information technology adoption. Decis. Support Syst. **22**, 15–29 (1998)
40. Agarwal, R., Prasad, J.: A conceptual and operational definition of personal innovativeness in the domain of information technology. Inf. Syst. Res. **9**, 204–215 (1998)
41. Rauschnabel, P.A., Ro, Y.K.: Augmented reality smart glasses: an investigation of technology acceptance drivers (2016)
42. Hair, J.F., Hult, G.T.M, Ringle, C.M., Sarstedt, M.: A Primer on Partial Least Squares Structural Equation Modeling (PLS-SEM), vol. 2. SAGE (2017)
43. Graser, S., Nielsen, L. H., Böhm, S.: Factors influencing the user experience of mobile augmented reality apps: an analysis of user feedback based on app store user reviews. In: Digital Media Transformation and Disruption (2023)

RSITS: Road Safety Intelligent Transport System in Deep Federated Learning Assisted Fog Cloud Networks

Tor-Morten Grønli[1], Abdullah Lakhan[1(✉)], and Muhammad Younas[2(✉)]

[1] Mobile Technology Lab (MOTEL), Department of Technology,
Kristiania University College, Kirkegata 24-26, 0153 Oslo, Norway
{Tor-Morten.Gronli,abdullah.lakhan}@kristiania.no
[2] School of Engineering, Computing and Mathematics, Oxford Brookes University,
Oxford, UK
m.younas@brookes.ac.uk

Abstract. This paper presents the road safety intelligent transport system (RSITS) based on deep federated learning-assisted fog cloud networks. RSITS offers mobile LiDAR sensors and vehicle LiDAR sensors-enabled applications to alert road safety mechanisms. To deal with the complex features of road safety, we trained the large pedestrian and vehicle detection dataset on different road safety fog servers and aggregated them on the centralized cloud. To ensure that constraints such as safety, the accuracy of alarms, response times, security, and deadlines are met, we present a deep federated learning scheduling scheme (DFLSS) that consists of different components: Initially, we bound all applications so that emergency tasks, such as moving an object within 5 m, should be processed locally with the minimum response time. Due to resource constraints and the limitations of devices, other tasks of applications are offloaded to the centralized cloud for processing. To ensure security, each computing node must encrypt and decrypt data before offloading and processing it in DFLSS. Simulation results show that the proposed DFLSS outperformed all existing approaches regarding accuracy, response time, and road safety application deadlines.

Keywords: Road Safety · Intelligent Transport System · Mobile and Vehicle Applications · Fog Computing · Cloud Computing

1 Introduction

In smart cities, the frequency of traffic collisions has been rising daily. More than half of all traffic-related deaths and injuries happen to people on the road due to public transportation. For instance, trams, buses, train passengers, cyclists, and motorcyclists. Most of the time, pedestrians use these modes of transportation while moving around smart cities and suffer different injuries during road accidents. According to the World Health Organization report published in 2018–2022, 1.3 million people died due to public transport accidents, and 30 to 50

M. Younas et al. (Eds.): MobiWIS 2023, LNCS 13977, pp. 20–37, 2023.
https://doi.org/10.1007/978-3-031-39764-6_2

million were injured [1]. But in these countries, the traffic systems on the roads are made up of sensors, cameras, and servers spread out. The goal is to detect objects, monitor the speed of the vehicles, and capture images of pedestrians from different angles on the roadside unit. There are tried-and-true ways to lower the risk of accidents and fatalities, and the Sustainable Development Plan 2023–2050 has set ambitious goals for reducing injuries from traffic accidents. For safer roads, [2] proposes an intelligent transport system (ITS) based on the Internet of Things. The goal is to detect vehicles' speed and alert them about objects to reduce accidents on the roads. In order to detect vehicle location and distance between pedestrians, the ITS system is presented in [3]. The automated traffic flow prediction based on artificial techniques is presented in [4]. The vehicle speed and driving pattern enabled ITS as presented in [5]. The microservices, 6G-enabled wireless communication, and vehicle- and pedestrian-enabled ITS are suggested in citer00000. These ITS consisted of different sensors, cameras, and servers, problems with traffic congestion in smart cities and rural areas, and improved road safety services [6]. But the suggested changes to traffic infrastructure haven't made a big difference in the number of people injured or eradicated in car accidents [7]. Also, these traffic deaths happened because different types of public transportation were going too fast, and pedestrians and motorcyclists moved without attention on the roads.

This study presents secure pedestrian and vehicle collision avoidance road safety intelligent transport system (RSITS) in deep reinforcement learning assisted fog networks. The paper makes the following contributions to the research questions. To address all questions mentioned above, this study presents secure pedestrian and vehicle collision avoidance by Road Safety Intelligent Transport Systems (RSITS) in deep reinforcement learning assisted fog networks. The paper makes the following contributions to the research questions.

- The study presents the RSITS, which offers mobile LiDAR sensors and vehicle LiDAR sensor-enabled applications to alert road safety mechanisms. To deal with the complex features of road safety, we trained the large pedestrian and vehicle detection dataset on different road safety fog servers and aggregated them on the centralized cloud.
- We have collected different dataset images of different public transport modes, vehicles, pedestrians, and routes, about 500000 images. We named this dataset the Road Safety Dataset (RS-Dataset). We divided the road safety dataset into sub-datasets and trained and validated them on different servers. These sub-datasets have pre-trained and real-time images in the proposed RSITS.
- We are considering different constraints such as security, deadline, response time, and an accurate safety alarm. So, we developed the deep federated learning scheduling scheme (DFLSS) to execute all applications based on the earlier constraints.
- We present a research product-based simulation tool with source code and a dataset for researchers to further analyze and develop road safety in smart cities.

The manuscript is organized in the following way. Section 2 discusses intelligent transport systems for road safety and their methods. Section 3 discusses the RSITS and mathematical model. Section 4 elaborates on the DFLSS algorithmic framework and its components. Section 5 shows the simulation part and discusses the implementation, dataset, and result analysis. Section 6 is about the conclusion and future work.

2   Related Work

We divided RSITS into applications, datasets, and methods in the related work studies. This prior work [8] presented the MuSLi: A multi-sensor LiDAR detection for Cloud-enabled vehicle to infrastructure (V2X) networks. The objective is to detect vehicles near 3 m to avoid any collision in distributed fog cloud networks. The primary objective is to design pedestrian and vehicle detection safety systems based on data from vision sensors [9]. There have been many attempts to make real-time algorithms that can find pedestrians and vehicles on the road quickly and accurately. Deep learning is the essential technology for using vision sensors on a roadside unit in a city to find pedestrian and vehicle objects [10]. The single-shot, multi-box [11], and faster region-enabled convolutional neural network-assisted [12] schemes were better at finding pedestrians and vehicles on the road. But these deep learning methods use much more power and resources and have many more parameters that must be tuned for computation. Therefore, deploying these methods on resource-constrained mobile devices and embedding gadgets takes a lot of work. So, statistically enabled feature-assisted object detection processes use more periodic resources and work well on mobile and gadget devices with limited resources [13].

Decentralized federated learning for road user classification in enhanced vehicle and infrastrucuture based on fog cloud networks is presented in [14]. In smart cities, vehicle and pedestrian real-time and training data become very large in velocity and size. Thus, work [15] presented a federated learning ITS for road safety problems in which security and processing delays were considered. A road service-enabled system based on edge fog cloud computing is presented in [16]. These services determined traffic prediction, vehicle detection, and pedestrian availability. Fog cloud-enabled road safety system based on secure Internet of Things (IoT) LiDAR sensors for vehicle speed, pedestrians, and other objects presented in [17–19].

To ensure security, these studies [20–24] suggested a different safety system by using the secure IoT and Internet of Vehicles (IoV) infrastructure to process vehicle and pedestrian image data in a fog cloud network. These studies optimized energy and security constraints based on deep learning methods. The data from the LiDAR and beacon sensors are also looked at to find and handle the transport data.

3   Proposed System

The study presents the RSITS based on the deep federated learning fog cloud network consisting of different components, as shown in Fig. 1. RSITS integrates different fog and cloud servers in distributed roadside units. Each fog cloud server cooperates and shares trained and secure data with the centralized cloud server. Different fog servers offer different services, such as pedestrian detection, vehicle detection, speed detection, route finding, safety alarms, and non-vehicle detection. RSITS integrated different sensors, such as LiDAR (e.g., mobile and vehicle devices), traffic, and wireless sensors. These sensors collect information about vehicles and pedestrians at the roadside unit. We trained the road safety dataset on different fog nodes and shared it with the central server for further analysis and decision-making. We have collected the route data from Reuters data source [25]. Different vehicles have different routes and are shown in different colors. The yellow line shows cars in smart cities as being on Route 1. The red, blue, and green lines show bus and tram routes in the smart city as Routes 2, 3, and 4. All routes are parts of the dataset, and we divided the dataset into subparts and trained them on different fog nodes optimally and efficiently over time. We trained the sub-datasets on different fog nodes based on deep federated learning schemes. All the considered vehicles and pedestrians offload and access data via various wireless networks (ws) in the smart city networks. In RSITS, each vehicle and mobile device has a LiDAR sensor. We designed the two

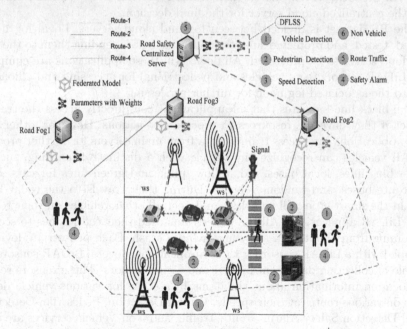

Fig. 1. RSITS: Road safety Intelligent Transport System in Deep Reinforcement Learning Assisted Fog Networks.

road safety applications, where applications can detect vehicles and pedestrians near and away from users. The progress of automated driving depends on these sensors. A laser LiDAR sensor that meets the standards for quality and safety set out by the transportation industry. In smart cities, LiDAR sensors help determine speed and distance, find a route, and handle traffic when people travel around the city. The study presents the DFLSS in the proposed architecture. The primary objective is to avoid collisions and detect objects with higher accuracy and an efficient response time for all services.

3.1 RSITS Dataset and Applications

The study discussed vehicle and pedestrian detection safety applications in RSITS with the different scenarios, as shown in Fig. 2. The mobile and vehicle applications are designed based on socket programming [26]. The socket has two main components: a client and a server socket. The client socket is integrated into the mobile and vehicle devices, and the server socket is integrated into the fog and cloud nodes for the execution flow of applications. The client and server socket can communicate via the common runtime environment (X86). We divided the dataset among different fog servers. For instance, we trained trams, local buses, long-route buses, cars, and random vehicles at different servers. In smart city networks, the goal is to improve training efficiency and lower the risk of resource shortages and slow response times when people call and get service data. All the local servers shared their trained and validated local sub-datasets with the centralized cloud server for the final decision.

The RS dataset is divided between fog and cloud servers. Local fog nodes trained, tested, and protected subsets of datasets before sending them to the central cloud server to be processed. All devices in these applications are equipped with LiDAR sensors (e.g., vehicles and pedestrians) for accessing and offloading data to the associated fog node for further processing.

The black line indicates that all applications can directly access the trained dataset if they have the resources to process any actions. However, otherwise, these applications can access trained data from main servers for further processing. All vehicles can recognize any vehicle with a distinctive marking, such as trams, blue lines, local buses, red, yellow, pink, and green lines for cars, local long-route buses, and random vehicles. During their travels to the radar locations in the smart cities, all vehicles can detect all other vehicles on their routes using LiDAR applications. All the pedestrians used their cell phones to see the car coming from about 30 m away and avoid a crash. Each pedestrian device is equipped with a LiDAR sensor for these applications. Several LiDAR sensors are capable of collecting data from LiDAR and signal sensors. These sensors record 3-D location information about the items in a scene for various vehicle detection's on various routes at their speeds. Vehicle Detection, Pedestrian Detection, Speed Detection Safety Alarm, Route Traffic, and Non-Vehicle services are integrated into both applications. These services data can be accessed through the smart city's wireless network (ws) during the flow of applications.

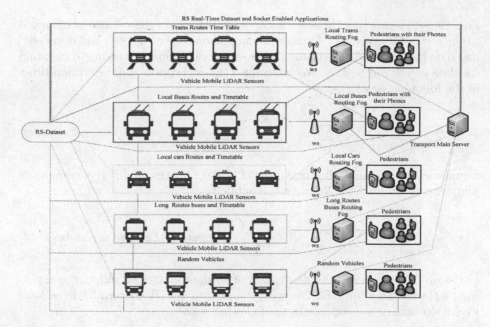

Fig. 2. Scenario:RSITS with Different Cases.

3.2   RSITS Problem Formulation

In this paper, the study considered the K number of computing nodes, e.g., $\{k = 1, \ldots, K\}$ where each node k has computing speed and resource capability ζ_k, ϵ_k, respectively. Each node k offers different road safety services, e.g., $\{j = 1, \ldots, J\}$. We assumed D is the road-safety dataset and divided it into sub-datasets, e.g., $\{d = 1, \ldots, D\}$. Each dataset consisted of different features, e.g., $\{f = 1, \ldots, F \in d\}$. The study considered A number of road safety applications. The application a consisted of T number of tasks, e.g., $\{t = 1, \ldots, T\}$ Each t consisted of different attributes, e.g., data d, deadline d_t, status s_t and required service t_j. The number of pedestrian users devices U and the number of vehicles devices V can exploit applications $a1, a2 \in A$ and following computing capability, e.g., $\zeta_u, \zeta_v \epsilon_u, \epsilon_v$. We show the user and vehicle-generated data in the following way, e.g., $i \in I, m \in M$.

We assumed that the trained dataset could be downloaded to mobile devices and vehicles for application usage locally. We determined the local assignment on pedestrian devices in the following.

$$x_{u,t,d,f,j} = \begin{cases} x_{u,t,d,f,j} = 0, local \\ x_{u,t,d,f,j} = 1, Offload \end{cases} \tag{1}$$

Equation (1) shows that the services can be run locally on the mobile or offloaded to the server for execution.

$$y_{v,t,d,f,j} = \begin{cases} y_{v,t,d,f,j} = 0, local \\ y_{v,t,d,f,j} = 1, Offload \end{cases} \tag{2}$$

Equation (2) shows that the services can be run locally in the vehicles or offloaded to the server for execution. Each data image should be encrypted and decrypted based on the AES-256 algorithm [27] in every node during processing to maintain the data security in RSITS. We determined the encryption and decryption times in the following way.

$$Enc = \sum_{a=1}^{A} \sum_{t=1,j=1}^{T,J} \sum_{i=1,m=1}^{I,M} \sum_{d=1,f=1}^{D,F} \sum_{u=1,v=1,k=1}^{U,V,K} EncryptionAES - 256(i, m, u, v, k, publickey)$$

(3)

Equation (3) determines the encryption of all data images on different computing platforms based on AES-256 with the public key.

$$Dec = \sum_{a=1}^{A} \sum_{t=1,j=1}^{T,J} \sum_{i=1,m=1}^{I,M} \sum_{d=1,f=1}^{D,F} \sum_{u=1,v=1,k=1}^{U,V,K} DecryptionAES(Enc, privatekey). \quad (4)$$

Equation (4) determines the decryption of all data images on different computing platforms based on AES-256 with the private key. We determined the local execution time of the services in the following way.

$$Local_p = \sum_{a=1}^{A} \sum_{t=1,j=1}^{T,J} \sum_{i=1}^{I} \sum_{d=1,f=1}^{D,F} \sum_{u=1}^{U} (\frac{(d \Leftrightarrow i/d \Leftrightarrow I)}{\zeta_u}).x_{a,u,t,d,f,j,u} + Enc + Dec.$$

(5)

Equation (5) determines the local execution time of tasks on the mobile devices based on trained and generated data. At the same time, $d \Leftrightarrow i$ predicts the mobile users.

$$Local_v = \sum_{a=1}^{A} \sum_{t=1,j=1}^{T,J} \sum_{d=1,f=1}^{D,F} \sum_{m=1}^{M} \sum_{v=1}^{V} \left(\frac{(d \Leftrightarrow m/d \Leftrightarrow M)}{\zeta_v} \right).y_{a,v,t,d,f,j,v} + Enc + Dec.$$

(6)

Equation (6) determines the local execution time of tasks on the vehicle devices based on trained and generated data. At the same time, $d \Leftrightarrow m$ predicts the vehicle devices.

$$com = \sum_{a=1}^{A} \sum_{t=1,j=1}^{T,J} \sum_{i=1}^{I} \sum_{d=1}^{D} \sum_{m=1}^{M} \left(\frac{d,m}{bw_{up}} + \frac{d,m}{bw_{down}} \right).a.u, v, t, d, f, j \quad (7)$$

Equation (7) determines the offloading and downloading time of tasks during execution.

$$remote = \sum_{a=1}^{A} \sum_{t=1,j=1}^{T,J} \sum_{i=1}^{I} \sum_{d=1}^{D} \sum_{m=1}^{M} \sum_{u=1}^{U} \left(\frac{(d \Leftrightarrow m, i/d \Leftrightarrow M, I)}{\zeta_k} \right).a, v, u, t, d, f, j, k + TT + Enc + Dec.$$

(8)

Equation (8) determined the execution time offloaded tasks on the different fog and cloud servers and the training and testing time of the sub-divided dataset. Furthermore, TT is the federated learning training and offloading time between fog and cloud nodes as determined as follows.

$$TT = \sum_{d=1}^{D}\sum_{k=1}^{K}\sum_{f=1}^{F}\sum_{r=1}^{R}(\frac{d,f}{\zeta_k}). \quad , \forall d = 1, \ldots, D. \qquad (9)$$

Equation (9) calculates the training and dataset validation time, where R number of iterations of training and testing of the dataset in the different nodes. The total time for prediction, processing, and training times for all applications is determined in Eq. (10).

$$Total = Local_p + Local_v + com + remote \quad , \forall a = 1, \ldots, A. \qquad (10)$$

The constraints of the problem are determined in the following way.

$$\min Total \quad , \forall a = 1, \ldots, A. \qquad (11)$$

Subject To

$$\sum_{a=1}^{A}\sum_{t=1}^{T}\sum_{i=1}^{I}\sum_{d=1}^{D}\sum_{u=1}^{U}(\frac{(d \Leftrightarrow i/d \Leftrightarrow I)}{\zeta_u}).x_{a,u,t,d,f,j,u} \leq \epsilon_u, \epsilon_v, \epsilon_k. \qquad (12)$$

Equation (12) determined that all the local devices must have enough resources for processing tasks; otherwise, they offloaded to the remote fog cloud servers.

$$\sum_{a=1}^{A}\sum_{t=1}^{T}\sum_{i=1}^{I}\sum_{d=1}^{D}\sum_{u=1}^{U}(\frac{(d \Leftrightarrow i/d \Leftrightarrow I)}{\zeta_u}).x_{a,u,t,d,f,j,u} \leq d_t, \forall t = 1, \ldots, T. \qquad (13)$$

Equation (13) determined that all the tasks must be less than the given deadlines.

4   Proposed DFLSS

We are considering different constraints such as security, deadline, response time, accurate prediction, and detection. So, we came up with the DFLSS to meet the needs of the research problem. The study presented the framework which consisted of different as shown in Algorithm 1. Algorithm 1 is the main algorithm which consists of different schemes such as local processing and deep federated learning to process the applications requests under their constrains.

Algorithm 1: DFLSS Algorithmic Framework

    Input : K, T, U, V, D, J, I, M

1 **begin**

2   **foreach** *(t = 1 as T)* **do**

3   Local Profiling for Tasks Execution;

4   Call Local Processing Based on Algorithm 2;

5   Call Federated Learning Processing Based on Algorithm 3;

6   Optimize Total $t \leftarrow K, T, U, V, D, J, I, M$;

4.1 Local Profiling for Tasks Execution

As shown in Algorithm 2 in our system, local profiling is the mechanism where decisions about tasks execution are made, as shown in Fig. 3. Two different interfaces, such as mobile and vehicle interfaces, are considered, which consist of various tasks as shown in Fig. 3. We assumed that the mobile application a_1 consisted of three tasks, such as $t1$=Vehicle Detection, $t3$=Speed Detection, and $t4$=Safety Alarm. The decision maker checks that the resources are sufficient and meet the deadline, and it returns the no offloading status to mobile devices for execution. However, otherwise, they will offload with a yes status to the fog and cloud networks. The near-emergency object detection tasks from the input camera, and LiDAR must be executed locally to avoid any collision with the safety alarm in our system. These tasks $t1$=Vehicle Detection $t2$=Pedestrian Detection, $t3$=Speed Detection, $t5$=route traffic, and $t6$=non vehicle are integrated with the vehicle application a_2. The local vehicle devices agent decides whether there are sufficient resources to meet the deadline or whether there is a need to offload to the fog cloud node for processing. The status of "no" means all tasks are executed locally, and "yes" means tasks are offloaded to the fog cloud servers for execution. These are all tasks t1=Vehicle Detection, t2=Pedestrian Detection, t3=Speed Detection, t4=Safety Alarm,t5=route Traffic, and t6=non vehicle will be executed on the cloud servers if the local mobile and vehicle inter-

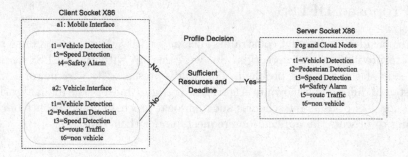

Fig. 3. Profiling Tasks Scheme.

faces do not have sufficient resources to meet all deadline requirements. The road safety applications are designed based on client and server sockets and executed on X86 run-time environments.

Algorithm 2: Local Processing

Input : K, T, U, V, D, J, I, M

1 **begin**
2   Input layer=3072,Conv1=608,Pool=14,14,8,softmax=850;
3   **foreach** *(t = 1 as T)* **do**
4   Apply profiling rules;
5   Determined the downloading time based on Eq. (7);
6       $\sum_{a=1}^{A} \sum_{t=1,j=1}^{T,J} \sum_{i=1}^{I} \sum_{d=1}^{D} \sum_{m=1}^{M} \left(\frac{d,m}{bw_{up}} + \frac{d,m}{bw_{down}} \right).a.u, v, t, d, f, j;$
7   **if** *(t ∼ i ← d ≤ ϵ_u)* **then**
8   Determine encryption and decryption based on Eq. (3) and Eq. (4);
9   Determined the local processing time based on Eq. (5);
10   Determined the available resources based on Eq. (12);
11         $\sum_{a=1}^{A} \sum_{t=1,j=1}^{T,J} \sum_{i=1}^{I} \sum_{d=1,f=1}^{D,F} \sum_{u=1}^{U} (\frac{(d \Leftrightarrow i/d \Leftrightarrow I)}{\zeta_u}).x_{a,u,t,d,f,j,u};$
12   **if** *(t ← local_p ≤ d_t)* **then**
13   Determined deadline based on Eq. (13);
14   **else if then**
15   Offloaded to the server;
16 **End Main**

4.2 Deep Federated Learning Assisted Fog and Cloud Networks

The Deep Federated Learning Assisted Fog and Cloud Networks enabled scheme trained and validated the sub-divided into different local servers and aggregated them with the centralized cloud server. Each node trained and shared data in the secure form based on encryption and decryption as determined in Eq. (3) and equation (4). We designed the fog and cloud networks based on deep federated learning schemes, as shown in Fig. 3. The dataset is divided among fog servers and aggregated to the centralized cloud node for processing, as shown in Algorithm 1. Each node can accept the real-time data and train and validate data on different nodes with a finite number of iterations. There are two kinds of iterations in federated learning: local and global iterations represented as $r \in R$. The output of each convolution is then sent through an activation function, such as a rectified linear unit (RELU), to produce better features F while maintaining positivity. The fully connected and merges all trained features of the road safety dataset, and Softmax makes the decision based on the vehicle speed analyzer and object detection. The locally trained sub-dataset merged to the aggregated dataset as shown in Fig. 4. All the nodes such as $k1, d1, k2, d2, k3, d4, \ldots D, K$

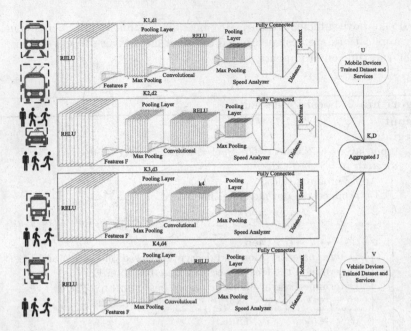

Fig. 4. DFLSS Training and Execution Mechanism.

trained dataset locally and shared to centralized server K. The mobile and vehicle applications can access the federated learning dataset at runtime.

Algorithm 3 determines the output dimensions of the given tasks in RSITS. The convolutional network is fully connected and merges all trained features of the road safety dataset, and Softmax makes the decision based on the vehicle speed analyzer and object detection. The locally trained sub-datasets merged to the aggregated dataset as shown in Fig. 4. All the nodes such as $k1, d1, k2, d2, k3, d4, \ldots D, K$ trained dataset locally and shared to centralized server K. The mobile and vehicle applications can access the federated learning dataset at runtime. The study presented the Algorithm 1, where profiling, local processing on mobile and vehicle, and remote processing for all tasks are done with the minimum response time. Based on profiling, all the local tasks are scheduled at the local level to handle the task processing based on available resources and deadlines.

5   Experimental Setting and Evaluation

The study designed the simulation environment based on collected datasets and road safety applications in distributed fog cloud networks. We designed the RSITS simulator using a cross-platform mechanism for all mobile and vehicle users. The simulator comprised mobile, vehicle, fog, and cloud computing nodes. The simulation parameters are defined in Table 1.

5.1   RS-Dataset

The trained RS-Dataset is the collection of Buses, Cars, Lorries, Motorcycles, Pedestrians, Trams, routes, and Trucks image objects during the execution of both applications in RSITS. The RS-Dataset consisted of Buses, Cars, Lorries, Motorcycles, Pedestrians, Trams, Trucks, and Vans with different images as defined in Table 2. The dataset consisted of additional features, e.g., F: Speed (km-h), Location, Route, Object, Distance (meter), Angles Detect, and Looking Object as defined in Table 2.

5.2   RSITS Application Development

We developed distributed road safety applications based on socket programming in a mobile fog cloud environment, as shown in Fig. 5. We have two kinds of applications: mobile and vehicle interfaces based on the X86 runtime environment. We integrated the TCP-IP protocols to transmit data between local devices and fog and cloud nodes. The mobile interface of the RSITS application

---

Algorithm 3: Federated Learning Enabled Remote Scheduling

Input : K, T, U, V, D, J, I, M

1 **begin**
2   Input layer=3072,Conv1=608,Pool=14,14,8,softmax=850;
3   **foreach** *(t = 1 as T)* **do**
4   Determine encryption and decryption based on Eq. (3) and Eq. (4);
5   **if** *($l \sim m \leftarrow d \leq \epsilon_v$)* **then**
6   Determined the available resources based on Eq. (12);
7   Determined the local processing time based on Eq. (6);
8              $\sum_{a=1}^{A} \sum_{t=1,j=1}^{T,J} \sum_{d=1,f=1}^{D,F} \sum_{m=1}^{M} \sum_{v=1}^{V} \left(\frac{(d \Leftrightarrow m/d \Leftrightarrow M)}{\zeta_v} \right).y_{a,v,t,d,f,j,v};$
9   **if** *($t \leftarrow local_v \leq d_t$)* **then**
10   Determined deadline based on Eq. (13);
11   **else if then**
12   Offloaded to the server;
13   **if** *($t \sim i, m \leftarrow d \leq \epsilon_k$)* **then**
14   Apply deep federated mechanism here;
15   Determined the remote processing time based on Eq. (8);
16   Determined the available resources based on Eq. (12);
17             $\sum_{a=1}^{A} \sum_{t=1,j=1}^{T,J} \sum_{i=1}^{I} \sum_{d=1}^{D} \sum_{m=1}^{M} \sum_{u=1}^{U} \left(\frac{(d \Leftrightarrow m, i/d \Leftrightarrow M, I)}{\zeta_k} \right).a, v, u, t, d, f, j, k+ TT;$
18   **if** *($t \leftarrow remote \leq d_t$)* **then**
19   Determined deadline based on Eq. (13);
20   Federated Learning Training;
21             $k1, kd1, k2, d2, k3, d3 \leftarrow K, D$ Input layer=3072,Conv1=608,Pool=14,14,8,softmax=850;
22   Optimize Total;
23   End Federated;
24   End Scheduling;
25 End Main

Table 1. Experiment Configuration.

Parameters	Description
Run-Time	X86
Language	Java, Kotlin and Python
$u = 1,500, \zeta_u, \epsilon_u$	AT Samsung Galaxy, A13 LTE,4 GB, 32 GB
$u = 1,500, \zeta_u, \epsilon_u$	AT iPhone 14 128 GB Midnight
$v = 1,500, \zeta_v, \epsilon_v$	Velodyne Lidar,4 GB,128 GB
k = 1	Virtual Server, 8 GB, 1000 GB
k = 2	Virtual Server, 16 GB, 1000 GB
k = 3	Virtual Server, 16 GB, 1000 GB
k = 4	Virtual Server, 32 GB, 5000 GB
Input layer	3072
Conv1	608
Pool	14,14,8
softmax	850
R	1000 per 30 min
Signals	200
Routes	4

Table 2. RS-Dataset 3D Images and Features.

Buses	Cars	Lorries	Motorcycles	Pedestrians	Trams	Trucks	Vans
3200	2200	2100	1800	20000	2000	1200	1500
Speed	Location	Route	Object	Distance	Angles	Detect	Looking Object
80	Frognerseteren	1	Tram	30	Building	Yes	Pedestrian
100	Frognerseteren	2	Tram	15	Building	Yes	Pedestrian
100	jernbanetorget	3	Tram	21	Building	yes	Vehicle
100	jernbanetorget	1	Tram	25	Building	Yes	Vehicle
80	Kirkegata	2	Car	30	Building	Yes	Vehicle
100	Kirkegata	4	Tram	15	Building	Yes	Pedestrian
100	Kirkegata	1	Car	21	Building	yes	Pedestrian
100	Kirkegata	1	Tram	25	Building	Yes	Pedestrian
80	Steinerud	2	Car	30	Building	Yes	Vehicle
100	Steinerud	4	Tram	15	Building	Yes	Pedestrian
100	Steinerud	1	Car	21	Building	yes	Pedestrian
100	Kolsas	1	Tram	25	Building	Yes	Pedestrian

(app) consisted of two primary services, vehicle detection, and safety alarm, with the following features. For instance, Speed (km-h), Location, Route, Object, Distance (meter), and Angles to Detect and Looking Object. The vehicle interface

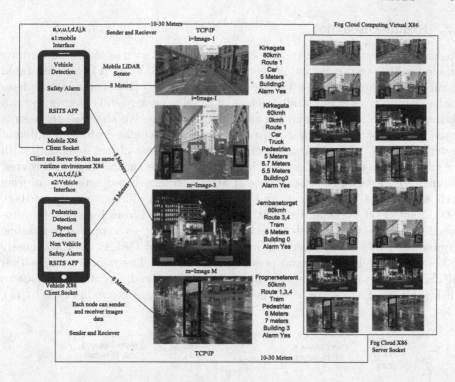

Fig. 5. RSITS Applications Implementation Based on Socket Programming.

RSITS application (app) consisted of pedestrian detection, vehicle speed detection, no vehicle objects, safety alarm with the Speed (km-h), Location, Route, Object, Distance (meter), Angles Detect, and Looking Object. Both applications have client and server sockets programming protocols. At the same time, the client-side mobile and vehicle applications can process only emergency objects nearby, such as 8-meters object detection with the safety alarm. The objects 10–30 meters away in smart will be offloaded to the fog and cloud network for analysis and results. The users and vehicle consisted of mobility features. Therefore, every request and response has different locations and different outcomes. For instance, mobile users process the $i = 1$ image-1 with $i = 1$ and obtain the following results based on the pre-trained dataset. For example, Kirkegata, 80kmh, Route 1, Car, 5 m, Building2, and Alarm Yes, as shown in Fig. 5. Furthermore, vehicles also detect the results based on $m = 1$ image-2 results. For instance, Kirkegata 60kmh, 0kmh (e.g., stay condition), Route 1, Car, Truck, Pedestrian, 5 m, 6.7 m, 5.5 m, Building3 and Alarm Yes. On the other hand, local mobiles and vehicles over 8 m in length can offload data if the sender and receiver meet their deadlines.

5.3   Result Discussion

The study implemented the two closely related studies such as federated learning enabled vehicle-to-vehicle and pedestrian detection (FLV2V) [14], and federated learning automated vehicle objective detection (FLAV) [15]. These studies have the same objectives as our study, such as processing latency and training and validating datasets in distributed fog and cloud networks. We analyzed the results based on sensor data generated from mobile and vehicle devices in different meter ranges: 5, 10, and 15 m. We analyzed the different object detections with the trained dataset on local and vehicle devices in different locations and routes. Figure 6(a) shows the performances of all algorithms based on given objects such as cars and Buses. Lorry, and Van Images with different numbers: 1000, 2000, 3000, 5000, 7000, and 10,000. It can be observed from Fig. 6(a), the proposed DFLSS performed with a higher ratio of accuracy as compared to baseline approaches FLV2V and FLAV. The proposed method DFLSS obtained nearly 98% in the mobile vehicle and pedestrian detection. The main reason is that DFLSS trained and executed the huge dataset on the different nodes. Due to the large dataset, the accuracy of the DFLSS increased, as shown in Fig. 6(b), (c),

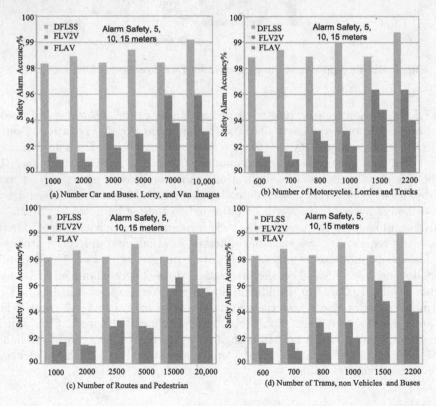

Fig. 6. Accuracy Performance of Object Detection and Generate Accuracy Safety Alarm on Trained Dataset.

and (d). We discuss the dataset and method limitation in the following way. (i) The existing studies only considered one type of service, such as random object detection in the baseline approaches. However, in our case, we are considering different kinds of objects according to our requirements. Therefore, with many service requirements, the accuracy of the existing baseline approaches decreases as the number of services increases in the RSITS. (ii) The second limitation is that existing approaches are adaptive and updated their models based on new data for further usage. Hence, therefore, our proposed DFLSS updated their models based on their new data images in the RSITS. We analyzed the different numbers of mobile and vehicle tasks, such as 100, 80, 200, 170, 300, and 500, during execution in the smart cities to obtain the safety alarm with the minimum total delays and deadlines. Figure 7(a) shows that the number of random tasks such as 100, 80, 200, 170, 300, and 500 was almost executed under their deadlines with the DFLSS as compared to baseline approaches. Figure 7(a) shows the performances of RSITS on mobile and vehicle devices with fixed ranges (5–10). We implemented profiling, where our method decides which tasks are executed locally and which are offloaded to the fog and centralized cloud servers for execution. As shown in Fig. 7(b), DFLSS obtained all executions under their deadlines on both local and remote computing with different ranges (5–30 meters) as compared to FLV2V and FLAV approaches. All existing approaches to RSITS did not include profiling for additional services. It leads to a higher failure rate of deadlines when the number of services increases, as shown in Fig. 7(a) and (b). Therefore, to trade-off between the deadline and total delay, we applied the profiling and reduced the risk of failure of tasks due to resource availability and deadlines in RSITS.

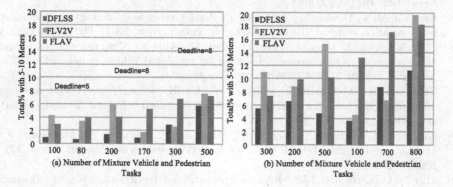

Fig. 7. Total% Performances of Methods with Different Objection Detection in Different Ranges.

6   Conclusion

The RSITS presented the road safety applications and trained datasets in mobile fog cloud networks. This study aims to identify vehicles' objectives, distances, and speeds to reduce accident risk and generate safety alerts with minimum processing time. We have collected different dataset images of various public transport vehicles, pedestrians, and routes, about 500000 images. We named this dataset the road safety dataset. We divided the road safety dataset into sub-datasets and trained and validated them on different servers. These sub-datasets have pre-trained and real-time images in the proposed RSITS. We consider constraints such as security, deadlines, response times, and accurate prediction objects for road safety applications. So, we came up with the deep federated learning scheduling scheme (DFLSS) to meet the needs of the research problem. Simulation results showed that the proposed DFLSS outperformed all existing approaches regarding accuracy by 5%, response time by 15%, and the deadline by 20% for road safety applications.

References

1. Organization, W.H. et al.: "Road safety" (2020)
2. Derawi, M., Dalveren, Y., Cheikh, F.A.: Internet-of-things-based smart transportation systems for safer roads. In: 2020 IEEE 6th World Forum on Internet of Things (WF-IoT), pp. 1–4. IEEE (2020)
3. Swarnamugi, M., Chinnaiyan, R.: Context—aware smart reliable service model for intelligent transportation system based on ontology. In: Singh, P.K., Kar, A.K., Singh, Y., Kolekar, M.H., Tanwar, S. (eds.) Proceedings of ICRIC 2019. LNEE, vol. 597, pp. 23–30. Springer, Cham (2020). https://doi.org/10.1007/978-3-030-29407-6_3
4. Boukerche, A., Tao, Y., Sun, P.: Artificial intelligence-based vehicular traffic flow prediction methods for supporting intelligent transportation systems. Comput. Netw. **182**, 107484 (2020)
5. Azadani, M.N., Boukerche, A.: Driving behavior analysis guidelines for intelligent transportation systems. IEEE Trans. Intell. Transp. Syst. **23**(7), 6027–6045 (2021)
6. Choe, C., Ahn, J., Choi, J., Park, D., Kim, M., Ahn, S.: A robust channel access using cooperative reinforcement learning for congested vehicular networks. IEEE Access **8**, 135540–135557 (2020)
7. Chakroun, R., Abdellatif, S., Villemur, T.: LAMD: location-based alert message dissemination scheme for emerging infrastructure-based vehicular networks. Internet Things **19**, 100510 (2022)
8. Giuliano, R., Vegni, A.M., Loscri, V., Innocenti, E., Vizzarri, A., Mazzenga, F.: MuSLi: a multi sensor LiDAR detection for C-V2X networks. Comput. Netw. **221**, 109514 (2023)
9. Murthy, C.B., Hashmi, M.F.: Real time pedestrian detection using robust enhanced YOLOv3+. In: 2020 21st International Arab Conference on Information Technology (ACIT), pp. 1–5. IEEE (2020)
10. Gao, F., Wang, C., Li, C.: A combined object detection method with application to pedestrian detection. IEEE Access **8**, 194457–194465 (2020)
11. Kumar, A., Zhang, Z.J., Lyu, H.: Object detection in real time based on improved single shot multi-box detector algorithm. EURASIP J. Wirel. Commun. Netw. **2020**(1), 1–18 (2020)
12. Song, L., Wang, X.: Faster region convolutional neural network for automated pavement distress detection. Road Mater. Pavement Des. **22**(1), 23–41 (2021)

13. Cui, J., Nie, G., et al.: Motion route planning and obstacle avoidance method for mobile robot based on deep learning. J. Electr. Comput. Eng. **2022**, 1–11 (2022)
14. Barbieri, L., Savazzi, S., Nicoli, M.: Decentralized federated learning for road user classification in enhanced V2X networks. In: 2021 IEEE International Conference on Communications Workshops (ICC Workshops), pp. 1–6. IEEE (2021)
15. Jallepalli, D., Ravikumar, N.C., Badarinath, P.V., Uchil, S., Suresh, M. A.: Federated learning for object detection in autonomous vehicles. In: 2021 IEEE Seventh International Conference on Big Data Computing Service and Applications (BigDataService), pp. 107–114. IEEE (2021)
16. Shin, S., Kim, J., Moon, C.: Road dynamic object mapping system based on edge-fog-cloud computing. Electronics **10**(22), 2825 (2021)
17. Lee, J., Lee, K., Yoo, A., Moon, C.: Design and implementation of edge-fog-cloud system through HD map generation from lidar data of autonomous vehicles. Electronics **9**(12), 2084 (2020)
18. Rocha, P.G., Souza, A., Silva, F.A., Rego, P.A.: Decision algorithm for computational offloading in vehicular fog computing with pedestrians. In: 2022 IEEE 11th International Conference on Cloud Networking (CloudNet), pp. 126–130. IEEE (2022)
19. Yin, H.: Public security video image detection system construction platform in cloud computing environment. Comput. Intell. Neurosci. **2022** (2022)
20. Concone, F., Lo Re, G., Morana, M.: SMCP: a secure mobile crowdsensing protocol for fog-based applications. Hum.-Centric Comput. Inf. Sci. **10**(1), 1–23 (2020)
21. Nahri, M., Boulmakoul, A., Karim, L.: Fog-based framework for improving IoT/IoV security and privacy. In: Security and Trust Issues in Internet of Things, pp. 165–183. CRC Press (2020)
22. Nouh, R., Singh, M., Singh, D.: SafeDrive: hybrid recommendation system architecture for early safety predication using internet of vehicles. Sensors **21**(11), 3893 (2021)
23. Broughton, G., Majer, F., Rouček, T., Ruichek, Y., Yan, Z., Krajník, T.: Learning to see through the haze: multi-sensor learning-fusion system for vulnerable traffic participant detection in fog. Robot. Auton. Syst. **136**, 103687 (2021)
24. Alemneh, E., Senouci, S.-M., Messous, M.-A.: An energy-efficient adaptive beaconing rate management for pedestrian safety: a fuzzy logic-based approach. Pervasive Mob. Comput. **69**, 101285 (2020)
25. Nordbakke, S., Phillips, R., Skollerud, K., Milch, V.: Health effects of ruter age-friendly transport. Transportøeconomic Institute (TØI), vol. 2020, 1810
26. Kalita, L.: Socket programming. Int. J. Comput. Sci. Inf. Technol. **5**(3), 4802–4807 (2014)
27. Shin, S., et al.: How to extend CTRT for AES-256 and AES-192. IEICE Trans. Fundam. Electron. Commun. Comput. Sci. **105**(8), 1121–1133 (2022)

Gamified DAOs as Blockchain-Based Catalysts for Prosocial and Environmentally Oriented Cities

Arturs Bernovskis[1($\boxtimes$)] (iD), Agnis Stibe[1,2,3] (iD), Deniss Sceulovs[1] (iD), Yan Zhang[4] (iD), and Jiajie Li[4] (iD)

[1] Riga Technical University, Riga, Latvia
arturs.bernovskis@rtu.lv
[2] INTERACT Research Unit, University of Oulu, Oulu, Finland
[3] Department of Informatics, Faculty of Engineering, Built Environment and Information Technology, University of Pretoria, Pretoria, South Africa
[4] MIT Media Lab, Massachusetts Institute of Technology, Cambridge, USA

Abstract. This paper explores the role of gamification in decentralized autonomous organizations (DAOs) that are run through rules encoded as computer programs called smart contracts rather than being managed by people. DAOs operate on a decentralized blockchain network and allow for secure and transparent decision-making processes without the need for intermediaries. Token holders typically govern them with voting rights to make decisions and allocate resources within the organization. In the context of ever-growing cities, previous research has shown that prosocial behavior and a positive mental attitude toward the environment are not always related. People without motivation tend not to take meaningful and valuable actions for their societies. Over the past decade, gamification has offered new strategies and tactics for encouraging and sustaining positive change. More recently, advances in blockchain technology have enabled the rise of DAOs. Therefore, this research aims to review and discuss the potential of gamification to support DAOs aiming at prosocial and pro-environmental transformations in cities, as well as the role of blockchain as a technology that fosters such societal improvements and enables organizations to better align with sustainability goals.

Keywords: Decentralized Autonomous Organization · Gamification · Blockchain · Smart Cities · Prosocial · Ecology · Non-Fungible Token · NFT · DAO

1 Introduction

Nowadays, 55% of the world's population lives in cities, and this number is growing, expecting 80% of the population will live in urban areas by 2050 [38]. By that time, with the urban population, more than doubling its current size, nearly 7 of 10 people worldwide will live in cities [23]. Fast urbanization has brought about various urban issues – high traffic, density, pollution, and the overproduction of waste [29]. However,

M. Younas et al. (Eds.): MobiWIS 2023, LNCS 13977, pp. 38–51, 2023.
https://doi.org/10.1007/978-3-031-39764-6_3

as the city gets more, these issues become harder to be solved, centralized just with government laws. Not all citizens trust the government [10], and a lack of trust could be an issue in participating in sustainable activities [21]. Therefore, there is an urgent need to find additional solutions to motivate residents to choose pro-social and sustainable behaviors and not be satisfied only with solutions that rely on regulation. Blockchain technology can be a solution for decentralized actions.

The blockchain market is predicted to grow from USD 7,4 billion in 2022 to USD 94.0 billion by 2027 [22]. A key application of blockchain is to store financial data with a secure exchange; there have been attempts to explore and extend the applications of blockchain beyond payments like Blockchain 1.0 is generally associated with cryptocurrency and payment (Bitcoin, Ethereum), Blockchain 2.0 is associated with automated digital finance using smart contracts, and the more recent Blockchain 3.0 trend is focused on addressing the needs of the digital society, such as smart cities and Industry 4.0 [2].

Sustainable living is the answer to long-term city development [35], but how do motivate citizens to be prosocial? Prosocial behavior is defined as behavior through which people benefit others, including helping, cooperating, comforting, sharing, and donating [14]. According to research, prosocial behavior and positive mental attitude toward the environment are not related, from 97% of participants who declared they had the environment in mind, only 2% picked up garbage that had been left on the ground near a trash can [4]. Without motivation, most citizens will not be prosocially active and will not act with a sustainable mindset.

This paper presents a conceptual framework for utilizing gamification in DAOs to motivate residents toward pro-social and sustainable behaviors and to enhance international business operations. Specifically, the authors suggest that tokenizing assets within a blockchain could effectively incentivize such strategies. Our methodology involves a comprehensive literature review of research on DAOs, gamification, and blockchain. By proposing and elaborating on this framework, we contribute to the existing literature on blockchain technology and provide insights into the potential of DAOs and tokenization in promoting sustainability and enhancing social transformation [34].

2   Background Literature

Research [4] shows that prosocial behavior and a positive mental attitude to the environment are not related, and humans without motivation are not willing to pick up garbage that had been left on the ground near a trash can. Governments mostly use centralized *Stick* and *Carrot* motivation – give penalties or discounts to citizens to take care of the city environment.

In this obstacle arises a question: How can decentralized autonomous organizations effectively incorporate blockchain-based gamification into their operations to promote prosocial and environmental behavior?

The "Industry 4.0" initiative was launched by the German government in 2011 as part of its high-tech strategy to tackle new challenges and ensure the future competitiveness of the German manufacturing industry [19]. The new evolution of the production and industrial process called Industry 4.0, and its related technologies, such as the Internet of Things, big data analytics, and cyber–physical systems, among others, still have an unknown potential impact on sustainability and the environment [5].

A smart contract is a self-executing contract with the terms of the agreement between buyer and seller being directly written into lines of code. The code and the agreements contained therein exist across a distributed, decentralized blockchain network. The code controls the execution, and transactions are trackable and irreversible. Smart contracts permit trusted transactions and agreements to be carried out among disparate, anonymous parties without needing a central authority, legal system, or external enforcement mechanism. Thanks to the characteristics of running automatically on the blockchain, smart contracts have the advantages of being safe, fast, decentralized, and protecting the privacy of both parties involved.

Blockchain technologies are categorized as permissioned (*i.e.,* only authorized users can access the blockchain applications in private, consortium, or cloud-based settings) or permissionless (*i.e.,* publicly accessible for all users via the Internet) systems [32]. Data is stored in the form of cryptographically protected 'blocks' that are linked together in a 'chain.' Blockchain is a type of distributed database managed over peer-to-peer networks, with transaction data ledgers not stored in a centralized server but across multiple nodes all connected by blockchain networks [9].

Gamification has gained enormous popularity in recent years, and the idea has also moved into a broad discourse in policymaking and the public sphere [37], among other things, to promote sustainability in local authorities [30, 33]. The use of gamification makes it possible to design game elements in non-game contexts [11] to motivate desired behavior.

3   Research Methodology

The methodology of this research involves a comprehensive literature review of research on gamification, decentralized autonomous organizations (DAOs), and blockchain technology. Blockchain is a system of recording information that makes it difficult or impossible to change, hack, or cheat the system. A blockchain is the system's distributed and immutable electronic database – a ledger of all transactions that have ever occurred on the network.

The research focuses on understanding the potential of gamification in DAOs to motivate residents toward pro-social and sustainable behaviors. To achieve this, the authors first explored the concept of gamification and its impact on behavior, especially in the context of sustainable living and pro-social behavior. The study then examines the potential of DAQs and tokenization in promoting sustainability and enhancing environmentally oriented societies.

The research also highlights the types of DAOs, their governance and ownership structures, and how tokens play a crucial role in facilitating the exchange of value within DAOs. Finally, the authors propose the utilization of a Mixed DAO, which incorporates two or more DAO types, for sustainable DAO development in urban settings. The DAO Type map proposed by the authors serves as a framework for understanding different types of DAOs and their specific features, allowing researchers and practitioners to design and analyze DAOs more effectively. The proposed conceptual framework and methodology provide valuable insights into the potential of gamification in DAOs to promote sustainable behavior.

To identify gamification in DAOs, authors have researched this theory since it was developed over a decade ago. Since this field is relatively new most of the literature was selected from the last decade. Authors of the paper mainly searched the Web of Science and Scopus databases for targeted articles, using the keywords "gamification", "prosocial", "sustainable" and "blockchain".

4 Decentralized Autonomous Organizations

Bitcoin and Ethereum (a popular smart contract-supported platform) are, perhaps, the two most widely recognized implementations of blockchain. Ethereum founder Buterin and researchers [16] argue that Bitcoin is effectively the first DAO [8] and the Ethereum white paper defines a DAO as a virtual entity that has a certain set of members or shareholders and has the right to spend the entity's funds and modify its code [7].

However, Ethereum is not only a cryptocurrency; in fact, Ethereum introduces four main features in its system:

- Tokens: different currencies living in the blockchain,
- Smart Contracts: digital contracts where rules are stated through code,
- Smart Property: a way to assert the ownership of a real (non-digital) asset,
- DAO: a decentralized autonomous organization structured as a set of smart contracts that define the organization's tokens, properties, and government regulations [40].

The latter is a continuously growing cryptographically linked list of immutable data records. Within the blockchain, a (public) ledger is used to record each transaction's data and information. Information about each completed transaction is stored in a distributed ledger and shared across all the participating nodes of the blockchain network [2]. Blockchain can efficiently record transactions between two or more involved parties on a distributed peer-to-peer (P2P) network, with the stored data co-owned by all members of the network and permanently unmodifiable [25]. Although Bitcoin was the initial usage of blockchain, cryptocurrencies are only one of its numerous applications. Government record-keeping, tracking the flow of products and services along supply chains, voting, and validating citizens' identities are all examples of blockchain uses. Because blockchain technology employs algorithms to facilitate 'smart contracts,' it has powers much beyond those of any standard database. Self-executing code enables safe electronic cooperation techniques that do not rely on a central authority to mediate between transacting parties. These parties, who may or may not trust one other, may rely on the accuracy of the information stored in their shared databases. In a word, blockchain is a type of Distributed Ledger Technology (DLT) in which transactions are recorded with an immutable cryptographic signature.

Generally, DAOs are designed based on their founding members' vision and mission, and as such, have no canonical structure [39] and governance, and ownership structure could be established at the inception of the project or dependent on held utility, security, or governance tokens [1]:

A) *Utility tokens* is an asset based on cryptography that generates or is expected to generate future cash flows [24], serving as the medium of exchange in DAO platforms. These tokens are fungible and could be nonfungible, e.g., concert tickets.

B) Security tokens are tokens that represent ownership of an external tradeable asset, such as real estate and collectibles. They can be fungible or nonfungible, unique tokens used to prove asset ownership [3].

C) Governance tokens are fungible tokens that usually double as utility or security tokens; however, they can be minted separately [1].

An Initial Coin Offering (ICO) is an innovative way to raise funds and an opportunity to take part in a project or in a DAO [17].

Research papers have described several types of DAO like daostack, daohaus, aragon for dao operation systems, maker dao, compound uniswap as protocol dao to govern a decentralized protocol with voting, bitdao for investment, moloch dao for grants. Our research fund two more types of DAO - philanthropy dao like biggreendao and social dao like friendswithbenefits and flamingodao. The authors have created a map of DAO types in Fig. 1.

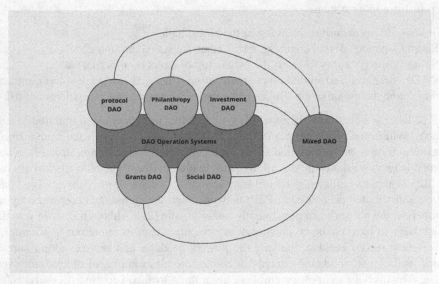

Fig. 1. Types of DAOs

The map of DAO types serves as a framework for understanding the different types of DAOs and their specific features, allowing researchers and practitioners to design and analyze DAOs more effectively. The authors propose the utilization of a Mixed DAO – with two or more DAO types – for sustainable DAO development in urban settings, given the existence of multiple DAO types.

DAOs can be structured in various ways, with governance and ownership structures established at inception or dependent on held utility, security, or governance tokens. Tokens facilitate value exchange within DAOs, represent external asset ownership, and enable governance. ICOs provide an innovative fundraising mechanism and a means to participate in a project or DAO. Researchers and practitioners can leverage the DAO types map as a framework for comprehending various DAO types and their specific characteristics, which can aid in designing and analyzing DAOs more effectively. Furthermore, Mixed DAOs, which incorporate two or more DAO types, may be particularly useful for sustainable DAO development in urban settings, given the existence of various DAO types.

5 DAO Policy Design for Urban Contexts

Technologies like blockchain can help introduce access tracking and control, secure device discovery, prevention of spoofing, and data loss while ensuring that end-to-end encryption is also used [36]. Collaborating parties on blockchains can trust that transactions are recorded accurately and cannot be altered and that all participants follow the system's rules. Thus, the importance of the identity of collaborating parties in blockchains is less significant than in relational governance.

To establish a new paradigm for incentive policy to promote prosocial behaviors at an individual level, these four aspects are critical:

- It shall be capable of the quantification of diverse behaviors,
- Its incentive mechanism shall be user-driven,
- It shall have a distribution system of equity and equality,
- It shall operate with an ecosystem instead of input from a singular party.

The diagram in Fig. 2 shows how it works. The policy's design and decision-making will involve all participants' participation, collectively determining how the reward system operates. Once collectively designed, the reward system will incentivize each individual to make behavioral changes.

Individualized and Performance-Based Distribution of Incentives. DAOs utilize tokens as incentives to motivate intrinsic motivation for prosocial behaviors, providing extrinsic and reputational values. In this framework, incentive distribution is personalized based on individual behavior, departing from uniform or average-based approaches. The objective is to balance equity and equality by utilizing performance-based, individualized incentive distribution.

Collective Decision-Making. The decentralized voting mechanism in DAOs enables each participant to participate in policy and incentive decision-making, promoting consensus-building among participants. The voting power of each participant is based on their contributions and relevance to the issues being voted on. The decision-making process covers a wide range of topics, such as incentive distribution patterns, token values, token usage scenarios, and activities. In a decentralized decision-making process, every stakeholder can be heard instead of limited to small groups of people. Thus, the decisions are:

More Fine-Grained and Contextual: A neighborhood's requirements can vary significantly due to the individuals living there, even if they share the same urban fabric.

Dynamic and Resilient: The decision made in such a decentralized way no longer relies on the opinions of a small group of people, thus avoiding bias and becoming more resilient.

Results of Consensus: The smart contract system, which all parties trust, enables secure sharing, storage, and data processing using blockchain technology.

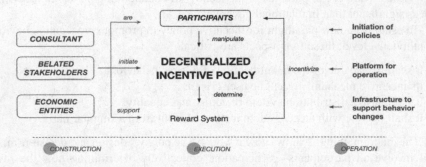

Fig. 2. Decentralized incentive policy

The blockchain market is expected to grow exponentially in the coming years, with the potential for use cases beyond payments and financial data storage. The Industry 4.0 initiative has led to the development of blockchain technologies that address the needs of the digital society, such as smart cities and sustainability. Smart contracts, which are self-executing agreements written in code and executed on a decentralized blockchain network, provide a trusted and efficient way for parties to carry out transactions and agreements without the need for a central authority.

The authors propose a new incentive policy paradigm that quantifies diverse behaviors, user-driven incentive mechanisms, distribution systems of equity and equality, and an ecosystem-based operation to promote prosocial behaviors at an individual level. A decentralized decision-making process, where every stakeholder can participate, leads to fine-grained and contextual decisions that are dynamic, resilient, and based on consensus. Furthermore, secure data and information management are provided using blockchain technology. By implementing these critical aspects, DAOs can effectively incentivize prosocial behaviors and promote sustainable practices in urban settings.

6 Application of Gamified DAOs in Cities

Gamification can help encourage residents to behave that care for the environment, thus creating more sustainable and durable cities [35]. Cities that use this way of intervention will be able to achieve sustainable behavior that is better for the environment and reduce costs [27], much more than traditional methods such as the stick and carrot method [34]. The gamification works exceptionally well when it creates human and community interactions around it [6] and is, therefore, particularly suitable for use in cities and communities within cities.

Blockchain technologies with gamification elements could motivate city stakeholders to be more active in sustainable activities. A sustainable mindset is habit change, and stakeholders need to learn that gamification blockchain or GamiChain can help as it increases students' and teachers' motivation to build a more transparent, safe, and enjoyable educational environment [26]. On blockchain technology, stakeholders can create a cryptocurrency or NFT (Non-Fungible Token) as a motivational reward for sustainable choices and activities. Cryptocurrency is a decentralized tradable digital asset or digital form of money built on blockchain technology. Cryptocurrency uses encryption to verify and protect transactions without the need for monetary authority. A cryptocurrency wallet is a tool that can store, transfer and receive crypto. It accepts and sends cryptocurrency through interaction with the blockchain. Most cryptocurrencies are fungible assets, which is an important property, the same with currencies. One Bitcoin you receive from a buyer does not need to be the same one you send to the merchant, which means that each crypto unit has an equal market value.

6.1 Advantages of DAOs in Cities

An advantage of the NFT implementation is that it allows the seller of energy assets to set different prices for different tokens of the same token type. Similarly, this implementation permits the actor offering rewards to set different conditions for rewards of the same type. However, in cases where asset standardization is required, the FT implementation offers an advantage as it ensures uniformity between tokens of the same token type [18].

Gaming is the Future's language that can sensitize and stimulate a hypothetical world to the people giving them an immersive experience with the power to change the dynamics of the complex system. The players' decisions in the game self-organize the system's dynamics, making the consequences of connected choices visible to the player. This provides the best learning-by-doing experience to constantly observe and reflect upon an individual's role in the self-organizing complex systems. This experience can encourage people to participate in collective prosperity actively [13].

Gamification methods have shown good results in impacting human behavior and can be used to solve sustainable issues in cities. Blockchain technologies can bring trust and transparent solutions, thus making decentralized gamified motivational programs for municipalities. Decentralized autonomous systems with gamification based on Blockchain can bring an alternative environment for citizens to motivate prosocial behavior. What differentiates gamification from other persuasion techniques is its entertaining design, which makes users perceive a fun and entertaining action and thus creates a positive association with the activity [20, 33]. This is particularly important because previous studies have shown that prosocial behavior and a positive mental attitude toward the environment are not always related. Only motivated people tend to take actions that are meaningful and valuable to their society. Therefore, it is necessary to strengthen motivation in other ways.

The possibility of the community managing the game and learning the behavior distinguishes gamification use of Blockchain in DAO. It enables the management of the networks to promote a broad public value. The fact that everything is transparent and does not require central management (but a network) reduces the problem of distrust of the residents that exist in gamification that the municipality or the government entirely manages. In addition, it also involves the residents more cooperatively, giving them more responsibility and a "voice."

DAO builds a tokenomy that ensures a robust system both inside the platform DAO, as well as inside every initiative (if they use our modules), by the composition of different types of tokens, reasonable regulation of issuance and currency valuing, the ratio of circulation amount and reserve amount, and control of liquidity and fungibility. The potential healthy inter-initiative economic communications will also be built by the exchange with DAO tokens exchange, which will be the hard currency for all protocols in the DAO ecosystem, both platform DAO and initiatives.

6.2 Concerns for DAOs in Cities

Another criticism of this intervention, as in others, is the harmful effect of external rewards on internal motivation [28]. In such a case, where the community manages the game thanks to this technology of decentralized management, the internal motivation will increase.

The ethical implications of using gamification as a policy tool are also a concern. While gamification is often used to encourage pro-social behavior in cities that prioritize environmental sustainability, such initiatives are often implemented top-down, raising questions about who defines the criteria for "good" purposes. It is possible that citizens who are affected by the intervention will not always define "good" in the way that the policymakers will explain it. In authoritarian regimes, it may also lead to implementing government goals that do not align with the social goal [15]. The blockchain also offers excellent transparency, preventing ethical problems and misuse.

Another criticism of gamification is that sometimes the use of game elements may create a lack of seriousness [12]. We believe that the transparency and involvement of the community in this type of gamification will increase the sense of seriousness towards the social and environmental goal, even though it is a "game".

In addition, sometimes, there is an imbalance between the rewards and the "punishments," which motivates some users to circumvent the game's rules. Thus, they are rewarded for adopting habits opposite to the game's goal [12]. This technology saves all the moves, which are transparently presented to everyone, so there is less chance of circumventing the game's rules.

Finally, as in other ways of intervention, sometimes the creation of gamification requires resources of money and knowledge, which not every city and community has. Thus, instead of reducing gaps, it may widen them. And here is the place for the cities and the government to intervene in places where more help is needed with knowledge and financial resources.

6.3 Meaningful DAOs in Cities

Gamification possesses mechanics, dynamics, and aesthetics that share similarities with DAO features. The authors depict DAO as a gamified structure that exhibits resemblances with Ruhi's [31] gamification mechanics, such as challenges, opportunities, competition, cooperation, feedback, resource acquisition, rewards, transactions, shifts, win states, badges, levels, points, social interaction, as well as game dynamic elements including competition, collaboration, community, collection, achievements, and progress. Figure 3 illustrates a comparison of meaningful enterprise gamification with the DAO framework.

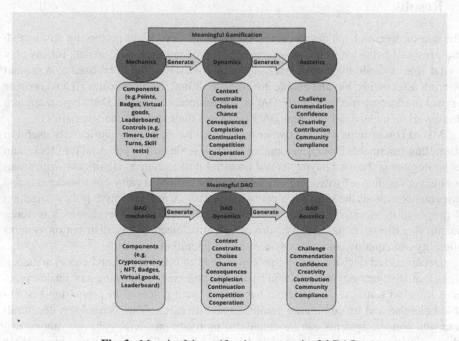

Fig. 3. Meaningful gamification vs meaningful DAO

DAO framework has many similarities with a meaningful enterprise gamification framework, and it could bring a more meaningful prosocial platform for citizens than a regular open government framework.

This paper argues that gamification, which involves using game elements in non-game contexts to motivate desired behavior, can be a powerful tool for promoting sustainability in cities. By combining gamification with blockchain technology, decentralized autonomous systems can be created to motivate prosocial behavior among residents, resulting in a more transparent and cooperative environment. The authors assert that such systems can also bring trust and transparency to solutions, making them more effective and less susceptible to problems of distrust that can occur when the government or municipality is solely responsible for the management of the game.

Furthermore, the transparency provided by the blockchain can help prevent ethical problems and misuse. However, the authors acknowledge that there are still some concerns and criticisms of gamification, such as the harmful effect of external rewards on internal motivation and the imbalance between rewards and punishments. Nonetheless, the authors believe this can be addressed by involving the community in gamification. The authors conclude that the combination of gamification and blockchain technology can create a more meaningful prosocial platform for citizens than a regular open government framework.

7 Results

The use of decentralized autonomous organizations (DAOs) in promoting sustainable and prosocial behavior in urban settings is a promising area of research. Tokens play a vital role in facilitating value exchange within DAOs and can be used to represent external asset ownership and enable governance. Initial Coin Offerings (ICOs) provide a novel fundraising mechanism for DAOs, and researchers can use DAO type maps as a framework to understand different DAO types and their specific characteristics.

Mixed DAOs, incorporating two or more DAO types, may be particularly useful in promoting sustainable DAO development in urban settings. The potential for blockchain technology to go beyond payments and financial data storage is significant, with smart contracts providing a trusted and efficient way for parties to carry out transactions and agreements without the need for a central authority. A new incentive policy paradigm is proposed to incentivize prosocial behavior at the individual level, which includes quantifying diverse behaviors, user-driven incentive mechanisms, distribution systems of equity and equality, and an ecosystem-based operation.

Decentralized decision-making processes lead to fine-grained and contextual decisions that are dynamic, resilient, and based on consensus, promoting sustainable practices in urban settings. Gamification has shown great potential in promoting sustainable behavior, and by combining gamification with blockchain technology, decentralized autonomous systems can be created to motivate prosocial behavior among residents. The community can be involved in the gamification process to address these concerns. International corporations can participate in city DAO token economies and use blockchain-based loyalty programs to reward customers and employees.

The platform can track the carbon impact of distribution channels. However, challenges such as greenwashing, limited resources for implementation, and ethical concerns must be considered. This paper provides insights and ideas for future research and implementation of DAOs in the sustainable development sectors. By creating more meaningful prosocial platforms for citizens, DAOs have the potential to promote sustainable practices and empower individuals and enterprises in sustainable activities.

8 Conclusions

In conclusion, accelerated urbanization has led to several environmental and social challenges. The conventional approaches, including regulations and laws, financial incentives, and carrot-and-stick methods, have proven insufficient to address these issues.

Even newer solutions, such as those based on behavioral economics and technologies like gamification, face criticism due to ethical concerns, issues of trust between residents and the government, and more. In this paper, we recommend integrating blockchain technology also into the urban realm.

The integration of blockchain technology can enable transparent and decentralized management by communities, under the guidance of the municipality, to promote pro-social and sustainable behaviors, which in turn can contribute to a better world for all. In the present times, with environmental and social challenges posing concerns for several cities worldwide, a method is required that can stimulate motivation and responsibility among all stakeholders. The authors contend that the utilization of gamification and Mixed DAO in cities, as recommended in this paper, can substantially aid in addressing these challenges.

DAOs can also offer opportunities for collaboration, innovation, and disruption of traditional business models. Moreover, DAOs can offer several benefits, such as cost savings, increased trust, and access to global markets. However, several challenges are associated with implementing DAOs in cities, including regulatory and legal barriers, issues of governance and decision-making, and potential security risks. Thus, further research is needed to develop best practices for implementing DAOs in cities and to address the challenges associated with their adoption.

References

1. Alao, O., Cuffe, P.: Structuring special purpose vehicles for financing renewable generators on a blockchain marketplace. IEEE Trans. Ind. Appl. **58**(2), 1478–1489 (2022). https://doi.org/10.1109/TIA.2021.3135252
2. Alladi, T., Chamola, V., Parizi, R., Choo, K.: Blockchain applications for industry 4.0 and industrial IoT: a review. IEEE Access **7**, 176935–176951 (2019). https://doi.org/10.1109/ACCESS.2019.2956748
3. Di Angelo, M., Salzer, G.: Towards the identification of security tokens on ethereum. In: Proceedings of the 11th IFIP International Conference New Technologies Mobility Security, pp. 1–5 (2021)
4. Bickman, L.: Environmental attitudes and actions. J. Soc. Psychol. **87**, 323–324 (1972). https://doi.org/10.1080/00224545.1972.9922533
5. Bonilla S., Silva H., Terra M., Franco R., Sacomano J.: Industry 4.0 and sustainability implications: a scenario-based analysis of the impacts and challenges. Sustainability **10**(10), 3740 (2018)
6. Buckley, P., Doyle, E.: Individualising gamification: an investigation of the impact of learning styles and personality traits on the efficacy of gamification using a prediction market. Comput. Educ. **106**, 43–55 (2017)
7. Buterin, V.: Ethereum whitepaper: A next-generation smart contract and decentralized application platform [White Paper] (2013).https://blockchainlab.com/pdf/Ethereum_white_paper-a_next_generation_smart_contract_and_decentralized_application_platform-vitalik-buterin.pdf
8. Buterin, V.: DAOs, DACs, DAs and More: An Incomplete Terminology Guide [Blog post]. Ethereum Foundation Blog (2014).https://blog.ethereum.org/2014/05/06/daos-dacs-das-and-more-an-incomplete-terminology-guide/
9. Choi, E., Choi, Y., Park, N.: Blockchain-centered educational program embodies and advances 2030 sustainable development goals. Sustainability **14**(7), 3761 (2022)

10. Dalton, R.J.: The social transformation of trust in government. Int. Rev. Sociol. **15**(1), 133–154 (2005)
11. Deterding, S., Sicart, M., Nacke, L., O'Hara, K., Dixon, D.: Gamification. using game-design elements in non-gaming contexts. In: Proceedings of the 2011 Conference on Human Factors in Computing Systems, ACM, 2011, pp. 2425–2428 (2011)
12. Diefenbach, S., Müssig, A.: Counterproductive effects of gamification: an analysis on the example of the gamified task manager Habitica. Int. J. Hum Comput Stud. **127**, 190–210 (2019)
13. Duke, R.D.: Toward a general theory of gaming. Simul. Games. **5**(2), 131–146 (1974). https://doi.org/10.1177/003755007452001
14. Eisenberg, N., Fabes, R.A.: Prosocial development. In: Damon, W., Eisenberg, N. (eds.) Handbook of Child Psychology, 5th edn, vol. 3, pp. 701–778. Wiley, New York (1998)
15. Harviainen, J.T., Hassan, L.: Governmental service gamification: central principles. Int. J. Innov. Digital Econ. (IJIDE) **10**(3), 1–12 (2019)
16. Hsieh, Y.-Y., Vergne, J.-P.: Bitcoin and the rise of decentralized autonomous organizations. J. Organ. Des. **7**(1), 1–16 (2018). https://doi.org/10.1186/s41469-018-0038-1
17. Ibba, S., Pinna, A., Baralla, G., Marchesi, M.: ICOs overview: should investors choose an ICO developed with the lean startup methodology? In: Garbajosa, J., Wang, X., Aguiar, A. (eds.) XP 2018. LNBIP, vol. 314, pp. 293–308. Springer, Cham (2018). https://doi.org/10.1007/978-3-319-91602-6_21
18. Karandikar, N., Chakravorty, A., Rong, C.: Blockchain based transaction system with fungible and non-fungible tokens for a community-based energy infrastructure. Sensors. **21**(11), 3822 (2021). https://doi.org/10.3390/s21113822
19. Kagermann, H., Wahlster, W., Helbig, J.: Recommendations for Implementing the Strategic Initiative Industrie 4.0: Final Report of the Industrie 4.0 Working Group Forschungsunion, Berlin, Germany (2013)
20. Kurani, K.S., et al.: Plug-in hybrid electric vehicle (PHEV) demonstration and consumer education, outreach, and market research program: Volumes I and II. Plugin Hybrid Electric Vehicle Research Center. Institute of Transportation Studies, University of California, Davis (2010)
21. Liu, L., Bouman, T., Perlaviciute, G., Steg, L.: Effects of trust and public participation on acceptability of renewable energy projects in the Netherlands and China. Energy Res. Soc. Sci. **53**, 137–144 (2019)
22. MarketsandMarkets: Blockchain Market Analysis & Report (2023). https://www.marketsandmarkets.com/Market-Reports/blockchain-technology-market-90100890.html. Accessed 2 May 2023
23. Minovi S.: Shaping the future of transport and climate action with four words (2022). https://blogs.worldbank.org/transport/shaping-future-transport-and-climate-action-four-words. Accessed 10 June 2022
24. Pazos J.: Valuation of utility tokens based on the quantity theory of money. J. Br. Blockchain Assoc. **1**(2), 2516–3957 (2018). https://doi.org/10.31585/jbba-1-2-(2)2018. WOS: 000776575700001
25. Puthal, D., Malik, N., Mohanty, S., Kougianos, E., Das, G.: Everything you wanted to know about the blockchain: its promise component processes and problems. IEEE Consum. Electron. Mag. **7**, 6–14 (2018)
26. Qurotul, A., Nur, A., Rahmat, S., Nuke, S., Shofiyul, M.: iLearning education based on gamification blockchain. Indonesian J. Electr. Eng. Comput. Sci. **26**(1), 531–538 (2022)
27. Rajanen, M., Rajanen, D.: Usability benefits in gamification. In: GamiFIN, vol, 87, p. 95 (2017)
28. Rapp, A.: From games to gamification: a classification of rewards in world of Warcraft for the design of gamified systems. Simul. Gaming **48**(3), 381–401 (2017)

29. Ren, Y., Li, H., Shen, L., Zhang, Y., Chen, Y., Wang, J.: What is the efficiency of fast urbanization? A China study. Sustainability **10**(9), 3180 (2018)

30. Robson, K., Plangger, K., Kietzmann, J.H., McCarthy, I., Pitt, L.: Is it all a game? Understanding the principles of gamification. Bus. Horiz. **58**(4), 411–420 (2015). https://doi.org/10.1016/j.bushor.2015.03.006

31. Ruhi, U.: Level up your strategy: towards a descriptive framework for meaningful enterprise gamification. Technol. Innov. Manage. Rev. **5**, 5–16 (2015). https://doi.org/10.22215/timreview/918

32. Salah, K., Rehman, M.H.U., Nizamuddin, N., Al-Fuqaha, A.: Blockchain for AI: review and open research challenges. IEEE Access **7**, 10127–10149 (2019). https://doi.org/10.1109/ACCESS.2018.2890507

33. Spanellis, A., Harviainen, J.T.: Transforming Society and Organizations through Gamification. From the Sustainable Development Goals to Inclusive Workplaces. Springer, Cham (2021).https://doi.org/10.1007/978-3-030-68207-1

34. Stibe, A., Cugelman, B.: Social influence scale for technology design and transformation. In: Lamas, D., Loizides, F., Nacke, L., Petrie, H., Winckler, M., Zaphiris, P. (eds.) INTERACT 2019. LNCS, vol. 11748, pp. 561–577. Springer, Cham (2019). https://doi.org/10.1007/978-3-030-29387-1_33

35. Stibe, A., Larson, K.: Persuasive cities for sustainable wellbeing: quantified communities. In: Younas, M., Awan, I., Kryvinska, N., Strauss, C., Thanh, D.V. (eds.) MobiWIS 2016. LNCS, vol. 9847, pp. 271–282. Springer, Cham (2016). https://doi.org/10.1007/978-3-319-44215-0_22

36. Syed, A., Sierra-Sosa, D., Kumar, A., Elmaghraby, A.: IoT in smart cities: a survey of technologies, practices and challenges. Smart Cities **4**(2), 429–475 (2021). https://doi.org/10.3390/smartcities4020024

37. Vanolo, A.: Cities and the politics of gamification. Cities **74**, 320–326 (2018)

38. Venditti, B.: United Nation, How Material Consumption is Calculated (2022). https://www.weforum.org/agenda/2022/04/global-urbanization-material-consumption/. Accessed 10 Jan 2023

39. Wang, S., Ding, W., Li, J., Yuan, Y., Ouyang, L., Wang, F.-Y.: Decentralized autonomous organizations: Concept model and applications. IEEE Trans. Comput. Soc. Syst. **6**(5), 870–878 (2019)

40. Zichichi, M., Contu, M., Ferretti, S., D'Angelo, G.: LikeStarter: a smart-contract based social DAO for crowdfunding, pp. 313–318 (2019). https://doi.org/10.1109/INFCOMW.2019.8845133

Digital Systems in Healthcare Services

Harnessing the Digital Revolution: A Comprehensive Review of mHealth Applications for Remote Monitoring in Transforming Healthcare Delivery

Avnish Singh Jat[(✉)] [iD] and Tor-Morten Grønli [iD]

School of Economics, Innovation, and Technology, Kristiania University College, Oslo, Norway
avnishsingh.jat@kristiania.no

Abstract. The utilization of mHealth applications for remote monitoring has the potential to revolutionize healthcare delivery by enhancing patient outcomes, increasing access to healthcare services, and reducing healthcare costs. This literature review aims to provide a comprehensive overview of the current state of knowledge on mHealth applications for remote monitoring, including their types, benefits, challenges, and limitations, as well as future directions and research gaps. A systematic search of databases such as PubMed, MEDLINE, EMBASE, CINAHL, and Google Scholar was conducted to identify relevant articles published within the last 5 years. Thematic analysis was used to synthesize the findings.

The review highlights various types of mHealth applications used for remote monitoring, such as telemedicine platforms, mobile apps for chronic disease management, and wearable devices. The benefits of these applications include improved patient outcomes, increased access to healthcare, reduced healthcare costs, and addressing healthcare disparities. However, challenges and limitations, such as privacy and security concerns, lack of technical infrastructure, regulatory issues, data accuracy, user adherence, and the digital divide, need to be addressed to ensure successful adoption and utilization of mHealth applications.

Further research is required in areas such as the long-term effects of mHealth applications on patient outcomes, integration of mHealth data with electronic health records, and the development of artificial intelligence-driven mHealth applications. By harnessing the potential of mHealth applications and addressing the existing challenges, healthcare delivery can be transformed towards a more accessible, cost-effective, and patient-centered model.

Keywords: mHealth · mobile health · remote monitoring · telemedicine · digital health · healthcare applications · chronic disease management · wearable devices · electronic health records · artificial intelligence · digital divide

1 Introduction

The rapid advancement of technology has transformed various aspects of our lives, and healthcare is no exception. The intersection of healthcare and technology has led to the development of innovative solutions that can improve healthcare delivery, enhance

M. Younas et al. (Eds.): MobiWIS 2023, LNCS 13977, pp. 55–67, 2023.
https://doi.org/10.1007/978-3-031-39764-6_4

patient outcomes, and reduce costs. One such innovation is the use of mobile health (mHealth) applications for remote monitoring. This literature review aims to explore the current state of knowledge on the utilization of mHealth applications for remote monitoring and to identify research gaps and future directions in this field.

mHealth applications refer to the use of mobile and wireless devices, such as smartphones, tablets, and wearable sensors, to support medical and public health practices. These applications enable the collection, transmission, analysis, and presentation of health-related data, facilitating better healthcare management and decision-making.[1] Remote monitoring, on the other hand, is a healthcare delivery method that allows healthcare providers to continuously monitor patients' health status and provide timely interventions without the need for in-person visits. Remote monitoring is particularly relevant for managing chronic diseases, such as diabetes, hypertension, and heart failure, where continuous monitoring and timely interventions are crucial for improving patient outcomes.[2] The significance of mHealth applications for remote monitoring in healthcare delivery cannot be overstated. As the global population ages and the prevalence of chronic diseases increases, there is a growing demand for cost-effective, accessible, and patient-centered healthcare solutions.[3] mHealth applications have the potential to address these needs by providing real-time monitoring, personalized feedback, and enhanced communication between patients and healthcare providers.[4] Furthermore, these applications can help bridge the gap in healthcare access, particularly in rural and low-resource settings, where traditional healthcare delivery methods may be limited [5].

The purpose of this literature review is to synthesize existing research on the utilization of mHealth applications for remote monitoring and to identify research gaps and future directions in this field. Specifically, the literature review seeks to answer the following research questions:

a) *What types of mHealth applications are currently being used for remote monitoring, and what are their key features and functionalities?*
b) *What are the benefits of using mHealth applications for remote monitoring in terms of patient outcomes, healthcare access, and cost reduction?*
c) *What are the challenges and limitations associated with the adoption and utilization of mHealth applications for remote monitoring?*
d) *What are the potential solutions to overcome these challenges and limitations, and what are the emerging trends and technologies that could shape the future of mHealth applications for remote monitoring?*

By examining the existing literature on mHealth applications for remote monitoring, this review aims to provide a comprehensive understanding of the current state of knowledge in this field, inform future research, and contribute to the ongoing discourse on the role of technology in transforming healthcare delivery.

2 Background

The development of mHealth applications and the growth of remote monitoring in healthcare have evolved over the past few decades, driven by the convergence of various technological advancements and the growing need for more accessible and cost-effective healthcare solutions. This section provides an overview of the evolution of mHealth applications and the factors contributing to their increased adoption in remote monitoring.

The origins of mHealth can be traced back to the 1990s, when mobile devices were first used for basic healthcare purposes, such as sending short message service (SMS) reminders for medication adherence or appointment scheduling.[6] With the advent of smartphones in the late 2000s, mHealth applications started to gain traction as these devices offered enhanced processing capabilities, larger screens, and an expanding ecosystem of applications.[7] Around the same time, the proliferation of wearable devices and sensors capable of collecting and transmitting health-related data further fueled the development of mHealth applications [8].

The growth of remote monitoring in healthcare can be attributed to several factors, including the rising prevalence of chronic diseases, an aging global population, and the increasing burden on healthcare systems. Remote monitoring has emerged as a viable solution to address these challenges, as it allows healthcare providers to monitor patients' health status continuously and intervene in a timely manner, thus improving outcomes and reducing hospitalizations [9].

There are several key factors driving the increased adoption of mHealth applications for remote monitoring in healthcare:

Technological advancements: The rapid evolution of mobile and wireless technologies, such as smartphones, wearable devices, and sensors, has enabled the development of sophisticated mHealth applications that can collect, analyze, and transmit health-related data in real-time. Additionally, advancements in data analytics, artificial intelligence, and cloud computing have further enhanced the capabilities of mHealth applications in remote monitoring [10].

Growing smartphone penetration: The widespread adoption of smartphones has made it easier for both patients and healthcare providers to access mHealth applications. According to the Pew Research Center, smartphone ownership has grown significantly over the past decade, with more than 5 billion people worldwide now using smartphones. This increased accessibility has facilitated the adoption of mHealth applications for remote monitoring across various demographic groups and geographical regions [11].

Need for cost-effective healthcare solutions: The rising costs of healthcare have become a significant concern for governments, healthcare providers, and patients alike. mHealth applications for remote monitoring offer a cost-effective solution by reducing the need for in-person visits, minimizing hospital readmissions, and enabling more efficient use of healthcare resources. Studies have shown that mHealth applications can lead to significant cost savings, particularly in the management of chronic diseases [12, 13].

Patient empowerment and demand for personalized care: There has been a growing trend towards patient empowerment and a demand for personalized healthcare solutions. mHealth applications for remote monitoring empower patients to actively participate in their healthcare management and enable healthcare providers to deliver personalized interventions based on real-time data. This shift towards patient-centered care has contributed to the increased adoption of mHealth applications for remote monitoring [14].

The development of mHealth applications and the growth of remote monitoring in healthcare have been driven by a combination of technological advancements, increasing smartphone penetration, and the need for cost-effective and personalized healthcare solutions. As these trends continue to evolve, it is expected that mHealth applications for remote monitoring will play an increasingly critical role in healthcare delivery.

3   Methodology

This section provides an overview of the approach taken to collect, analyze, and synthesize the relevant research on the utilization of mHealth applications for remote monitoring. The methodology section will discuss the search strategy, inclusion and exclusion criteria, data extraction, and analysis process.

3.1   Search Strategy

To identify relevant articles and studies on mHealth applications for remote monitoring, a comprehensive search of databases such as PubMed, MEDLINE, EMBASE, CINAHL, and Google Scholar was conducted. The search terms used included combinations of keywords such as "mHealth," "mobile health," "remote monitoring," "telemedicine," "digital health," and "healthcare applications." Additionally, reference lists of the included articles were reviewed to identify any other relevant publications.

3.2   Inclusion and Exclusion Criteria

To ensure the relevance and quality of the literature included in the review, specific inclusion and exclusion criteria were established. Studies were included if they:

a) Were published in English.
b) Focused on mHealth applications used for remote monitoring in healthcare settings.
c) Presented primary research, such as clinical trials, observational studies, or qualitative research.

Were published within the last 5 years to ensure the relevance of the technology and findings.

Exclusion criteria were applied to remove studies that:

a) Did not focus on mHealth applications or remote monitoring.
b) Were reviews, editorials, or opinion pieces without primary data.
c) Focused on telehealth interventions that did not involve mobile or digital technology.

3.3   Data Extraction

After the identification of relevant articles and studies, data were extracted using a standardized data extraction form. The extracted information included the study's objectives, design, population, mHealth application type, intervention details, outcome measures, and main findings.

3.4 Data Analysis

The extracted data were analyzed and synthesized using a thematic approach. This involved identifying common themes, patterns, and trends across the included studies. [15] The analysis was organized into sections that addressed the different aspects of mHealth applications for remote monitoring, such as types of applications, benefits, challenges and limitations, future directions, and research gaps.

By following a rigorous methodology, the literature review aims to provide a comprehensive and up-to-date overview of the current state of knowledge on the utilization of mHealth applications for remote monitoring in healthcare. This approach ensures that the review's findings are based on a thorough examination of the available evidence, which can serve as a foundation for further research and inform policy and practice decisions in this rapidly evolving field.

4 MHealth Applications for Remote Monitoring

mHealth applications for remote monitoring encompass a wide range of tools and platforms designed to facilitate healthcare delivery and improve patient outcomes. These applications as per our review can be broadly categorized into three main types: telemedicine platforms, mobile apps for chronic disease management, and wearable devices. This section will discuss each of these categories, their key features and functionalities, and examples of successful mHealth applications used in various medical fields.

4.1 Telemedicine Platforms

Telemedicine platforms allow healthcare providers to conduct virtual consultations with patients, enabling remote diagnosis, treatment planning, and follow-up care. These platforms often include features such as video conferencing, secure messaging, electronic health record (EHR) integration, and appointment scheduling. [16] Telemedicine platforms have become particularly useful during the COVID-19 pandemic, as they have enabled healthcare providers to continue delivering care while minimizing the risk of infection [17].

Practo is a leading telemedicine platform in India that connects patients with healthcare providers through video consultations, allowing for remote diagnosis and treatment of various medical conditions, including dermatological issues, mental health concerns, and chronic disease management [18].

4.2 Mobile Apps for Chronic Disease Management

Mobile apps for chronic disease management are designed to help patients and healthcare providers monitor and manage chronic conditions, such as diabetes, hypertension, and heart failure. These apps typically include features such as medication reminders, symptom tracking, personalized feedback, and educational resources. Some apps also integrate with wearable devices or external sensors to collect real-time health data, which can be shared with healthcare providers for analysis and intervention [19, 20].

MySugr is a mobile app designed for diabetes management, allowing patients to track their blood glucose levels, insulin doses, and carbohydrate intake. The app provides personalized feedback and insights to help users maintain optimal blood sugar control and integrates with various glucose meters and insulin pumps for seamless data collection [21].

4.3 Wearable Devices

Wearable devices, such as fitness trackers and smartwatches, are increasingly being used for remote monitoring purposes, as they can collect and transmit various health-related data, including heart rate, physical activity, sleep patterns, and more. Some wearable devices also incorporate specialized sensors to monitor specific health parameters, such as blood glucose levels or blood pressure, making them particularly useful for managing chronic diseases [10, 22].

Apple Watch Series 7 features an FDA-cleared electrocardiogram (ECG) app that can detect atrial fibrillation, a common form of irregular heartbeat. Users can share their ECG data with their healthcare providers, allowing for remote monitoring and timely interventions when necessary [23].

4.4 Features of mHealth Applications

The key features and functionalities of mHealth applications for remote monitoring include:

Data collection: mHealth applications collect various types of health-related data, such as vital signs, symptoms, medication adherence, and lifestyle factors, to provide a comprehensive view of a patient's health status [24].

Patient-provider communication: These applications often facilitate secure communication between patients and healthcare providers, enabling remote consultations, real-time feedback, and timely interventions [25].

Data analysis: mHealth applications typically incorporate data analytics and artificial intelligence capabilities to analyze health data, identify trends and patterns, and generate personalized insights and recommendations [24].

mHealth applications for remote monitoring have been successfully used in various medical fields, including:

Cardiology: AliveCor's KardiaMobile is a portable ECG device that connects to a smartphone app, enabling patients to monitor their heart rhythm and share the data with their healthcare providers for remote monitoring and intervention [26].

Diabetes management: Dexcom G6 is a continuous glucose monitoring (CGM) system that tracks blood glucose levels in real-time, sends alerts when levels are too high or low, and shares the data with healthcare providers for remote monitoring and personalized feedback [27].

Mental health: Headspace is a meditation and mindfulness app that offers guided sessions, tools, and resources to help users manage stress, anxiety, and depression. While Headspace does not directly provide remote monitoring by healthcare providers, the app allows users to track their progress and share their mental health data with therapists or other healthcare professionals, facilitating remote support and personalized interventions. Headspace has been shown to be effective in reducing stress, improving focus, and promoting overall mental well-being [28].

mHealth applications for remote monitoring encompass a diverse range of tools and platforms, such as telemedicine platforms, mobile apps for chronic disease management, and wearable devices. These applications offer various features and functionalities, including data collection, patient-provider communication, and data analysis, to facilitate remote healthcare delivery and improve patient outcomes. Examples of successful mHealth applications in various medical fields demonstrate the potential of these technologies in transforming healthcare delivery and addressing the growing demand for cost-effective, accessible, and patient-centered care.

5   Benefits of mHealth Applications for Remote Monitoring

The utilization of mHealth applications for remote monitoring offers several advantages that can transform healthcare delivery and improve patient outcomes. This section will discuss the key benefits of mHealth applications for remote monitoring, review the evidence supporting their effectiveness, and explore their potential to address healthcare disparities in rural and low-resource settings.

Improved patient outcomes

mHealth applications for remote monitoring enable continuous monitoring of patients' health status, allowing healthcare providers to intervene in a timely manner and prevent complications. This is particularly beneficial for patients with chronic conditions, where early detection and intervention can significantly improve outcomes.[29] Several studies and trials have demonstrated the effectiveness of mHealth applications in improving patient outcomes. A study published in JAMA found that patients using a mobile app for heart failure management experienced fewer hospitalizations and improved quality of life compared to those receiving standard care [30].

Increased access to healthcare

mHealth applications can bridge geographical barriers and provide access to healthcare services for individuals in remote or underserved areas. Telemedicine platforms, for instance, enable virtual consultations with healthcare providers, reducing the need for patients to travel long distances for in-person visits [31]. Moreover, mHealth applications can facilitate access to specialized care for patients with rare or complex conditions, who may not have access to expert care in their local communities. A systematic review published in the Journal of Medical Internet Research found that telemedicine interventions can improve access to healthcare and patient satisfaction, particularly in rural and remote areas [32].

Reduced healthcare costs

By enabling remote monitoring and reducing the need for in-person visits, mHealth applications can lead to significant cost savings for both patients and healthcare providers. [33] A study published in Journal of Medical Internet Research: Cardiovascular Quality and Outcomes found that a telemonitoring program for heart failure patients resulted in a 30% reduction in hospitalization costs.[34] Furthermore, mHealth applications can streamline healthcare processes, such as appointment scheduling and medication management, leading to increased efficiency and reduced administrative costs [33].

Addressing healthcare disparities

mHealth applications have the potential to address healthcare disparities by providing access to healthcare services for traditionally underserved populations, such as those in rural or low-resource settings. By leveraging mobile and wireless technologies, mHealth applications can overcome infrastructure limitations, such as the lack of healthcare facilities and healthcare providers and offer cost-effective healthcare solutions for these populations. [35] A study published in the International Journal of Medical Informatics found that a mobile health intervention targeting rural populations with chronic diseases led to improved medication adherence and disease-specific knowledge [36].

mHealth applications for remote monitoring offer several advantages, including improved patient outcomes, increased access to healthcare, reduced healthcare costs, and the potential to address healthcare disparities. The evidence from studies and trials supports the effectiveness of mHealth applications in improving patient outcomes and healthcare delivery, particularly for individuals in rural and low-resource settings. As technology continues to advance and mHealth applications become more sophisticated, their role in transforming healthcare delivery and addressing healthcare disparities is expected to grow.

6 Challenges and Limitations

While mHealth applications for remote monitoring offer numerous benefits, they also face several challenges and limitations that can hinder their adoption and utilization. This section will identify the key barriers, discuss the limitations of mHealth applications, and explore potential solutions to overcome these challenges.

Privacy and security concerns

One of the primary challenges associated with mHealth applications is ensuring the privacy and security of sensitive health information. Patients and healthcare providers may be hesitant to adopt mHealth applications due to concerns about unauthorized access to personal health data, data breaches, or misuse of information.[37] To address these concerns, developers of mHealth applications must adhere to strict data protection standards, implement robust encryption methods, and comply with relevant regulations, such as the Health Insurance Portability and Accountability Act (HIPAA) in the United States.[38] Additionally, one research reviewed mentioned the integration of technologies like blockchain for security can help enhance data protection and increase confidence in the use of mHealth applications for remote monitoring [39].

Lack of technical infrastructure

The successful implementation of mHealth applications for remote monitoring requires a robust technical infrastructure, including reliable internet connectivity, compatible devices, and interoperable systems. In some rural or low-resource settings, the lack of adequate infrastructure can hinder the adoption of mHealth applications. To overcome this challenge, governments and organizations should invest in improving connectivity and infrastructure in underserved areas, while developers should design mHealth applications that can function with limited resources or in offline mode [40, 41].

Regulatory issues

Navigating the complex regulatory landscape for mHealth applications can be challenging for developers and healthcare providers alike. Different countries and regions have varying regulations regarding the approval, use, and reimbursement of mHealth applications, which can create confusion and slow down the adoption process. To address this issue, stakeholders should advocate for harmonized regulatory frameworks and clear guidelines for the development and deployment of mHealth applications [42, 43].

Data accuracy

Ensuring the accuracy and reliability of health data collected through mHealth applications is critical for effective remote monitoring. Some wearable devices or sensors may not be as accurate as traditional medical devices, which can compromise the quality of care provided. To overcome this limitation, developers should prioritize the validation and calibration of mHealth applications and devices, while healthcare providers should be cautious when interpreting data from these sources [44, 45].

User adherence

The effectiveness of mHealth applications for remote monitoring largely depends on user adherence, which can be influenced by factors such as usability, user engagement, and perceived value. To enhance user adherence, developers should design mHealth applications that are user-friendly, customizable, and incorporate gamification or motivational strategies to encourage sustained use [46].

Digital divide

The digital divide, or the gap between those with access to digital technologies and those without, can limit the reach of mHealth applications for remote monitoring. Individuals from low-income, elderly, or rural populations may face barriers in accessing or using mHealth applications due to factors such as affordability, digital literacy, or lack of infrastructure. To bridge the digital divide, stakeholders should promote digital literacy initiatives, subsidize the cost of devices or internet access, and develop low-cost mHealth solutions tailored to the needs of these populations [47].

Addressing the challenges and limitations of mHealth applications for remote monitoring is essential to ensure their successful adoption and utilization. By developing standardized protocols, promoting digital literacy, ensuring data privacy, and investing in infrastructure improvements, stakeholders can help overcome these barriers and unlock the full potential of mHealth applications in transforming healthcare delivery and improving patient outcomes.

7   Future Directions and Research Gaps

As mHealth applications for remote monitoring continue to evolve and gain traction, there are several areas where further research is needed to better understand their impact and potential. This section will highlight key research gaps and discuss emerging trends and technologies that could shape the future of mHealth applications for remote monitoring.

Integration of mHealth data with electronic health records.

The seamless integration of mHealth data with electronic health records (EHRs) is crucial for optimizing healthcare delivery and facilitating data-driven decision-making. Research is needed to develop interoperable systems, data standards, and protocols that enable efficient and secure sharing of mHealth data across different healthcare providers and platforms.

Artificial intelligence-driven mHealth applications.

The integration of artificial intelligence (AI) and machine learning algorithms into mHealth applications holds significant promise for enhancing remote monitoring capabilities, personalizing care, and predicting patient outcomes. Further research is needed to develop and validate AI-driven mHealth applications, as well as to understand the ethical, legal, and social implications of their use in healthcare.

Internet of Things (IoT) and remote monitoring.

The Internet of Things (IoT) refers to the interconnected network of devices and sensors that can collect, share, and analyze data. IoT has the potential to transform mHealth applications for remote monitoring by enabling the seamless integration of wearable devices, home monitoring systems, and environmental sensors. Research is needed to develop IoT-based mHealth applications, evaluate their effectiveness, and address the associated privacy and security challenges.

Advanced data analytics.

As mHealth applications generate vast amounts of health data, there is a growing need for advanced data analytics techniques to process, analyze, and interpret this information. Research is needed to develop novel analytics algorithms and tools that can identify trends, patterns, and correlations in mHealth data, enabling healthcare providers to make more informed decisions and deliver personalized care.

8 Conclusion

In conclusion, mHealth applications for remote monitoring have the potential to transform healthcare delivery by offering several benefits, including improved patient outcomes, increased access to healthcare services, reduced healthcare costs, and addressing healthcare disparities. Despite the challenges and limitations, such as privacy and security concerns, lack of technical infrastructure, regulatory issues, data accuracy, user adherence, and the digital divide, potential solutions like standardized protocols, digital literacy promotion, and ensuring data privacy can help overcome these barriers.

As the field continues to grow, further research is required to address gaps in areas like long-term effects on patient outcomes, integration of mHealth data with electronic health records, and the development of artificial intelligence-driven mHealth applications. Emerging trends and technologies, such as 5G, the Internet of Things, and advanced data analytics, will shape the future of mHealth applications for remote monitoring, enabling more sophisticated and personalized care.

Collaboration among stakeholders, ongoing research, and investment in infrastructure improvements will be crucial to ensure that mHealth applications remain responsive to the changing needs of patients and healthcare providers. By harnessing the potential of mHealth applications for remote monitoring, we can work towards a future where healthcare is more accessible, cost-effective, and patient-centered.

References

1. Sadiku, M.N.O., Shadare, A.E., Musa, S.M.: Mobile Health. Int. J. Eng. Res. **6**, 450 (2017). https://doi.org/10.5958/2319-6890.2017.00061.7
2. Coulby, G., Clear, A., Jones, O., Young, F., Stuart, S., Godfrey, A.: Towards remote healthcare monitoring using accessible IoT technology: state-of-the-art, insights and experimental design. Biomed. Eng. Online **19**, 80 (2020). https://doi.org/10.1186/s12938-020-00825-9
3. Milani, R.V., Lavie, C.J.: Health care 2020: reengineering health care delivery to combat chronic disease. Am. J. Med. **128**, 337–343 (2015). https://doi.org/10.1016/j.amjmed.2014.10.047
4. Abaza, H., Marschollek, M.: mHealth application areas and technology combinations. Meth. Inf. Med. **56**, e105–e122 (2017). https://doi.org/10.3414/ME17-05-0003
5. Kyriacou, E.C., Pattichis, C.S., Pattichis, M.S.: An overview of recent health care support systems for eEmergency and mHealth applications. In: 2009 Annual International Conference of the IEEE Engineering in Medicine and Biology Society, pp. 1246–1249 (2009). https://doi.org/10.1109/IEMBS.2009.5333913
6. Nilsen, W., et al.: Advancing the science of mHealth. J. Health Commun. **17**, 5–10 (2012). https://doi.org/10.1080/10810730.2012.677394
7. Fiordelli, M., et al.: Mapping mHealth research: a decade of evolution. J. Med. Internet Res. **15**(5), e95 (2013). https://doi.org/10.2196/JMIR.2430
8. Rowland, S.P., et al.: What is the clinical value of mHealth for patients. NPJ Digit. Med. **3**(1), 4 (2020). https://doi.org/10.1038/S41746-019-0206-X
9. Liao, Y., et al.: The future of wearable technologies and remote monitoring in health care. Am. Soc. Clin. Oncol. Educ. Book **39**, 115–121 (2019). https://doi.org/10.1200/EDBK_238919
10. Jat, A.S., Grønli, T.-M.: Smart watch for smart health monitoring: a literature review. In: Rojas, I., Valenzuela, O., Rojas, F., Herrera, L.J., Ortuño, F. (eds.) Bioinformatics and Biomedical Engineering, pp. 256–268. Springer, Cham (2022). https://doi.org/10.1007/978-3-031-07704-3_21
11. Marshall, J.M., Dunstan, D.A., Bartik, W.: Clinical or gimmickal: the use and effectiveness of mobile mental health apps for treating anxiety and depression (2020). https://doi.org/10.1177/0004867419876700. Accessed 17 June 2023
12. Barlow, R., Diop, F.: Increasing the utilization of cost-effective health services through changes in demand. Health Policy Plan. **10**, 284–295 (1995)
13. Pettoello-Mantovani, M., Namazova-Baranova, L., Ehrich, J.: Integrating and rationalizing public healthcare services as a source of cost containment in times of economic crises. Ital. J. Pediatr. **42**, 18 (2016). https://doi.org/10.1186/s13052-016-0231-1
14. Chen, H., Compton, S., Hsiao, O.: DiabeticLink: a health big data system for patient empowerment and personalized healthcare. In: Zeng, D., et al. (eds.) ICSH 2013. LNCS, vol. 8040, pp. 71–83. Springer, Heidelberg (2013). https://doi.org/10.1007/978-3-642-39844-5_10
15. Blenner, S.R., Köllmer, M., Rouse, A.J., Daneshvar, N., Williams, C., Andrews, L.B.: Privacy policies of android diabetes apps and sharing of health information. JAMA **315**(10), 1051–1052 (2016). https://doi.org/10.1001/jama.2015.19426
16. Ting, D.S., Gunasekeran, D.V., Wickham, L., Wong, T.Y.: Next generation telemedicine platforms to screen and triage. Br. J. Ophthalmol. **104**, 299–300 (2020). https://doi.org/10.1136/bjophthalmol-2019-315066
17. Lin, J.C., Humphries, M.D., Shutze, W.P., Aalami, O.O., Fischer, U.M., Hodgson, K.J.: Telemedicine platforms and their use in the coronavirus disease-19 era to deliver comprehensive vascular care. J. Vasc. Surg. **73**, 392–398 (2021). https://doi.org/10.1016/j.jvs.2020.06.051

18. Srinivasan, R.: Practo. In: Srinivasan, R. (ed.) Platform Business Models: Frameworks, Concepts and Design, pp. 131–135. Springer, Singapore (2021).https://doi.org/10.1007/978-981-16-2838-2_10
19. Bardhan, I., Chen, H., Karahanna, E.: Connecting systems, data, and people: a multidisciplinary research roadmap for chronic disease management. MIS Q.: Manag. Inf. Syst. **44**, 185–200 (2020). https://doi.org/10.25300/MISQ/2020/14644
20. Pham, Q., et al.: A Library of analytic indicators to evaluate effective engagement with consumer mhealth apps for chronic conditions: scoping review. JMIR Mhealth Uhealth **7**, e11941 (2019). https://doi.org/10.2196/11941
21. Debong, F., Mayer, H., Kober, J.: Real-world assessments of mySugr mobile health app. Diabetes Technol. Ther. **21**, S2–35https://doi.org/10.1089/dia.2019.0019
22. Smuck, M., Odonkor, C.A., Wilt, J.K., Schmidt, N., Swiernik, M.A.: The emerging clinical role of wearables: factors for successful implementation in healthcare. NPJ Digit. Med. **4**, 1–8 (2021). https://doi.org/10.1038/s41746-021-00418-3
23. Ruiz, A.M.: Validity and Reliability of the Apple Series 6 and 7 Smartwatches and Polar H-10 Monitor on Heart Rate (Doctoral dissertation, The University of Texas at El Paso) (2022)
24. MacKinnon, G.E., Brittain, E.L.: Mobile Health technologies in cardiopulmonary disease. Chest **157**, 654–664 (2020). https://doi.org/10.1016/j.chest.2019.10.015
25. Shaik, T., et al.: Remote patient monitoring using artificial intelligence: current state, applications, and challenges. WIREs Data Min. Knowl. Discov. **13**, e1485 (2023). https://doi.org/10.1002/widm.1485
26. Girvin, Z.P., Silver, E.S., Liberman, L.: Comparison of AliveCor KardiaMobile Six-Lead ECG with standard ECG in pediatric patients. Pediatr. Cardiol. **44**, 689–694 (2023). https://doi.org/10.1007/s00246-022-02998-7
27. Akturk, H.K., Dowd, R., Shankar, K., Derdzinski, M.: Real-world evidence and glycemic improvement using dexcom G6 features. Diab. Technol. Ther. **23**, S–21 (2021). https://doi.org/10.1089/dia.2020.0654
28. Militello, L., Sobolev, M., Okeke, F., Adler, D.A., Nahum-Shani, I.: Digital prompts to increase engagement with the headspace app and for stress regulation among parents: feasibility study. JMIR Formative Res. **6**, e30606 (2022). https://doi.org/10.2196/30606
29. Chang, H.-Y., Hou, Y.-P., Yeh, F.-H., Lee, S.-S.: The impact of an mHealth app on knowledge, skills and anxiety about dressing changes: a randomized controlled trial. J. Adv. Nurs. **76**, 1046–1056 (2020). https://doi.org/10.1111/jan.14287
30. Schmaderer, M., Miller, J.N., Mollard, E.: Experiences of using a self-management mobile app among individuals with heart failure: qualitative study. JMIR Nurs. **4**, e28139 (2021). https://doi.org/10.2196/28139
31. Sahoo, S.: Mobile phone bridges health divide: exploring possibilities in health care services delivery in Odisha. Odisha Rev. 48–53 (2019)
32. Jiang, X., Ming, W.-K., You, J.H.: The cost-effectiveness of digital health interventions on the management of cardiovascular diseases: systematic review. J. Med. Internet Res. **21**, e13166 (2019). https://doi.org/10.2196/13166
33. Rowland, S.P., Fitzgerald, J.E., Holme, T., Powell, J., McGregor, A.: What is the clinical value of mHealth for patients? NPJ Digit. Med **3**, 1–6 (2020). https://doi.org/10.1038/s41746-019-0206-x
34. Ware, P., Ross, H.J., Cafazzo, J.A., Boodoo, C., Munnery, M., Seto, E.: Outcomes of a heart failure telemonitoring program implemented as the standard of care in an outpatient heart function clinic: pretest-posttest pragmatic study. J. Med. Internet Res. **22**, e16538 (2020). https://doi.org/10.2196/16538
35. Aguilera, A., et al.: mHealth app using machine learning to increase physical activity in diabetes and depression: clinical trial protocol for the DIAMANTE study. BMJ Open **10**, e034723 (2020). https://doi.org/10.1136/bmjopen-2019-034723

36. Lorca-Cabrera, J., Martí-Arques, R., Albacar-Riobóo, N., Raigal-Aran, L., Roldan-Merino, J., Ferré-Grau, C.: Mobile applications for caregivers of individuals with chronic conditions and/or diseases: quantitative content analysis. Int. J. Med. Inform. **145**, 104310 (2021). https://doi.org/10.1016/j.ijmedinf.2020.104310

37. Nurgalieva, L., O'Callaghan, D., Doherty, G.: Security and privacy of mHealth applications: a scoping review. IEEE Access **8**, 104247–104268 (2020). https://doi.org/10.1109/ACCESS.2020.2999934

38. Feld, A.D.: The health insurance portability and accountability act (HIPAA): its broad effect on practice. Official J. Am. Coll. Gastroenterol. | ACG. **100**, 1440 (2005)

39. Jat, A.S., Grønli, T.-M.: Blockchain for cybersecure healthcare. In: Awan, I., Younas, M., Poniszewska-Marańda, A. (eds.) Mobile Web and Intelligent Information Systems, pp. 106–117. Springer, Cham (2022). https://doi.org/10.1007/978-3-031-14391-5_8

40. Byambasuren, O., Beller, E., Hoffmann, T., Glasziou, P.: Barriers to and facilitators of the prescription of mHealth apps in Australian general practice: qualitative study. JMIR Mhealth Uhealth **8**, e17447 (2020). https://doi.org/10.2196/17447

41. Galetsi, P., Katsaliaki, K., Kumar, S.: Exploring benefits and ethical challenges in the rise of mHealth (mobile healthcare) technology for the common good: an analysis of mobile applications for health specialists. Technovation **121**, 102598 (2023)

42. Jogova, M., Shaw, J., Jamieson, T.: The regulatory challenge of mobile health: lessons for Canada. Healthc. Policy. **14**, 19 (2019)

43. Carmi, L., Zohar, M., Riva, G.M.: The European general data protection regulation (GDPR) in mHealth: theoretical and practical aspects for practitioners' use. Med Sci Law. **63**, 61–68 (2023). https://doi.org/10.1177/00258024221118411

44. Giebel, G.D., Gissel, C.: Accuracy of mHealth devices for atrial fibrillation screening: systematic review. JMIR Mhealth Uhealth **7**, e13641 (2019). https://doi.org/10.2196/13641

45. Vijayan, V., Connolly, J.P., Condell, J., McKelvey, N., Gardiner, P.: Review of Wearable devices and data collection considerations for connected health. Sensors **21**, 5589 (2021). https://doi.org/10.3390/s21165589

46. Jakob, R., et al.: Factors Influencing adherence to mhealth apps for prevention or management of noncommunicable diseases: systematic review. J. Med. Internet Res. **24**, e35371 (2022). https://doi.org/10.2196/35371

47. Paglialonga, A., Mastropietro, A., Scalco, E., Rizzo, G.: The mHealth. In: Andreoni, G., Perego, P., Frumento, E. (eds.) m_Health Current and Future Applications. EICC, pp. 5–17. Springer, Cham (2019). https://doi.org/10.1007/978-3-030-02182-5_2

Medical Test Results Management System Based on Blockchain, Smart Contracts, and NFT Technologies

Hieu T. Nguyen[1,3(✉)], Ngan N. T. Kim[2,3], N. M. Triet[1,3], Khanh H. Vo[1,3],
Quy T. Lu[1,3], Phuc N. Trong[1,3], Khoa T. Dang[1,3], Khiem H. Gia[1,3],
Nguyen D. P. Trong[1,3], Loc V. C. Phu[1,3], Anh N. The[1,3], Huynh T. Nghia[1,3],
Bang L. Khanh[1,3], and Huong H. Luong[1,3(✉)]

[1] FPT University, Can Tho, Vietnam
hieunt239@fe.edu.vn, huonghoangluong@gmail.com
[2] FPT Polytechnic, Can Tho, Vietnam
nganntkpc06789@fpt.edu.vn
[3] University of Insubria, Varese, Italy

Abstract. The current diagnostic and treatment process is highly dependent on the results of medical tests (i.e., current and past addiction tests). This information directly affects the doctor's decisions regarding the treatment regimen for each disease and the patient's condition. However, current centralized storage methods pose a major barrier for patients (i.e., changing medical facilities). Medical information is extremely private and affects the patient directly if left unprotected, so it is constrained to retrieve this information from another treatment facility. Many previous approaches have proposed a decentralized storage model based on blockchain, smart contracts technologies to solve the above problems. However, the security of personal information is a potential risk for the above systems due to the openness of data stored on the chain. Based on the above limitations, we propose the NFT combination model to create document sets based on test results for easy sharing by patients in the medical environment.

Keywords: Medical test results · Blockchain · Smart contracts · NFT · Ethereum · Fantom · Polygon · Binance Smart Chain

1 Introduction

Today, the diagnosis and treatment of diseases are getting smarter. It contributes to reducing the number of patients coming to medical facilities for examination and treatment. Specifically, the apps installed on smartphones support remote health monitoring under the supervision of family doctors/healthcare facilities (i.e., real people or AI platforms) [27]. However, to be able to replace the entire traditional health care system, several directions of research have shown the essential steps that must be taken [13]. Among the above risks, the problem related to the management of medical information in each individual is extremely challenging (i.e., medical treatment process, medical history). In particular, the medical history must be recorded accurately to ensure the diagnosis and treatment of disease [4].

To gradually replace traditional healthcare systems, a series of studies draws on the utility of today's advanced technologies to replace supply chain processes [9,10], as well as diagnosis and treatment of disease. The above solutions focus on decentralized storage (e.g., distributed) to ensure that data is not overloaded when users access [19]. Specifically, there have been several proposed models for managing patient's medical examination and treatment information based on Blockchain technology. For example, HealthBank[1] introduced in 2018 proposes a patient information management model based on Blockchain technology, where users can easily store all information trust on the blockchain. Similarly, Health-Nautica and Factom Announce Partnership.[2] exploited the transparency of stored data on-chain storage to build a system that protects the integrity of medical data (e.g. personal information, health status). Any stored information cannot be deleted or edited. All access requests are logged and stored on-chain.

However, storing all patient information on-chain faces two main problems: i) reduced system-wide performance and increased transaction fees per access; ii) does not guarantee patient privacy as all information is publicly available and easily accessible by the stakeholders. Indeed, for the first problem (i), too much information is stored leading to redundant and unnecessary [28]. Specifically, Thanh et al. [15] have stated that not all collected data has to be stored and processed on-chain (i.e., most of it is redundant and unnecessary). In addition, Trieu et al. [14] have provided a similar claim that personal data not directly related to treatment or diagnosis may be stored off-chain (e.g., IPFS). Besides, the transaction cost is also a concern when the more information and data on the chain, the more the processing or execution of the commands also increases the corresponding fee [1]. As for privacy risk (ii), it is easy to see that any stored data (i.e., unencrypted) can be exploited and corrupted by other users (i.e., same system). In particular, insurance companies can exploit information related to a patient's current medical history and refuse to sell coverage to them [26]. To solve this problem, some approaches based on Blockchain technology and IPFS, (e.g., Misbhauddin et al. [18] and Zyskind et al. [32]) have stored personal information of users (i.e., sensitive data) off-chain. This information is only stored as a one-way hash on the blockchain to minimize the risk of revealing personal data.

However, the above approach still faces problems when sharing their medical records with medical centers (i.e., medical staff: doctors, nurses, laboratory staff). To solve this problem, this paper proposes an approach based on a series of advanced technologies, namely blockchain, smart contracts, and NFT. Specifically, the patient's personal information and treatment history are stored as an NFT. Information related to medical test results is stored off-chain. Each test is generated corresponding NFTs and is shared with the required address

---

[1] https://www.healthbank.coop.

[2] https://www.factom.com/company-updates/healthnautica-factom-announce-partnership/.

(e.g., nurse, doctor). In addition, each patient will have a unique identifier to distinguish it from other patients.

Therefore, our work contributes on four aspects, namely (a) proposing a mechanism for sharing test results based on blockchain and smart contracts technologies; (b) proposing a medical test results generation based on the NFT tool; (c) implementing the proof-of-concept based on the proposed model on the EVM-supported platforms; and (d) deploying proof-of-concept on those platforms, i.e., BNB Smart Chain, Fantom, Polygon, and Celo to select the most suitable platform for our proposed model.[3]

2   Related Work

2.1   Patient-Centric Health Information Management Model

These approaches focus on exploiting the privacy preferences of individuals (i.e., patients). Specifically, the information is related not only to treatment (e.g., heart rate, blood pressure) but also other personal information (e.g., location, phone), so not all of them are useful in the process disease treatment. For example, a model of medical information extraction based on sensors and iodine devices implanted directly into the patient was proposed by Chen et al. [6]. Specifically, they proposed a model based on Blockchain technology applied to healthcare environments to store and control mining data from IoT devices. These devices store real-time medical data. The information is collected and sent directly to cloud servers (these data is encrypted before leaving the patient's control). Similarly, instead of empowering medical centers (i.e. hospitals) to store data and manage access to patient information, the approaches propose a new paradigm, where empowering patient control (e.g., [7,21,23]). Specifically, patients are allowed to share data with trusted subjects.

Similar to the above approaches, Makubalo et al. [17] has compiled approaches to empowering the sharing of health information to owners (i.e., patients) in their publication. To prevent re-sharing of shared information (i.e., doctors or nurses may share medical records with an untrusted third party), Yin et al. [31] introduced a system to protect data privacy by applying attribute-based encryption (ABE). Specifically, patients define their data access policies. These policies are defined as attributes of the object (e.g., accessor role, place of work) or context (e.g., time, location). Depending on the different context, medical staff may or may not be able to access the personal data of the patient. Similarly, Barua et al. [3] also proposes an ABE-based access control model to control accesses to patient data. In addition, based on the Role-based Access Control model Chen et al. [5] described a requester role-based access management model. Besides, some methods apply dynamic policy model to increase flexibility in medical environment [11,25] or design two layers of policy, i.e., i) security policy - protect data patient data from intrusion by users outside the system, and ii) privacy policy that protects patient information from agents in the system [28].

---

[3] We do not deploy smart contracts on ETH because the execution fee of smart contracts is too high.

2.2   Blockchain-Based Medical Information Management Model

This section focuses on articles based on i) blockchain technology to build a decentralized management model of patient medical data (including laboratory information) and ii) personal data storage. User kernel to IPFS to minimize the amount of information stored on-chain. For example, Madine et al. [16] has proposed a model of storing medical record information on blockchain and storing details of that information on IPFS. The purpose of this group of authors is to protect the privacy of patient data (i.e., limit access from users of the same system). For actual deployed solutions, HealthBank[4] combined blockchain and IPFS to propose a patient-centric model for sharing medical data. In addition to the above two approaches, several solutions are introduced to comply with privacy constraints (e.g., GDPR). For example, HealthNautica and Factom Announce Partnership[5] presented a decentralized data storage solution. and protect personal information based on Blockchain technology.

Also based on Blockchain and IPFS, MedAccess introduced patient Health Records management system [18]. The proposed system focuses on protecting patient information from being altered (i.e., transparency) and privacy (offchain storage). Similar to the approach of [18], to minimize the amount of information stored on the chain, Zyskind et al. [32] presents an onchain and offchain patient data and information storage model. Specifically, the information related to personnel management (i.e., patients, medical staff) for the treatment process is stored onchain; in contrast, sensitive information (i.e., medical data) is encrypted and stored on a centralized server. However, the above approaches only provide a way to store rather than share necessary information with other authorized subjects (i.e., doctors and nurses at health centers).

Understanding this disadvantage, the FHIRChain platform has proposed an approach that allows patients to share their medical data with a trusted delegate [30]. Specifically, instead of sharing the entire information stored on-chain, patients only need to share a part (off-chain storage). One of the approaches to off-chain processing of health information and data is proposed by Patel et al. [20], they demonstrate how patients can share their personal data to their respective destinations (i.e., healthcare centres). Another approach based on data streaming is also proposed by IRYO[6] based on NuCypher KMS (i.e., [8]).

During the Covid-19 pandemic, several approaches to exploiting remote disease diagnosis problems based on blockchain technology were proposed by Ahmad [2]. To address the problems of disease treatment during the pandemic, they presented a five-step approach: i) managing unsolicited access to patient records; ii) telemedicine diagnosis and treatment; iii) traceability of medical treatment devices used in households; iv) allowing access and patient health records to authorized subjects; and v) paymenting for health care services (e.g., prescriptions and doctor's consultation fees). The above approaches are only

---

[4] https://www.healthbank.coop/2018/10/30/healthbank-creates-the-first-patient-centric-healthcare-trust-ecosystem/.

[5] https://www.factom.com/company-updates/healthnautica-factom-announce-partnership/.

[6] https://iryo.network/iryo_whitepaper.pdf.

interested in subjects in the medical environment (i.e., patients and medical staff) but ignore other groups of subjects indirectly related to the treatment process (i.e., insurance companies and regulators). To address this shortcoming, Kassab et al. [12] proposed an extended medical model to store other processing between a patient and an insurance company, or between a hospital/medical facility and a drug or medical device provider.

All of the above evaluation directions face two major challenges for both the user-centric approach and based on Blockchain and IPFS technologies. Specifically, with the first approach of empowering users based on access policies, the approaches are limited when users have to create a series of policies to control access accordingly. These policies are prone to conflicts or redundancies if the number of access objects is large and there are many properties [26]. Moreover, getting used to a completely new system (i.e., user-centric) also causes users to encounter some obstacles due to lack of necessary background (i.e., average users). As for the second approach (blockchain and IPFS-based), it is agreed that this method brings a lot of efficiency in the process of storing and processing medical data, but on-chain data storage solutions and out-of-string also bring a lot of complications for the average user when they want to share [1,22]. To limit the above risks, in the framework of sharing medical test results, we combine a series of modern platforms including blockchain, smart contract, NFT. Specifically, instead of sharing policies to define groups of people who can retrieve test results or patient history, we create corresponding NFTs. This approach restricts the strict requirements of the technology platform, such as security policy-based methods. The next section presents our proposed model based on NFT technology (i.e., ERC721) to share information to the respective objects.

3   The Blockchain-Based Medical Test Results Management System

In this section, we present traditional medical test results management models before proposing an approach based on Blockchain technology, smart contract, and NFT.

3.1   Traditional Medical Test Results Management Model

Figure 1 shows the traditional process of testing and getting results based on four steps. Specifically, the patient creates an archive of health information (i.e., electronic or paper) called medical record book at the medical center. All information related to the treatment process, test results are recorded in the medical record book. The patient undergoes the necessary medical examinations before proceeding with the treatment. This information is extremely important - the doctor's diagnoses and judgments are based on the changes in the patient's health status through the test results. In developing countries, the testing phase often takes a long time to provide samples and receive test results due to limitations in infrastructure and supporting medical equipment. After receiving the

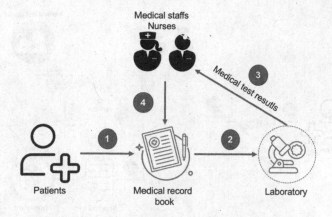

Fig. 1. Traditional medical test results management model.

results from the laboratory staff, the patient brings the results to the doctors and nurses to make judgments about their health status and corresponding treatments. All information about the diagnosis and treatment results are updated in the medical record book. Therefore, the loss of the patient's medical record book seriously affects the treatment process. For the electronic versions, the medical record book is stored locally at a separate hospital/health care facility. Due to the risky nature of medical data, sharing this information with other institutions is highly unlikely. Therefore, there is a need for a comprehensive solution to the problems related to the storage and sharing of patients' medical record books for both electronic and paper formats. The following section presents our solution based on popular technologies today: blockchain, smart contract and NFT.

3.2 Medical Test Results Management Model Based on Blockchain Technology, Smart Contract, and NFT

Figure 2 shows our approach based on blockchain technology, smart contract and NFT, consisting of nine steps. Users can create a system-wide shared identifier (call patience_ID global) to use across all medical systems (step 1). In addition, this identifier is associated with a medical record book that stores all information about the medical record and test results as well as the patient's medical history (step 2). Steps 3–6 are directly linked to UI services (i.e., User-Interface services), which provide interfaces for each user group of the system to limit complex operations (i.e., backend processing). These interactions are linked through smart contracts containing corresponding functions for storing and processing data (step 7). In this section we build functions related to contract creation/NFT or transfer of NFTs (see Introduction). All transactions are updated and stored and distributed in a distributed ledger, including information about visitors, time and location, etc. The information related to the test results is generated in the corresponding NFTs and forwarded to the physicians responsible for treating the patient (step 9).

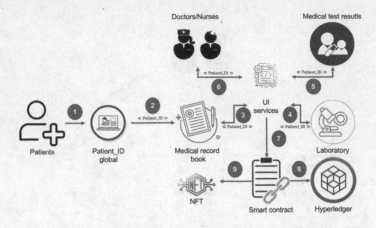

Fig. 2. Medical test results management model based on blockchain technology, smart contract, and NFT.

4   Implementation

Our reality model focuses on two main purposes i) data manipulation (i.e., medical test results) - creation, query and update - on blockchain platform and ii) creation of NFT for medical test results for easy sharing by patients (e.g., doctors, nurses).

4.1   Initialize Data/NFT

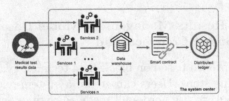

Fig. 3. Initialize data/NFT.

Figure 3 shows the data initialization steps involved in the medical test results. These types of medical test results include information about the type of test, time, testing facility, test results, consultation results, and the corresponding method and duration of treatment. In addition, information about the type of patient as well as the medical staff supporting the test is also added to the metadata of the test results. As for the storage process, services support concurrent storage (i.e., distributed processing as a peer-to-peer network) on a distributed ledger - supporting more than one user for concurrent storage reduce system latency. In general, the data on medical test results is organized as follows:

```
medicalTestResultsObject = {
"patientID": patientID,
"medicalTestID": medicalTestID,
"medicalStaffID": medicalStaffID,
"type": type of test,
"numbers": numbers of treatments,
"results": results of the medical test,
"diagnose": diagnosis of the illness,
"institution": institutionID,
"date": time and date,
"times": times of test,
"period": period of the treatment,
"state": Null};
```

Specifically, in addition to the information for content extraction (i.e., medical staff, test results, diagnostic results, etc.), we also store information related to the treatment status of patients hospital patient (i.e., "state" - defaults to Null). Specifically, "state" changes to a value of 1 if the respective patient has completed the treatment and left the medical center (i.e., numbers increases by 1); value 0 - patient is in treatment. In addition, we store the treatment interval and number of tests through two parameters "period" and "times". Then the pre-designed constraints in the Smart Contract are called through the API (i.e., name of function) to sync them up the chain. This role of validation is extremely important because they directly affect the process of storing medical information (i.e., medical test results), as well as the treatment of patients. For processes that initiate NFTs (i.e., store only test results), the contents of the NFT are defined as follows:

```
NFT MEDICAL_RECORD = {
"medicalRecordID": medicalRecordID,
"patientID": patientID,
"medicalTestID": medicalTestID,
"type": type of test,
"medicalStaffID": medicalStaffID,
"results": results of the medical test,
"institution": institutionID,
"date": time and date};
```

The above information is extracted from the original data stored on the string - our previous model built a property-based access control (RBAC) system, so it cannot be accessed directly from non-objects have ownership or access rights. In addition, a patient will perform many of their health assessments/checks before diagnosing the disease, so the information extracted limits the risk of data loss. For example, a doctor diagnosing blood problems does not need access to a patient's bone X-ray.

4.2   Data Query

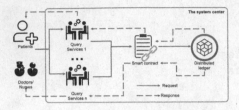 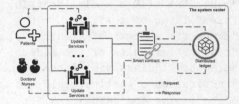

Fig. 4. Data query.   **Fig. 5.** Data updated.

Similar to the data initialization steps, the data query process also supports many simultaneous participants in the system for access (i.e., distributed model). Support services receive requests from medical staff (i.e., nurses/doctors), patients to access data. Depending on the query object we have different access purposes. Specifically, medical staff queries for the purpose of checking the medical testing process (i.e., test results). In contrast, patients can query the data to find information regarding the new owners of their NFTs. Figure 4 shows the steps to query medical test result data. These requests are sent as requests (i.e., pre-designed services as API calls) from the user to the smart contracts available in the system (i.e., name of function) before retrieving the data from the distributed ledger. All retrieval requests are also saved as query history for each individual or organization. In case the corresponding information is not found (e.g., wrong ID), the system will send a message not found results. For the NFT query process, all support services are provided as APIs.

4.3   Data Updated

The data update routine is invoked only after verifying that the data exists on the thread (i.e., after executing the corresponding data query procedure). In this section, we assume that the search data exists on the string. Where none exists, the system sends the same message to the user (see Sect. 4.2 for details). Similar to the two processes of query and data initialization, we support update services in the form of APIs to receive requests from users before passing them to smart contract (i.e., name of function) for processing. The purpose of this process is to update test results to reduce patient wait times at medical treatment facilities. In addition, it is also easy for doctors to track their treatment route based on the corresponding sequence of NFTs. Figure 5 shows the procedure for updating medical test results. For NFTs (i.e., available) the update process includes only moving from the owner's address to the new (i.e., new owner). If any information is updated on an existing NFT, it will be stored as a new NFT (see Sect. 4.1 for details).

5 Evaluation Scenarios

Fig. 6. The transaction info (e.g., BNB Smart Chain).

Fig. 7. NFT creation.   **Fig. 8.** NFT transfer.

Because the model for generating medical test results makes it easy for patients to manage test results (i.e., can be extended to medical records) as well as easily share them with other objects that users want. We want instead of defining security policies (e.g., access control), we implement the proposed model on EVM-enabled blockchain platforms instead of exploiting Hyperledger eco-system platforms because they are easy to open wide (i.e., using existing platforms and systems). In addition, assessments based on system responsiveness (i.e., number of requests responded successfully/failed, system latency - min, max, average) have been evaluated by us in the previous research paper. Therefore, in this paper, we determine the suitable platform for our proposed model. Specifically, we install a recommendation system on four popular blockchain platforms today, supporting Ethereum Virtual Machine (EVM), including Binance Smart Chain (BNB Smart Chain)[7]; Polygon[8]; Fantom[9]; and Celo[10]. Our implementations on these four platforms are also shared as a contribution to the article to collect transaction fees corresponding to the four platforms' supporting coins[11], i.e., BNB[12]; MATIC[13]; FTM[14]; and CELO[15]. For example, Fig. 6 details our

---

[7] https://github.com/bnb-chain/whitepaper/blob/master/WHITEPAPER.md.

[8] https://polygon.technology/lightpaper-polygon.pdf.

[9] https://whitepaper.io/document/438/fantom-whitepaper.

[10] https://celo.org/papers/whitepaper.

[11] Implementation of theme models our release at 11/24/2022, 8:44:53 AM UTC.

[12] https://testnet.bscscan.com/address/0xafa3888d1dfbfe957b1cd68c36ede4991e104 a53.

[13] https://mumbai.polygonscan.com/address/0xd9ee80d850ef3c4978dd0b099a45a559f d7c5ef4.

[14] https://testnet.ftmscan.com/address/0x4a2573478c67a894e32d806c8dd23ee8e26f7 847.

[15] https://explorer.celo.org/alfajores/address/0x4a2573478C67a894E32D806c8Dd23E E8E26f7847/transactions.

three assessments of a successful installation on BNB Smart Chain (i.e., similar settings are shown for the other three platforms). Our implementations to evaluate the execution cost of smart contracts (i.e., designed based on Solidity language) run on testnet environments of four platforms in order to choose the most cost-effective platform to deploy. Our detailed assessments focus on the cost of performing contract creation, NFT generation (see Fig. 7) and NFT retrieval/transfer (i.e., updating NFT ownership address - see Fig. 8) presented in the respective subsections related to i) Transaction Fee; ii) Gas limit; iii) Gas Used by Transaction; and iv) Gas Price.

5.1   Transaction Fee

Table 1. Transaction fee.

	Contract Creation	Create NFT	Transfer NFT
BNB Smart Chain	0.0273134 BNB ($8.43)	0.00109162 BNB ($0.34)	0.00057003 BNB ($0.18)
Fantom	0.00957754 FTM ($0.001849)	0.000405167 FTM ($0.000078)	0.0002380105 FTM ($0.000046)
Polygon	0.006840710032835408 MATIC ($0.01)	0.000289405001852192 MATIC ($0.00)	0.000170007501088048 MATIC ($0.00)
Celo	0.007097844 CELO ($0.004)	0.0002840812 CELO ($0.000)	0.0001554878 CELO ($0.000)

Table 1 shows the cost of creating contracts for the four platforms. It is easy to see that the highest transaction fee of the three requirements is contract creation for all four platforms. In which, the cost of BNB Smart Chain is the highest with the highest cost when creating a contract is 0.0273134 BNB ($8.43); whereas, the lowest cost recorded by the Fantom platform with the highest cost for contract initiation is less than 0.00957754 FTM ($0.001849). Meanwhile, the cost to enforce Celo's contract initiation requirement is lower than Polygon's with only $0.004 compared to $0.01. For the remaining two requirements (Create NFT and Transfer NFT), we note that the cost of implementing them for all three platforms, Polygon, Celo, and Fantom is very low (i.e., negligible) given the cost trades close to $0.00. However, this cost is still very high when deployed on BNB Smart Chain with 0.00109162 BNB ($0.34) and 0.00057003 BNB ($0.18) for Create NFT and Transfer NFT, respectively.

5.2   Gas Limit

Table 2 shows the gas limit for each transaction. Our observations show that the gas limits of the three platforms (i.e., BNB, Polygon, and Fantom) are roughly equivalent - where Polygon and Fantom are similar in all three transactions. The remaining platform (i.e., Celo) has the highest gas limit with 3,548,922; 142,040; and 85,673 for all three transaction types.

Table 2. Gas limit.

	Contract Creation	Create NFT	Transfer NFT
BNB Smart Chain	2,731,340	109,162	72,003
Fantom	2,736,440	115,762	72,803
Polygon	2,736,284	115,762	72,803
Celo	3,548,922	142,040	85,673

5.3 Gas Used by Transaction

Table 3. Gas Used by Transaction.

	Contract Creation	Create NFT	Transfer NFT
BNB Smart Chain	2,731,340 (100%)	109,162 (100%)	57,003 (79.17%)
Fantom	2,736,440 (100%)	115,762 (100%)	68,003 (93.41%)
Polygon	2,736,284 (100%)	115,762 (100%)	68,003 (93.41%)
Celo	2,729,940 (76.92%)	109,262 (76.92%)	59,803 (69.8%)

Table 3 shows the amount of gas used when executing the transaction (i.e., what percentage of gas in total gas is shown in Table 2). Specifically, three platforms BNB, Polygon, and Fantom use 100% of Gas Limit for two transactions Contract Creation and Create NFT. Meanwhile, Celo uses 76.92% of the Gas limit for the above two transactions. For the last transaction of Transfer NFT, the highest Gas level was recorded by Fantom and Polygon with 93.41% of Gas limit; while BNB and Celo use 79.17% and 69.8% of Gas limit.

5.4 Gas Price

Table 4. Gas Price.

	Contract Creation	Create NFT	Transfer NFT
BNB Smart Chain	0.00000001 BNB (10 Gwei)	0.00000001 BNB (10 Gwei)	0.00000001 BNB (10 Gwei)
Fantom	0.0000000035 FTM (3.5 Gwei)	0.0000000035 FTM (3.5 Gwei)	0.0000000035 FTM (3.5 Gwei)
Polygon	0.000000002500000012 MATIC (2.500000012 Gwei)	0.000000002500000016 MATIC (2.500000016 Gwei)	0.000000002500000016 MATIC (2.500000016 Gwei)
Celo	0.0000000026 CELO (Max Fee per Gas: 2.7 Gwei)	0.0000000026 CELO (Max Fee per Gas: 2.7 Gwei)	0.0000000026 CELO (Max Fee per Gas: 2.7 Gwei)

Table 4 shows the value of Gas for all four platforms. Specifically, BNB, Fantom, and Celo have the same Gas value in all three transactions with values of 10 Gwei (i.e., the highest of the three platforms), 3.5 Gwei, and 2.7 Gwei, respectively. Meanwhile, the Gas value of the Polygon platform (i.e., MATIC) has the lowest value and fluctuates around 2.5 Gwei.

6   Discussion

According to our observation, the transaction value depends on the market capitalization of the respective coin. The total market capitalization of the 4 platforms used in our review (i.e., BNB (Binance Smart Chain); MATIC (Polygon); FTM (Fantom); and CELO (Celo)) are \$50,959,673,206; \$7,652,386,190; \$486,510,485; and \$244,775,762, respectively.[16] This directly affects the coin value of that platform – although the number of coins issued at the time of system implementation also plays a huge role. The total issuance of the four coins BNB, MATIC, FTM, and CELO, is 163,276,974/163,276,974 coins, respectively; 8,868,740,690/10,000,000,000 coins; 2,541,152,731/3,175,000,000 coins and 473, 376,178/1,000,000,000 coins. The coin's value is based on the number of coins issued and the total market capitalization with a value of \$314.98; \$0.863099; \$0.1909; and \$0.528049 for BNB, MATIC, FTM, and CELO, respectively.

Based on the measurements and analysis in 5 section, we have concluded that the proposed model deployed on Faltom brings many benefits related to system operating costs. In particular, generating and receiving NFTs has an almost zero (i.e., negligible) fee. Also, the cost of creating contracts with transaction execution value is also meager (i.e., less than \$0.002).

In future work, we proceed to implement more complex methods/algorithms (i.e., encryption and decryption) as well as more complex data structures to observe the costs for the respective transactions. Deploying the proposed model in a real environment is also a possible approach (i.e., implementing the recommendation system on the FTM mainnet). In our current analysis, we have not considered issues related to the privacy policy of users (i.e., access control [25, 26], dynamic policy [24, 29]) - a possible approach would be implemented in upcoming research activities.

7   Conclusion

The article proposes a model for managing medical test results based on Blockchain technology and smart contract and sharing the results in the test process with doctors and nurses based on NFTs for care purposes and the treatment of disease. Our solutions are intended to replace complicated security policies when setting up a system. Specifically, in a health environment, information about test results can be shared with doctors and nurses without compromising patient privacy. In addition, NFTs also help patients easily manage access history and detect unwanted data retrieval behaviors. Our proposed model is implemented on the Ethereum platform, and the Solidity language is then deployed on four EVM-enabled platforms, including BNB, MATIC, FTM, and CELO. Our analysis and evaluation (i.e., presented in the evaluation section) have found that it is low-cost to install our transactions (i.e., contract creation, NFT creation, NFT transfer) on the Fantom platform best. Our explanations (i.e., based on market analysis at the time of system implementation) in the Discussion section

---

[16] Our observation time is 12:00PM - 11/26/2022.

give a full view of the above statements as well as future approaches for the proposed model.

References

1. Abou Jaoude, J., Saade, R.G.: Blockchain applications-usage in different domains. IEEE Access **7**, 45360–45381 (2019)
2. Ahmad, R.W., et al.: The role of blockchain technology in telehealth and telemedicine. Int. J. Med. Inform. **148**, 104399 (2021)
3. Barua, M., et al.: ESPAC: enabling security and patient-centric access control for eHealth in cloud computing. Int. J. Secur. Netw. **6**(2–3), 67–76 (2011)
4. Chan, K.S., Fowles, J.B., Weiner, J.P.: Electronic health records and the reliability and validity of quality measures: a review of the literature. Med. Care Res. Rev. **67**(5), 503–527 (2010)
5. Chen, L., Hoang, D.B.: Novel data protection model in healthcare cloud. In: 2011 IEEE International Conference on High Performance Computing and Communications, pp. 550–555. IEEE (2011)
6. Chen, Z., et al.: A blockchain-based preserving and sharing system for medical data privacy. Future Gener. Comput. Syst. **124**, 338–350 (2021)
7. Du, M., et al.: Supply chain finance innovation using blockchain. IEEE Trans. Eng. Manag. **67**(4), 1045–1058 (2020)
8. Egorov, M., Wilkison, M., Nuñez, D.: NuCypher KMS: decentralized key management system. arXiv preprint arXiv:1707.06140 (2017)
9. Ha, X.S., et al.: DeM-CoD: novel access-control-based cash on delivery mechanism for decentralized marketplace. In: IEEE 19th International Conference on Trust, Security and Privacy in Computing and Communications, pp. 71–78. IEEE (2020)
10. Ha, X.S., Le, T.H., Phan, T.T., Nguyen, H.H.D., Vo, H.K., Duong-Trung, N.: Scrutinizing trust and transparency in cash on delivery systems. In: Wang, G., Chen, B., Li, W., Di Pietro, R., Yan, X., Han, H. (eds.) SpaCCS 2020. LNCS, vol. 12382, pp. 214–227. Springer, Cham (2021). https://doi.org/10.1007/978-3-030-68851-6_15
11. Hoang, N.M., Son, H.X.: A dynamic solution for fine-grained policy conflict resolution. In: Proceedings of the 3rd International Conference on Cryptography, Security and Privacy, pp. 116–120 (2019)
12. Kassab, M., et al.: Exploring research in blockchain for healthcare and a roadmap for the future. IEEE Trans. Emerg. Top. Comput. **9**(4), 1835–1852 (2019)
13. Kyrarini, M., et al.: A survey of robots in healthcare. Technologies **9**(1), 8 (2021)
14. Le, H.T., et al.: Patient-chain: patient-centered healthcare system a blockchain-based technology in dealing with emergencies. In: Shen, H., et al. (eds.) PDCAT 2021. LNCS, vol. 13148, pp. 576–583. Springer, Cham (2022). https://doi.org/10.1007/978-3-030-96772-7_54
15. Le, N.T.T., et al.: Assuring non-fraudulent transactions in cash on delivery by introducing double smart contracts. Int. J. Adv. Comput. Sci. Appl. **10**(5), 677–684 (2019)
16. Madine, M.M., et al.: Blockchain for giving patients control over their medical records. IEEE Access **8**, 193102–193115 (2020)
17. Makubalo, T., Scholtz, B., Tokosi, T.O.: Blockchain technology for empowering patient-centred healthcare: a pilot study. In: Hattingh, M., Matthee, M., Smuts, H., Pappas, I., Dwivedi, Y.K., Mäntymäki, M. (eds.) I3E 2020. LNCS, vol. 12066, pp. 15–26. Springer, Cham (2020). https://doi.org/10.1007/978-3-030-44999-5_2

18. Misbhauddin, M., et al.: MedAccess: a scalable architecture for blockchain-based health record management. In: 2020 2nd International Conference on Computer and Information Sciences (ICCIS), pp. 1–5. IEEE (2020)
19. Nakamoto, S.: Bitcoin: a peer-to-peer electronic cash system. Decentralized Bus. Rev. 21260 (2008)
20. Patel, V.: A framework for secure and decentralized sharing of medical imaging data via blockchain consensus. Health Inform. J. **25**(4), 1398–1411 (2019)
21. Patra, M.R., Das, R.K., Padhy, R.P.: CRHIS: cloud based rural healthcare information system. In: Proceedings of the 6th International Conference on Theory and Practice of Electronic Governance, pp. 402–405 (2012)
22. Quoc, K.L., et al.: SSSB: an approach to insurance for cross-border exchange by using smart contracts. In: Awan, I., Younas, M., Poniszewska-Marańda, A. (eds.) MobiWIS 2022. LNCS, vol. 13475, pp. 179–192. Springer, Cham (2022). https://doi.org/10.1007/978-3-031-14391-5_14
23. Rolim, C.O., et al.: A cloud computing solution for patient's data collection in health care institutions. In: 2010 Second International Conference on eHealth, Telemedicine, and Social Medicine, pp. 95–99. IEEE (2010)
24. Son, H.X., Dang, T.K., Massacci, F.: REW-SMT: a new approach for rewriting XACML request with dynamic big data security policies. In: Wang, G., Atiquzzaman, M., Yan, Z., Choo, K.-K.R. (eds.) SpaCCS 2017. LNCS, vol. 10656, pp. 501–515. Springer, Cham (2017). https://doi.org/10.1007/978-3-319-72389-1_40
25. Son, H.X., Hoang, N.M.: A novel attribute-based access control system for fine-grained privacy protection. In: Proceedings of the 3rd International Conference on Cryptography, Security and Privacy, pp. 76–80 (2019)
26. Son, H.X., Nguyen, M.H., Vo, H.K., Nguyen, T.P.: Toward an privacy protection based on access control model in hybrid cloud for healthcare systems. In: Martínez Álvarez, F., Troncoso Lora, A., Sáez Muñoz, J.A., Quintián, H., Corchado, E. (eds.) CISIS/ICEUTE -2019. AISC, vol. 951, pp. 77–86. Springer, Cham (2020). https://doi.org/10.1007/978-3-030-20005-3_8
27. Su, C.J., Wu, C.Y.: JADE implemented mobile multi-agent based, distributed information platform for pervasive health care monitoring. Appl. Soft Comput. **11**(1), 315–325 (2011)
28. Thi, Q.N.T., Dang, T.K., Van, H.L., Son, H.X.: Using JSON to specify privacy preserving-enabled attribute-based access control policies. In: Wang, G., Atiquzzaman, M., Yan, Z., Choo, K.-K.R. (eds.) SpaCCS 2017. LNCS, vol. 10656, pp. 561–570. Springer, Cham (2017). https://doi.org/10.1007/978-3-319-72389-1_44
29. Xuan, S.H., et al.: Rew-XAC: an approach to rewriting request for elastic ABAC enforcement with dynamic policies. In: 2016 International Conference on Advanced Computing and Applications (ACOMP), pp. 25–31. IEEE (2016)
30. Zhang, P., et al.: FHIRChain: applying blockchain to securely and scalably share clinical data. Comput. Struct. Biotechnol. J. **16**, 267–278 (2018)
31. Zhang, Y., et al.: Health-CPS: healthcare cyber-physical system assisted by cloud and big data. IEEE Syst. J. **11**(1), 88–95 (2015)
32. Zyskind, G., et al.: Decentralizing privacy: using blockchain to protect personal data. In: 2015 IEEE Security and Privacy Workshops, pp. 180–184. IEEE (2015)

Intelligent Identification of Respiratory Diseases: Covid-19 and Similar Virus Cases

Dawit Teklu Weldeslasie[1]([✉]), Mohamed Ahmed[1], Gebremariam Assres[2]([✉]),
Tor-Morten Grønli[2], and Gheorghita Ghinea[2,3]

[1] Aksum University, Tigray, Ethiopia
dawit.tekulu@gmail.com
[2] Kristiania University College, Oslo, Norway
mesfin.assres@gmail.com
[3] Brunel University London, Uxbridge, UK

Abstract. The World Health Organization (WHO) has declared an end to the emergency phase of the COVID-19 pandemic. However, it is still negatively impacting countries like Ethiopia. Thus, exploring the identification and treatment mechanisms for COVID-19 from similar disease has still paramount importance. COVID-19 testing is still expensive, not easily available and time consuming, particularly in the conflict hit Tigray region. In this study, our main goal is to explore, design, implement and evaluate intelligent software that identifies COVID-19 from similar diseases, namely, Common Cold, Measles, Flu, COVID-19, and Chicken Pox. Furthermore, we point out the benefits of implementing such software to replace shortage of manpower given the circumstances in Tigray region. The software, hereafter named CKBS (COVID-19 Knowledge-based System), has been evaluated to ensure whether it is accurate and usable. In this study, 25 patients participated for each of the five different diseases to test the effectiveness of the developed knowledge base. The dataset was split in such a way that 70% is used for training while the remaining 30% for testing. Accordingly, we found out that the resulting software can successfully identify the five diseases at 98% accuracy and getting 96% community acceptance rate. This implies that our use of the tree model in the development was effective and resulting software has been accepted to be used by the local community to tackle the COVID-19 and related challenges that Ethiopia (particularly Tigray) is still facing.

Keywords: COVID-19 · Similar Virus Cases (SVC) · Intelligent Systems · Identification · Learning and Memorization

1 Introduction

A study in [26] showed that the community practice toward COVID-19 and its preventive measure was poor in Tigray thereby negatively affected the effort for combating the virus. Therefore, continuous public health programs in the region are urgently needed to improve knowledge, attitude, and practices. The application of intelligent systems is also low and the awareness of the people towards respiratory diseases is not good. So, for successful implementation a respiratory diseases control, a community-based technology should be developed. Hence, working on identification of respiratory diseases should be a priority and feasible research intervention.

Now a day, healthcare institutions are experiencing an increase of technological innovations purposed at enhancing life expectancy, quality of life, diagnostic and treatment options, as well as the efficiency and cost effectiveness of the healthcare system [1]. Moreover, primary health care contributes a central role in health care systems worldwide. It can offer families cost effective services close to their home [2]. Particularly in developing countries community health centers usually offer a broad range of services, including prenatal care, immunizations, treatment of childhood illnesses, treatment of malaria, tuberculosis, leishmaniasis and other common infectious diseases, and other basic medical care [3].

Ethiopia is one of the under developing countries which have been experiencing a heavy burden of disease mainly attributed to communicable infectious diseases (including COVID-19) and nutritional deficiencies. Shortage and high turnover of human resource; inadequacy of essential drugs and supplies have also contributed to the burden [4]. According to the report of WHO [5], there are several symptoms of COVID-19 and among the most common symptoms include Fever, coughing, sneezing, and losing sense of smelling and testing. In line to such health problems, Computer and Smart-Mobile technique are increasingly used to improve the quality of medical services. Mostly the remote areas, the population are deprived of the facilities of having experts to identify and treat COVID-19 disease [25].

So, it is the need of the day to store the expertise of specialists in computers through using computerized technology. Knowledge-based technology is certainly helpful for inexperienced physicians in making medical identification as well as for experienced physicians in supporting complex decisions [6]. Moreover, Knowledge-based technology has become an attractive tool to help physicians in retrieving medical information as well as in making decision faced in today's COVID-19 complications [18]. The underdeveloped countries like Ethiopia having shortage of medical experts and infrastructures are still at their early stage in terms of the consequences of the disease [19]. According to the report of Ethiopian ministry of health the ratio of the existing medical experts to the population is 1:10000, which is unthinkable and impossible to handle COVID-19 cases appropriate by the existing medical experts unless the possible precautions are taken place properly by the community [7]. Moreover, the main reason behind the fast spreading of COVID-19 is lack of health workers and minimum flow of information towards the virus [5].

Even though top priority is given to prevention of COVID-19 in Ethiopia now, there is a technological gap against the time which are facing to contain the virus very fast [20]. For this reason, we propose a software for identification and treatment of COVID-19 and related diseases. The software also provides proper advice to all communities in short period of time which is also evident for people living in places other than Ethiopia.

2 Literature Review

Studies indicate that there is an association between massive population displacements because of the war in Tigray and the emergence of respiratory diseases. Most diseases occurred among refugees and displaced persons living in humanitarian crisis settings [27]. During outbreaks of influenza, COVID-19, and other respiratory diseases, technology is a tool to promote social distancing and prevent the spread of disease. For instance, Smart phones have created a new means of respiratory disease control that affects the lungs and other parts of the human body.

Corona virus disease (COVID-19) is an infectious disease caused by the severe acute respiratory syndrome corona virus 2 virus [28]. Due to the nobility of COVID-19 several research have been done so far to help mankind through technology. We found the following research that can automate COVID-19:

First, Salman et al. [8] describes COVID-19 Detection using Artificial Intelligence. In an article level this is the pioneer which is published in 2020. Unfortunately, this research does not include the concept of "Treatment". What the researchers do focus was on "Diagnosis" process only. Moreover, X-rays imaging was one of the possible methods implemented in this research for detecting COVID-19. Moreover, Salman et al. does not find an optimal choice for handling evaluation of experts. Therefore, we suggest an effective approach for implementing multiple experts' opinions or sorting experts' responses in addition to the 260 X-Ray Imaging in order to improve the performance. In their next consecutive publication Salman et al. [9] developed Knowledge-Based System for COVID-19 Diagnosis. Unfortunately, its performance is not measured at all. In addition, the researchers do not consider the context of multilingual in their research.

Then, Almadhoun et al. [10] developed An Expert System for Diagnosing Corona virus (COVID-19) Using SL5. Regrettably, the performance of the developed system is not evaluated at all. Moreover, the research methodology applied in this research is unclear and there is no literature review part in this paper.

Next, a knowledge-based self-pre-diagnosis system to predict Covid-19 in smart phone users using personal data and observed symptoms was developed by Çelik Ertuğrul et al. [21]. The system can be suitable for diagnosing and monitoring of positive cases in the areas other than clinics and hospitals during the Covid-19 pandemic. But, Similar Virus Cases are not incorporated in this research. This means, significant work is ignored. A pre-screening approach for COVID-19 testing is done by T Arora, R Soni [22] based on Belief Rule-Based Expert System. It focuses mainly on Prediction, Decision-Making, and its Impacts. The above researches don't consider native languages during their implementation. For instance, English language cannot be used by most of the population in the world. To be community inclusive, we develop a multilingual system that includes Tigrigna/ ትግርኛand Ahmaric/ አማርኛlanguages. Moreover, a robust methodology is not yet used by the above authors as their research approach, that's why we believe the performance of the systems still needs to be improved better.

Finally, Kiros et al. [26] was able to assess the level of knowledge, attitudes, and practices in Mekelle, Tigray towards COVID-19 and its prevention measures. However, the results of the study did not cover other cities as well as rural areas of the region. In addition, the study did not include any recommended technological solutions. Thus, our focus is to design the technological solution, include other cities and rural areas thereby overcome these limitations of the existing literature.

3 Research Methodology

Our research is motivated by the desire to improve the health system in controlling COVID-19 and similar diseases through the introduction and process of building a new prototype. So, design science research methodology is found suitable and robust for our research because it relies on existing kernel theories that are applied, tested, modified, and extended through the experience, creativity, intuition, and problem-solving capabilities the researchers. The research methodology is shown in Fig. 1. Accordingly, we review literatures to have deep understanding on the problem of COVID-19 and SVC (Similar Virus Cases). Additionally, doctors were consulted with an aim to understand the health system.

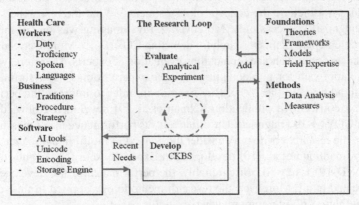

Fig. 1. The research methodology, modified [11]

The research environment is Covid-19 and Similar Virus Cases. It is composed of health care workers, business, software, the research loop, foundations and methods. The diagram of the research methodology shown in Fig. 1 is articulated below.

1. Recent needs of health care workers are assessed and identified within the context of business traditions, procedure, and strategy to be supported by AI tools, Unicode Encoding and Storage engines. The most common attributes of health workers are duty, proficiency, and language.
2. Our research loop addresses the gap of respiratory disease via development/evaluation of COVID-19 Knowledge-Base System (CKBS). The identified weaknesses in CKBS are refined and reassessed to be efficient with the help of health care workers. In its execution we learn about the nature of the problem, the environment, and the possible solutions to COVID-19 and SVC.
3. Relevance of our methodology is ensured by applying suitable foundations. Accordingly, theories, frameworks, models, and field expertise are added to the research loop for determining how well the software works. Moreover, statistical analysis and measures has been conducted using SPSS software.

4   Prototype Development

The architecture of the software consists of a user, user interface, inference engine, Unicode compiler, permanent memory and explanation facility as shown in Fig. 2.

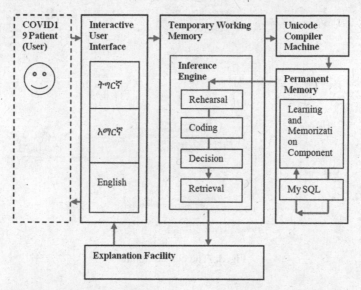

Fig. 2. Architecture of the COVID-19 and similar virus cases (SVC)

The software is developed using Prolog and MySQL. In order to enter Tigrigna/ ትግርኛor Ahmaric/ አማርኛalphabets into the software, Power Geez is installed into the machine. We incorporated English, Tigrigna/ ትግርኛ, and Ahmaric/ አማርኛlanguages in order to help users to communicate with the software easily.

4.1   Learning and Memorization Component

COVID-19 is a new virus which changes its behaviors very fast. Scientists around the world are learning about Corona virus dynamics by drawing different algorithms [24]. So, it's mandatory to incorporate "Learning and Memorization" component into our architecture. The class diagram in Fig. 3 represents the capability of the software to learn and remember from previous disease history. The "Learning and Memorization" architecture shown in Fig. 2 works as the following:

1. Patient enters name through the user interface.
2. The inference engine finds previous patient history from learning and memorization component.
3. Next, patients enter their recent symptoms.
4. When new virus behavior is detected, then inference engine creates link with learning and memorization component to store the new virus case.
5. Then, user completes all the identification and treatment steps.

6. Finally, the learning and memorization component stores the new virus behavior permanently in its permanent memory.

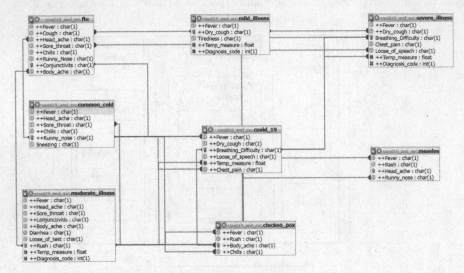

Fig. 3. The class diagram

4.2 Knowledge Uncertainty Technique

In our research, we apply fuzzy logic uncertainty technique, because fuzzy logic is a very popular uncertainty handling technique which assigns a value between 0 and 1 to a variable [12]. Table1 shows the weight or accuracy of the deducted result, or action by the proposed software which is a "quality value". The software detects imprecise or inaccurate disease information range in between 0 and 1 variables.

Table 1. Knowledge uncertainty for COVID-19 and similar virus cases (SVC)

No	Disease Name	Symptoms	Fussy Logic Range
1	Common Cold	Sneezing, Chills, Runny Nose, Sore Throat	[0.0,0.25), [0.25,0.50), [0.50,0.75), [0.75,1.0)
2	Measles	Fever, Rush, Runny Nose	[0.0,0.33), [0.33,0.66), [0.66,1.0)
3	Flu	Fever, Chills, Runny Nose, Cough	[0.0,0.25), [0.25,0.50), [0.50,0.75), [0.75,1.0)
4	COVID_19	Fever, Dry Cough, Difficulty of Breathing, Chest Pain, Loose of Speech/Movement, Body Temperature Greater than 38 Deg.Cel (100Deg.Far)	[0.0,0.16), [0.16,0.28), [0.28,0.48), [0.48,0.64), [0.64,0.8), [0.8,0.96), [0.96,1.0)
5	Chicken Pox	Fever, Rush, Chills	[0.0,0.33), [0.33,0.66), [0.66,1.0)

4.3   Tree Model for COVID-19 and Similar Virus Cases (SVC)

In this research, we model the diseases using decision tree. Decision tree is a classification scheme which generates a tree and a set of rules from a given dataset [13]. As shown in Fig. 5, the identification process of COVID-19 and SVC is modeled by using decision tree structures. This tree provides a procedural guidance and shows block diagram of decisions made by doctors during identification of COVID-19 and related disease.

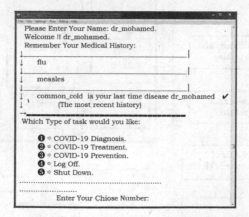

Fig. 4. Diagnosis results of a patient

The sample interfaces shown in Fig. 4 and Fig. 6 are implemented by applying the tree model shown in Fig. 5. Note that necessary knowledge was extracted from doctors and important credentials for drawing the decision tree model and developing the class diagram.

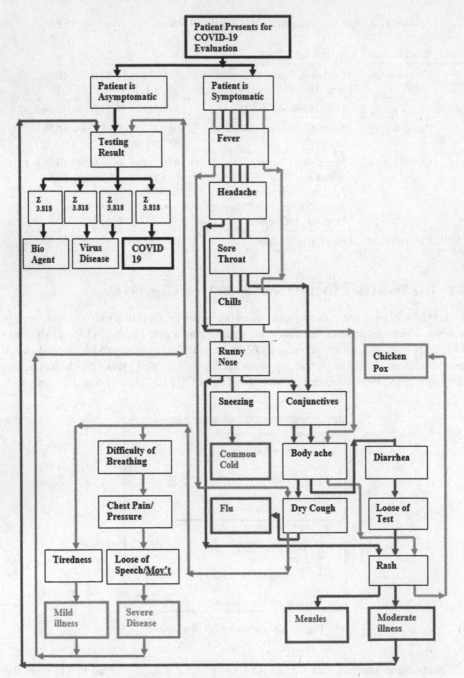

Fig. 5. Tree model for COVID-19 and similar virus cases

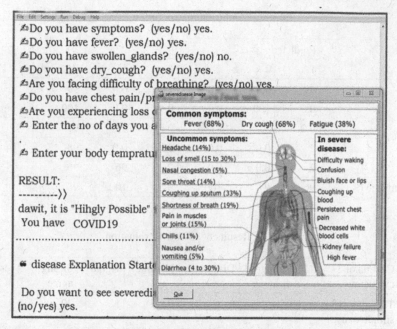

Fig. 6. Past history of a patient

5 Results and Discussion

Health centers found in Wukro-Maray, Selekleka and Gendebta are considered as our focus area to evaluate the software in Tigray. From the total data set of each disease, 70% was used to build training and the remaining 30% of the total was used for testing data. After the training, the performance of the software was tested by using 30% of the total workers registered at the three health centers. The software is evaluated in terms of accuracy from the *confusion matrix* and user *acceptance testing*.

First, we perform computing the *confusion matrix*. Confusion matrix is used to derive true positives, true negatives, false positives and false negatives indicating the correct/incorrect allotment of samples into their respective disease classes [15]. The measures are computed by using the equations Accuracy = TP + TN/(TP + FP + FN + TN).

From Table 2 confusion matrix 1, 2, 3, 4, 5 represent Common Cold, Measles, Flu, COVID-19 and Chicken Pox respectively. The identification accuracy for Common Cold, Measles, Flu, COVID-19 and Chicken Pox are 96%, 97%, 100%, 97% and 100% respectively. The disease that is affected by Common Cold was identified as COVID-19 virus (4%). This shows that some diseases that are affected by Common Cold and COVID-19 have a strong similarity between their virus features. In addition, the disease that is affected by COVID-19 virus was identified as Flu (3%). This shows that there is a slight similarity between the virus features of COVID-19 disease and Flu. In general, from the total test set that we have used to test the software 98% are identified "correct" diseases and 2% are "incorrect" diseases.

Table 2. Confusion matrix of test data

Actual	Predicted					
	1	2	3	4	5	Performance (%)
1	99	0.0	0.0	1	0.0	99
2	0.0	100	0.0	0.0	0.0	100
3	0.0	3	97	0.0	0.0	97
4	2	0.0	0.0	98	0.0	98
5	2	0.0	0.0	2	96	96
Performance (%)	96	97	100	97	100	98

Table 3. Results of software evaluation

No	Criteria of evaluation	Strong disagree	Disagree	Neutral	Agree	Strong agree	Average
1	The software is simple to use	0	0	0	5	20	4.8
2	The software is attractive	0	0	5	3	17	4.48
3	The software is efficiency in time	0	0	0	2	23	4.92
4	The software is accurate in reaching a decision	0	0	0	1	24	4.96
5	The software has adequate knowledge about the diseases	0	0	0	2	23	4.92
6	The software has the ability of making right conclusions and recommendations	0	0	3	3	19	4.52
7	The software detects the diseases properly	0	0	2	0	23	4.84
8	You can understand the functions of software	0	0	1	0	24	4.92

(*continued*)

Table 3. (*continued*)

No	Criteria of evaluation	Strong disagree	Disagree	Neutral	Agree	Strong agree	Average
9	The software is important for health domain	0	0	0	1	24	4.96
							4.81

Next, we perform user *acceptance testing*. The value of this research focuses on ISO9241-110 usability metrics [14]. As a result, how these criteria influence the software is presented in Table 3. The researchers assigned values as strongly agree = 5, agree = 4, neutral = 3, disagree = 2 and strongly disagree = 1. A total of twenty-five (25) domain experts are participated in the software evaluation.

As shown in Table 3 above, 80% of the evaluators scored the simplicity of the software as strong agree and 20% as agree. The second criteria (attractiveness of the software) scored 68% as strong agree, 12% as agree and 20% as neutral. The score for efficiency of the software with respect to time was 92% as strong agree and 8% as agree. Moreover, equal scores were given for both the accuracy of the software in reaching a decision to identify diseases and importance of the software in the domain area with 96% strongly agree and 4% as agree. 92% of the evaluators rated strongly agree and 8% as agree if the software has adequate knowledge of treatment about those diseases. For evaluation criteria 7 it was found that most of the respondents agreed on the ability of the software to detect the diseases properly with 92% as strong agree and 8% as neutral. For evaluation criteria 9 it was found that most of the respondents agreed the software is important for health domain (96% as strong agree and 4% as agree).

Finally, the average performance of the software according to the evaluation results filled by the health experts is 4.80 out of 5 or 96%, which shows the health workers are satisfied with the identification of the diseases by the software.

6 Conclusions

In today's technological development, human expertise can be represented as knowledge base on the computer and mobile systems [16]. Furthermore, digital knowledge penetration rate is increasing in many countries including Ethiopia. Nowadays, families found in many countries can afford to buy computer or smart phones [17]. However, the use of these devices for the treatment of COVID-19 and related diseases in the local community has not been sufficiently studied. Thus, in this research, we show how to reduce the spread of COVID-19 and related diseases by implementing intelligent software at the health institutions of Ethiopia, particularly in Tigray region. The software is developed using tree model and it is found to be capable of identifying COVID-19 and other viruses such as Common Cold, Measles, Flu and Chicken Pox. In addition, the performance of the software is improved by incorporating SVC, model training utility and local languages. Hence, given the shortage of human expertise at the health institutions [23], the software offers relevant advice to patients, just like a personal digital assistant, on how to identify COVID-19 from similar disease.

References

1. Lee, S.M., Lee, D.: Opportunities and challenges for contactless healthcare services in the post-COVID-19 Era. Technol. Forecast. Soc. Chang. **167**, 120712 (2021)
2. Kumpunen, S., et al.: Transformations in the landscape of primary health care during COVID-19: themes from the European region. Health policy **126**(5), 391–397 (2022)
3. Desjeux, P.: The increase of risk factors for leishmaniasis WHO (2014)
4. Abdi, et al.: Knowledge based system researches and applications. AI Mag. (2010)
5. World Health Organization (WHO). Press Conference (2020)
6. Dipanwita, B.: Knowledge-based system to diagnose disease (2011)
7. Ethiopian. Ministry of Health Document (2020)
8. Salman, F.M., Abu-Naser, S.S., Alajrami, E., Abu-Nasser, B.S., Alashqar, B.A.: Covid-19 detection using artificial intelligence (2020)
9. Salman, F.M., Abu-Naser, S.S.: Knowledge-based system for COVID-19 diagnosis (2020)
10. Almadhoun, H.R., Abu-Naser, S.S.: An expert system for diagnosing corona virus (COVID-19) using SL5 (2020)
11. Hevner, A., Chatterjee, S.: Design science research in information systems. In: Design Research in Information Systems. Integrated Series in Information Systems, vol. 22, pp. 9–22. Springer, Boston (2010). https://doi.org/10.1007/978-1-4419-5653-8_2
12. Al-Hammadi, D.A.A.: Developing an expert system for diabetes mellitus patients. Masters degree thesis (2010)
13. Hasan, M.R., et al.: Single decision tree classifiers' accuracy on medical data. In: Proceedings of the 5th International Conference on Computing and Informatics, ICOCI, vol. 2015 (2015)
14. García Frey, A., et al.: QUIMERA: a quality metamodel to improve design rationale. In: Proceedings of the 3rd ACM SIGCHI Symposium on Engineering Interactive Computing Systems (2011)
15. Ruuska, S., et al.: Evaluation of the confusion matrix method in the validation of an automated system for measuring feeding behavior of cattle. Behav. Process. **148**, 56–62 (2018)
16. Kendal, S.L., Creen, M.: An Introduction to Knowledge Engineering. Springer, London (2007). https://doi.org/10.1007/978-1-84628-667-4
17. Andrade, A.D., Bill, D.: Information and communication technology and the social inclusion of refugees. Mis. Q. **40**(2), 405–416 (2016)
18. Tiwari, S.P.: Covid-19: knowledge development, exchange, and emerging technologies. Int. J. Soc. Sci. Res. Rev. **5**(5), 310–314 (2022)
19. Memirie, S.T., et al.:Addressing the impact of noncommunicable diseases and injuries (NCDIs) in Ethiopia: findings and recommendations from the Ethiopia NCDI Commission. Ethiop. J. Health Sci. **32**(1) (2022)
20. Baye, K.: COVID-19 Prevention Measures in Ethiopia: Current Realities and Prospects, vol. 141. Intl Food Policy Res Inst (2020)
21. ÇelikErtuğrul, D., Celik Ulusoy, D.: A knowledge-based self-pre-diagnosis system to predict Covid-19 in smartphone users using personal data and observed symptoms. Expert Syst. **39**(3), e12716 (2022)
22. Arora, T., Soni, R.: A pre-screening approach for COVID-19 testing based on belief rule-based expert system. In: Santosh, K., Joshi, A. (eds.) COVID-19: Prediction, Decision-Making, and its Impacts. Lecture Notes on Data Engineering and Communications Technologies, vol. 60, pp. 19–28. Springer, Singapore (2021). https://doi.org/10.1007/978-981-15-9682-7_3

23. Tesfa, M., et al.: Growth monitoring practice and associated factors among health professionals at public health facilities of Bahir Dar Health Centers, Northwest Ethiopia, 2021. Pediatr. Health Med. Ther. **13**, 195–215 (2022)

24. Galluccio, F., et al.: Treatment algorithm for COVID-19: a multidisciplinary point of view. Clin. Rheumatol. **39**(7), 2077–2084 (2020). https://doi.org/10.1007/s10067-020-05179-0

25. Mohammed, R., et al.: COVID-19 vaccine hesitancy among Ethiopian healthcare workers. PloS one **16**(12), e0261125 (2021)

26. Kiros, M., Gebru, S.B., Tewelde, B.: Knowledge, attitude, practice and associated factors towards COVID-19 and its prevention measures among residents of Mekelle City, Tigray Region, Northern Ethiopia: a community-based cross sectional study. J. Public Health 1–16 (2023). https://doi.org/10.1007/s10389-023-01826-3

27. Ahmed, A., et al.: Hepatitis E virus outbreak among Tigray war refugees from Ethiopia, Sudan (Response). Emerg. Infect. Dis. **29**(2) (2023)

28. World Health Organization. COVID-19 weekly epidemiological update, edition 143, 18 May 2023. World Health Organization (2023). https://apps.who.int/iris/handle/10665/367938

SDN, IoT and Edge Computing

Minimizing User Connectivity Costs and Latency Between Controllers and Switch-Controllers for Software Defined Networking

Andres Viveros[1] , Pablo Adasme[1(✉)] , and Ali Dehghan Firoozabadi[2]

[1] Department of Electrical Engineering, Universidad de Santiago de Chile,
Avenida Víctor Jara No 3519, 9170124 Santiago, Chile
{andres.viveros11,pablo.adasme}@usach.cl
[2] Department of Electricity, Universidad Tecnológica Metropolitana,
Av. Jose Pedro Alessandri 1242, 7800002 Santiago, Chile
adehghanfirouzabadi@utem.cl

Abstract. In this paper, we consider the problem of assigning users to switches and controllers at minimum connectivity costs. We simultaneously minimize the existing latency between controllers and switch controllers for software-defined networks (SDN). In particular, we propose two mixed-integer quadratic programming formulations and their standard linearization counterparts. All the proposed models are solved with the CPLEX solver. More precisely, the quadratic models are solved with the branch and cut (B&C) algorithm of the solver. Whilst the linear ones are solved with both, the B&C and with the automatic Bender's decomposition algorithmic option of the CPLEX solver. To the best of our knowledge, this work constitutes a first attempt to propose mathematical formulations while including user connectivity to a backbone software-defined network. Notice that we consider which is the best strategy for connecting users to the backbone, either connecting them to switches or to the controller nodes of the network. Our preliminary numerical results indicate that for most of the benchmark instances considered the second strategy which connects users to switches has a better performance in terms of objective function values. On the other hand, we observe that the linear models offer better performance in terms of CPU times to get the optimal or best objective values. Finally, we see that the linear models can be solved faster with the branch and cut algorithm than using Bender's decomposition approach.

Keywords: Minimizing user connectivity for software-defined networks · Minimizing latency · Mixed-integer quadratic and linear programming · Branch and cut and automatic Bender's decomposition · Software-defined networks

M. Younas et al. (Eds.): MobiWIS 2023, LNCS 13977, pp. 99–111, 2023.
https://doi.org/10.1007/978-3-031-39764-6_7

1   Introduction

In order to deal with the growing user demand for being capable of connecting users to different types of wireless networks, it is mandatorily required that all these types of networks operate optimally. In particular, software-defined networks (SDNs) is a type of wireless network that separates the transmission plane from the control plane. One of the main differences between SDNs with traditional ones is that SDNs are software-based, while traditional networks are based on hardware architecture. Since the control plane uses software instead of hardware, it is significantly more flexible than a traditional wireless network. As such a network operator can control the whole network traffic, and change its configuration settings to increase the network capacity while using a centralized user interface, and without using more hardware devices. On the other side, it offers a higher security level as it can use a centralized controller which is crucial for maintaining a secure network. From the literature, some brief related works which are closer to our proposed formulations can be described as follows. In [1], a review of the best architecture configurations and designs for open-source and open-flow SDN controllers, such as Nox, Beacon, Maestro, and Floodlight, is presented. A brief review of other controllers, such as RYU, Trema, SNAC, OMNI, McNettle, and OpenDayLight, are also presented, and their features and applications are described. In addition, to be able to flexibly manage the increasing range of services that are requested by the diverse set of users, network fragmentation emerges as a plausible alternative as well in reference [2] which addresses the challenge by proposing a logical architecture for network slicing based on SDNs. As such an SDN can control the network slicing process in a centralized manner with the help of a slicing manager. In [3], the authors consider the problem of optimizing both the latency between the controller and its associated switches and the latency between controllers themselves. A mathematical model is formulated as a mixed-integer linear programming problem subject to a latency constraint. Next in reference [4], the problem of co-location of switches and controllers in a hybrid SDN, which is an intermediate step to transform a traditional backbone network into a pure SDN, is addressed. For a hybrid SDN, the quality of service becomes a primary concern to ensure the service of a traditional network while providing additional software benefits.

Other problems related to SDNs are the routing and mapping problem of a network (EARMLP). In [5], this problem is addressed to minimize the total energy consumption in SDNs. To enforce network utilization towards green policy design for data centers, SDN leverages the protocol configurations for available routing in the infrastructure. Therefore, the proposed mechanism aims to design an optimal routing strategy that takes into account the system configuration and traffic demand between the data and control planes in the networks. Similarly, in [6], the existing complexity of a single controller is not sufficient to solve the scalability and reliability problems to be addressed. In fact, it is shown in [6] that solving these problems requires a significantly larger number of controllers in the network. Notice that the latency mainly comprises processing, queuing, propagation, and transmission of the data. In a wide area network, propagation latency is an important metric that includes the average and the worst-case propagation situations between switches and controllers. In order to meet the required quality of service parameters such as scalability and flexibility of the underlying network, SDNs emerge as an appropriate approach. In [7], a mathematical model for link failure prediction of control placement problem is also proposed to minimize the control latency jitter in case of link failure.

In particular, in this paper, we consider the problem of assigning users to switches or controllers at minimum connectivity costs. We also minimize the existing latency between controllers and between switch-controller pairs for software-defined networks (SDN) simultaneously. More precisely, to efficiently handle an SDN, we propose two mixed-integer quadratic programming formulations together with their standard linearization counterparts. All the proposed models are solved with the CPLEX solver. In particular, the quadratic models are solved with the branch and cut (B&C) algorithm of the solver. At the same time, the linear ones are solved with both, with the B&C and with the automatic Bender's decomposition algorithmic options of the CPLEX solver. To the best of our knowledge, this work constitutes a first attempt to propose mathematical formulations while including user connectivity to a backbone SDN. Notice that we further study which would be the best strategy for connecting users to the backbone, either by connecting users to switches or connecting them only to controller nodes of the network. In particular, Bender's approach has been used in various applications. For instance in communication networks and machine learning domains. However, the master problem in Bender's decomposition remains NP-hard. In [8], a hybrid quantum-classical algorithm is proposed by transferring the master problem of Bender's decomposition to the unconstrained binary quadratic optimization model.

Notice that our paper emerges as an extension of a previous work already published in [9] in which mathematical programming models for SDNs were proposed by placing controllers in a network in such a way that each switch node can connect to at least one of the controllers with minimum latency cost. In [9], this is achieved by seeking to minimize the worst latency between the switch-controller and controller-controller pairs. In this paper, we incorporate the additional dimension of connecting a set of users to the backbone SDN considering two situations. The first one corresponds to the fact that users can only connect to one controller of the SDN. Whilst in the second strategy, users can only connect to one switch of the SDN. Consequently, the function to be optimized in our new models includes the sum of latencies of switch-controller pairs, the sum of latencies between controllers themselves, the connectivity cost of installing a switch or a controller in a particular node of the graph, and the distance cost of connecting each user to a unique switch or controller. Finally, our numerical results are analyzed while comparing their performances on 13 selected benchmark networks http://www.topology-zoo.org/.

The organization of the paper is as follows. First, in Sect. 2, we present two generic quadratic programming formulations. Subsequently, we obtain the standard linearization counterparts [10]. Next, in Sect. 3, we present the numerical results obtained from the proposed models and compare their performances. Finally, in Sect. 4, we report the conclusions obtained and briefly discuss future research work.

2 Brief System Description and Mathematical Formulations

In this section, we assume that the backbone SDN can be represented by means of an undirected connected graph. Let $G = (S, L)$ represent such an SDN graph with a set of nodes (switches or controllers) $S = \{1, 2, \ldots, n\}$ and with a set of connection links $L = \{\{i, j\} | i, j \in S\}$ between them. Notice that the set S represents the set of candidate location sites where a switch or a controller can be installed. Finally, we denote by $K = \{1, 2, 3, \ldots, |K|\}$, the set of users with cardinality $|K|$ which are to be connected to the SDN. Notice that we assume that they can either be connected to switch or controller-type nodes of the backbone SDN.

2.1 Brief System Description

For the sake of clarity, in Figs. 1 and 2, we plot the optimal solutions obtained for 200 users which are connected only to controller and switch-type nodes for the Abiline benchmark network (http://www.topology-zoo.org/), respectively.

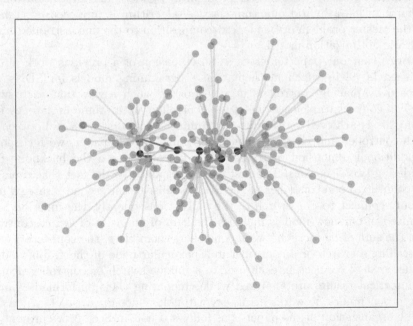

Fig. 1. This is an optimal solution to the Abiline Network, the blue dots correspond to switches, the red squares represent network controllers, and the pink dots are network users. Notice that each user is connected to a unique controller. The number of users connected to the network is 200. (Color figure online)

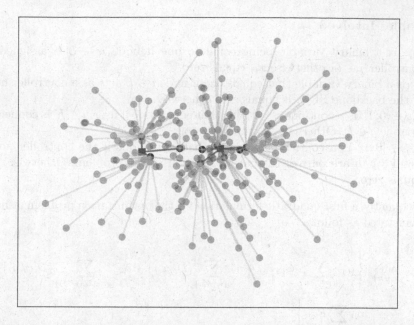

Fig. 2. This is an optimal solution to the Abiline Network, the blue dots correspond to switches, the red squares represent network controllers, and the pink dots are network users. Notice that each user is connected to a unique Switch node. The number of users connected to the network is 200. (Color figure online)

In these figures, at first sight, we observe that there is less number of controllers than switches which suggests that it is cheaper to connect users to the switch-type nodes. Finally, we recall that in both of these figures, we are simultaneously minimizing the connection costs of users to switches and/or controllers, the latencies in terms of the distances required to connect switch-controller and controller-controller pairs of nodes, and the costs of installing controllers in the SDN.

2.2 Mathematical Formulations

Now, we present and explain our proposed mathematical formulations. For this purpose, first, we present and describe the input parameters and variables involved in our mathematical models, respectively.

Input Parameters

- D_{ij}: The shortest path distance between nodes i and $j \in L$ in the network. Notice that matrix $D = (D_{ij})$ is symmetric and its diagonal has only zero values. Also, notice that these distances are computed with Dijkstra's algorithm [11].
- E_i: denotes the installation cost of controller $i \in L$.
- C_{uj}: Euclidean distance from user $u \in K$ to controller $j \in L$.

Variables Involved

- x_{ij}: is a binary variable being equal to one if node $i \in L$ is assigned to controller $j \in L$, otherwise x_{ij} equals zero.
- y_i: is a binary variable that equals one if node $i \in L$ acts as a controller node in the backbone SDN, it equals zero otherwise.
- $z_{uj} \in [0; 1]$: is a continuous variable that equals one if user $u \in K$ is connected to node $j \in L$. Otherwise, z_{uj} equals zero.
- $w_{ij} \in [0; 1]$: is a continuous variable that equals one if the controller nodes i and $j \in L$ are part of the output solution of the problem. Otherwise, w_{ij} equals zero.

Consequently, a first quadratic formulation for the optimization problem at hand can be stated as follows.

$$M_1 : \min_{\{x,y,z\}} \left\{ \alpha_1 \sum_{u \in K, j \in L} C_{uj} z_{uj} + \alpha_2 \sum_{\{i,j \in L\}} \{D_{ij} x_{ij}\} + \alpha_3 \sum_{\{i,j \in L, (i<j)\}} \{D_{ij} y_i y_j\} + \right.$$

$$\left. \alpha_4 \sum_{i \in L} E_i y_i \right\} \tag{1}$$

$$\text{st} : \sum_{j \in L} x_{ij} = 1, \quad \forall i \in L \tag{2}$$

$$x_{ij} <= y_j, \quad \forall i, j \in L \tag{3}$$

$$x_{ij} <= 1 - y_i y_j, \quad \forall i, j \in L, (i \neq j) \tag{4}$$

$$\sum_{j \in L} z_{uj} = 1, \quad \forall u \in K \tag{5}$$

$$z_{uj} <= y_j, \quad \forall j \in L, u \in K \tag{6}$$

$$x \in \{0,1\}^{|L|^2}, y \in \{0,1\}^{|L|}, z \in [0,1]^{|K||L|} \tag{7}$$

In model M_1, the objective function (1) minimizes the connection costs of users to controllers (or switches), the latencies in terms of the distances required to connect switch-controller and controller-controller pairs of nodes, and the costs of installing controllers in the SDN. The parameters α_1, α_2, α_3, and α_4 represent weighting factors that allow to vary the degree of importance of each of the objective terms. Each one of them belongs to the interval $[0; 4]$ and the sum of them must be equal to four. Subsequently, the constraints in (2) force the fact that each node should be connected to a unique controller. Naturally, the latter can be achieved only if a controller node $j \in L$ is active. This is ensured with the constraints (3). Next, the constraints in (4) guarantee that if both nodes i and $j \in L$ are acting as controllers, then the variable x_{ij} must be equal to zero since node i is not a switch node. The constraints in (5) ensure that each user $u \in K$ must be connected to a controller. Notice that is ensured together with the occurrence of constraints (6). Finally, the constraints (7) are the domain constraints for the decision variables. Notice that model M_1 is a mixed-integer quadratic model as we have products of variables in the third term of the objective function and also in the constraints (4). Also, notice that model M_1 ensures that each user should be connected to a controller-type node. However, as mentioned in Sect. 1, we also consider the situation where each user can be connected to a switch-type node. Thus, we propose a similar model M_2 which arises by simply replacing the constraints (6) with the constraints (9) in M_2. This leads to writing the following equivalent model

$$M_2 : \min_{\{x,y,z\}} \left\{ \alpha_1 \sum_{u \in K, j \in L} C_{uj} z_{uj} + \alpha_2 \sum_{\{i,j \in L\}} \{D_{ij} x_{ij}\} + \alpha_3 \sum_{\{i,j \in L, (i<j)\}} \{D_{ij} y_i y_j\} + \right.$$

$$\left. \alpha_4 \sum_{i \in L} E_i y_i \right\}$$

$$\text{st}: \sum_{j \in L} x_{ij} = 1, \quad \forall i \in L$$

$$x_{ij} <= y_j, \quad \forall i,j \in L$$

$$x_{ij} <= 1 - y_i y_j, \quad \forall i,j \in L, (i \neq j)$$

$$\sum_{j \in L} z_{uj} = 1, \quad \forall u \in K$$

$$z_{uj} <= 1 - y_j, \quad \forall u \in K, j \in L \tag{8}$$

$$x \in \{0,1\}^{|L|^2}, y \in \{0,1\}^{|L|}, z \in [0,1]^{|K||L|}.$$

In order to write a standard linear version for both quadratic models M_1 and M_2, we introduce the variables w_{ij}, for each $i,j \in L$. This allows replacing the quadratic terms $y_i y_j$ for all $i,j \in L$. Thus, we let $w_{ij} = y_i y_j$ [12]. This allows writing the following equivalent linear model for M_1

$$M_3 : \min_{\{x,y,z,w\}} \left\{ \alpha_1 \sum_{u \in K, j \in L} C_{uj} z_{uj} + \alpha_2 \sum_{\{i,j \in L\}} \{D_{ij} x_{ij}\} + \alpha_3 \sum_{\{i,j \in L\}} \{D_{ij} w_{ij}\} + \right.$$

$$\left. \alpha_4 \sum_{i \in L} E_i y_i \right\} \tag{9}$$

$$\text{st}: \sum_{j \in L} x_{ij} = 1, \quad \forall i \in L$$

$$x_{ij} <= y_j, \quad \forall i,j \in L$$

$$x_{ij} <= 1 - w_{ij}, \quad \forall i,j \in L, (i \neq j)$$

$$w_{ij} \leq y_i, \quad \forall i,j \in L \tag{10}$$

$$w_{ij} \leq y_j, \quad \forall i,j \in L \tag{11}$$

$$w_{ij} \geq y_i + y_j - 1, \quad \forall i,j \in L \tag{12}$$

$$\sum_{j \in L} z_{uj} = 1, \quad \forall u \in K$$

$$z_{uj} <= y_j, \quad \forall u \in K, j \in L$$

$$x \in \{0,1\}^{|L|^2}, y \in \{0,1\}^{|L|}, z \in [0,1]^{|L|^2}, w \in [0,1]^{|L|^2} \tag{13}$$

where the constraints (10)–(12) are the standard linearization constraints [12]. Similarly, we arrive at the following equivalent model for M_2

$$M_4 : \min_{\{x,y,z,w\}} \left\{ \alpha_1 \sum_{u \in K, j \in L} C_{uj} z_{uj} + \alpha_2 \sum_{\{i,j \in L\}} \{D_{ij} x_{ij}\} + \alpha_3 \sum_{\{i,j \in L\}} \{D_{ij} w_{ij}\} + \right.$$

$$\left. \alpha_4 \sum_{i \in L} E_i y_i \right\}$$

$$\text{st} : \sum_{j \in L} x_{ij} = 1, \quad \forall i \in L$$

$$x_{ij} <= y_j, \quad \forall i, j \in L$$

$$x_{ij} <= 1 - w_{ij}, \quad \forall i, j \in L, (i \neq j)$$

$$w_{ij} \leq y_i, \quad \forall i, j \in L$$

$$w_{ij} \leq y_j, \quad \forall i, j \in L$$

$$w_{ij} > y_i + y_j - 1, \quad \forall i, j \in L$$

$$\sum_{j \in L} z_{uj} = 1, \quad \forall u \in K$$

$$z_{uj} <= 1 - y_j, \quad \forall u \in K, j \in L$$

$$x \in \{0,1\}^{|L|^2}, y \in \{0,1\}^{|L|}, z \in [0,1]^{|L|^2}, w \in [0,1]^{|L|^2}$$

Finally, notice that since the variables z_{uj}, for all $u \in K$, $j \in L$ are continuous and belong to the interval $[0;1]$. Then, we can apply the automatic Bender's decomposition algorithm of the CPLEX [13]. The underlying idea of this decomposition algorithm is that given a linear mathematical programming formulation, it is possible to decompose the optimization model into a single master and (possibly multiple) sub-problems. For this purpose, the CPLEX solver uses annotations that the user can supply for the model. In some cases, this algorithmic approach has proved to offer significant performance improvements when solving combinatorial optimization problems formulated as mixed-integer programming problems in the literature [14].

3   Computational Numerical Experiments

In this section, we conduct preliminary numerical experiments in order to compare all the proposed models using both the B&C and Bender's decomposition algorithms of the CPLEX solver [13]. To this end, we implement all the codes in Python using the CPLEX solver version 20.1.0 either for solving the mixed-integer quadratic and linear programming models. The numerical results have been obtained using a MAC computer with a 1.8 GHz Dual-Core Intel Core i5 processor with 8G of RAM under MacOS. As mentioned above, we consider in our numerical experiments 13 benchmark real graph networks from http://www.topology-zoo.org/ with different dimensions from 4 to 87 nodes. So far, we assume that each of the 4 terms in the objective functions of our proposed models has an equal degree of importance, i.e., we arbitrarily set α_1, α_2, α_3, and α_4 to be equal to one.

In Tables 1, 2, and 3, we present numerical results for the models M_1, M_2, M_3, and M_4, respectively. Notice that models M_1 and M_3 are equivalent as both connect users to controller-type nodes only. Similarly, the models M_2 and M_4 are also equivalent. Indeed, they are the quadratic and linear versions of the models that connect users to switch-type nodes. In particular, in Tables 1 and 2, we report numerical results for the proposed models while using the B&C algorithm of the CPLEX solver. Whereas in Table 3, we report numerical results for the models M_3 and M_4 when using the automatic Bender's decomposition approach of the CPLEX solver. Notice that the latter can be done only because these models have continuous variables which allow the use of Bender's approach. Otherwise, this is not possible to achieve [13]. More precisely, in Tables 1 and 2, column 1 reports the network name, next columns 2–4, and 5–7 report, for each model, the optimal or best solution found in at most one hour of CPU time, the CPU time in seconds, and the number of controllers of the solution obtained. Finally, the legends of columns 8–10, and 11–13 are exactly the same as for the model M_1, but for M_2 and M_4, respectively. Notice that we arbitrarily set the number of users, in each model, to the values of 35 and 200 users, respectively. In particular, the location of users was randomly generated from the middle point of all nodes of each network.

Table 1. Comparison of models M_1 and M_2 for Benchmark SDN instances. Each of these instances is solved with the B&C CPLEX solver.

| Network Name | M_1 | | | | | | M_2 | | | | | |
| | User = 35 | | | User = 200 | | | User = 35 | | | User = 200 | | |
	Best Sol	CPU(s)	NC	Best Sol	CPU(s)	NC	Best Sol	CPU(s)	NC	Best Sol	CPU(s)	NC
Arpanet196912	1032.28	0.16	3	6282.7	0.03	3	1004.78	0.09	1	6257.31	0.02	1
Abiline	1009.67	3.89	3	4929.68	5.07	5	840.54	3.05	2	4572.49	4.65	2
Aarnet	1050.29	5.38	3	5036.02	7.96	4	851.38	4.04	2	4615.5	5.47	2
Ans	1095.75	10.36	3	4957.12	21.04	5	934.61	8.12	2	4436.55	15.03	2
HurricaneElectric	2032.33	10.95	3	6915.56	27.02	3	1959.02	11.1	2	6603.24	20.66	2
Atmnet	1086.25	20.48	4	4954.26	29.59	5	925.59	19.3	2	4495.58	23.33	2
Bbnplanet	1109.99	3600.13	3	5041.73	348.51	5	962.73	60.88	3	4633.09	121.21	3
Bics	1128.95	254.21	4	5103.49	103.9	6	902.12	3600.36	3	4507.66	3600.05	3
CrlNetworkServices	1160.97	3600.41	3	4957.65	1355.18	6	980.86	3600.42	3	4401.03	912.79	3
Internet2 OS3E	1219.23	3600.08	4	4947.39	1262.31	6	983.78	3600.23	3	4320.33	3600.23	3
Geant2009	1287.58	234.6	4	4934.19	273.97	6	935.72	3600.07	3	3774.75	3600.04	3
NetworkUsa	1104.12	3600.09	4	6480.89	90.59	5	1066.81	3600.11	3	6411.55	3600.15	3
VtlWavenet2008	1424.22	3600.21	4	6750.55	3600.15	6	1568.42	3600.1	8	6492.87	3601.63	6

From these two tables, we mainly observe that the objective function values are smaller for M_2 and M_4 when compared to the values obtained with the models M_1 and M_3, respectively, for all tested instances. This occurs either when using 35 or 200 users. This clearly suggests that it is less expensive to connect

Table 2. Comparison of models M_3 and M_4 for Benchmark SDN instances. Each of these instances is solved with the B&C CPLEX solver.

Network Name	M_3						M_4					
	User = 35			User = 200			User = 35			User = 200		
	Best Sol	CPU(s)	NC	Best Sol	CPU(s)	NC	Best Sol	CPU(s)	NC	Best Sol	CPU(s)	NC
Arpanet196912	1032.28	0.05	3	6282.7	0.03	3	1004.78	0.02	1	6257.31	0.04	1
Abiline	1009.67	0.17	3	4929.68	0.37	5	840.54	0.15	2	4572.49	0.31	2
Aarnet	1050.29	0.18	3	5036.02	0.31	4	851.38	0.14	2	4615.5	0.31	2
Ans	1095.75	0.46	3	4957.12	0.73	5	934.61	0.4	2	4436.55	0.73	2
HurricaneElectric	2032.33	0.34	3	6915.56	0.78	3	1959.02	0.42	2	6603.24	0.87	2
Atmnet	1086.25	1.55	4	4954.26	1.41	5	925.59	1.03	2	4495.58	0.85	2
Bbnplanet	1109.99	1.79	3	5041.73	4.15	5	962.73	0.93	3	4633.09	2.41	3
Bics	1128.95	3.71	4	5103.49	2.86	6	901.99	1.03	3	4504.87	2.35	3
CrlNetworkServices	1160.97	3.2	3	4957.65	6.86	6	978.97	2.87	3	4401.03	4.03	3
Internet2 OS3E	1208.29	5.58	4	4947.39	9.45	6	983.78	3.94	3	4310.16	3.68	3
Geant2009	1287.58	5.15	4	4934.19	15.97	6	935.72	2.99	3	3774.75	3.53	3
NetworkUsa	1100.44	2.4	4	6480.89	2.22	5	1066.81	1.79	3	6411.55	14.22	3
VtlWavenet2008	1332.02	913.93	4	6520.07	186.38	6	1296.93	3600.04	5	6390.21	2846.2	4

users to switch-type nodes rather than to connect users to controller-type nodes. Regarding the CPU times, we observe similar trends for both models M_1 and M_2, and M_3 and M_4 in Tables 1 and 2, respectively. Subsequently, we also see that the number of controller nodes remains in the range of 1 and 8. Notice that the latter depends on the number of nodes each backbone SDN contains. Finally, a last observation is that most of the instances can be solved optimally with the models M_3 and M_4, i.e., with the linear ones. In Table 3, the legend is analogous to the previous Tables 1, and 2. Notice that the only difference is that in Table 3 we add an extra column reporting the number of cuts required by the CPLEX Bender's decomposition approach [13].

Table 3. Comparison of models M_3 and M_4 for Benchmark SDN instances. Each of these instances is solved with Bender's decomposition algorithm of CPLEX solver.

Network Name	M_3								M_4							
	User = 35				User = 200				User = 35				User = 200			
	Best Sol	CPU(s)	NC	cuts	Best Sol	CPU(s)	NC	cuts	Best Sol	CPU(s)	NC	cuts	Best Sol	CPU(s)	NC	cuts
Arpanet196912	1032.28	0.03	3	5	6282.7	0.07	3	6	1004.78	0.02	1	0	6257.31	0.07	1	210
Abiline	1009.67	1.08	3	51	4929.68	4.26	5	52	840.54	1.06	2	28	4572.49	4.16	2	199
Aarnet	1050.29	1.48	3	67	5036.02	12.75	4	38	851.38	1.37	2	44	4615.5	4.36	2	220
Ans	1095.75	4.91	3	140	4957.12	13.96	5	131	934.61	5.4	2	124	4436.55	15.32	2	200
HurricaneElectric	2032.33	5.68	3	172	6603.24	36.97	2	143	1959.02	5.24	2	165	6603.24	36.2	2	200
Atmnet	1086.25	8.22	4	190	4954.26	25.27	5	197	925.59	7.51	2	165	4495.58	29.83	2	214
Bbnplanet	1109.99	21.51	3	291	5041.73	95.79	5	297	962.73	27.63	3	281	4633.09	146.17	3	221
Bics	1128.95	42.33	4	425	5103.49	163.96	6	376	901.99	48.43	3	335	4504.87	255.84	3	200
CrlNetworkServices	1160.97	54.33	3	450	4957.65	207.41	6	458	978.97	59.41	3	411	4401.03	391.74	3	214
Internet2 OS3E	1208.29	61.75	4	494	4947.39	265.02	6	476	983.78	57.55	3	434	4310.16	479.19	3	205
Geant2009	1287.58	57.52	4	499	4934.19	198.63	6	472	935.72	60.5	3	426	3774.75	236.87	3	220
NetworkUsa	1100.44	61.04	4	347	6480.89	486.35	5	212	1066.81	58.27	3	289	6411.55	1158.85	3	199
VtlWavenet2008	–	–	–	–	–	–	–	–	–	–	–	–	–	–	–	–

No solution found due to a CPLEX shortage of memory

From Table 3, we observe similar trends concerning the objective function values reported in Table 2. Regarding the CPU time values in seconds, we observe slightly larger values, but we also see that almost all the instances are solved optimally. Another observation is that the number of Bender's cuts required to solve the instances optimally does not grow significantly with the number of users. In order to give more insight related to the numerical results obtained, in Figs. 3 and 4, we respectively report optimal objective function and CPU time values in seconds obtained for M_3 and M_4 for the benchmark network known as Abiline while varying the number of users from 100 to 1000. These values are obtained using the B&C algorithm. We choose these models as they solve this benchmark instance more rapidly than the rest of the models. In particular, from Fig. 3, we observe that the objective function values of both models increase linearly with the number of users. We further notice that the objective function values obtained with model M_4 are lower than those obtained with model M_3. This suggests that it is still cheaper to connect users to switch-type nodes rather than to connect users to controller-type nodes of the backbone SDN network. Finally, from Fig. 4, we see that the CPU times required to solve model M_3 optimally are mostly higher than those required for solving optimally model M_4.

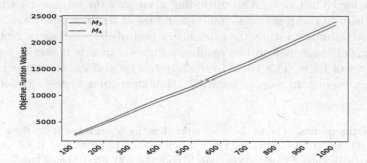

Fig. 3. Optimal objective function values obtained for M_3 and M_4 for the benchmark Abiline network while varying the number of users from 100 to 1000. The values are obtained using B&C algorithm.

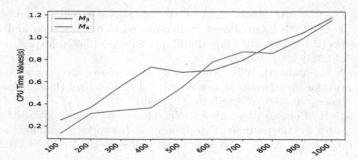

Fig. 4. Optimal CPU time values in seconds required for solving M_3 and M_4 for the benchmark Abiline network while varying the number of users from 100 to 1000. The values are obtained using B&C algorithm.

4 Conclusion

In this paper, we propose mathematical models to efficiently connect users to a backbone SDN architecture. In particular, we consider the problem of connecting users to either controller or switch-type nodes. For this purpose, we propose mixed-integer quadratic and mixed-integer linear programming formulations while taking into account the sum of the total existing latency between controller-controller and switch-controller pairs of nodes, the connection cost from users to controllers or switches, and the total installation costs of controllers in the network. For solving each of the proposed quadratic models, we use the B&C algorithm of the CPLEX solver. Whilst for solving the proposed linear models, we use both the B&C as well as Bender's decomposition algorithms of the CPLEX solver. From the numerical results obtained, it can be observed that the linear models have a notable improvement in processing times compared to the quadratic ones. In general, we see that it is cheaper to connect users to switch-type nodes rather than connecting users to controller-type nodes. Finally, we see that the CPU times required by Bender's approach seem to be a bit larger than the B&C method.

In future research, we plan to investigate the performance of Bender's algorithm for larger instances. Also, including a larger number of users while connecting them to controller or switch-type nodes of the backbone SDN. Finally, we are also planning to study the existence of multiple types of users. Notice that considering different user profiles requires a different quality of service treatment for each set of users. This should be addressed by performing network slicing. Ultimately, we plan to propose approximation algorithms to deal efficiently with large SDNs.

Acknowledgements. The authors acknowledge the financial support from Projects Dicyt 062313AS, ANID/FONDECYT Iniciación No. 11230129, and the Competition for Research Regular Projects, year 2021, code LPR21-02; Universidad Tecnológica Metropolitana.

References

1. Prabha, C., Goel, A., Singh, J.: A survey on SDN controller evolution: a brief review. In: 2022 7th International Conference on Communication and Electronics Systems (ICCES), Coimbatore, India, pp. 569–575 (2022). https://doi.org/10.1109/ICCES54183.2022.9835810
2. Hlophe, M.C., Maharaj, B.T.: An SDN controller-based network slicing scheme using constrained reinforcement learning. IEEE Access **10**, 134848–134869 (2022). https://doi.org/10.1109/ACCESS.2022.3228804
3. Rasol, K.A.R., Domingo-Pascual, J.: Joint placement latency optimization of the control plane. In: International Symposium on Networks, Computers and Communications (ISNCC), pp. 1–6 (2020). https://doi.org/10.1109/ISNCC49221.2020.9297271
4. Maity, I., Misra, S., Mandal, C.: SCOPE: cost-efficient QoS-aware switch and controller placement in hybrid SDN. IEEE Syst. J. **16**(3), 4873–4880 (2022). https://doi.org/10.1109/JSYST.2021.3124280

5. Ibrahim, A.A.Z., Hashim, F., Sali, A., Noordin, N.K., Fadul, S.M.E.: A multi-objective routing mechanism for energy management optimization in SDN multi-control architecture. IEEE Access **10**, 20312–20327 (2022). https://doi.org/10.1109/ACCESS.2022.3149795

6. Mohanty, S., Shekhawat, A.S., Sahoo, B., Apat, H.K., Khare, P.: Minimizing latency for controller placement problem in SDN. In: 2021 19th OITS International Conference on Information Technology (OCIT), pp. 393–398 (2021). https://doi.org/10.1109/OCIT53463.2021.00083

7. Wang, T., Chen, H.: Optimal model for link failure foresight controller placement in SDN. In: 2021 IEEE 4th International Conference on Electronics Technology (ICET), pp. 727–730 (2021). https://doi.org/10.1109/ICET51757.2021.9450905

8. Zhao, Z., Fan, L., Han, Z.: Hybrid quantum benders' decomposition for mixed-integer linear programming. In: IEEE Wireless Communications and Networking Conference (WCNC), Austin, TX, USA 2022, pp. 2536–2540 (2022). https://doi.org/10.1109/WCNC51071.2022.9771632

9. Viveros, A., Adasme, P., Urrutia, E.S.J.: Minimizing latency and number of controllers in software defined networking. In: 2022 IEEE International Conference on Automation/XXV Congress of the Chilean Association of Automatic Control (ICA-ACCA), Curicó, Chile, pp. 1–6 (2022). https://doi.org/10.1109/ICA-ACCA56767.2022.10006004

10. Adasme, P., Viveros, A.: Ali Dehghan Firoozabadi. Mathematical Models for Minimizing Latency in Software-Defined Networks, pp. 131–142. MobiWIS, Ismael Soto (2022)

11. Cormen, T.H., Leiserson, C.E., Rivest, R.L., Stein, C.: Section 24.3: Dijkstra's algorithm. Introduction to Algorithms (Second edn), pp. 595–601. MIT Press and McGraw-Hill (2001). ISBN: 0-262-03293-7

12. Fortet, R.: Applications de l'algebre de boole en recherche operationelle. Revue Francaise d'Automatique, d'Informatique et de Recherche Opérationnelle **4**, 17–26 (1960)

13. IBM Ilog: CPLEX high-performance mathematical programming engine (2021). http://www.ibm.com/software/integration/optimization/cplex/, https://www.ibm.com/docs/en/icos/20.1.0?topic=optimization-benders-algorithm

14. Rahmaniani, R.: Teodor gabriel crainic, michel gendreau, walter rei: the benders decomposition algorithm: a literature review. Eur. J. Oper. Res. **259**(3), 801–817 (2017)

Fuzzy Data Deduplication at Edge Nodes in Connected Environments

Sylvana Yakhni[1], Joe Tekli[1(✉)], Elio Mansour[2], and Richard Chbeir[3]

[1] E.C.E. Department, Lebanese American University, Byblos 36, Lebanon
silvana.yakhni@lau.edu, joe.tekli@lau.edu.lb
[2] Scient Analytics, 75007 Paris, France
elio.mansour@scient.io
[3] University of Pau and Pays Adour, 64600 Anglet, France
richard.chbeir@univ-pau.fr

Abstract. The Internet of Things (IoT) is ushering-in the era of connected environments, i.e., networks of physical objects that are embedded with sensors and softwar, connecting and exchanging data with other devices and systems. The huge amount of data produced by such systems calls for solutions to reduce the amount of data being handled and transmitted over the network. In this study, we investigate data deduplication as a prominent pre-processing method that can address such a challenge. Data deduplication techniques have been traditionally developed for data storage and data warehousing applications, and aim at identifying and eliminating redundant data items. Few recent approaches have been designed for sensor networks and connected environments, yet existing solutions mostly rely on crisp thresholds and provide minimum-to-no expert control over the deduplication process, disregarding the domain expert's needs in defining redundancy. In this study, we propose a new approach for Fuzzy Redundancy Elimination for Data Deduplication in a connected environment. We use simple natural language rules to represent domain knowledge and expert preferences regarding data duplication boundaries. We then apply pattern codes and fuzzy reasoning to detect duplicate data items at the outer-most edge (sensor node) level of the network. This reduces the time required to hard-code the deduplication process, while adapting to the domain expert's needs for different data sources and applications. Experiments on a real-world dataset highlight our solutions' potential and improvement compared with existing solutions.

Keywords: Connected Environments · Fuzzy Reasoning · Data Redundancy · Data Deduplication · Internet of Things (IoT) · Wireless Sensor Networks

1 Introduction

The Internet of Things (IoT) is ushering-in the era of connected environments, i.e., networks of physical objects that are embedded with sensors, software, and other technologies for the purpose of connecting and exchanging data with other devices and systems (e.g., smart hospitals, smart buildings, and smart cities) [1, 2]. According to

M. Younas et al. (Eds.): MobiWIS 2023, LNCS 13977, pp. 112–128, 2023.
https://doi.org/10.1007/978-3-031-39764-6_8

a recent survey conducted by VoucherCloud in [3], 2.5+ quintillions of sensory data are currently generated every day, and over 123×10^9 IoT devices are expected to be connected within the next 10 years [4]. This huge amount of data highlights several challenges including network bandwidth, consumption of network energy, cloud storage, and I/O throughput. These call for data pre-processing and filtering techniques to reduce the amount of data being handled and transmitted over the network. In this study, we investigate data deduplication as a prominent pre-processing method that can address such challenges. Data Deduplication techniques have been traditionally developed for data storage and data warehousing applications, and aim at identifying and eliminating redundant data items, where only one unique copy of the data is stored [5]. Similarly, data deduplication in connected environments aims at eliminating redundant measurements produced by sensing devices. For instance, there is no need to store and transmit similar temperature measurements produced by a sensor if they are almost identical within a given timespan. Such measurements would be considered redundant and need to be eliminated, where only relevant changes are processed by the system. In this context, few recent approaches have been designed for handling data in connected environments, e.g., [5–9], yet most existing solutions rely on crisp evaluation thresholds and provide the domain expert with minimum-to-no control over the deduplication process (i.e., which data need to be duplicated and which data should be kept intact) hence overlooking the expert's requirements and application needs in defining redundancy, e.g., [6, 9].

In this study, we propose a new approach for Fuzzy Redundancy Elimination for Data Deduplication (FREDD) in a connected environment. It uses simple natural language rules to represent domain knowledge and expert preferences regarding data duplication boundaries. It then applies pattern codes and fuzzy reasoning to detect duplicates on the edge of the network. This reduces the time required to hard-code the deduplication process, while adapting to the domain expert's needs and application requirements. Experiments on a real-world dataset highlight our solution's potential and improvement compared with existing approaches.

The remainder of this paper is organized as follows. Section 2 briefly reviews the related works. Section 3 describes our framework. Section 4 describes our experimental evaluation and results, before concluding in Sect. 5 with ongoing directions.

2 Related Works

Data deduplication techniques have been initially developed for data storage and data warehousing systems, e.g., [10–12], and have been recently investigated in the context of IoT and connected environments.

In [9], the authors address data redundancies at the core of the network using a supervised machine learning solution based on Support Vector Machines (SVM). They build an aggregation tree for the given size of the network and then apply SVM to recognize data redundancies. The authors target temporal and spatial redundancies once the data is consolidated in a central node, which provides a redundancy-free data repository that can be mined using dedicated data processing techniques (cf. *Challenge 1*). However, redundancies are not handled at the edge level, and data exchange between devices at the edge remains costly due to unnecessary communications. In [13], the authors provide a data deduplication technique in healthcare-based IoT, and introduce a Controlled

Window-size based Chunking Algorithm (CWCA) to identify cut-points in sensor data distributions. Yet similarly to [9], the solution in [13] only performs data deduplication at sink nodes and does consider redundancies at edge devices (cf. *Challenge 1*). In [14], the authors focus on the spatial distribution of sensors in the environment, and how it can be managed to prevent redundancies. The authors build a graph of nodes and events in order to detect "redundant" nodes: i.e., nodes producing identical events. Redundant nodes are either relocated or put into sleep mode using a circle packing technique to enhance coverage, while minimizing energy usage during relocation. This work only handles redundancy from a sensor deployment perspective (i.e., avoiding deploying sensors that provide the same type of data in the same area).

In a continuous sensing setup, triggering mechanisms are available to restrict the number of transmissions between the sensor node and the monitoring node without degrading the tracking of the sensed measurements, e.g., [15, 16]. These mechanisms can also be used for filtering redundant spatial-temporal data, in order to trigger transmissions from sensor node (edge) to monitoring node (sink) only when there are changes in the sensed measurements. These approaches fall into the category of edge-based data deduplication solutions, and rely on a simple crisp deviation threshold δ_v. More recently, the authors in [6, 17] proposed a Data Redundancy Management Framework (DRMF) that handles data redundancies at the edge device level considering both static and mobile devices. It clusters the data based on expert/system defined crisp deviation threshold, while also keeping track of the temporal and spatial-temporal spread (or coverage) of each cluster (i.e., sets of redundant data). The algorithm sorts all data tokens and checks if the current token belongs to the current cluster by comparing it with the cluster's centroid, considering a expert-defined deviation threshold δv. Otherwise, a new cluster is created with the current data item added as its centroid. In another relevant study in [18], the authors introduce the Redundancy Elimination Data Aggregation (REDA) algorithm to perform deduplication at individual edge nodes and also among nodes in the same cluster. Assuming that data is presented as a set of scalar values (e.g., temperature, humidity), the range of numbers is divided into crisp intervals that depend on the domain expert requirements, then a lookup table is generated for each cluster containing the ranges of each interval and their associated pattern codes (e.g., 10–15 °C are associated with pattern code 1, 16–20° are associated with pattern code 2). Note that both [6, 18] rely on crisp deviation thresholds, and share the same limitations of crisp processing.

Discussion: Few recent solutions have been designed to handle data deduplication in connected environments. They utilize crisp thresholds where even the slightest variations in the sensed measurements are processed similarly to extremely large variations (e.g., given a temperature variation threshold $\delta_v = 1$ °C, variations of 1.5 °C and 20.5 °C are processed exactly the same). Similarly, variations which are slightly below the threshold are entirely ignored (e.g., given a temperature variation threshold $\delta_v = 1$ °C, a variation of 0.99 °C goes unprocessed). Relying on crisp thresholds leads to i) missing certain relevant redundancies or ii) removing certain data values that might not be redundant. Also, existing solutions provide minimum-to-no expert intervention and adaptability in the deduplication process.

3 FREDD Framework

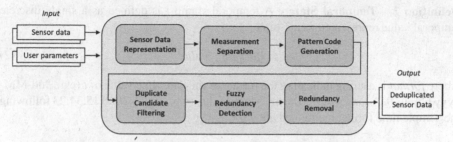

Fig. 1. Simplified diagram describing FREDD's architecture

To address the aforementioned challenges, we introduce FREDD: a new framework for Fuzzy Redundancy Elimination for Data Deduplication in a connected environment. FREDD detects data duplicates at edge (source) nodes, in order to minimize network traffic and bandwidth consumption. It combines simple natural language rules with a fuzzy inference mechanism designed to adapt the deduplication process following the expert's needs. FREDD's core architecture is depicted in Fig. 1. It consists of six main modules: i) *sensor data representation* which defines the spatial and temporal representations of data measurements/items, ii) *measurement separation* which separates the input data into measurement-based data collections, iii) *pattern code generation* which associates data items with pattern codes based on expert-defined lookup tables, iv) *duplicate candidate filtering* which determines whether data items are candidates for fuzzy duplication, v) *fuzzy redundancy detection* which identifies duplicate data items using fuzzy reasoning based on expert-defined condition-action rules, and vi) *redundancy removal* which eliminates redundant data items and produces deduplicated data.

3.1 Sensor Data Representation

Connected environments contain diverse devices each embedding one or more sensors that provide data from the real world. Static devices are immobile; therefore, the data generated by such devices can be redundant temporally. Mobile devices produce data while moving around the environment, which potentially generates spatial-temporal redundancies. Here, we restrict our presentation to static devices dealing with temporal redundancies, and report spatial-temporal redundancies to a later dedicated study. We adopt a set of formal definitions from [6] that allows us to describe data items considering the temporal dimension:

Definition 1 - **Data Items**: A data item d is defined as a 4-tuple:

$$d = \langle m; v; t; s \rangle \tag{1}$$

where m is the data measurement, v is the data value, t is the creation temporal stamp of d (cf. Definition 2), and s is the data source that sensed/created d •

Definition 2 - **Temporal Stamp**: A temporal stamp t is defined as a single discrete temporal value represented as a 2-tuple:

$$t = \langle format : value \rangle \tag{2}$$

where *format* is a string indicating the format of the date-time value of t (e.g., "dd-MM-yyyy hh:mm:ss"), and *value* is the timestamp value (e.g., 10-11-2020 15:34:23 following the sample time format mentioned above) •

Table 1. Sample sensory data items

Measurement m	Value v	Time stamp t		Source s
		format	*value*	
Humidity	92 µg/m³	dd/MM/yyyy hh:mm:ss	10/02/2019 10:00:00	S1
Temperature	16 °C	dd/MM/yyyy hh:mm:ss	10/02/2019 10:01:00	S1
Humidity	94 µg/m³	dd/MM/yyyy hh:mm:ss	10/02/2019 10:02:00	S1
Temperature	19.5 °C	dd/MM/yyyy hh:mm:ss	10/02/2019 10:02:00	S1
Temperature	21 °C	dd/MM/yyyy hh:mm:ss	10/02/2019 10:03:00	S1
Humidity	103 µg/m³	dd/MM/yyyy hh:mm:ss	10/02/2019 10:05:00	S1
Temperature	21 °C	dd/MM/yyyy hh:mm:ss	10/02/2019 10:05:00	S1
Humidity	104 µg/m³	dd/MM/yyyy hh:mm:ss	10/02/2019 10:06:00	S1

Consider the motivating example of a smart building, hosting a set of static sensing devices that provide *humidity* and *temperature* measurements (among others) from the environment. Devices have built-in memories to buffer chunks of sensory data before transmission to the network's sink nodes. Table 1 shows the representation of sample sensory data after being sensed/produced by an edge device (source) S_1 embedding two sensors producing *humidity* and *temperature* measurements respectively.

3.2 Measurement Separation

Since the device can embed various sensors, its internal memory might store different measurements (i.e., features such as *humidity* and *temperature* in Table 1). Therefore, in order to detect redundancies in the data stored locally on the edge device, we start by filtering the data into collections having the same measurements. To illustrate the measurement filtering process, the data shown in Table 1 produces two distinct data collections: the first for *humidity* data (first four tuples - cf. Table 2), and the second for *temperature* data (containing the last tuples). Consequently, the measurement data collections are processed separately for data deduplication. Note that the domain expert decides about the selection of measurements to be processed for deduplication.

Table 2. Measurement separation of the data from Table 1

a. *Humidity* data collection

Measurement m	Value v	Time stamp t		Source s
		format	*value*	
Humidity	92 μg/m^3	dd/MM/yyyy hh:mm:ss	10/02/2019 10:00:00	S1
Humidity	94 μg/m^3	dd/MM/yyyy hh:mm:ss	10/02/2019 10:02:00	S1
Humidity	103 μg/m^3	dd/MM/yyyy hh:mm:ss	10/02/2019 10:05:00	S1
Humidity	104 μg/m^3	dd/MM/yyyy hh:mm:ss	10/02/2019 10:06:00	S1

b. *Temperature* data collection

Measurement m	Value v	Time stamp t		Source s
		format	*value*	
Temperature	16 °C	dd/MM/yyyy hh:mm:ss	10/02/2019 10:01:00	S1
Temperature	19.5 °C	dd/MM/yyyy hh:mm:ss	10/02/2019 10:02:00	S1
Temperature	21 °C	dd/MM/yyyy hh:mm:ss	10/02/2019 10:03:00	S1
Temperature	21 °C	dd/MM/yyyy hh:mm:ss	10/02/2019 10:05:00	S1

3.3 Pattern Generation Code

The pattern code generation module transforms ranges of data item values for a given measurement (e.g., *humidity*, *temperature*) into interval values that are defined based on reference lookup tables. Edge and sink devices handling the same measurements refer to the corresponding measurement lookup tables (e.g., *humidity* lookup table, or *temperature* lookup table), where lookup tables are created based on expert preferences or application requirements. Here, we distinguish between two kinds of lookup tables allowing: i) *disjoint* data ranges, and ii) *intersecting* data ranges.

Table 3. Sample *disjoint* value lookup tables for *humidity* and *temperature* measurements, considering ranges 90–110 μg/m[1] and 15–28 °C respectively

a. Disjoint *humidity* data ranges

Interval values	[90, 96] μg/m^3	]96, 104] μg/m^3	]104, 110] μg/m^3
Pattern code	H1	H2	H3

b. Disjoint *temperature* data ranges

Interval values	[15-19] °C	]19-24] °C	]24-28] °C
Pattern code	T1	T2	T3

Disjoint data ranges (cf. Table 3) allow simple pattern code generation, yet they produce disconnected pattern codes where values on the range boundaries might be misrepresented (e.g., it is not clear which pattern code can be assigned with values 96.2 μg/m^3 or 104.7 μg/m^3 following Table 3). *Intersecting* data ranges (cf. Table 4) allow the generation of combined pattern codes when the target value belongs to more than one range (e.g., *humidity* values 103, 104, and 105 μg/m^3 belong to both H2 and H3 pattern codes following Table 4).

---

[1] Microgram Per Cubic Meter.

Table 4. Sample *intersecting* value lookup tables for *humidity* and *temperature* measurements, considering ranges 90–110 μg/m³ and 15–28 °C respectively

<table>
<tr><td colspan="4">a. Intersecting humidity data ranges</td><td colspan="4">b. Intersecting temperature data ranges</td></tr>
<tr><td>Interval values</td><td>[90, 98] μg/m³</td><td>[94, 106] μg/m³</td><td>[102, 110] μg/m³</td><td>Interval values</td><td>[15-20] °C</td><td>[18-25] °C</td><td>[23-28] °C</td></tr>
<tr><td>Pattern code</td><td>H1</td><td>H2</td><td>H3</td><td>Pattern code</td><td>T1</td><td>T2</td><td>T3</td></tr>
</table>

In this study, we consider *intersecting* ranges to allow more efficient processing (duplicate candidate filtering, cf. Section 3.4) and more accurate data deduplication (fuzzy redundancy detection, cf. Section 3.5).

Table 5 shows the pattern codes generated for the data items from our running example in Table 2, considering the above look-up tables.

Table 5. Value, zone, and combined pattern codes for sample data from Table 1

a. *Humidity* data collection

Measurement m	Value v	Value Pattern Code	Time stamp t		Source s
			format	*value*	
Humidity	92 μg/m³	{H1}	dd/MM/yyyy hh:mm:ss	10/02/2019 10:00:00	S1
Humidity	94 μg/m³	{H1}	dd/MM/yyyy hh:mm:ss	10/02/2019 10:02:00	S1
Humidity	103 μg/m³	{H2,H3}	dd/MM/yyyy hh:mm:ss	10/02/2019 10:05:00	S1
Humidity	104 μg/m³	{H2,H3}	dd/MM/yyyy hh:mm:ss	10/02/2019 10:06:00	S1

b. *Temperature* data collection

Measurement m	Value v	Value Pattern Code	Time stamp t		Source s
			format	*value*	
Temperature	16 °C	{T1}	dd/MM/yyyy hh:mm:ss	10/02/2019 10:01:00	S1
Temperature	19.5 °C	{T1,T2}	dd/MM/yyyy hh:mm:ss	10/02/2019 10:02:00	S1
Temperature	21 °C	{T2}	dd/MM/yyyy hh:mm:ss	10/02/2019 10:03:00	S1
Temperature	21 °C	{T2}	dd/MM/yyyy hh:mm:ss	10/02/2019 10:05:00	S1

3.4 Duplicate Candidate Filtering

Since sensor data items are produced and ordered per sensing time stamp, each data item to be deduplicated is evaluated with its previous one to check if the data is duplicate or not. Our duplicate candidate filtering algorithm is depicted in Fig. 2. It accepts as input two consecutive data items and produces as output a decision of whether the data items are duplicates, non-duplicates, or candidates for deduplication, based on the following rules: i) if two data items share one value-zone pattern code, then they are considered duplicates (cf. Figure 2, lines 4–5), ii) if the data items share one or more value-zone pattern codes, they are considered as candidates for deduplication (lines 6–7), and iii) if the data items do not share any value-zone pattern code, they are considered as non-duplicates (lines 8–9),

Table 6 shows the output of the filtering algorithm applied on the input data from Table 5, where 6 data items are identified as either duplicates/non-duplicates, such that 2 of the original 8 items need to be further considered for fuzzy deduplication. Depending on the data patterns generated in the target connected environment, duplicate filtering can significantly reduce the number of data items to be processed for fuzzy redundancy detection, thus significantly improving overall processing performance especially at the device level (cf. Experimental results in Sect. 4).

Algorithm 1 – Duplicate Candidate Filtering
Input: DataItem1, DataItem2
Output: DeduplicationStatus
Begin
1   *pattern1* ← pattern code for DataItem1
2   *pattern1* ← pattern code for DataItem2
3   *interLen* ← length of intersection between DataItem1 and DataItem2
4   **if** (pattern1 = pattern2) **and** (interLen =1) **then**
5   DeduplicationStatus ← Duplicates
6   **else if** interLen > 1 **then**
7   DeduplicationStatus ← Candidates
8   **else**
9   DeduplicationStatus ← NotDuplicates
End

Fig. 2. Pseudocode of our *duplicate candidate filtering* algorithm

3.5 Fuzzy Redundancy Detection

The fuzzy redundancy detection module's overall process is shown in Fig. 3. It accepts as input data items that are candidates for redundancy detection, and then produces as output their deduplication status (i.e., *duplicates* or *non-duplicates*).

Fuzzification: First, the scalar data item values are fuzzified, producing linguistic values associated with fuzzy membership degrees (e.g., *humidity* value 103 $\mu g/m^3$ becomes 75% H2 and 25% H3 following Fig. 4). The fuzzy partitions for every measurement are defined based on the corresponding lookup table ranges, where the fuzzy membership functions can be defined following the expert and application needs (cf. Figure 4.a and b). The output *deduplication status* variable represents a percentage value using one membership function varying from 0-to-100% duplication (cf. Figure 4.c).

Condition-Action Rules: As for the fuzzy agent's condition-action rules, they reflect the common sense logic applied by an domain expert to determine whether two data items are duplicates or not, based on their measurement's look-up tables:

Rule 1. **IF** (Humidity_Item1 is H1) **AND** (Humidity _Item2 is H1) **THEN** DedupStatus is *Duplicate*
Rule 2. **IF** (Humidity_Item1 is H2) **AND** (Humidity _Item2 is H2) **THEN** DedupStatus is *Duplicate*

Table 6. Output of the filtering algorithm applied on input data from Table 5

▨ Duplicate   ▢ Candidate for Deduplication   ▨ Non-Duplicate

a. *Humidity* data collection

Measurement m	Value v	Value Pattern Code	Time stamp t		Source s	
			format	*value*		
Humidity	92 µg/m³	H1	dd/MM/yyyy hh:mm:ss	10/02/2019 10:00:00	S1	Duplicates
Humidity	94 µg/m³	H1	dd/MM/yyyy hh:mm:ss	10/02/2019 10:02:00	S1	Non-Duplicates
Humidity	103 µg/m³	H2 H3	dd/MM/yyyy hh:mm:ss	10/02/2019 10:05:00	S1	Candidates
Humidity	104 µg/m³	H2 H3	dd/MM/yyyy hh:mm:ss	10/02/2019 10:06:00	S1	

b. *Temperature* data collection

Measurement m	Value v	Value Pattern Code	Time stamp t		Source s	
			format	*value*		
Temperature	16 °C	{T1}	dd/MM/yyyy hh:mm:ss	10/02/2019 10:01:00	S1	Non-Duplicates
Temperature	19.5 °C	{T1,T2}	dd/MM/yyyy hh:mm:ss	10/02/2019 10:02:00	S1	Candidates
Temperature	21 °C	{T2}	dd/MM/yyyy hh:mm:ss	10/02/2019 10:03:00	S1	Duplicates
Temperature	21 °C	{T2}	dd/MM/yyyy hh:mm:ss	10/02/2019 10:05:00	S1	

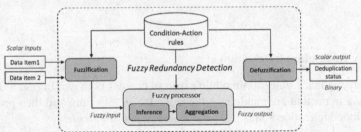

Fig. 3. Simplified diagram describing the *fuzzy redundancy detection* module's process

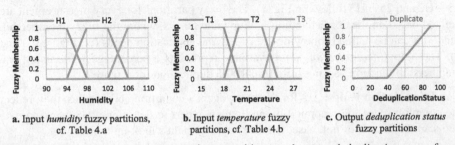

a. Input *humidity* fuzzy partitions, cf. Table 4.a

b. Input *temperature* fuzzy partitions, cf. Table 4.b

c. Output *deduplication status* fuzzy partitions

Fig. 4. Input *humidity* and *temperature* fuzzy partitions, and output *deduplication status* fuzzy partitions defined using the trapezoidal function following the lookup tables in Table 4

Rule 3. **IF** (Humidity_Item1 is H3) **AND** (Humidity_Item2 is H3) **THEN** DedupStatus is *Duplicate*

Rule 4. **IF** (Temp_Item1 is T1) **AND** (Temp_Item2 is T1) **THEN** DedupStatus is *Duplicate*

Rule 5. **IF** (Temp_Item1 is T2) **AND** (Temp_Item2 is T2) **THEN** DedupStatus is *Duplicate*

Rule 6. **IF** (Temp_Item1 is T3) **AND** (Temp_Item2 is T3) **THEN** DedupStatus is *Duplicate*

Inference: Fuzzy inference consists in applying the concerned condition-action rules on the fuzzified data in order to produce fuzzy outputs. The logical connectors in the condition-action rules are translated into mathematical formulas that operate on the fuzzy data. In our agent, we adopt *Mamdani's implication* operator as the default inference function given its common usage in the literature [19, 20].

Aggregation: It allows grouping the outputs of multiple inference operations executed on multiple condition-action rules, in order to produce on single fuzzy output result. In our agent, we adopt the *maximization* aggregation function (Formula 5) given its usage in the literature [19, 21]. Others formulas like *bounded sum* and *weighted sum* can be utilized.

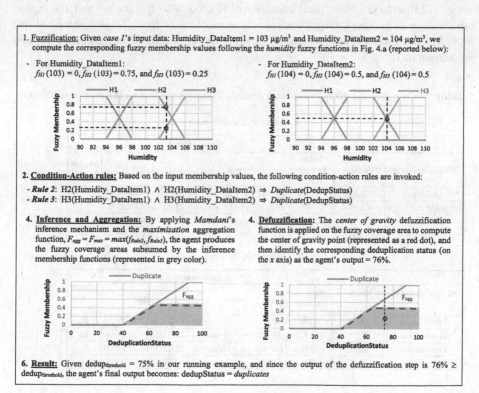

1. **Fuzzification:** Given *case 1*'s input data: Humidity_DataItem1 = 103 μg/m³ and Humidity_DataItem2 = 104 μg/m³, we compute the corresponding fuzzy membership values following the *humidity* fuzzy functions in Fig. 4.a (reported below):

- For Humidity_DataItem1:
$f_{H1}(103) = 0$, $f_{H2}(103) = 0.75$, and $f_{H3}(103) = 0.25$

- For Humidity_DataItem2:
$f_{H1}(104) = 0$, $f_{H2}(104) = 0.5$, and $f_{H3}(104) = 0.5$

2. **Condition-Action rules:** Based on the input membership values, the following condition-action rules are invoked:
- *Rule 2*: H2(Humidity_DataItem1) ∧ H2(Humidity_DataItem2) ⇒ *Duplicate*(DedupStatus)
- *Rule 3*: H3(Humidity_DataItem1) ∧ H3(Humidity_DataItem2) ⇒ *Duplicate*(DedupStatus)

4. **Inference and Aggregation:** By applying *Mamdani's* inference mechanism and the *maximization* aggregation function, $F_{agg} = F_{max} = max(f_{Rule2}, f_{Rule3})$, the agent produces the fuzzy coverage areas subsumed by the inference membership functions (represented in grey color).

4. **Defuzzification:** The *center of gravity* defuzzification function is applied on the fuzzy coverage area to compute the center of gravity point (represented as a red dot), and then identify the corresponding deduplication status (on the *x* axis) as the agent's output = 76%.

6. **Result:** Given dedup_threshold = 75% in our running example, and since the output of the defuzzification step is 76% ≥ dedup_threshold, the agent's final output becomes: dedupStatus = *duplicates*

Fig. 5. Fuzzy redundancy detection process for the *humidity* sample case (cf. Table 6)

Deduplication: It allows transforming the fuzzy output produced by the aggregation function into a crisp output that represents the final result of the agent. In our agent, we adopt *center of gravity* (Formula 6) given its common usage in the literature [19, 21]. Other formulas like *maximum to the left* and *maximum to the right* can be utilized.

Mamdani's implication:
Given fuzzy sets f_1, f_2 :

$$f_1 \implies {}_{Mamdani} f_2 \equiv f_1 \wedge \quad (4)$$
$$f_2 \equiv min(f_1, f_2)$$

where $\wedge$ is the AND fuzzy logic operator[1]

Maximization aggregation:
Given fuzzy sets f_1, $f_2, ..., f_n$:

$$F_{agg} = F_{Max} = \quad (5)$$
$$max(f_1, f_2, ..., f_n)$$

Center of gravity defuzzification:
Given aggregate fuzzy set F_{Agg}

$$x = \frac{\int x \times F_{agg}(x) \times dx}{\int F_{agg}(x) \times dx} \quad (6)$$

Computation example: We consider in Table 6 two cases for *humidity* and *temperature* measurements studied in our motivation scenario. The detailed computation process for *humidity* described in Fig. 5 (a similar computation process is executed for *temperature*). The agent recommends that input 103 μg/m^3 and 104 μg/m^3 data values are duplicates with a 76% fuzzy membership degree, which seems reasonable given the *humidity* lookup tables and value ranges defined in Table 4 (H2 and H3 fuzzy partitions intersect between [102, 106] μg/m^3, where 103 is much closer to the 102 μg/m^3 boundary of H2 than to the 106 μg/m^3 boundary of H3, but also 103 μg/m^3 and 104 μg/m^3 are close to each other). Given our running example data from Table 6, the identified *humidity* and *temporal* redundancies following the fuzzy redundancy detection process are shown in Table 7.

Table 7. Output of the fuzzy redundancy detection process applied on the data from Table 6

a. *Humidity* data collection

Measurement m	Value v	Value Pattern Code	Time stamp t		Source s	
			format	*value*		
Humidity	92 μg/m^3	H1	dd/MM/yyyy hh:mm:ss	10/02/2019 10:00:00	S1	⎫ Duplicates
Humidity	94 μg/m^3	H1	dd/MM/yyyy hh:mm:ss	10/02/2019 10:02:00	S1	⎭
Humidity	103 μg/m^3	H2 H3	dd/MM/yyyy hh:mm:ss	10/02/2019 10:05:00	S1	⎫ Duplicates
Humidity	104 μg/m^3	H2 H3	dd/MM/yyyy hh:mm:ss	10/02/2019 10:06:00	S1	⎭

b. *Temperature* data collection

Measurement m	Value v	Value Pattern Code	Time stamp t		Source s	
			format	*value*		
Temperature	16 °C	{T1}	dd/MM/yyyy hh:mm:ss	10/02/2019 10:01:00	S1	
Temperature	19.5 °C	{T1,T2}	dd/MM/yyyy hh:mm:ss	10/02/2019 10:02:00	S1	
Temperature	21 °C	{T2}	dd/MM/yyyy hh:mm:ss	10/02/2019 10:03:00	S1	⎫ Duplicates
Temperature	21 °C	{T2}	dd/MM/yyyy hh:mm:ss	10/02/2019 10:05:00	S1	⎭

3.6 Redundancy Removal

Once redundancies are identified, the redundancy removal process occurs. Here, domain experts might have different needs for redundancy removal. This component summarizes a sequence of redundancies into one representative data item following an expert-chosen redundancy removal function (e.g., *media, mean*, maximum, minumum,) representative. Experts provide their requirements in the form of simple consumer requests that the module processes to execute the required redundancy removal functions. For instance, Table 8 shows the *humidity* and *temporal* redundancies that are removed using the *median* function.

Table 8. Output of redundancy removal using the *median* function applied on Table 7

a. *Humidity* data collection

Measurement *m*	Value *v*	Time stamp *t*		Source *s*
		format	*value*	
Humidity	92 µg/m³	dd/MM/yyyy hh:mm:ss	10/02/2019 10:00:00	S1
Humidity	103 µg/m³	dd/MM/yyyy hh:mm:ss	10/02/2019 10:05:00	S1

b. *Temperature* data collection

Measurement *m*	Value *v*	Time stamp *t*		Source *s*
		format	*value*	
Temperature	16 °C	dd/MM/yyyy hh:mm:ss	10/02/2019 10:01:00	S1
Temperature	21 °C	dd/MM/yyyy hh:mm:ss	10/02/2019 10:05:00	S1

4 Experimental Evaluation

We have implemented our *FREDD* framework as a web-based application, using methods from the *jFuzzyLogic* open source library [22, 23] in implementing our fuzzy logic agent, to allow easy manipulation for domain experts in operating and evaluating the system[2]. We considered Intel Lab Berkeley dataset [24] obtained from 54 Micra2Dot sensors providing weather data including temperature, humidity, light, as well as the list of Cartesian coordinates for each of the 54 sensors, and the time when each data measurement is collected. In our empirical evaluation, we consider 20k *humidity* and *temperature* data measurements collected from sensor S1 on 28/2/2004.

We utilize four evaluation metrics: i) *deduplication accuracy* (acc): time series similarity between the original data and the deduplicated data [5], ii) *data reduction ratio* (*redu*) is defined as the ratio of the difference between the original data and the duplicated data, iii) *size of transmitted data* ($|data_{trans}|$) represents the size of the data transmitted

---

[2] We adopt a three-layer architecture: i) a *Web API* layer that allows client-side applications to communicate with the server to request data, etc.; ii) a *Business Logic* layer where *FREDD*'s main decision making processes are implemented; and iii) a *Data Access* layer where data storage and retrieval take place.

from the edge devices to the sink device (a good deduplication solution would reduce the size of data transmitted over the network in order to gain in network bandwidth), and iv) *size of stored data* ($|data_{stored}|$) represents the size of the data stored at the sink device (a good deduplication solution would reduce the size of the data stored at the sink to gain in processing speed and throughput at the sink level). The system implementation, experimental datasets, and test results are available online[3].

4.1 Fuzzy Deduplication Threshold Evaluation

We vary the fuzzy deduplication threshold, allowing the fuzzy redundancy detection process to decide on the deduplication status of candidate data items, and evaluate FREDD's behavior accordingly. Results in Fig. 6 show that when the threshold increases: i) *acc* increases while ii) *redu* decreases. This is due to the fact that a higher deduplication threshold means less candidate pairs are considered for duplication. Also, the size of data transmitted to the sink ($|data_{trans}|$) and the size of data stored at the sink ($|data_{stored}|$) are both increased with the increase in deduplication threshold. This is mainly due to the decrease in *redu*, resulting in more data being sent and processed at the sink node. Fine-tuning the evaluation metric values can be handled automatically as a multi-objective optimization problem, e.g., [25–27]. We report this to a dedicated study.

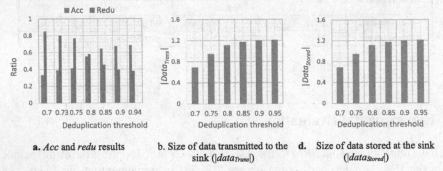

a. *Acc* and *redu* results

b. Size of data transmitted to the sink ($|data_{Trans}|$)

d. Size of data stored at the sink ($|data_{Stored}|$)

Fig. 6. Deduplication quality metrics obtained with varying fuzzy deduplication thresholds

4.2 Baseline Comparisin with Existing Approaches

We conducted a comparative study to assess FREDD's effectiveness with respect to recent alternatives in the literature: i.e., REDA [18] and DRMF [6]. To test REDA, we consider the crisp humidity ranges shown in Table 4. To test FREDD, we consider the fuzzy humidity ranges in Fig. 4 and we set the deduplication threshold to 0.8. We also consider two variations of DRMF: i) the first one with a deviation threshold equal to one quarter of the width of the crisp range $\delta = 3/4$ (which we refer to as DRMF_1), and ii) the second one with a deviation threshold equal to one eighth of the width of the

---

[3] http://sigappfr.acm.org/projects/fredd/

crisp range $\delta = 3/8$ (which we refer to as DRMF_2). Results in Fig. 7 show that FREDD consistently achieves the best *acc* results across all data variations compared with both REDA and DRMF1/2. This is due to FREDD's fuzzy processing capability, allowing to detect approximate redundancies and process them for deduplication, compared with the crisp decision-making processes performed by REDA and DRMF.

To further explain the results in Fig. 7, we conduct a second experiment where we compare the decision-making behavior of each algorithm applied on different pairs of humidity data measurement; the first data item is fixed at a certain value, while the second item is varied within a controlled range. Figure 8 shows the percentage of deduplication produced by each algorithm for a first humidity value of 39.5 $\mu g/m^3$, and the second value with a variation range of $\pm 2.5 \ \mu g/m^3$. Results for exising solutions show that all values that lie between [38, 41] $\mu g/m^3$ are considered automatic duplicates (i.e., 100% duplicates).

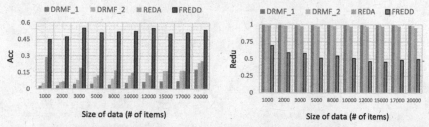

Fig. 7. Comparison of the deduplication quality metrics between RED, DRMF1/2 and FREDD, when varying the number of data measurements of *dataset1*

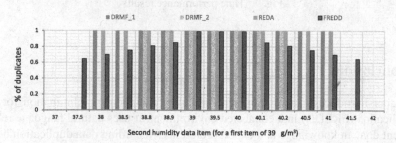

Fig. 8. Percentage of deduplicates with first humidity data fixed at 39.5 $\mu g/m^3$ and varying the second between [37, 42] $\mu g/m^3$

In contrast, each pattern code range in FREDD is divided into: i) a crisp range where pairs are automatically considered duplicates (i.e., from [39, 40] $\mu g/m^3$), and ii) a fuzzy range (i.e., between [37, 39] $\mu g/m^3$ and [40, 42] $\mu g/m^3$) where boundaries from different other ranges overlap. In the fuzzy range, the deduplication decision is made based on a fuzzy inference system and a set of fuzzy rules, allowing the percentage of duplicates to vary accordingly (e.g., for a second value of 38 $\mu g/m^3$, the percentage of duplicates is 70%). Less duplicate pairs are considered automatic duplicates and the accuracy of the deduplication process increases accordingly (as shown in Fig. 8).

4.3 Performance Evaluation

We have also compared FREDD's time complexity with its recent alternatives, REDA, DRMF_1 and DRMF_2. FREDD's complexity simplifies to: $O(N \times E^2)$ where N designates the number of data items considered per edge device, and E the number of edge devices considered per sink node. Tests were carried out on a PC with an *Intel I7* system with 2.9 GHz CPU/16 GB RAM. Figure 9.a highlights the linear complexity of FREDD's deduplication process when varying the number of data items per edge node, reflecting $O(N)$ time complexity. Figure 9.b shows running time results considering a fix data size per edge device = 1000 items and a fixed number of edges per sink node = 10. Results show that REDA is the most efficient approach due to its fast and crisp pattern code assignment approach. FREDD requires more processing time than REDA due to its fuzzy computation process. DRMF is seemingly the most time consuming approach due to its data clustering process.

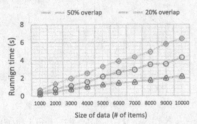 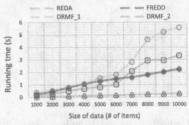

a. Edge-level processing time when varying the   **b.** Time performance compared with its alternatives,
number of data items   considering a fixed data size of 1000 items per edge

Fig. 9. Time performance results

5 Conclusion

This paper introduces a new approach for Fuzzy Redundancy Elimination for Data Deduplication (FREDD) in a connected environment. It uses natural language rules to represent domain knowledge and expert preferences regarding data duplication boundaries. It then applies pattern codes and fuzzy reasoning to detect duplicates on the general network infrastructure including both the edge level and the sink level of the network. Experiments highlight our solution's potential and improvement compared with existing solutions.

We are currently investigating the use of parametric learners [28, 29] and meta-heuristic algorithms [30, 31] to (semi) automatically configure the pattern codes' interval ranges and their fuzzy rules based on expert or data related features. We are currently investigating data deduplication at the sink level of the network [32], where data is aggregated from multiple edge nodes, including edge node mobility, edge node coverage area overlapping, and inter-edge collaboration. In the future, we plan to investigate data recovery [33, 34] in connected environments, including damage assessment and recovery from deduplicated data.

References

1. Nižetić, S., et al.: Internet of Things (IoT): opportunities, issues and challenges towards a smart and sustainable future. J. Clean. Prod. **274**, 122877 (2020)
2. Lytras, M., et al.: Enabling technologies and business infrastructures for next generation social media: big data, cloud computing, IoT and VR. J. Univ. Comput. Sci. **21**(11), 1379–1384 (2015)
3. VoucherCloud, The Uses of Big Data (2018). www.vouchercloud.com/resources/everyday-big-data
4. IoT Analytics, State of IoT 2021 (2021) https://iot-analytics.com/number-connected-iot-dev ices/. Accssed Feb 2023
5. Ismael, W., et al.: An in-networking double-layered data reduction for internet of things (IoT). Sensors **19**(4), 795 (2019)
6. Mansour E., et al.: Data redundancy management in connected environments. In: International Conference on Modeling, Analysis, and Simulation of Wireless and Mobile Systems (Q2SWinet), pp. 75–80 (2020)
7. Qutub B., et al.: Data Reduction in Low Powered Wireless Sensor Networks. Wireless Sensor Networks- Technology and Applications (2012). https://doi.org/10.5772/50178
8. Li, S., et al.: EF-Dedup: enabling collaborative data deduplication at the network edge.In: IEEE 39th International Conference on Distributed Computing Systems (ICDCS), pp. 986–996 (2019)
9. Patil, P., Kulkarni, U.: SVM-based data redundancy elimination for data aggregation in wireless sensor networks. In: Advances in Computing Communications Informatics (ICACCI), pp. 1309–1316 (2013)
10. Christen, P.: A survey of indexing techniques for scalable record linkage and deduplication. IEEE Trans. Knowl. Data Eng. **24**(9), 1537–1555 (2012)
11. Malhotra, J., Bakal, J.: A survey and comparative study of data deduplication techniques. In: International Conference on Pervasive Computing (ICPC), pp. 1–5 (2015)
12. Bhalerao, A., Pawar, A.: A survey on data deduplication for efficiently utilizing cloud storage for big data backups. In: Trends in Electronics and Informatics (ICEI), pp. 933–938 (2017)
13. Ullah, A., et al.: Secure healthcare data aggregation and deduplication scheme for FoG-orineted IoT. In: IEEE International Conference on Smart Internet of Things (SmartIoT), pp. 314–319 (2019)
14. Chowdhury, S., Benslimane, A.: Relocating redundant sensors in randomly deployed wireless sensor networks. In: IEEE Global Communications Conference (GLOBECOM), pp. 1–6 (2018)
15. Santini, S., Romer, K.: An adaptive strategy for quality-based data reduction in wireless sensor networks. In: International Conference on Networked Sensing Systems (INSS 2006), p.14407470 (2006)
16. Liansheng, T., Wu, M.: Data reduction in wireless sensor networks: a hierarchical LMS prediction approach. IEEE Sens. J. **16**(6), 1708–1715 (2015)
17. Shahzad, F., et al.: Data redundancy management framework for connected environments. Comput. J. **104**(7), 1565–1588 (2022)
18. Khriji, S., et al.: Redundancy elimination for data aggregation in wireless sensor networks. In: International Multi-Conference on Systems, Signals & Devices (SSD 2018), pp. 28–33 (2018)
19. Salloum, G., Tekli, J.: Automated and personalized nutrition health assessment, recommendation, and progress evaluation using fuzzy reasoning. Inter. J. Hum. Comput. Stud. **151**, 102610 (2021)

20. Bouchon-Meunier, B., et al.: Compositional rule of inference as an analogical scheme. Fuzzy Sets Syst. **138**(1), 53–65 (2003)
21. Ross, T.J.: Fuzzy Logic with Engineering Applications. 4th edn, p. 580 (2016)
22. Cingolani, P., Alcala-Fdez, J.: jFuzzyLogic: a robust and flexible fuzzy-logic inference system language implementation. In: IEEE International Conference on Fuzzy Systems, pp. 1–8 (2012)
23. Cingolani, P., Alcalá-Fdez, J.: jFuzzyLogic: a java library to design fuzzy logic controllers according to the standard for fuzzy control programming. Int. J. Comput. Intell. Syst. **6**(1), 61–75 (2013)
24. Bodik P., et al.: Intel Lab Data (2019). http://db.csail.mit.edu/labdata/labdata.html. Accessed Feb 2023
25. Hopfield, J.: The effectiveness of neural computing. In: IFIP World Computer Congress (WCC), pp. 402–409 (1989)
26. Zou, F., et al.: A reinforcement learning approach for dynamic multi-objective optimization. Inf. Sci. **546**, 815–834 (2021)
27. Salloum, G., Tekli, T.: Automated and personalized meal plan generation and relevance scoring using a multi-factor adaptation of the transportation problem. Soft. Comput. **26**(5), 2561–2585 (2022)
28. Abboud, R., Tekli, J.: Integration of non-parametric fuzzy classification with an evolutionary-developmental framework to perform music sentiment-based analysis and composition. Soft. Comput. **24**(13), 9875–9925 (2019)
29. Wen, X.: Using deep learning approach and IoT architecture to build the intelligent music recommendation system. Soft. Comput. **25**(4), 3087–3096 (2021)
30. Azar, D., et al.: A combined ant colony optimization and simulated annealing algorithm to assess stability and fault-proneness of classes based on internal software quality attributes. Inter. J. AI **14**, 2 (2016)
31. Nguyen, T.: A novel metaheuristic method based on artificial ecosystem-based optimization for optimization of network reconfiguration to reduce power loss. Soft. Comput. **25**(23), 14729–14740 (2021)
32. Yakhni, S., et al.: Using fuzzy reasoning to improve redundancy elimination for data deduplication in connected environments. Soft Comput. (2023). https://doi.org/10.1007/s00500-023-07880-z
33. Haraty, R., El Sai, M.: Information warfare: a lightweight matrix-based approach for database recovery. Knowl. Inf. Syst. 2017 **50**(1), 287–313 (2017)
34. Haraty, R., et al.: Data damage assessment and recovery algorithm from malicious attacks in healthcare data sharing systems. Peer Peer Netw. Appl. 2016 **9**(5), 812–823 (2016)

Towards Liquid AI in IoT with WebAssembly: A Prototype Implementation

Pyry Kotilainen[1]([✉]), Ville Heikkilä[2], Kari Systä[2], and Tommi Mikkonen[1]

[1] Faculty of Information Technology, University of Jyväskylä, Jyväskylä, Finland
{pyry.kotilainen,tommi.j.mikkonen}@jyu.fi
[2] Faculty of Information Technology and Communication Sciences,
Tampere University, Tampere, Finland
{ville.heikkila,kari.systa}@tuni.fi

Abstract. An Internet of Things (IoT) system typically comprises numerous subsystems and devices, such as sensors, actuators, gateways for internet connectivity, cloud services, end-user applications, and analytics. Currently, these subsystems are built using a wide range of programming technologies and tools, posing challenges in migrating functionality between them. In our previous work, we have proposed so-called liquid software, where different subsystems are developed using a consistent set of technologies and functions can flow from one computer to another. In this paper, we introduce a prototype implementation of liquid artificial intelligence features, which can be flexibly deployed at the cloud-edge continuum.

Keywords: Liquid software · Artificial intelligence · AI · Machine learning · ML · Web of Things · WoT · Internet of Things · IoT · Isomorphic software

1 Introduction

Contemporary Internet of Things (IoT) systems and their associated applications are capable of generating and managing vast volumes of data. This has paved the way for the utilization of Machine Learning (ML) and Artificial Intelligence (AI) in several application domains, including smart homes, smart cities, healthcare, retail, and industrial systems. However, not all data generated by IoT devices can be transmitted to the cloud for processing due to concerns related to privacy, latency, or limited connectivity. As a result, it becomes imperative to perform certain computations near the data source, while other computations can be offloaded to the cloud. Nevertheless, there are numerous use cases where seamless data and computation transfer between different system components is necessary.

Performing such transfer in the cloud-edge continuum has been one of the goals of so-called liquid software in the IoT domain [16]. A recent literature

M. Younas et al. (Eds.): MobiWIS 2023, LNCS 13977, pp. 129–141, 2023.
https://doi.org/10.1007/978-3-031-39764-6_9

study defined cloud continuum as "an extension of the traditional cloud towards multiple entities (e.g., edge, fog, IoT) that provide analysis, processing, storage, and data generation capabilities" [20]. Given the rapidly increasing use of ML technologies, we expect that the same technical challenges that apply to conventional computations shall emerge also in the context of ML technologies across the cloud-edge continuum.

In this paper, we report the first prototype of using AI/ML technologies in the liquid context, building on our previous work [15,16,18]. As the underlying technology framework, we use WebAssembly, a technique for running small memory virtual machines with binary bytecode [23], and neural networks, which are a commonly used technique in ML and has several practical use cases. Moreover, it is expected that new, improved hardware platforms will allow distributing ML functions between the cloud-fog-edge continuum.

The rest of the paper is structured as follows. In Sect. 2, we introduce the background of the paper. In Sect. 3, we present our prototype implementation, where we test AI/ML features in liquid fashion. In Sect. 4, we discuss the key findings. Finally, towards the end of the paper, in Sect. 5, we draw some conclusions.

2   Background and Motivation

2.1   Isomorphic IoT Systems

Using the term isomorphism – a well-established mathematical concept – in software development has emerged relatively recently. In the context of web applications, isomorphism refers to running the same code in both the backend (cloud) and frontend (web browser) [25].

In general, isomorphic software architectures include software components that do not need to be altered ('change their shape') while running on various hardware or software components of the system. Well-known examples of isomorphic systems are Java and its 'write once, run everywhere' guarantee [2], Unity 3D engine, Universal Windows platform, which allows running the same code on Windows 10, Xbox One gaming machines, and HoloLens devices, and liquid web applications [19].

There are several levels of isomorphism that can be identified [18]. Static, development-level isomorphism allows using the same development technologies consistently throughout the entire system's different computational elements. In contrast, *dynamic* isomorphism allows the usage of a common runtime engine or virtualization solution to enable running the same code on various computational elements without the need for recompilation. In a more sophisticated system, dynamic code migration from one computational element to another is also possible.

In the IoT context, we are interested in dynamic isomorphism, allowing the deployment of the same, isomorphic software throughout the end-to-end system to run on edge devices, gateways, mobile clients and cloud services, instead of them all running separate software (Fig. 1 [27]). Such facilities would liberate

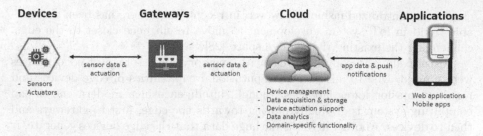

Fig. 1. Elements of a typical IoT end-to-end system, with each element featuring their own implementation technologies.

the developers from designing dedicated applications for individual nodes in the network taking into account the associated implementation technologies [28], and only create one implementation that can be deployed to various locations [18].

2.2 Liquid Software

Liquid software [10,11,19,29] is a paradigm that builds on isomorphic software, allowing the migration of software from one computer to another on the fly. In the context of the web, the main use case has been experience roaming from one display to another [19], whereas in the context of IoT, liquid software enables flexible configurations of applications, instead of rigid architectures that are associated with traditional technologies [28].

It has been pointed out that there are various ways to build liquid software, depending on what are the desired characteristics and use cases [7,8]. These characteristics and use cases have an impact on various technical decisions, including topology, replication and migration techniques, thickness of the client, and user interface adaptation, to name some examples.

To support isomorphic, liquid software deployment, a runtime environment is needed where the same infrastructure is made available across the cloud-edge continuum. In our previous work, we have used WebAssembly, with some early results published in [12]. This setup allows using various programming languages to create the software, but the infrastructure maps everything to the WebAssembly virtual machine. This virtual machine can be included in various nodes in the cloud-edge continuum, so that the actual code can be flexibly run in different locations. This added flexibility then enables orchestrating functions so that energy consumption, communication bandwidth, and performance and memory requirements can be taken into account. In fact, similar executions could be run in different configurations at different times, if the circumstances change.

2.3 Liquid AI/ML

One important use case for liquid software is edge intelligence [21]. In "classic" IoT systems, the majority of computation and analytics are performed in the cloud in a centralized fashion. However, in recent years there has been a noticeable trend in IoT system development to move intelligence closer to the edge, challenging the existing rigid design space [28].

Historically, the computing capacity, memory and storage of edge devices were limited. Due to increasing computational capabilities of edge devices and requirements for lower latencies, though, intelligence in a modern end-to-end computing system is gradually moving towards the edge, first to gateways and then to devices. Another driver is the huge data that the edge devices generate. It is often reasonable to process data on the edge devices for performance reasons, but privacy and data ownership concerns also support placing of the computation to edge devices.

This trend towards edge includes both generic software functions, and – more importantly – time critical AI/ML features for processing data available on the edge with minimal latency. The requirement to run advanced AI/ML and analytics algorithms on the edge increases the demand for consistent programming technologies across the end-to-end system. Hence, in addition to liquid software, we also need liquid AI/ML [26], allowing flexible deployment of intelligent components in different nodes of the IoT network.

2.4   WebAssembly and WASI

WebAssembly (Wasm) is a binary instruction format for a stack-based virtual machine designed for efficiency together with hardware- and platform-independence among other things [22]. WebAssembly offers dynamic isomorphism, as a standard runtime interpreter is used to execute the code. Therefore, WebAssembly can be used as a runtime environment for applications developed using different languages, but compiled for the WebAssembly stack machine.

While the origins of WebAssembly are inside the browser, the developer community has started to realise its significance outside the browser, in particular as a unifying environment for heterogeneous devices [4,14,34,35]. WebAssembly's conservative memory usage and somewhat near-native performance make it a good candidate for constrained environments like IoT devices [9].

Moreover, extensions such as *WebAssembly System Interface* (WASI) [5] have been introduced to access system resources when running WebAssembly outside the browser. This is particularly pertinent to our research, as access to host functions from the WebAssembly runtime offers a way to outsource running AI/ML models to a host runtime with potentially significant performance gains. This approach has been formalized in a WASI proposal called wasi-nn [3], an extension for the WebAssembly System Interface to provide an API to run ML models on a native ML runtime (Fig. 2).

The motivation for the wasi-nn proposal are the challenges that would arise from trying to ensure high-performance AI/ML inference in WebAssembly – AI/ML requires special hardware support (GPU, TPU, and special CPU instructions in particular) for maximal performance. Support for these would be challenging to implement for WebAssembly. In addition machine learning still evolves rapidly, with new computational operations getting introduced. These new operations would need added support to run new models which are using

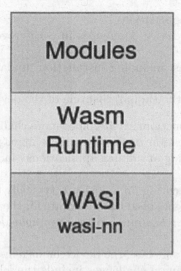
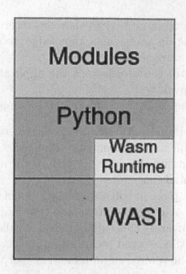

Fig. 2. Two WebAssembly use cases: one where WASI extended with wasi-nn is sufficient to run the module, and other where Python is used to embed WebAssembly runtime and provide more interfacing options with the host than WASI.

these operations. The wasi-nn proposal therefore leaves the ML runtime implementation details outside WebAssembly domain. This approach has the benefit of protecting the model intellectual property, as the WebAssembly module and runtime do not need to know anything about the inner workings of the model. Essentially wasi-nn treats AI/ML model as a virtualized I/O type, with defined operations such as load and compute.

The proposal has initial focus on only supporting inference, as it is the main AI/ML use case, not training. However, adding support for training has not been excluded from forthcoming implementations. The API provided by wasi-nn is a simple model loader API, inspired by WebNN's model loader proposal [33]. The proposal is framework and model format agnostic, but runtime implementations need to make decisions about what ML runtimes and model formats to support.

The first experimental implementation of wasi-nn for the Wasmtime WebAssembly runtime only supports OpenVINO ML runtime [30]. The implementation is however not considered production quality and Wasmtime needs to be compiled with wasi-nn support enabled to have access to it. However, at present the WasmEdge [6] runtime seems to have the most extensive implementation for wasi-nn, with support for OpenVINO, PyTorch [31] and TensorFlow-Lite [32] ML runtimes.

2.5 Device Management and Orchestration

IoT systems are often composed of many headless devices that need to be remotely managed, and thus most commercial IoT platform have a device management functionality. This functionality keeps track of the devices and the software in them. From the application point of view the device management should

- keep track of devices that can receive applications
- maintain and utilize knowledge about device differences in a heterogeneous fleet of devices,
- control the life-cycle of the applications, including installation, update and removal, and
- in the context of this research manage the (liquid) lifecycle of the devices.

For liquid software this management functionality becomes more challenging since the computation may change its location dynamically. The management functionality should support dynamic moving of running applications - including ML models.

The piece of software or ML model executing on a device is typically a component of a bigger system, and the components need to collaborate for the overall goal. Ensuring this collaboration is called *orchestration* or *choreography* depending on the selected technical approach.

In the context of liquid and isomorphic software, the device management and orchestration are closely coupled. The common challenges include the following two key points:

- ensuring reliability and trustworthiness a distributed system where stateful components roam between locations
- minimizing disturbances to overall functionality while the software components behave in a liquid fashion.

Some of these issues have been addressed in our earlier work. Integration development and dynamic deployment to devices was address in [1] where IoT application development was addressed in DevOps spirit. The research challenges on managing Liquid AI applications have been discussed in [26]. In this paper we address installation of ML models similarly to traditional applications. In the future we plan to complement the system with full device management and orchestration functionalities.

3 Design and Implementation

3.1 Development Goals

The goal of our development approach was to investigate and hopefully demonstrate liquid deployment of AI/ML models on heterogeneous fleet of IoT devices. In a more technical sense, the target was two-fold:

G1: Demonstrate the feasibility of using WebAssembly to run AI/ML models on edge devices.
G2: Demonstrate the potential for liquid AI/ML software deployment on IoT devices.

The technical framing for the system was to use a microservice architecture consisting of various IoT devices building on our previous work [13]. Within this architecture, heterogeneous devices could easily be discovered and used in accordance to their characteristics, such as varying processing power, available peripherals and ML/AI hardware functions, because application code could move inside the system. Computations would then be executed when and where best suited, taking into account the state of the system and the present capacity of the different nodes.

3.2   Implementation

As the baseline implementation technology we have used WebAssembly. This is the key enabling technology to achieve the free deployment of software modules across different hardware platforms, since as discussed, WebAssembly can be used as a runtime environment for applications developed using different languages, but compiled for the WebAssembly interpreter. It is also the technology we have used in our previous work, and the architecture to support liquid migration of functions followed the requirements identified in [13]. As a new challenge in the implementation, the applications that are deployed to devices include ML components.

To support freely moving code, a specific element in the architecture is a package-manager-housing orchestration server or *orchestrator*, whose functionality is depicted in Fig. 3. While running, the orchestrator gathers 1) descriptions of devices available and 2) deployment *manifests* from users, that each hold the information needed for setting up an execution process/task as described in [13] where an application composed together from WebAssembly modules is run in the distributed system of heterogeneous devices.

The proposed system shown in Fig. 3 consists of an orchestration server or *orchestrator* and a variable amount of heterogeneous node devices in the same local area network. An actor (user or another system that interacts with our system) can control the system through the orchestrator.

Aside from communication and application logic, the orchestration server consists of three components, presented below:

- *Device database* contains the hardware configurations of the various devices, and it is populated by listening to mDNS messages and requesting information from the associated devices.
- *Deployment registry* contains all executed deployments by the orchestrator, with each deployment listing the devices involved and the services they provide in it.
- *Package manager* maintains a database of all available WebAssembly software modules that can be sent to the devices. It is also capable of resolving dependencies to provide a complete list of required modules for a given module to run.

The system functionality can be split into three phases: device discovery, deployment and execution. Upon first discovery, the orchestrator requests configuration information from the device and adds it to the device database the

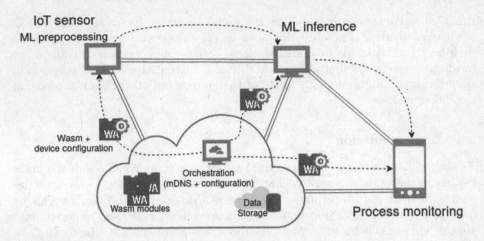

Fig. 3. Overview of the proposed system. In this example, an IoT sensor runs ML preprocessing on measurements, sending the results to an intermediary device with resources for ML inference based on the measurements. The results are then sent to a device with a screen for monitoring.

server maintains. Upon a request for deployment, the orchestration server generates a setup that is a feasible deployment solution, and sends out the deployment configuration to involved devices. The devices pull the required microservices and start serving them according to the deployment information.

Device discovery is performed with mDNS which each device uses to advertise their availability to the orchestrator. For querying the capabilities of discovered devices, a ReSTful endpoint providing the answers is available on each IoT device. ReSTful endpoints are currently also used for machine-to-machine (M2M) communication between the IoT-devices. A move to CoAP has been planned, to demonstrate that IoT specific protocols are feasible. Finally, all functionality running on the different IoT devices – in particular executing WebAssembly binaries – is controlled by the host process running on the device, which we call *supervisor*. The supervisor was implemented in Python, based on our earlier work, and the WebAssembly runtime for the moving code modules is Wasm3 [17].

The move to support AI/ML modules with our existing system necessitated changes to the ReSTful interface on the supervisor to facilitate upload of ML model files. Endpoints for uploading a pre-trained protocol buffer model file and running ML inference with supplied binary data were added. Additions were also required to the interface between the WebAssembly runtime and the host to enable loading of modules and input data to the linear memory of the runtime.

There are two ways to run ML models with WebAssembly. These are porting a ML framework to WebAssembly and running the model entirely in WebAssembly runtime, or outsourcing the ML model execution to a host-provided native ML runtime. As discussed earlier, latter approach has been formalized in a WASI proposal called wasi-nn, an extension for the WebAssembly System Interface to provide an API to run ML models on a native ML runtime. The first experimental implementation of wasi-nn is for the Wasmtime WebAssembly runtime and uses the OpenVINO ML runtime. The experimental status of the implementation as well as lack of Python bindings for wasi-nn deterred us from starting with Wasmtime.

WasmEdge runtime implementation of wasi-nn has wider support for different ML runtimes including PyTorch, OpenVINO and Tensorflow-Lite, but Python bindings are a work in progress. Both Wasmtime and WasmEdge also have limited platform support compared to the Wasm3 runtime we have used in previous work.

Because of the current limitations of wasi-nn support addressed above, the supervisor prototype was done with ML framework compiled to WebAssembly, and run without a host ML runtime, using Wasm3 as the WebAssembly runtime.

The WebAssembly modules for AI/ML inference were written in Rust and the ML framework used was Tract [24], but these are of course interchangeable as long as the supplied model files are in the correct format for the used framework.

3.3   Results and Observations

We were able to realise a rudimentary system of orchestrating AI/ML applications across varied devices using WebAssembly.

We tested our system using pre-trained MobileNetV2 model for image classification. As expected using a framework compiled to WebAssembly results in poor performance. What was more surprising was the difference between different WebAssembly runtimes visible in Table 1, as we also ran simple tests between Wasm3 and Wasmtime. Tests were run on a laptop with Intel Core i7-1165G7 and 16 GB of RAM. The results highlight the disparate state of WebAssembly runtimes, but also the need for an extension like wasi-nn, as the pure WebAssembly approach will not be performant enough for all applications.

Table 1. MobileNetV2 execution times on tested runtimes, Wasmtime and Wasm3.

Runtime	Execution time (s)
Wasmtime	0.42
Wasm3	5.85

Building the system revealed a promising but still lacking framework for building liquid software systems with WebAssembly. The planned additions to WASI will likely alleviate the problems encountered in our implementation. Specifically standardized and extensive support for wasi-nn should enable an out-of-the-box solution for deploying AI/ML applications across different hardware platforms.

With the current state of affairs however, we encountered a myriad of issues in trying to implement our system. While some projects like WasmEdge were close to being useful, each had some drawbacks, such as narrow platform support or lack of bindings in our language of choice. While the lack of language bindings can in the WebAssembly ecosystem be mostly eliminated by using Rust, the lack of platform support or features like wasi-nn will likely continue to be a problem for some time.

4 Discussion

With the experience gained from our work so far it seems that the best supported language for working with WebAssembly is Rust, possibly owing to the fact that the reference runtime Wasmtime is implemented in Rust. The support for embedding WebAssembly in Rust as well as the tooling for compiling Rust to WebAssembly are more developed and better documented than Python, which we used for our supervisor implementation. Future development could benefit from moving to Rust as the development language. This could also ease turning developed functionality into contributions to existing WebAssembly ecosystem.

The lackluster performance of AI/ML inference on pure WebAssembly also motivates a move to wasi-nn-style paradigm of running the models, and will likely be necessary for wider adoption. This is however hindered by the lack of implementations in WebAssembly runtimes, but will hopefully improve as the wasi-nn proposal matures. As mentioned, currently the best support for running AI/ML models on host runtimes seems to be on WasmEdge runtime. Previously discussed move to rust would also allow us to change the WebAssembly runtime to WasmEdge, which would enable us to take advantage of WasmEdge's wasi-nn implementation.

In future we also hope to expand the functionality of the orchestrator. For example, the deployment requests need not be as specific as outlined above. The server could make decisions about device selection and deployment topology based on device availability and their dynamic state according to a deployment task describing desired deployment outcome without necessarily naming specific devices or their arrangement.

Including dynamic state for devices could also enable improved persistence and self-healing properties, as detection of failed devices could trigger a change in deployment topology and either a replacement device could be selected or the responsibilities of the failed device could be moved to another available device.

5 Conclusions

WebAssembly has been gaining attention outside the browser as a technique to speed up execution [4]. Its ability to support liquid deployment where applications can roam from one computer to another in an isomorphic fashion seems ideal for AI/ML applications that typically run in isolation, but may introduce strict requirements for performance.

In this paper, we have introduced a prototype system for isomorphic microservices based architecture for liquid deployment of AI/ML applications using WebAssembly, to test the limits of the above view. It was found out that executing AI/ML applications as WebAssembly modules in a WebAssembly runtime that there is a serious performance hit in comparison to running native code, and that running the applications using WebAssembly runtime requires both more working memory and persistent storage [9]. The runtime also complicates deploying applications that have real-time requirements, which are an integral part of many IoT use cases.

In the future, with increasing computational power and memory of IoT devices, the trade-off for ease of development and flexibility of deployment will likely become less and less of a problem for traditional applications. This in turn will liberate developers from considering some of the necessary practicalities during the development and deployment of services. Furthermore, in connection with AI/ML applications in particular, we expect that with emerging WASI extensions, such as wasi-nn, and host-bound specialised ML runtimes can be used to bring execution to near-native performance. However, this in turn can have impact on the isomorphic, liquid nature of the functions.

Acknowledgments. This work has been supported by Business Finland (project LiquidAI, 8542/31/2022).

References

1. Ahmadighohandizi, F., Systä, K.: Application development and deployment for IoT devices. In: Lazovik, A., Schulte, S. (eds.) ESOCC 2016. CCIS, pp. 74–85. Springer International Publishing, Cham (2018). https://doi.org/10.1007/978-3-319-72125-5_6
2. Arnold, K., Gosling, J., Holmes, D.: The Java Programming Language. Addison Wesley Professional, Boston (2005)
3. Andrew, B., Sun, M.: Neural Network proposal for WASI. https://github.com/WebAssembly/wasi-nn. Accessed 09 May 2023
4. Bryant, D.: WebAssembly outside the browser: a new foundation for pervasive computing. In: Keynote at ICWE 2020, June 9–12, Helsinki, Finland (2020)
5. Bytecode Alliance: Welcome to WASI. https://github.com/bytecodealliance/wasmtime/blob/main/docs/WASI-intro.md. Accessed 05 Dec 2022
6. Cloud Native Computing Foundation: WasmEdgeRuntime. https://wasmedge.org/, Accessed 09 May 2023
7. Gallidabino, A., Pautasso, C., Ilvonen, V., Mikkonen, T., Systä, K., Voutilainen, J.P., Taivalsaari, A.: On the architecture of liquid software: technology alternatives and design space. In: 2016 13th Working IEEE/IFIP Conference on Software Architecture (WICSA), pp. 122–127. IEEE (2016)
8. Gallidabino, A., Pautasso, C., Mikkonen, T., Systa, K., Voutilainen, J.P., Taivalsaari, A.: Architecting liquid software. J. Web Eng. **16**, 433–470 (2017)
9. Hall, A., Ramachandran, U.: An execution model for serverless functions at the edge. In: Proceedings of the International Conference on Internet of Things Design and Implementation, pp. 225–236. IoTDI 2019, Association for Computing Machinery, New York, NY, USA (2019). https://doi.org/10.1145/3302505.3310084

140   P. Kotilainen et al.

10. Hartman, J., Manber, U., Peterson, L., Proebsting, T.: Liquid software: A new paradigm for networked systems. Technical report, Technical Report 96 (1996)
11. Hartman, J.J., et al.: Joust: a platform for liquid software. Computer **32**(4), 50–56 (1999)
12. Kotilainen, P., Järvinen, V., Tarkkanen, J., Autto, T., Das, T., Waseem, M., Mikkonen, T.: WebAssembly in IoT: beyond toy examples. In: Garrigós, I., Murillo Rodríguez, J.M., Wimmer, M. (eds.) Web Engineering. ICWE 2023. LNCS, vol. 13893, pp. 93–100 Springer, Cham (2023). https://doi.org/10.1007/978-3-031-34444-2_7
13. Kotilainen, P., Autto, T., Järvinen, V., Das, T., Tarkkanen, J.: Proposing isomorphic microservices based architecture for heterogeneous IoT environments. In: Taibi, D., Kuhrmann, M., Mikkonen, T., Klünder, J., Abrahamsson, P. (eds.) PROFES 2022. LNCS, vol. 13709, pp. 621–627. Springer, Cham (2022)
14. Losant IoT Inc: Embedded Edge Agent. https://docs.losant.com/edge-compute/embedded-edge-agent/overview/. Accessed 09 Nov 2022
15. Mäkitalo, N., Bankowski, V., Daubaris, P., Mikkola, R., Beletski, O., Mikkonen, T.: Bringing WebAssembly up to speed with dynamic linking. In: Proceedings of the 36th Annual ACM Symposium on Applied Computing, pp. 1727–1735 (2021)
16. Mäkitalo, N., et al.: WebAssembly modules as lightweight containers for liquid IoT applications. In: Brambilla, M., Chbeir, R., Frasincar, F., Manolescu, I. (eds.) ICWE 2021. LNCS, vol. 12706, pp. 328–336. Springer, Cham (2021). https://doi.org/10.1007/978-3-030-74296-6_25
17. Massey, S., Shymanskyy, V.: wasm3: the fastest WebAssembly interpreter, and the most universal runtime. https://github.com/wasm3/wasm3. Accessed 209 Dec 2022
18. Mikkonen, T., Pautasso, C., Taivalsaari, A.: Isomorphic Internet of Things architectures with web technologies. Computer **54**(7), 69–78 (2021)
19. Mikkonen, T., Systä, K., Pautasso, C.: Towards liquid web applications. In: Cimiano, P., Frasincar, F., Houben, G.-J., Schwabe, D. (eds.) ICWE 2015. LNCS, vol. 9114, pp. 134–143. Springer, Cham (2015). https://doi.org/10.1007/978-3-319-19890-3_10
20. Moreschini, S., Pecorelli, F., Li, X., Naz, S., Hästbacka, D., Taibi, D.: Cloud continuum: the definition. IEEE Access **10**, 131876–131886 (2022)
21. Peltonen, E., et al.: The many faces of edge intelligence. IEEE Access **10**, 104769–104782 (2022)
22. Rossberg, A.: Introduction - WebAssembly 1.1 (Draft 2022–04-05). https://www.w3.org/TR/wasm-core-2/intro/introduction.html. Accessed 12 Jan 2023
23. Rossberg, A.: WebAssembly Core Specification. https://www.w3.org/TR/wasm-core-2/. Accessed 09 Dec 2022
24. Sonos: Tract. https://github.com/sonos/tract. Accessed 09 May 2023
25. Strimpel, J., Najim, M.: Building Isomorphic JavaScript Apps: From Concept to Implementation to Real-World Solutions. O'Reilly Media, Sebastopol (2016)
26. Systä, K., Pautasso, C., Taivalsaari, A., Mikkonen, T.: LiquidAI: towards an isomorphic AI/ML system architecture for the cloud-edge continuum. In: Garrigós, I., Murillo Rodríguez, J.M., Wimmer, M. (eds.) ICWE 2023. LNCS, vol. 13893, pp. 67–74. Springer, Cham (2023). https://doi.org/10.1007/978-3-031-34444-2_5
27. Taivalsaari, A., Mikkonen, T.: A roadmap to the programmable world: software challenges in the IoT era. IEEE Softw. **34**(1), 72–80 (2017)
28. Taivalsaari, A., Mikkonen, T.: On the development of IoT systems. In: 2018 Third International Conference on Fog and Mobile Edge Computing (FMEC), pp. 13–19. IEEE (2018)

29. Taivalsaari, A., Mikkonen, T., Systä, K.: Liquid software manifesto: the era of multiple device ownership and its implications for software architecture. In: 2014 IEEE 38th Annual Computer Software and Applications Conference, pp. 338–343. IEEE (2014)
30. The OpenVino Project: OpenVino documentation. https://docs.openvino.ai/. Accessed 13 June 2023
31. The PyTorch Project: PyTorch. https://pytorch.org/. Accessed 13 June 2023
32. The TensorFlow Project: TensorFlow for Mobile & Edge. https://www.tensorflow.org/lite. Accessed 13 June 2023
33. The World Wide Web Consortium (W3C): Web Neural Network API. https://www.w3.org/TR/webnn/. Accessed13 June 2023
34. Vetere, P.: Why wasm is the future of cloud computing. https://www.infoworld.com/article/3678208/why-wasm-is-the-future-of-cloud-computing.html. Accessed 09 Dec 2022
35. wasmCloud Project: wasmCloud. https://wasmcloud.com/. Accessed 30 Nov 2022

Mobile Interfaces and Interactivity

Interactive Behavior Change Model (IBCM 8.0): Theory and Ontology

Brian Cugelman[1](✉) (iD) and Agnis Stibe[2,3] (iD)

[1] Statistical Cybermetrics and Research Evaluation Group, University of Wolverhampton, Wolverhampton, UK
brian@alterspark.com
[2] Department of Informatics, Faculty of Engineering, Built Environment and Information Technology, University of Pretoria, Pretoria, South Africa
[3] INTERACT Research Unit, University of Oulu, Oulu, Finland

Abstract. This paper presents the Interactive Behavior Change Model (IBCM 8.0), a system that integrates behavior change principles from neuroscience, psychology, and behavioral science into a behavioral meta-theory. With its broad, application-agnostic nature, the IBCM provides insight into behavior change, how it operates, and offers an alternative explanation for why various behavior change models work or do not work. It has applications as a behavioral system for education, research, analysis, intervention design, and implementation in various technologies, especially self-adaptive systems run by rule-based engines or artificial intelligence (AI). Due to space limits, this paper covers the model structure and theory with a limited high-level overview of its ontology.

Keywords: Behavioral Science · Behavior Change · Persuasive Technology · Affective Computing · Artificial Intelligence · Personalization · Science Philosophy · Evolutionary Psychology

1 Introduction

In recent years, there has been growing interest in implementation science, where scientific models are used for understanding, building, and evaluating real-world products and services [1]. Behavior change systems and taxonomies, herein referred to as behavioral systems, are arguably the most popular scientific tools for use in research and the construction of interventions. They typically contain a model, a taxonomy of behavior change principles, or both. These behavioral systems are usually developed for distinct fields, with behavioral taxonomies curated for specific applications [2–6].

However, many behavioral models are built from abstract constructs that do not explain behavior, despite opportunities to ground these systems in neuroscience, psychology, sociology, etc. Taxonomies tend to be arbitrary, author-curated lists, incomplete,

---

The original version of this chapter was revised: The placement of two sections 3.5 and 3.6 was presented incorrectly. This was corrected. The correction to this chapter is available at
https://doi.org/10.1007/978-3-031-39764-6_19

M. Younas et al. (Eds.): MobiWIS 2023, LNCS 13977, pp. 145–160, 2023.
https://doi.org/10.1007/978-3-031-39764-6_10

and full of overlapping, redundant principles. Domain-specific systems that work in one area may be ineffective or trigger backfires when misapplied [7].

Recognizing these limitations, this paper introduces a universal behavioral meta-system based on neurobiology and psychology. This system merges various behavior change theories and principles into an intuitive format, optimally structured for implementation by adaptive, rule-based systems or artificial intelligence (AI).

2 Behavioral System Challenges

2.1 Popular Behavioral Systems

Researchers and practitioners often utilize *behavioral systems*, science-based models and taxonomies of principles proven to impact people's emotions, thoughts, and actions. People apply behavioral systems in many ways, such as using them for education, research, intervention design, or in impact evaluations.

There are several popular behavioral systems, each with a distinct philosophy, serving a range of applications and taking various forms. In technology are the systems of *CAPTOLOGY* [8] and *persuasive systems designs* [9]. Notable persuasion systems include the extensive work of O'Keefe [10] and Cialdini's simple sales-oriented six principles [11]. Broad theories, such as *stages of change,* provide extensive lists of narrowly focused principles [12, 13]. However, narrow models offer small groupings of broadly applicable principles, such as Ajzen's early persuasion research [14].

Social marketing systems provide simple catalogs to help intervention designers, such as *tools of change* [15] and *community-based social marketing* [16]. *Evidence-based behavioral medicine* began with large taxonomies of health behavior change principles and techniques [17–19], then adapted their earlier systems for practitioners [20]. Perhaps due to problems of behavioral economists inventing and repackaging hundreds of principles, scholars are using data reduction techniques to reduce the massively redundant and ever-expanding cognitive bias taxonomies [21].

2.2 Overcoming Behavioral System Limits

These behavioral systems have made a sizeable impact on scientific research and practice. However, despite their popularity, each suffers at least one of the following shortcomings. Theory-based models like Stages of Change explain behavior through its stage model and offer techniques to facilitate change, with the minor shortcoming that it is domain-focused, limiting its use to situations where a stage model applies.

However, many behavior change systems employ abstractions such as the Behavior change wheel, rendering them a list of principles without a unifying theory. This makes them practical, and grounded in proven behavior/social change strategies. But their structure does not explain what drives individual and social behavior.

In the worst case, most behavioral systems have no central theory, often resembling arbitrary curated lists of principles, like Cialdini's six or seven principles. With no central theory, there are no criteria for deeming the system complete or incomplete–other than when the author arbitrarily decides.

Many behavioral systems are inadequately short, and contain redundant, overlapping principles. Some include principles that authors invented, with no scientific merit. The popular Wikipedia-based cognitive bias wheel is an example of practitioner models that gained massive popularity, despite violating standard scientific criteria.

In this paper, we discuss the Interactive Behavior Change Model (IBCM), a theory-based system for structuring behavior change principles, that can overcome each of these challenges. The IBCM was initially developed as a comprehensive system for studying how behavior change operates in the technology [22, 23], then used in a statistical meta-analysis [5], and used for education and product design in the Behavioral Design Academy (https://www.behavioraldesign.academy). This paper presents the latest edition, its nomenclature, theory, philosophy, and a high-level ontology.

3   Interactive Behavior Change Model

The IBCM's central tenet is that feedback loops provide a wid-reaching mechanism for understanding behavior change from multiple perspectives. It organizes behavior change principles into domains unified by common theories, influence mechanisms, and where we have evidence, psychometrically robust factor structures. The IBCM explains behavior change principles from evolutionary, neurobiological, psychological, and behavioral science perspectives. It offers an alternative explanation for the efficacy of various behavior change principles, theories, models, and practices. It can also be scaled to explain influence within a person, between people, and through complex social interactions. This section describes the IBCM 8.0.

3.1   Nine Domains of Communications and Influence

Presented in Fig. 1, the IBCM encompasses nine communication domains, representing the factors that matter in human interactions and influence. Each domain doubles as an influence sphere when we use those factors for behavior change. This model portrays communication as a flow, one-way from source to audience, or two-way with feedback loops between actors.

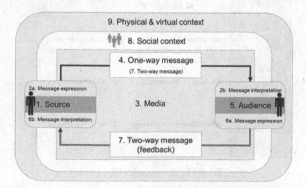

Fig. 1. Interactive Behavior Change Model (IBCM)

The model explains behavior change as the outcome of a two-way feedback loop between agents, that fosters positive feedback leading to adaptive learning that produces a change, we call influence, behavior change, training, nudging, etc... Each domain plays a distinct role in fostering change, with clusters of correlated principles.

The IBCM is built from communication theory. Traditionally, one-way communication, introduced by Aristotle for rhetoric, later extended to signal transmission by the Shannon-Weaver model [24], has been the default model for persuasive messaging. However, the Osgood and Schramm Model introduced the concept of two-way human communication [25], used for interpersonal communication and adaptive self-learning technologies. Communication occurs within a medium and is influenced by the persuasive communication context [10, 14]. It takes place within a social and physical/virtual spatial contexts, and we use the term "spatial" intentionally, as the human brain utilizes spatial processing for both physical and social relationships [26], in both real and virtual environments [27].

3.2 Eight Communication Modes

Behavior change happens within a communication context. The eight communication modes, represented in Fig. 2, describe the macro-level structure of all behavior change contexts. There are eight communication modes, where one or many sources attempt to influence one or many audiences in a one or two-way context. Each mode has practical benefits and drawbacks, depending on the context and behavioral goals.

We treat the actors (sources and audiences) as anything with agency, be they human groups, brands, technology, AI agents, etc... The source (S) is the entity intending to exert influence, while the audience (A) is the target of influence. However, in two-way communication, the audience also influences the source.

The flow of communication may be one or two-way. The shorthand *to* describes one-way communication flow from actor to actor. The shorthand *with* describes two-way communication flow, between actors in a cyclical, iterative loop.

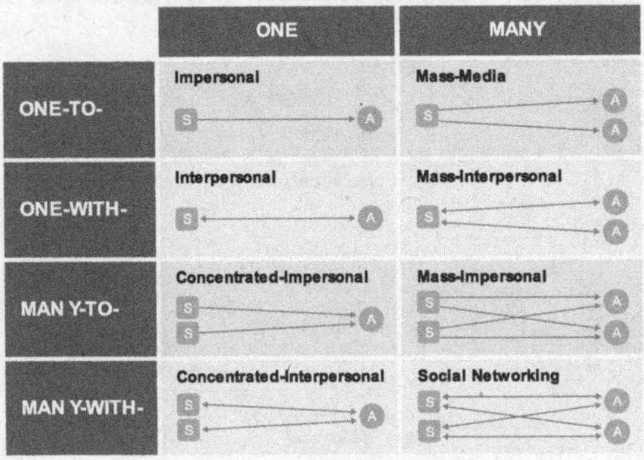

Fig. 2. Eight communication modes

Modes Control Domains of Influence: A core premise is that communication modes govern behavior change principles. There is no feedback in one-way modes, making it difficult and usually impossible to use two-way message principles in a one-way communication mode. Employing reinforcement learning, tailoring, or any adaptive strategy with no audience information is impossible except by luck. Modes that include single versus group contexts have different social influence opportunities and limits.

Description of Each Mode: This model describes various influence contexts, from individual-level interventions like therapist-client relationships to population-level inter-actions between organizations and their members. It also includes the models utilized by swarm-style network influence campaigns, such as those employed by lobby groups to inundate targets with messages of public disagreement or the multi-nodal covert actions governments run to divide adversarial populations and influence their elections. Here are the eight modes:

The *impersonal mode* (one-to-one) describes the early one-way models where information and influence flow from the source to an audience, such as when the boss dictates what he/she must do to an employee. The *mass-media mode* (one-to-many) describes the traditional mass-media communication flow from one source to many audience members, such as when an organization puts out an advertisement to influence audiences through TV, radio, or newspapers. The *interpersonal mode* (one-with-one) describes two-way communication between a source and an audience, such as a discussion between a salesperson and a potential customer. The *mass-interpersonal mode* (one-with-many) describes a situation where a source conducts two-way communication with multiple audience members, such as an online coaching platform, that supports multiple relationships.

The *concentrated-impersonal mode* (many-to-one) describes a situation where many sources send messages to one audience, such as an advocacy campaign that channels public sentiment to one organization to convey public will. The *mass-impersonal mode* (many-to-many) describes when many sources send messages to audiences, such as a crime network distributing multiple phishing email campaigns, to deceive the audiences. The *concentrated-interpersonal mode* (many-with-one) describes when multiple sources engage in two-way communication with one audience, such as an advocacy campaign encouraging citizens to engage in two-way dialogue with targeted politicians to sway their stance. And finally, the *social networking mode* (many-with-many) describes the two-way relations between multiple sources and audiences, describing a social network where influence is in constant flux.

3.3 Three Communication Methods

Across the eight domains of influence, there are three common ways that intervention designers may leverage behavioral science in direct or mediated communication [28]. Figure 3 presents a generic edition of the three communication methods. This model contains a source (S), that sends behavioral principles (P), through a communication medium (M), to a target audience (A).

The *direct* method is where the source interacts directly with the audience, such as in face-to-face communication, where a politician goes door-to-door. In the case

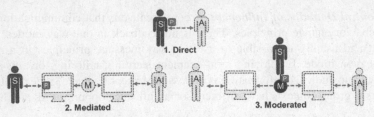

Fig. 3. Communication connectivity

of technology, it is when some interact directly with their smart wearable technology device. The *mediated* method is when the source attempts to influence the audience through technology, such as a salesperson working through online video chat. This also includes using technologies such as a health coaching app, or AI-driven sales agents using telephones to engage and sway a target audience.

The *moderated* method is where the source controls the platform other people use for communication and structures their communication to influence their behavior—a form of "non-choice" architecture. For instance, Twitter didn't have success until they reduced the message size limit from large text to just 140 characters. Social media platform owners routinely abuse this method by placing false words in users' digital mouths by sending misleading messages to users' friends, implying the user wants their friends to take all sorts of actions.

3.4 Communication-Based Influence Components

Many have proposed an "atomic theory" for the behavioral sciences, arguing for the existence of deeper drivers of behavior. This concept has been termed the evidence-based kernels [29]. Susan Michie adopted this philosophy in her pioneering work, where she gathered scientists together for a consensus-based approach to reducing multiple overlapping theories to a set of core theoretical constructs associated with behavior change [18]. She later used a combined approach with methods that were closer to grounded theory combined with scientific consensus to develop high-quality taxonomy of behavior change techniques [17].

The quest to isolate kernels, the factors driving behavior change, is a sacred mission for many. While evolution may have shaped our susceptibilities to influence, evolutionary explanations do not specify the detailed structure of those kernels.

To develop its ontology at the threshold of psychology and neuroscience, the IBCM rests on the hypothesis that the closest we can get to the kernel of behavior is to isolate the latent variables that reflect a web of interacting components, displayed in Fig. 4 and described below.

Physics: At the lowest level, exist our perspectives on the world shaped by atomic theory, chemistry, electromagnetism, and the laws of physics. Though behavioral science rarely reaches this level, behavioral neuroscience works at this level.

Without specialists operating at this level, we would not understand many links between matter, chemistry, electromagnetism, and their impact on people. For example, by understanding the physics of electromagnetic energy, we can better understand the

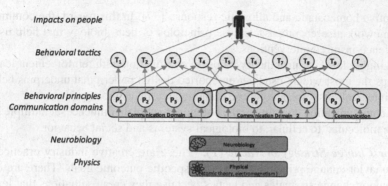

Fig. 4. Influence-components model

visible light spectrum and later translate it into design strategies that impact users through circadian light impacts. Similarly, the first brain-to-brain transmission over the internet came about by using EEG (electrical potential difference) to express a thought, that was transmitted electronically to another person, with transcranial magnetic stimulation used to send a signal into a second person's brain [36].

Neurobiological Predisposition (N): This is the domain of neuroscience, where there should be the fewest mechanical explanations for what behavior change principles are, how they work, and how they operate between physical processes and psychologically conscious experience. We believe the fewest number of principles exist here. For instance, there is only one emotional reward system for motivating and reinforcing behavior, which helps us understand motivation and techniques for shaping behavior. The sympathetic and parasympathetic nervous systems operate simultaneously, creating the conscious experience of a uni-dimensional nervous system response that ranges from low to high-states of arousal, creating a single variable that is present in every emotion.

Behavior Change Principle (P): These are semi-limited principles of behavior change tied to psychology, where the field of Evidence-based Behavioral Medicine provides a helpful metaphor that explains how this mechanism works. According to the field, a behavior change intervention can be built by adding active ingredients proven to elicit a particular outcome, similar to how medicine works. When added to medicine, active ingredients produce a predictable outcome. The medicine will no longer work without active ingredients at an adequate dose [19, 29].

Communication Domain (D): In the communication domains, one-way communication involves the transmission of signals from one entity to another, resulting in an impact of some kind. Conversely, two-way communication involves bi-directional feedback, which is crucial for the evolution of molecular structures, coordinated cellular activity, and the evolution of species, their nervous systems and social behaviors.

This is why communication theory has widespread application for explaining how the body itself adapts to change, such as through its hormone systems which employ chemical messengers delivered via the bloodstream, or its neuronal system that utilizes electro-chemical messages conveyed through neural circuits, as two key systems behind our adaptive homeostatic and allostatic response [37]. In this regard, the communication framework also encompasses those principles of neurobiology that help us build neuroscience-inspired interventions.

At a higher level, control theory loops, in conjunction with reinforcement learning, is perhaps the most widely used yet unreported design pattern that underpins behavior change interventions, especially those implemented in technology.

The communication domain has the potential to explain influence, at multiple levels, from the molecular, to cellular, to biological systems and social behavior.

Behavior Change Strategy or Tactic (T): These are creative industry practices that apply behavior change principles to achieve specific outcome goals. There are unlimited behavior change strategies and tactics because they create situations that leverage behavior change principles. For instance, asking someone to make a public commitment to support sustainability is a tactic that uses a range of principles, such as committing, being held accountable for commitments, social normative influence, and other possible factors that may emerge depending on the context and implementation details.

3.5 Building Behavioral Theories from Influence Components

As a meta-behavioral system, the IBCM's influence components model follows a simple recipe model, ingredients (influence components that foster change), can be combined into recipes which are groups of principles that deliver impacts greater than the sum of their parts. We further follow the idea that the intensity in which an ingredient is applied, ranges from too weak to make an impact, or so strong that it appears tasteless (manipulative, cliche, annoying)—with a perfect spot calibrated based on what's appropriate for the audience.

Ingredients (Influence Components): In the IBCM, *ingredients* are the components that exert influence on how people perceive, classify information, respond emotionally, respond habitually, deliberate, decide, appraise, and act. No universally accepted phenomenon qualifies as the ultimate causal factor driving these outcomes. IBCM includes physical, neurobiological, and psychological principles as the core ingredients. We generally avoid using tactics, which are usually tied to specific applications and contexts.

Recipes (Conventions, Models, Theories): Individual ingredients are rarely enough to elicit change. For example, to get citizens involved in an issue, McKenzie-Mohr and Smith (1999) did not just advocate obtaining commitments from people; instead, they recommended making those commitments public and encouraging people to see themselves as concerned citizens. In other words, the authors advocated combining three distinct influence strategies: obtaining a commitment, leveraging social influence, and playing on a person's self-identity and consistency.

This combination of success factors is a behavioral recipe. Combinations of principles that produce effects greater than the sum of their parts are likely candidates for becoming conventional pairings or theories of change.

Figure 5 presents a model of the relationship between the number of ingredients and a product's potential influence. Within this model, a product with too few ingredients may not have enough to influence behavior. Conversely, a product with too many ingredients may overwhelm audiences or users with too much irrelevant content. Somewhere

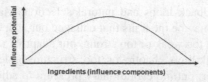

Fig. 5. Theories and models as optimized ingredient groups

in-between is a middle ground where a few relevant, mutually reinforcing influence strategies are most effective [5].

In the IBCM, behavioral design conventions and theories combine broad principles that work well in general, or may offer exceptional benefits in particular contexts. For instance, popular ingredient pairings include costs and benefits [38], punishments and rewards [39], threats and self-efficacy [40]. Popular ingredient triplets include: motivation, ability, and triggers [41]; and motivation, ability/efficacy, and opportunity [42].

Conversely, behavioral models are more practical, and with that, they often use more lay terms and focus on specific industry applications that are popular at the time. These models are often developed quickly and spread through professional networks.

Rather than offering specific recipes, IBCM catalogs principles and recommends theories (combinations of principles) based on the particular applications, following the principle that there are a handful of optimal theories for each application. IBCM also uses tailored psychometrics based on audience demographics and psychographics.

3.6 Influence Principles as Population-level Adaptive Traits

Behavioral scientists hold different views on the factors that shape human behavior. Some favoring a pragmatic approach prefer to isolate scientifically validated principles of influence without getting trapped in wasteful debates about their cause.

Conversely, others pursue deep insight into the essence of behavior change, employing perspectives from neuroscience, psychology, and sociology. Dennis Embry theorizes that the genesis of evidence-based behavioral kernels could be rooted in many sources, like anthropology, and evolution, among others [29].

The IBCM might also shed light on the origin of some behavior change principles via social feedback loops that evolved our species' psychology. Feedback loops are used to explain the existence of ordered physical matter and life in our universe [31]. Some believe feedback loops are an overlooked mechanism of evolution, with positive feedback as a supplementary process to natural selection, contributing to the development of diverse traits (genetic variation) in social organisms, their mating behaviors and social structure [30]. Others focus on the detailed role of positive feedback as the fundamental mechanism driving the evolution of social behaviors and structures [32]. Feedback loops also lay at the crux of cybernetic adaptive technologies [33] and AI [34].

While many focus on behavior change principles as things used by the source, others treat them as traits of the target audience [35]. We theorize that behavior change principles are innate or learned strategies of the source matched to trait variation in audiences, calibrated by social feedback loops and natural selection. Many traits that make us susceptible to influence may be the traits that enhance our adaptability as a species.

When those traits are too weak or too strong, our adaptive social structure becomes too relaxed or too weak (too chaotic or too structured), leading to mal-adaptive population-level behavior, putting evolutionary pressure to adjust the human distribution of traits till our population either adapts, changes, or disintegrates through social entropy.

Human social structures can be depicted along a spectrum from chaos to order (entropy to negentropy), encapsulating four states: (1) unstructured chaos, (2) structure-emerging positive feedback, (3) structure-dissolving negative feedback, and (4) equilibrium, a stabile state that oscillates between competing forces. We are never static.

Imagine a thought experiment using the IBCM to demonstrate the model's potential. We can use the IBCM to study one-with-one and many-with-many relations, linking individual predispositions to population impacts.

Imagine five separate islands, each inhabited by 10,000 genetically engineered people. We will engineer each population to have a unique predisposition across five levels of susceptibility to persuasion and later examine the population-level impacts. In all social interactions, when sources use influence tactics, their influence is a function of the population distribution of that trait in audiences, causing population-level impacts.

For our first study, we will engineer five populations of 10,000 people with different susceptibilities to social normative influence. Island-1 inhabitants lack this predisposition entirely, rendering social normative influence ineffective. Island-2 exhibits a reduced susceptibility to social normative influence. Island-3, serving as our control, possesses an average predisposition. Island-4 possesses an enhanced susceptibility. And island-5 exhibits maximum susceptibility, with social normative influence operating flawlessly every time it is employed.

Next, we will evaluate the long-term effects of these traits on the population, considering impacts on individuals, families, society, and humanity itself, in time frames of 1, 1,000, 10,000, and 100,000 years. We also measure if the population goes extinct or evolves into another species, or singularity entity.

We speculate that island-1, with no social normative influence, may decline into extreme individualism, weakening from eroded social cohesion as negative feedback cascades social entropy, disintegrating its social structure, preventing adaption due to chaos. Island-5, with maximum normative influence, could become overly structured, losing adaptability due to excessive positive feedback. However, the balanced island-3 would maintain an adaptive equilibrium, achieving optimal adaptability.

Continuing this thought experiment, we next evaluate self-efficacy. We hypothesize that islands with low self-efficacy might struggle due to a lack of confidence, innovation, effort, and risk-taking. Conversely, the island with excessive self-efficacy might display reckless behavior, likely to be detrimental to any population. And the middle island maintains an optimal social structure for adaptation.

We extend our thought experiment to other behavioral change principles like goal setting, source credibility, and social learning. Our speculative findings suggest that traits we call too weak or too strong can lead to maladaptive social structures, either too chaotic or overly rigid. In contrast, susceptibilities to influence deemed healthy or normal fall within an oscillating equilibrium range, optimized by social feedback and natural selection. Thus the IBCM may help explain the essence of some behavior change principles. We share this hypothesis for broader discussion and theory testing.

4 IBCM Ontology

This section presents the IBCM's ontology of influence principles and tactics, which are organized within the nine domains of communication and influence.

The ontology was initially developed by extracting principles and tactics from the influence systems, systematic reviews, and meta-analyses, with the minimum criteria being proven effective across multiple studies [4, 5, 17, 18, 43–47]. These were clustered and lined to the domains of communication and in some cases, subject to model fit through factor analysis and structural equation modeling [44, 48]. Additional work included linking the principles to theories and using content analysis to associate the principles with applied behavioral science [49].

We use the term ontology, as the ultimate goal of the IBCM is to isolate the fundamental factors of behavior change, which we hypothesize, is clustered around the models' structure, an interactive feedback loop.

IBCM is adaptable, backward compatible, and numbered for research and technology use. This is version IBCM 8.0, with unique numbers for each influence component. Here is the ontology, with a list of principles to demonstrate its organizing structure.

Domain 1. Source
A source is any entity with whom a target audience holds a relationship and interacts. Sources are typically people, organizations, or brands. However, in an abstract sense, a source is anything that can possess a reputation and be trusted or mistrusted, such as a person, organization, brand, product, or technology such as an app, robot, or AI agent.

Ingredients: 101. Source representation; 102. Credibility; 102a. Competence; 102b. Honesty; 103. Charm; 103a. Surface appeal; 103b. Likeable; 103c. Similar; 104. Familiarity.

Domain 2. Source expression and audience interpretation (source to audience)
This domain pertains to how the source constructs a message in media, which is transmitted and then understood by the audience. It encompasses psychological principles that guide effective communication strategies, regardless of the message's content. For example, it covers visual design principles, content organization, shape, size, and other non-content elements where style matters more than substance.

Ingredients: 201. Cognitive ease and strain; 201a. Cognitive ease (fluence); 201b. Cognitive strain; 202. Preattentive processing (salience); 203. Visual cognition (Gestalt); 203a. Proximity; 203b. Connectivity; 203c. Enclosure; 203d. Similarity; 203e. Continuity; 203f. Closure; 203g. Symmetry; 203h. Figure-ground; 204. Ordering; 204a. Serial position: primacy & recency; 204b. Priming (relative to the context); 204c. Anchoring (relative to the anchor); 205. Framing; 205a. Concrete versus abstract framing; 205b. Gain versus loss framing; 205c. Decoy effect; 205d. Zero, one, or two-sided arguments;

205e. Endowment framing; 205f. Defaults; 206. Timing; 206a. Single-session; 206b. Multi-session.

Domain 3. Media

Media is anything we use to record a message and give to another person who can then interpret and understand the message. Single-media is any media that the audience interprets through one distinct sense, such as written words conveyed through the eyes, or audio interpreted through the ears. Multi-media are any media interpreted through multiple senses, such as video interpreted through the eyes and ears. The persuasive qualities of different media come from the different cognitive and emotional artifacts associated with each sensory system.

Ingredients: 301. Images (sight); 302. Words (sight); 303. Numbers (sight); 304. Audio (hearing); 305. Video (sight, hearing); 306. Haptic (touch).

Domain 4. One-way message

A one-way message is when the source expresses its message without prior knowledge of the audience, in a "point and shoot" approach. Although the core elements needed to influence people can be conveyed through one-way messaging, it is hard to have much impact with truly one-way messaging, because there is no ability to judge when a message is relevant. For this reason, one-way messaging describes the core factors required for influence, but does not contain those iterative, feedback-based strategies that exist in two-way communication. Some of these principles are two-way, violating the theoretical basis. However, these violations were introduced to aid education.

Ingredients: 401. Focus; 402. Persuade; 402a. Educate; 402b. Motivate; 402c. Nudge; 402d. Assure; 403. Facilitate; 403a. Pave; 403b. Guide; 403c. Reinforce; 404. Re-engage; 404a. Support (for ability or self-efficacy deficits); 404b. Re-motivate (for motivation deficit); 404c. Restore trust (for source damage).

Domain 5. Audience

This domain describes the target outcomes that we typically use in stage-based models, which tend to be "deal breakers", where failures in any of these usually result in failed influence. The key target outcomes include raising our audience's awareness, comprehension, motivation, intention, confidence, and both short-term and long-term action. However, it's normal for our audience to disengage during the process, which is why abandonment is also a key outcome that should be anticipated from the onset.

Ingredients: 501. Concentrating (aware); 502. Comprehending (informed); 503. Desiring (motivated); 504. Deciding (intent); 505. Trusting (confident); 506. Acting (short-term behavior); 507. Maintaining (long-term behavior); 508. Abandoning (no behavior).

Domain 6. Audience expression and source interpretation feedback

This domain covers the capture, storage, and interpretation of data through research, data science, and algorithms. This is a prerequisite for using many of the feedback psychology principles listed in the two-way message domain.

Ingredients: 601. Research-based feedback; 602. Manual data capture; 603. Interaction-based data capture; 604. Automated data porting; 605. Sensor-based data capture.

Domain 7. Two-way message (adaptive techniques)

This domain covers feedback psychology principles that can only be applied when the source is able to capture and process information from the audience, and deploy strategies inspired by the principles in this domain. In situations where the source is unable to gather information, or has a messy feedback system, the risk of backfiring is great, as many of the worst behavioral science backfires come from failures in data collection, classification, and prediction [7].

Ingredients: 701. Sequential gifts and requests; 701a. Reciprocity; 701b. Foot-in-the-door; 701c. Door-in-the-face; 702. Reminders & prompts; 703. Engaging at the right time; 704. Targeting (segmenting); 705. Personalization; 706. Tailoring; 707. Setting goals & making commitments (intentions); 708. Personal action plan; 709. Personal barriers and friction; 709a. Remove personal barriers & friction; 709b. Add personal barriers & friction; 710. Feedback on performance; 711. Reinforcement; 711a. Reward on success; 711b. Punish on failure.

Domain 8. Social context

A large part of influence comes from the audience's social context, where other people can be more influential than the source. However, there are several distinct forms of social influence that may be leveraged, with social facilitation operating like the ultimate control switch, for turning social influence on/off, just by making the audience aware of others or pushing awareness of others out of sight and out of mind [50].

Ingredients: 801. Anonymity; 802. Social affiliation; 803. Self-identity & expression; 804. Social curiosity & concern; 805. Social facilitation; 806. Social learning (modeling); 807. Social norms (normative influence); 808. Psychological safety; 809. Social recognition (approval/disapproval); 810. Social comparison (upward / downward); 811. Co-ompetition; 811a. Cooperation; 811b. Competition; 812. Social diffusion facilitation.

Domain 9. Physical & virtual context

This domain describes the physical and virtual environment, which covers the built environment, objects, and the availability of things in space and time. This also covers virtual environments, as evidence suggests grid and place cells in the brain, operate the same for physical and virtual environments, underpinning the psychological evidence that we apply spatial navigation to virtual environments. The ingredients in this domain cover spatial navigation, organizing the environment, and resource availability.

Ingredients: 901. Spatial metaphor design; 902. Environmental restructuring; 903. Stimulus control; 904. Scarcity (resource limits); 905. Urgency (time limits).

5 Conclusion

The IBCM is a theory-based behavioral meta-system with diverse applications, bridging work in psychology, neuroscience, and behavioral science. If further validated, its theoretical underpinning could provide substantial insight into human behavior. As a universal meta-system, it can support behavioural science research, education, design, and the management of behavioral interventions by people, algorithms, and AI.

References

1. Nilsen, P.: Making sense of implementation theories, models, and frameworks. Implement. Sci. **30**, 53–79 (2020)
2. Wantland, D., Portillo, C., Holzemer, W., Slaughter, R., McGhee, E.: The effectiveness of web-based vs. non-web-based interventions: a meta-analysis of behavioural change outcomes. J. Med. Internet Res. **6** (2004)
3. Portnoy, D., Scott-Sheldon, L., Johnson, B., Carey, M.: Computer-delivered interventions for health promotion and behavioral risk reduction: a meta-analysis of 75 randomized controlled trials, 1988–2007. Prev. Med. **47**, 3–16 (2008)
4. Webb, T., Joseph, J., Yardley, L., Michie, S.: Using the internet to promote health behavior change: a systematic review and meta-analysis of the impact of theoretical basis, use of behavior change techniques, and mode of delivery on efficacy. J. Med. Internet Res. **12**, e4 (2010). https://doi.org/10.2196/jmir.1376
5. Cugelman, B., Thelwall, M., Dawes, P.: Online interventions for social marketing health behavior change campaigns: a meta-analysis of psychological architectures and adherence factors. J. Med. Internet Res. **13**, e17 (2011). https://doi.org/10.2196/jmir.1367
6. Kelders, S.M., Kok, R.N., Ossebaard, H.C., Van Gemert-Pijnen, J.E.: Persuasive system design does matter: a systematic review of adherence to web-based interventions. J. Med. Internet Res. **14** (2012)
7. Stibe, A., Cugelman, B.: Persuasive backfiring: when behavior change interventions trigger unintended negative outcomes. In: Meschtscherjakov, A., De Ruyter, B., Fuchsberger, V., Murer, M., Tscheligi, M. (eds.) PERSUASIVE 2016. LNCS, vol. 9638, pp. 65–77. Springer, Cham (2016). https://doi.org/10.1007/978-3-319-31510-2_6
8. Fogg, B.J.: Persuasive Technology: Using Computers to Change What We Think and Do. Morgan Kaufmann Publishers, San Francisco (2003)
9. Oinas-Kukkonen, H., Harjumaa, M.: Persuasive systems design: key issues, process model, and system features. Commun. Assoc. Inf. Syst. Forthcom. **24**, 485–500 (2009)
10. O'Keefe, D.: Persuasion: Theory and Research. Sage Publications Inc., London (2002)
11. Cialdini, R.: Influence: Science and Practice. Pearson/Allyn and Bacon, Boston (2008)
12. Prochaska, J., Norcross, J., DiClemente, C.: Changing for Good: A Revolutionary Six-Stage Program for Overcoming Bad Habits and Moving Your Life Positively Forward. Collins (1995)
13. Prochaska, J., Norcross, J.: Stages of change. Psychotherapy **38**, 443–448 (2001)
14. Ajzen, I.: Persuasive communication theory in social psychology: a historical perspective. In: Manfredo, J. (ed.) Influencing Human Behavior: Theory and Applications in Recreation, Tourism, and Natural Resources Management, pp. 1–16. Sagamore Publishing, Illinois (1992)
15. Kassirer, J., McKenzie-Mohr, D.: Tools of change: proven methods for promoting environmental citizenship. National Round Table on the Environment and the Economy, Ottawa (1998)
16. McKenzie-Mohr, D., Smith, W.: Fostering Sustainable Behavior–An Introduction to Community-Based Social Marketing. New Society Publishers, Gabriola Island, Canada (1999)
17. Abraham, C., Michie, S.: A taxonomy of behavior change techniques used in interventions. Health Psychol. **27**, 379–387 (2008)

18. Michie, S., Johnston, M., Abraham, C., Lawton, R., Parker, D., Walker, A.: Making psychological theory useful for implementing evidence based practice: a consensus approach. Qual. Saf. Health Care **14**, 26–33 (2005)
19. Michie, S., Johnston, M., Francis, J., Hardeman, W., Eccles, M.: From theory to intervention: mapping theoretically derived behavioural determinants to behaviour change. Appl. Psychol. **57**, 660–680 (2008)
20. Michie, S., van Stralen, M.M., West, R.: The behaviour change wheel: a new method for characterising and designing behaviour change interventions. Implement. Sci. **6**, 42 (2011)
21. Ceschi, A., Costantini, A., Sartori, R., Weller, J., Di Fabio, A.: Dimensions of decision-making: an evidence-based classification of heuristics and biases. Personal. Individ. Differ. **146**, 188–200 (2019)
22. Cugelman, B.: Online Social Marketing: Website Factors in Behavioural Change (2010)
23. Cugelman, B., Thelwall, M., Dawes, P.: Communication-based influence components model. Presented at the Persuasive 2009 (2009)
24. Shannon, C., Weaver, W.: A mathematical theory of communications. Bell Syst. Tech. J. **27**, 632–656 (1948)
25. Schramm, W.: How communications works. In: Wells, A., Hakanen, E. (eds.) Mass Media & Society. Ablex Pub (1955)
26. Tavares, R.M., et al.: A map for social navigation in the human brain. Neuron **87**, 231–243 (2015)
27. Harvey, C.D., Collman, F., Dombeck, D.A., Tank, D.W.: Intracellular dynamics of hippocampal place cells during virtual navigation. Nature **461**, 941–946 (2009)
28. Stibe, A.: Advancing typology of computer-supported influence: moderation effects in socially influencing systems. In: MacTavish, T., Basapur, S. (eds.) PERSUASIVE 2015. LNCS, vol. 9072, pp. 253–264. Springer, Cham (2015). https://doi.org/10.1007/978-3-319-20306-5_23
29. Embry, D., Biglan, A.: Evidence-based kernels: fundamental units of behavioral influence. Clin. Child Fam. Psychol. Rev. **11**, 75 (2008)
30. Crespi, B.J.: Vicious circles: positive feedback in major evolutionary and ecological transitions. Trends Ecol. Evol. **19**, 627–633 (2004)
31. Funk, R.H.: Understanding the feedback loops between energy, matter and life. Front. Biosci.-Elite. **14**, 29 (2022)
32. Taborsky, B.: A positive feedback loop between sociality and social competence. Ethology **127**, 774–789 (2021)
33. Brun, Y., et al.: Engineering self-adaptive systems through feedback loops. Softw. Eng. Self-Adapt. Syst. 48–70 (2009)
34. Rosenblatt, F.: The perceptron: a probabilistic model for information storage and organization in the brain. Psychol. Rev. **65**, 386 (1958)
35. Kaptein, M., Markopoulos, P., de Ruyter, B., Aarts, E.: Can you be persuaded? Individual differences in susceptibility to persuasion. In: Gross, T., et al. (eds.) INTERACT 2009. LNCS, vol. 5726, pp. 115–118. Springer, Heidelberg (2009). https://doi.org/10.1007/978-3-642-03655-2_13
36. Grau, C., et al.: Conscious brain-to-brain communication in humans using non-invasive technologies. PLoS ONE **9**, e105225 (2014)
37. Sterling, P.: Allostasis: a model of predictive regulation. Physiol. Behav. **106**, 5–15 (2012)
38. Bagozzi, R.: Marketing as an organized behavioral system of exchange. J. Mark. **38**, 77–81 (1974)
39. Andreoni, J., Harbaugh, W., Vesterlund, L.: The carrot or the stick: rewards, punishments, and cooperation. Am. Econ. Rev. **93**, 893–902 (2003)
40. Witte, K.: Putting the fear back into fear appeals: the extended parallel process model. Commun. Monogr. **59**, 329–349 (1992)

41. Fogg, B.J.: A behavior model for persuasive design. Presented at the Proceedings of the 4th International Conference on Persuasive Technology (2009)
42. Rothschild, M.: Carrots, sticks, and promises: a conceptual framework for the management of public health and social issue behaviors. J. Mark. **63**, 24–37 (1999)
43. Bandura, A.: Human agency in social cognitive theory. Am. Psychol. **44**, 1175–1184 (1989)
44. Cugelman, B., Thelwall, M., Dawes, P.: The dimensions of web site credibility and their relation to active trust and behavioural impact. Commun. Assoc. Inf. Syst. **24**, 455–472 (2009)
45. Krishna, A., Briesch, R., Lehmann, D.R., Yuan, H.: A meta-analysis of the impact of price presentation on perceived savings. J. Retail. **78**, 101–118 (2002)
46. Tversky, A., Kahneman, D., Choice, R.: The framing of decisions. Science **211**, 453–458 (1981)
47. Wilson, E.J., Sherrell, D.L.: Source effects in communication and persuasion research: a meta-analysis of effect size. J. Acad. Mark. Sci. **21**, 101–112 (1993)
48. Stibe, A., Cugelman, B.: Social influence scale for technology design and transformation. In: Lamas, D., Loizides, F., Nacke, L., Petrie, H., Winckler, M., Zaphiris, P. (eds.) INTERACT 2019. LNCS, vol. 11748, pp. 561–577. Springer, Cham (2019). https://doi.org/10.1007/978-3-030-29387-1_33
49. Neuendorf, K.: The Content Analysis Guidebook. Sage (2005)
50. Stibe, A.: Towards a framework for socially influencing systems: meta-analysis of four PLS-SEM based studies. In: MacTavish, T., Basapur, S. (eds.) PERSUASIVE 2015. LNCS, vol. 9072, pp. 172–183. Springer, Cham (2015). https://doi.org/10.1007/978-3-319-20306-5_16

A Comparison of YOLOv5 and YOLOv8 in the Context of Mobile UI Detection

Burcu Selcuk[✉] and Tacha Serif

Yeditepe University, 34755 Atasehir, Turkey
{bselcuk,tserif}@cse.yeditepe.edu.tr

Abstract. With ever increasing technological capabilities, nowadays artificially intelligent systems solve mathematical equations, write poems and songs. However, to this day, many companies who build native mobile applications replicate their work and increase their workload by implementing the same user interface for each one of their target mobile platforms. Accordingly, this study aims to design, train and test a GUI element recognition model by utilizing the latest, state-of-the-art YOLOv8 and Roboflow Object Detection (Fast) algorithm, which then can be used to implement a multi-platform user interface generator. For evaluation purposes, a study in the same domain is set as a benchmark so that the newly obtained results can be interpreted meaningfully and put into a perspective. Accordingly, the results showed that the newly proposed YOLOv8s and YOLOv8n models have performed with a 3.32% and 1.62% better mAP respectively, than the benchmark study. On the other hand, the Roboflow Object Detection (Fast) model performed with a 1.08% lower mAP than the YOLOv5s benchmark study.

Keywords: Object Detection · Graphical User Interface · Deep Learning · Mobile Systems

1 Introduction

Smartphone ownership has been growing rapidly over the past decade, making it a crucial platform for businesses and individuals to reach their customers and audiences [1]. A well-designed user interface (UI) on a smartphone is essential in providing a positive user experience [2]. With the limited screen real estate available on a smartphone, it is important to design a UI that is easy to use, navigate and understand. With the continued growth of smartphone use, the importance of a well-designed UI cannot be overstated. However, this comes with the generation of GUI elements that are both aesthetically pleasing and compatible with different operating systems is both a tedious process as the developers have to port and convert each UI design from one target platform to another. On the other hand, this is also a redundant and expensive process as the software companies need to absorb the cost of the UI redesigning process for each one of their target mobile application platforms. Hence, automating UI generation is a key target that would speed up mobile application development and deployment life cycle for native developers and software companies targeting native mobile platforms. As a result, there are a significant number of studies in the literature that propose various approaches to develop a system that detects UI elements and generates Graphical UI (GUI) elements automatically using new models or algorithms. However, to the best of our knowledge, the YOLOv8 object detection algorithm has not been utilized by any work in the mobile GUI element detection domain. Therefore, this study pursues to train a model that identifies a set of GUI elements and detects their location within a UI image.

Accordingly, this paper is structured as follows; the second section describes the previous work done in GUI element recognition; the third section discusses the methodology and the fourth section contains the details about the dataset utilized. The fifth section represents the details of the implementation and the sixth section defines the tests and evaluation of the proposed system. Last but not least, in the seventh section, conclusions will be drawn and future works for the proposed method will be discussed.

2   Background

A significant amount of studies have been undertaken in the field of GUI element detection. Accordingly, the following section provides an overview of comparable studies to gain a more profound understanding of the GUI component recognition domain. To address the challenges of detecting GUI elements, various methods have been evaluated, primarily utilizing computer vision (CV) techniques, machine learning (ML), and deep learning (DL) methods.

Cheng et al. [3] present a new algorithm called YOLOv5-MGC, which is designed for recognizing interface elements in mobile applications using computer vision. The algorithm enhances the YOLOv5 [4] by incorporating the K-means++ [5] algorithm for generating target anchor boxes. In the study, an attention mechanism is employed and a microscale detection layer is added while Ghost bottleneck module is introduced [6]. Additionally, the proposed algorithm is also able to detect small elements more effectively, addressing the drawbacks of existing target detection algorithms. Results of the study show that the YOLOv5-MGC algorithm outperforms YOLOv5 in recognizing GUI elements, with a mean average precision (mAP) of 89.8% and a recognition precision of 80.8%.

From a different perspective, Zhang et al. [7] propose the use of deep learning algorithms to recognise GUI elements. As part of the study, the data is classified into various software interfaces. Based on this classification, a unified annotation specification is developed. For this purpose, a dataset was constructed that would include ten GUI element classes - namely 'Button', 'Toggle Button', 'Adjustment Button', 'Combo Box', 'Scroll Bar', 'Table View', 'Text Field', 'Menu Item', 'Tool Strip Button' and 'Link Label' - containing 30003 GUI images in total. Their dataset was trained using Mask R-CNN [8] and YOLOv3 [9] and then compared. The findings of this study indicate that the Mask R-CNN network performs barely better than YOLOv3 based on Average Precision (AP) if the same number of data is introduced to the model.

Combining multiple methodologies, Xie et al. [10] came up with a mechanism that utilizes computer vision (CV) and object detection techniques such as YOLOv3 [9], Faster R-CNN [11] and CenterNet [12] to accurately locate GUI elements and identify their types. The proposed solution is intended to reverse engineer GUI screen captures and test its precision. As part of their work, CV algorithms are utilized for the purpose of detecting the position of non-text GUI components. Furthermore, techniques such as flood-filling [13] and shape recognition were used to identify layout blocks, and the connected component labeling method [14] was applied to identify regions of GUI components. Lastly, a ResNet50 [15] classifier, trained with 90,000 GUI elements, was utilized to classify each GUI element in the identified regions into 15 categories. The results revealed that their technique - UIED - surpassed other object detection methods, YOLOv3, Faster-RCNN [11] and CenterNet [12] in terms of F1-score.

With a very different objective, Serna et al. [16] implemented an image detection-based planetary exploration system for unmanned aerial vehicles. The main aim of the image detection system was to recognise biosignatures. The prototype was implemented using three models - YOLOv5, YOLOv7, and Roboflow 2.0 Object Detection (Fast) - and their outcomes were compared. All three models are reported to be trained for 500 epochs, except for the Roboflow Object Detection method, as it automatically stopped when the overfitting point of the model is reached. The results of this study showed that the YOLOv5s model offered the highest average precision, thus, it is documented to be the best-performing approach for this study. Another study which concerns a similar comparison is done by Peter Bloch [17], where they proposed a computer vision model for real-time tracking of the apples utilizing Faster-RCNN and YOLOv5. While comparing these two networks, Roboflow 2.0 Object Detection (Fast) is also compared as more of a novel approach. The Roboflow network delivered some promising results with a score of 0.1721 mAP@0.5 while YOLOv5 scored 0.2219 mAP@0.5. However, YOLOv5 is documented to be the best-performing network, as the inference speeds of the Roboflow network are unknown.

3   Methodologies

The following section highlights the primary algorithms that are employed for GUI element recognition. Furthermore, details regarding these algorithms are discussed.

3.1   SSD

SSD [18] is a single-shot detector that takes only one shot to detect multiple objects using a multi-box in a given image. As the name implies, SSD and the You Only Look Once (YOLO) model family is essentially the result of the same ideal view. If the SSD family such as SSD300, SSD500 is compared to different object detection methods, Faster R-CNN [11], YOLO [19] and SSD500 outperformed the other approaches in terms of mAP. With the use of differently sized filters and multiple boxes, high detection accuracy is accomplished. In the later stages of the network, SSD applies these filters to various feature maps, which makes it possible to perform detection at multiple scales. SSD has a base neural network to extract features. For this purpose, the VGG-16 [20] base network is employed. However, this network is only utilized for feature extraction and not for classification. The additional convolutional layers of SSD are used for detecting objects and they are added to the network base for object detection. For every feature layer, the convolutional model used for detection changes. However, at the end of the base network VGG-16, these layers gradually reduces in size which results in a decreasing feature map size, as well as an increasing depth. The deeper layers can cover bigger receptive fields and are able to construct more conceptual representations, which results in a more accurate detection of large objects. The shallower layers contain smaller receptive fields and they are cruical for detecting smaller objects.

3.2   You Only Look Once (YOLO)

The initial YOLO model is presented by Redmon et al. [19] in 2015, where in that specific paper they present a custom framework called the Darknet that is the foundation of a sequence of the best real-time object detection networks to this day - namely YOLOv2 [21], YOLOv3 [9], YOLOv4 [22], YOLOv5 [4], YOLOv7 [23] and its latest variant, YOLOv8 [24]. Notably, before YOLO models, Region-Based Convolutional Neural Networks (R-CNN) [8] were utilized for object detection. However, in their work, Redmon et al. assert that if compared to the state-of-the-art models of that time, such as the deformable parts model (DPM) [25] and R-CNN, YOLO seriously reduces inference times while producing fewer false positive detections in the background. The initial YOLO is considered to be the first object detection model to attach the process of predicting bounding boxes with class labels at an end-to-end differentiable network. The YOLO model family is a series of object detection models that approach object detection like it is a regression problem. The input image is passed through a CNN to extract features, which is performed using architectures such as Darknet or FPN (Feature Pyramid Network). The output of this layer is given to the detection head, which predicts the coordinates as well as the class probabilities of the objects in the image. After the detection head predicts the bounding boxes and class probabilities, a non-maximum suppression (NMS) algorithm is applied to remove identical detections and improve the overall accuracy of the model. The last output of the YOLO model is a bounding box set, class probabilities, and objectness scores per detected object in the image. The YOLO models have evolved with advancements to the backbone network, detection head, and other techniques such as anchor boxes which enhance the accuracy and improve the speed of object detection.

3.3 YOLOv5

YOLOv5 (You Only Look Once version 5) is an object detection algorithm that employs a single deep neural network to predict bounding boxes and class probabilities for objects within an image. This algorithm, developed by Ultralytics, represents an evolution of previous YOLO versions, which were also designed to facilitate real-time object detection. The algorithm is trained on a large dataset of images, and it learns to identify objects by analyzing features at varying scales within the image. To accomplish this, YOLOv5 utilizes a series of convolutional layers to extract features from the input image, and subsequently predicts bounding boxes and class probabilities from these features.

- Input Image: The input image is adjusted to a specified size and normalized.
- Backbone network: This network is utilized for extracting features from the images. YOLOv5 employs FPN as the backbone.
- Neck: This module in YOLOv5 is a set of convolutional layers that helps to fuse features from different layers of the backbone network.
- Head: The head module in YOLOv5 is responsible for predicting the bounding boxes, objectness scores, and class probabilities. It contains a set of fully linked layers after a set of convolutional layers.
- Non-maximum suppression: After the head module predicts the bounding boxes, objectness scores, and class probabilities, the non-maximum suppression (NMS) technique is used for the removal of duplicate detections and boosts the model's overall accuracy.
- Output: For each detected object in the image, YOLOv5 produces a set of bounding boxes, objectness scores, and class probabilities as its final output (Fig. 1).

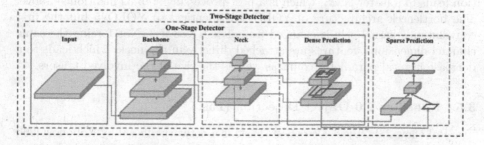

Fig. 1. YOLO model illustration in terms of backbone, neck and head pieces. [22].

3.4 YOLOv8

YOLOv8 is the most recent addition to the YOLO model family which can be used for object detection, image classification, and instance segmentation as shown in Fig. 4. It is also developed by Glenn Jocher, who also produced the YOLOv5 model. The working principle of the YOLOv8 model is essentially the same as YOLOv5, as it also contains an FNP that consists of backbone, neck, and head pieces. However, the modules are altered. For the backbone network and neck modules, the kernel of the first convolutional layer is 3×3 for YOLOv8, whereas it was 6×6 for YOLOv5 and all of the C3 modules present in YOLOv5 are replaced by C2f in YOLOv8; this approach is based on the YOLOv7 ELAN concept. More skip connections and split operations are performed and two convolutional connection layers are removed from the neck module. Nonetheless, the most significant difference between YOLOv5 and YOLOv8 lay in the head module. The original coupling structure that was present in YOLOv5 is changed to a decoupling one in YOLOv8. Furthermore, the YOLOv8 is an anchor-free model, whereas the YOLOv5 is an anchor-based model. An anchor-based model, like YOLOv5, uses a predefined set of anchor boxes of various sizes and aspect ratios. The model predicts the location and size of the bounding boxes relative to these anchor boxes. The predicted bounding boxes are then adjusted based on the offset between the anchor boxes and the ground-truth boxes. This method helps the model to accurately detect objects of different sizes and aspect ratios. On the other hand, an anchor-free model, like YOLOv8, does not use anchor boxes. Instead, it directly predicts the center point and size of the bounding boxes. This method reduces the complexity of the model and eliminates the need for manually defining anchor boxes. Regardless, as far as the training strategies are concerned, YOLOv5 and YOLOv8 perform similar operations. The most significant difference is that the total number of training epochs for YOLOv8 has been raised to 500, which was 300 for YOLOv5.

YOLOv8 is known to be an anchor-free model, which means that the model predicts the center of an object rather than the offset from a comprehended anchor box. This approach lowers the number of box predictions and this reduction leads to a faster NMS, which is a post-processing step as mentioned above. The bottleneck architecture of YOLOv8 is identical to YOLOv5 but the first convolution's kernel size is changed from 1×1 to 3×3. Not forcing the same channel dimensions, features are attached directly in the neck, which leads to a decrease in total parameter count as well as the size of the involved tensors.

3.5   Roboflow 2.0 Object Detection (Fast)

The Roboflow 2.0 Object Detection (Fast) is a network offered by Roboflow [26], which suggests an effortless answer to the problem of training and deploying a model. The training itself is conducted on Google Cloud AutoML. Depending on the image and annotation count, the training duration can vary. It is worth noting that the epoch number and the batch size are automatically chosen by Roboflow and once the model reaches an overfitting point in training, the training stops, which can be considered a less error-prone operation in some cases. However, being a proprietary product, the algorithmic details about the network are not available to the public.

4 Datasets

In the past, many researchers have generated and employed various datasets for the purpose of GUI element detection. GUI recognition-related studies mostly utilize datasets that consist of various design attributes of different applications. One of these is The Rico dataset [27]. It consists of 72000 UI screenshots from approximately 9700 different Android applications. The Android applications are classified into 27 different categories. Another popular example is the ReDraw Dataset, which was introduced in their paper by Moran et al. [28] that was released with the dataset. This dataset is used to train and evaluate the machine learning techniques based on K-Nearest-Neighbour (KNN) and Convolutional Neural Networks (CNN). The ReDraw dataset contains a total of 119.000 different images which are grouped in 15 different classes. Part of the images in the dataset are organic, meaning that they have been captured by applications directly, while the other part is synthetic, they are augmented from the organic data to expand the dataset. Last but not least, the VINS dataset [29] is another bundle of UI images that can be used to train algorithms for GUI detection. It is built upon the previously discussed Rico UI image bundle.

The procedure done by Bunian has two phases. The first phase is locating and identifying UI elements using a model trained with the SSD algorithm while the second phase is to recall the most similar image based on UI element hierarchies. In order to have a consistent and comparable dataset, the full content used by Altinbas and Serif [30] was obtained. The work by Altinbas and Serif follows the initial phase of Bunian's procedure faithfully, using YOLOv5 instead of the SSD algorithm. Accordingly, this study utilizes the same dataset with YOLOv8n, YOLOv8s and RoboFlow Object Detection 2.0 (Fast) models for training. Therefore, each image is kept in its same, respective classification when they are split into three sets: training, validation, and testing. Moreover, the class names are labeled as follows: Text, Text Button, Image, Background Image, Icon, Input Field, Checked View, Sliding Menu, Page Indicator, Pop-Up Window, Switch, and Upper TaskBar. In the final dataset, there are a total of 63,554 annotations, with an average of 14 annotations per image. The annotation heatmap for the Switch class (Fig. 2a) and Text Button class (Fig. 2b) indicates where most of the annotations are placed for their respective classes.

5 Implementation

This section highlights the phases of development for the YOLOv8n and YOLOv8s GUI identification models. The training could have been executed using Google Colab, however, in Altinbas and Serif's existing study, the training was performed using a Mac mini, which has a specification of 3 GHz 6-Core 8th generation Intel core i5 and 32 GB memory. In order to eliminate any hardware disparities and achieve a consistent comparison, the same hardware is utilized for both of the GUI element recognition models in this study.

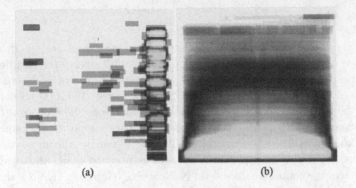

(a)   (b)

Fig. 2. Annotation heatmaps for (a) Switch and (b) TextButton elements.

5.1 YOLOv8s Training

Initially, to conduct the training of the YOLOv8 GUI element detection model, the YOLOv8 repository is cloned to the computer. Furthermore, any additional dependencies and libraries are also installed to the standalone computer. Similar to YOLOv5, there are several versions of the YOLOv8 family model - YOLOv8n is the smallest model and on the other end of the spectrum YOLOv8x is the largest one. For consistency purposes, as in the previous study the authors have used the smallest version of YOLOv5 (YOLOv5s), similarly in this study YOLOv8's smallest model (YOLOv8s) is utilized. The model is trained for 100 epochs on the same computer with the same specifications, where the batch size is chosen to be 16 training images. Once the model has completed training, a couple of test batch images, matrices and graphs are obtained. The training was completed in a total of 34.68 h. The immediate results show that the mean average precision is 0.927 across all classes.

5.2 YOLOv8n Training

Furthermore, in order to get another perspective, the YOLOv8n version is also chosen for training. It is the smallest version available in the YOLOv8 framework with a total of 3.2 million parameters, thus, it is expected to be faster and smaller compared to its bigger counterpart, YOLOv8s, which has a total of 11.2 million parameters. YOLOv8n is optimized for inference on edge devices. Similar to YOLOv8s training, the model is trained for 100 epochs with the same hardware specifications. The batch size is chosen to be 16 training images once again. The training was completed in a total of 29.87 h. The immediate results show that the mean average precision is 0.937 across all classes involved.

6 Evaluation

In this section of the study, the trained models, YOLOv8s and YOLOv8n, are compared with each other and the benchmark study by Altinbas and Serif, which utilizes YOLOv5s. The rest of this section includes some graphs that indicate precision, recall, and confusion findings, as well as mean average comparisons.

6.1   Confusion Matrices

A confusion matrix is frequently used to assess how well a classification model is working. It compares the actual class label to the anticipated class label using the test images. Confusion matrices can be used to compute a number of performance metrics, including F1 score, accuracy, precision, and recall. Figure 3 shows the confusion matrix for the YOLOv8n model.

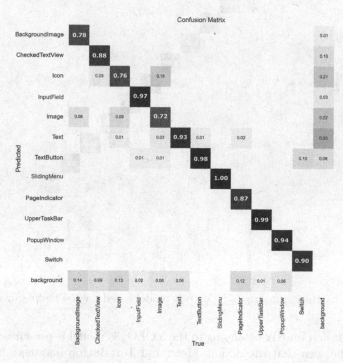

Fig. 3. Confusion matrix of YOLOv8n model based on 450 testing images.

It can be observed from the matrix that all test images which contain Sliding Menu and Upper TaskBar elements have been matched with the corresponding class. Furthermore, most of the Input Field and Pop Up Window instances have also been classified into their correct relative classes for the most part. However, UI test images that contain Image and Background Image instances have not performed as well. It is believed that there could be two reasons for this distinction, the first being the under-representation of this element in the dataset, and the second could be due to the UI element's relative size compared to the image size. Background Image is not a small UI component compared to other items, such as Switch or checkedView. However, it does not have many instances in the dataset as it does not appear in every single UI sample. On the other hand, even though most of the UI images in the dataset contain images, most of them are quite small in size, thus they have a tendency to be harder to locate and detect. It can also be observed that other elements, such as Icon and Text, can get false positives. This is due to the fact that they have some look-alike attributes.

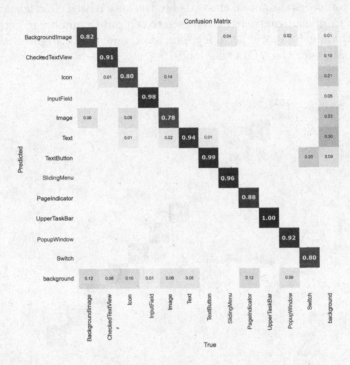

Fig. 4. Confusion matrix of YOLOv8s model based on 450 testing images.

The confusion matrix belonging to the YOLOv8s model is presented in Fig. 4 and it can be seen that the Sliding Menu and TextButton instances have been detected practically as successfully as they were in the YOLOv8n model. Following suit with the results of the YOLOv8s model, Background Image and Image classes did not perform well in the YOLOv8n model. However, when compared with each other, YOLOv8s outperformed the YOLOv8n. In the YOLOv8s model, Background Image examples were detected with 8.3% better accuracy, while Image examples were detected with 5.1% better accuracy compared to the YOLOv8n model. Thus, it can be concluded that YOLOv8s not only detects all test instances at least as well as YOLOv8n but also surpasses it in some cases.

6.2 Precision-Confidence Curves

A precision-confidence curve is a graphical representation of the relationship between the confidence level of a classifier and the precision of the classifier's predictions. It is often used in object detection and classification tasks to visualize the trade-off between the number of correct predictions and the number of incorrect predictions made by a model at different levels of confidence. The curve indicates the quality of the model's predictions at different confidence values. A high precision at a particular threshold indicates that the classifier is making relatively few false positive predictions at that confidence level, but it may also be missing some true positive predictions. Conversely, a low precision at a particular threshold indicates that the classifier is making more false positive predictions, but it may also be detecting more true positive predictions. Based on Fig. 5, it can be concluded that at the same confidence level, YOLOv8n is slightly more precise compared to the YOLOv8s model.

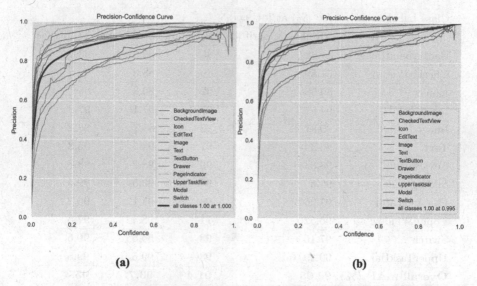

(a)   (b)

Fig. 5. (a) YOLOv8n (b) YOLOv8s Precision Confidence curve.

6.3 Comparison of Mean Average Precisions

One often employed metric for assessing object identification algorithms is average precision (AP). It measures how well the model is able to detect objects and accurately predict their location. The mAP value ranges from 0 to 1, and higher numbers denote better performance. In object detection, AP is a widely used evaluation metric that quantifies the ability of an algorithm to accurately detect and localize objects of interest in an image or video. Averaging the precision values across a range of recall values yields the AP value. Precision is the proportion of accurate detections among all detected objects, and recall is the proportion of accurate detections among all ground truth objects. The lowest amount of overlap between the anticipated result and ground-truth bounding boxes that must exist for a detection to be deemed a true positive is specified by the Intersection over Union (IoU) threshold. The AP is commonly calculated at multiple IoU thresholds ranging from 0 to 1, with 0.5 being a popular choice when evaluating the performance of an object detection model. The average precision (AP) at IoU = 0.5, or where the predicted bounding box coincides with the ground-truth bounding box by at least 50%, is determined when only taking into account detections with IoU $\geq$ 0.5. Table 1 depicts the average precision calculations at IoU = 0.5 for each one of the classes in all models trained in this study and the benchmark study by Altinbas and Serif [30].

Table 1. Comparison table.

Class Label	AP (%) at IoU = 0.5			
	Altinbas & Serif [30]	Roboflow	YOLOv8n	YOLOv8s
BackgroundImage	84.62	85	90.5	93.4
CheckedView	67.59	86	88.8	92.8
Icon	89.58	92	80.3	86
InputField	94.57	97	97.1	97.8
Image	83.87	82	85.7	88.2
Text	96.3	97	94.5	95.3
TextButton	98.83	99	98.2	98.8
SlidingMenu	99.5	99	99.5	99.5
PageIndicator	97.96	98	95.1	96.2
PopupWindow	95.52	71	98.4	97.5
Switch	97.16	93	96.6	99.5
UpperTaskBar	99.49	98	99.5	99.5
Overall mAP (%)	**92.08**	**91.4**	**93.7**	**95.4**

Considering the data provided in Table 1, it can be observed that all models trained within the scope of this study have surpassed our benchmark study in terms of mAP. If the numbers are dissected, 5 classes have yielded a better precision while 4 classes had similar APs. On the other hand, however, the YOLOv8 models have performed considerably worse than the benchmark study in Icon, Text, and PageIndex classes. All of these class items tend to be smaller UI entities, this could be seen as an indication that the YOLOv5 performs better with these types of elements. On the other hand, it is noteworthy to mention that larger GUI elements are recognized with better precision scores using YOLOv8n and YOLOv8s. Overall, the YOLOv5 model has outperformed the Roboflow Object Detection (Fast) model by 1.08% while YOLOv8n exceeded Altinbas and Serif's model by 1.62%. Furthermore, the YOLOv8s has surpassed the YOLOv8n model by 2.24% and the YOLOv5 model by 3.32%.

7   Conclusion and Future Work

This study designs, implements and tests a revamped model for GUI element recognition by utilizing a more recent, state-of-the-art algorithm - namely YOLOv8. For evaluation purposes it sets an existing study as a benchmark and compares the findings with its results. In order to obtain a comparable result, the study follows the same guidelines (same number of classes, same number of training images and same type of training model) as the benchmark has and utilizes the same VINS dataset. Furthermore, in addition to the benchmark model, two additional models - RoboFlow Object Detection 2.0 (Fast) and YOLOv8n - were trained with the same dataset. Accordingly, the findings showed that the newly proposed YOLOv8s and YOLOv8n models have performed with a higher mAP than the benchmark study - with 3.32% and 1.62% higher mAP respectively. On the other hand, the Roboflow Object Detection (Fast) model performed 1.08% worse mAP than the YOLOv5s benchmark study. The next step from this point would be using these models to create an automated UI file code generator, which can be utilized to recognize UI elements and generate UI scripts for multiple mobile platforms such as iOS, Android and Linux Mobile.

References

1. Norman, D.A., Nielsen, J.: The definition of user experience. Interactions **17**(4), 50–60 (2010)
2. Norman, D.A.: Emotion & design: attractive things work better. Interactions **9**(4), 36–42 (2002)
3. Cheng, et al.: YOLOv5-MGC: GUI Element Identification for Mobile Applications Based on Improved YOLOv5. Mobile Information Systems (2022)
4. GitHub. https://github.com/ultralytics/yolov5. Accessed 30 Mar 2023
5. Bahmani, B., et al.: Scalable k-means++. arXiv preprint arXiv:1203.6402 (2012)
6. Han, K., et al.: GhostNet: more features from cheap operations. In: Proceedings of the IEEE/CVF Conference on Computer Vision and Pattern Recognition (2020)
7. Zhang, T., et al.: Deep learning-based mobile application isomorphic GUI identification for automated robotic testing. IEEE Softw. **37**(4), 67–74 (2020)
8. He, K., et al.: Mask R-CNN. In: Proceedings of the IEEE International Conference on Computer Vision (2017)
9. Redmon, J., Farhadi, A.: YOLOv3: an incremental improvement. arXiv preprint arXiv:1804.02767 (2018)
10. Xie, M., et al.: UIED: a hybrid tool for GUI element detection. In: Proceedings of the 28th ACM Joint Meeting on European Software Engineering Conference and Symposium on the Foundations of Software Engineering (2020)
11. Girshick, R.: Fast R-CNN. In: Proceedings of the IEEE International Conference on Computer Vision (2015)
12. Duan, K., et al.: CenterNet: keypoint triplets for object detection. In: Proceedings of the IEEE/CVF International Conference on Computer Vision (2019)
13. Burtsev, S.V., Kuzmin, Y.P.: An efficient flood-filling algorithm. Comput. Graph. **17**(5), 549–561 (1993)
14. He, L., et al.: The connected-component labeling problem: a review of state-of-the-art algorithms. Pattern Recogn. **70**, 25–43 (2017)

15. He, K., et al.: Deep residual learning for image recognition. In: Proceedings of the IEEE Conference on Computer Vision and Pattern Recognition (2016)
16. Galvez Serna, J., et al.: Towards a biosignatures image detection system for planetary exploration with UAVs. In: IEEE Aerospace Conference (2023)
17. Bloch, P.J.: Computer Vision Model Selection for Real-Time Tracking of Apples (2022)
18. Liu, W., et al.: SSD: single shot multibox detector. In: Leibe, B., Matas, J., Sebe, N., Welling, M. (eds.) ECCV 2016. LNCS, vol. 9905, pp. 21–37. Springer, Cham (2016). https://doi.org/10.1007/978-3-319-46448-0_2
19. Redmon, J., et al.: You only look once: unified, real-time object detection. In: Proceedings of the IEEE Conference on Computer Vision and Pattern Recognition (2016)
20. Simonyan, K., Zisserman, A.: Very deep convolutional networks for large-scale image recognition. arXiv preprint arXiv:1409.1556 (2014)
21. Redmon, J., Farhadi, A.: YOLO9000: better, faster, stronger. In: Proceedings of the IEEE Conference on Computer Vision and Pattern Recognition (2017)
22. Bochkovskiy, A., Wang, C.-Y., Liao, H.-Y.M.: YOLOv4: optimal speed and accuracy of object detection. arXiv preprint arXiv:2004.10934 (2020)
23. Wang, C.-Y., Bochkovskiy, A., Liao, H.-Y.M.: YOLOv7: trainable bag-of-freebies sets new state-of-the-art for real-time object detectors. arXiv preprint arXiv:2207.02696 (2022)
24. GitHub https://github.com/ultralytics/ultralytics. Accessed 30 Mar 2023
25. Felzenszwalb, P., McAllester, D., Ramanan, D.: A discriminatively trained, multi-scale, deformable part model. In: 2008 IEEE Conference on Computer Vision and Pattern Recognition. IEEE (2008)
26. Roboflow. https://roboflow.com/. Accessed 30 Mar 2023
27. Deka, B., et al.: Rico: a mobile app dataset for building data-driven design applications. In: Proceedings of the 30th Annual ACM Symposium on User Interface Software and Technology (2017)
28. Moran, K., et al.: Machine learning-based prototyping of graphical user interfaces for mobile apps. IEEE Trans. Softw. Eng. **46**(2), 196–221 (2018)
29. Bunian, S., et al.: VINS: visual search for mobile user interface design. In: Proceedings of the 2021 CHI Conference on Human Factors in Computing Systems (2021)
30. Altinbas, M.D., Serif, T.: GUI element detection from mobile UI images using YOLOv5. In: Awan, I., Younas, M., Poniszewska-Marańda, A. (eds.) MobiWIS 2022. LNCS, vol. 13475, pp. 32–45. Springer, Cham (2022). https://doi.org/10.1007/978-3-031-14391-5_3

Urban Data Platforms as Added-Value Systems for Citizens

Yasmina Tajja[✉] and Ludger Martin

RheinMain University of Applied Sciences, Wiesbaden, Germany
{yasmina.tajja,ludger.martin}@hs-rm.de

Abstract. Efforts to develop the necessary infrastructure for Smart Cities are increasingly being discussed to improve urban life by making it greener and more pleasant. At the center of a Smart City are urban data platforms that are used to consolidate all the necessary urban data on a single platform. When designing these platforms, the user group of citizens is often left out, which is why these platforms do not find much appeal among them. This work aims to develop a design pattern to provide citizens with added value when using urban data platforms. To achieve this, techniques of user-centered design are applied to identify added value functions based on a user analysis. The results are the formulation of three core functional groups and an interaction framework based on them. The identified function groups Discover, Accumulate and Broaden were evaluated using a usability test, which indicates a positive evaluation of the functional groups in terms of value creation, with potential for improvement in the areas of learnability, labeling, and human relevance.

Keywords: Smart City · Urban Data Platform · Usability · Mobile Web-App · HCI

1 Introduction

To make urban life better, greener, and generally more pleasant, efforts for the development of the necessary infrastructure of smart cities are increasingly being discussed. The core of a smart city are urban data platforms. As the name suggests, these platforms should act as a hub for all urban data, including information on the city's environmental situation, traffic development, administrative data, and data collected from sensors, among others. However, there is currently no uniform definition for the functional scope of such a platform. In general, many urban data platforms collect and make data available. A few platforms offer additional services such as visualization of selected data or a collection of smart services. But when it comes to a fixed definition, it often changes from platform to platform. When analyzing urban data platforms, the focus is often on the technical functionalities they offer or their adherence to open data standards, as in the study of the Fraunhofer Institute [9]. This technical perspective

M. Younas et al. (Eds.): MobiWIS 2023, LNCS 13977, pp. 175–184, 2023.
https://doi.org/10.1007/978-3-031-39764-6_12

is reflected in the actual user group of these platforms. It is noticeable that urban data platforms are often used by technology-savvy users, while less technically experienced users like the actual citizens of a smart city are often not directly considered in the development of these platforms.

However, it is important to consider the needs of all potential users, not just those who are technologically inclined. Given that urban data platforms have the potential to inform and empower citizens, it is crucial that they are accessible and user-friendly for the general public. This paper contributes:

1. Conducting an analysis of user requirements for an urban data platform targeting the "Citizen" group
2. Identifying key functional groups to effectively deliver value to citizens
3. Performing an evaluation and testing of a prototype to validate its efficacy in meeting the identified user requirements

To achieve this, the following sections present the analysis steps and results that emerged during the investigation of the design of an urban data platform for citizens. For this purpose, a detailed analysis of the target group was conducted in order to design an interaction framework based on their requirements. The resulting wireframes of the interaction framework served as a template for a click dummy, which was used in a usability test to examine the resulting added value of the design. Finally, the results are discussed and future work is considered.

2   Related Work

In Germany, a standardized specification for a reference architecture for open urban data platforms (OUPs) has been formulated [4]. This architecture proposes to divide the tasks of urban data platforms into microservice-like packages, categorized according to the competence areas of a Smart City [5]. There is a lot of research on the technical side of urban data platforms, such as the design of a data platform for the model city of Santander [1] with a focus on IoT systems, or the design of a platform with a focus on the reuse of existing resources in Australia [8]. Osagie et al. [7] made a similar observation in evaluating usability for urban data platforms, arguing that many OUPs are "designed by developers for developers." According to Cooper et al. [3], software designed by developers often only represents the implemented functions and deviates from the actual vision of the user. This means that technically proficient users can handle most OUPs better than less proficient users, such as citizens of a city. Osagie et al. [7] also point out that research on OUPs often focuses on technical topics, such as implementing open data requirements or system architectures.

However, while these works identify the problem, they do not present a solution approach for the required functions that developers can use as a guide when designing an urban data platform. This study highlights the functional groups that may be of particular interest to non-technical users and how to leverage them. When aiming to create added value with software, it is important to consider and involve the target audience. The essential question is: for whom should the added value be created? Therefore, it is crucial to have a clear idea of the target groups and individual actors who interact with the software. The development of a system that tries to solve this problem can be achieved using techniques of user-centered design (UCD).

In the context of UCD, when discussing added value for users, the terms utility, usability, and user experience (UX) [10] are crucial. Utility forms the core of the actual functionalities of a system that cover the users' goals. Usability builds on the core functionalities and describes the ease of use of the implemented core functionalities. Building on both the utility and usability of a system, UX describes the user experience when interacting with the system. The task is to design an urban data platform as an added-value system for citizens by maximizing the usability for citizens when using the designed urban data platform.

3   Concept

The process methodologies described by Cooper et al. [3] were used as a process template. Cooper et al. outline a user-centered design approach with a focus on creating an interaction framework for software. This aligns with the goal of designing a value-added system for the citizens of a smart city, where understanding the needs and preferences of the target audience is crucial. The methodologies introduced by Cooper et al. [3] are applied to effectively integrate user analysis, persona development, scenario definition, and the creation of functional groups, laying the groundwork for the development of a user-centric urban data platform. In their work, the authors describe a six-stage user-centered design process aimed at creating an interaction framework for software. This process is preceded by a detailed user analysis.

Since the goal is to design a value-added system for the citizens of a smart city, the target audience must be closely examined. Figure 1 shows the relationship of all human actors in the context of the urban data platform. The citizens were divided into three demographic focus groups, and their goals and needs were studied in more detail. Three personas and related scenarios were defined with the help of brainstorming in expert groups and analysis of existing smart applications. The defined scenarios provide examples of use cases within a citizen-centered OUP, covering requirements for smart systems and general system requirements.

The proposed design process by Cooper et al. [3] includes six steps in which the underlying form of the software and various wireframes are developed using pattern analysis. The following sections highlight the key points of the design process.

The *form factor* of an OUP is not strictly defined. Many OUPs are used as web applications, such as the Helsinki 3D+ platform [6]. However, there are also efforts to offer OUP-like software products as smartphone apps. For example, the Citykey app [2] is intended to provide a smartphone app for citizens. After analyzing the personas, it became clear that the user group would like to use

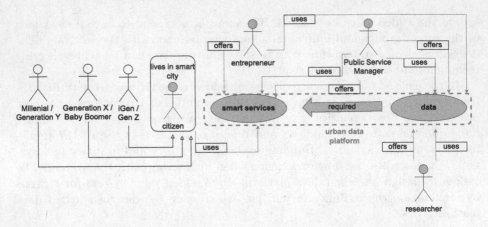

Fig. 1. Interaction of all actors based on benefits and offerings.

the OUP at home on their desktop and on the go on their smartphone devices. Therefore, a hybrid web app design is recommended, which means that a web application is developed that can also be used on a smartphone.

Cooper et al. [3] describe the *posture* of software as the underlying nature of software. The nature of the software describes the appearance, feeling, which the software conveys, while the user is using it. This includes factors such as frequency of use and the environment in which the software is used. For web applications, the authors describe two types of software posture or nature. "Transient" web applications are described as fleeting or short-lived, which are occasionally used for their service and then closed quickly. Web applications with this nature require clear and simple navigation structures to quickly provide users with the functionalities they need for a short period of time. The second nature is described as "sovereign". This type of web application should feel like its own environment with plenty of functionality that is used for a long time, similar to enterprise applications or desktop applications. Regarding the OUP, from the perspective of the target group "citizens", a classification as transient can be made. The developed personas want to use the OUP for a short period of time for specific functionalities in the user stories.

In the design process, the use cases were examined in more detail and existing solutions were critically evaluated. It was found that existing urban data platforms often offer dashboards and map views in which selected data can be viewed. A crucial point for generating added value with such views should be personalization. In the age of social media and personally tailored algorithms for consuming content, it is not enough to simply offer the user a wealth of data to work through. Personalization should ensure that users can create their own experiences to tailor the platform's offerings to their personal daily lives. The personalization approach should be simplified using pre-made templates, as described by Cooper et al. [3]. For example, dashboard and map views should offer a series of predefined templates to group health, environmental, or mobility topics. In addition, the creation of personal templates should be enabled so that citizens can create a dashboard that displays a news feed, weather, opening hours of specific restaurants, and available parking spaces within a certain radius. Personalizable dashboards are not conceptually new, however the key point for urban data platforms that belong to public government institutions is to enable such personalization. One problem with this is often issues related to data protection. It is necessary to decide which data is stored where and what costs are incurred when each citizen can create as many templates as they want. The proposed solution involves storing the data on the end devices themselves. The citizen can therefore generate as many templates on the smartphone app as the smartphone's storage allows. On the desktop, the local storage of the browser can be used to save templates. With this method, no user accounts or additional storage are necessary for personalization, and the data provided remains with the user and does not land on any servers. This approach should also ensure that technology-critical users are confronted with a lower hurdle, as they do not have to create an additional account. The described personalization is only one part of the defined functional groups for creating added value for citizens in designing an urban data platform. In total, three functional groups were defined, which are depicted in Fig. 2.

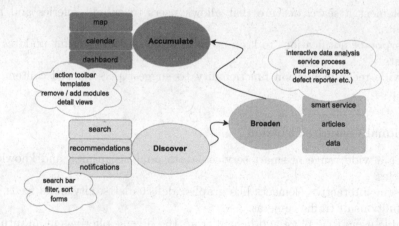

Fig. 2. Three main function groups to achieve an added-value for citizens.

The functional group *"Discover"* includes the functionalities that enable the user to explore the OUP. The search feature, notifications, and recommendation functionality are designed to leverage the underlying services and data of the OUP and offer the user a greater degree of flexibility in resolving their concerns, without being limited to pre-made service solutions. This category necessitates a means to submit queries to the OUP, filter these queries, and access a list of the resultant set.

The category *"Broaden"* contains the actual smart services, data and knowledge articles with which the user can expand his horizons. In this group, many different subject areas come together, making it more difficult to conceptualize a universal usage flow. The functionalities of this group are only partially implemented by many OUPs. OUPs often provide pure data without offering appropriate analysis results in the form of interactable graphs or services. This category includes functionalities such as defect alerts, city news feeds or evaluations of traffic cameras. Based on this, the most important functions can be collected in the "Accumulate" category.

The functional group *"Accumulate"* aims to provide the user with a single location to access relevant data and services. Once the user has identified the services that they require for their personal enrichment through the "Discover" and "Broaden" functionalities, they can be aggregated and presented in a dashboard, calendar, or map view. These three views require a wide window to display their content, an additional detail view, a toolbar with actions that can be performed on the content, and a selection of pre-made templates to simplify the personalization step.

To implement the described functional groups in a hybrid website for an urban data platform, focus on the following key aspects:

Functional Group: "Discover"

1. Implement a search feature that allows users to submit queries and filter results.
2. Incorporate notifications to keep users informed about relevant updates and events.
3. Provide recommendation functionality to suggest personalized content and services.

Functional Group: "Broaden"

1. Offer a wide range of smart services, data analysis results, and knowledge articles.
2. Present interactive elements like graphs, defect alerts, city news feeds, and evaluations of traffic cameras.
3. Enable users to explore and benefit from the diverse offerings in an intuitive and user-friendly manner.

Functional Group: "Accumulate"

1. Design dashboards, calendar views, and map views for users to access relevant data and services.
2. Provide a wide window to display content, along with additional detail views.
3. Offer a toolbar with actions specific to the content and a selection of pre-made templates for easy personalization.

Overall Website Design:

1. Adopt a hybrid web app approach to ensure a seamless user experience across desktop and smartphone devices.
2. Focus on clear and simple navigation structures for quick access to desired functionalities.
3. Prioritize personalization by allowing users to create customized dashboards and templates.
4. Store personalized data on end devices to address data protection concerns.

A user study was conducted using a click dummy implementation of these functionalities to validate the concept as a viable foundation for future citizen-centered urban data platforms.

4   User Study

Based on the concept, a usability test was conducted to evaluate the three groups using a simple click dummy. The usability test was task-based with two subsequent post-test questionnaires. The 5 subjects each tested one functionality of the three main function groups and were asked to implement thinking aloud. Before the test was conducted, each subject was given a brief introduction explaining what a smart city is, what an urban data platform is, and what the goal of the user test is. The goal was defined as whether the selected user scenarios for the developed functional groups create added value for the users. After each functional group's test, the subjects were asked to rate on a scale of one to five whether the tested use cases of this group provide added value for them, with one meaning "no added value" and five meaning "high added value".

For the "Accumulate" group, a customizable dashboard with different modules was tested, in which subjects should recognize the functions of the modules and perform simple customization. The generated added value was rated for this group with an average of 3.8, which is a generally positive result. It was particularly evident that subjects expected a function for sharing on social networks. For example, one subject stated that the function of the dashboard reminded them of the pinboard function of Pinterest and that sharing the dashboard was therefore the next expected step.

For the "Discover" group, a planning module was tested in which intelligent suggestions for leisure activities in the city are made by filling out a form. The average added value rating was 4. The main criticism was that the layout of the form was unclear and not self-explanatory, but the actual functionality behind it was very positively received.

For the "Broaden" group, a service of smart mobility was tested. Subjects could locate a free parking space nearby on a map and explore further statistics on the data set. The added value was rated here with an average of 3.6. The main point of criticism was also the labeling and layout, as subjects had difficulty finding individual statistics on the overview page.

The evaluation of the AttrakDiff questionnaire and the statements from the thinking-aloud technique support these results. The AttrakDiff is a questionnaire developed in 2003 by Hassenzahl, Burmeister, and Koller. It allows users to subjectively evaluate the usability and aesthetics of a product, as well as assess the usefulness of identified functional groups. It allows users to subjectively evaluate the usability, aesthetics, and usefulness of a product, which aligns with the goal of assessing the added value provided by the developed functional groups. The questionnaire's evaluation, along with the feedback obtained through the thinking-aloud technique, supports the findings of the usability test and provides insights into areas that require improvement in the design. In Fig. 3, the average results of the AttrakDiff dimensions and their standard deviation can be seen. Hedonic Quality - Stimulation (HQ-S) performed the worst, followed by Pragmatic Quality (PQ), both of which have a standard deviation of about 1. When evaluating the word pairs, it is striking that these are the only categories that each contain a negatively rated word pair. The prototype was rated as too technical and harmless. The classification as technical can be explained by the lack of reference to other people. Subjects expressed that they would like to see a sense of communities within neighborhoods reflected in an urban data platform and not just handle data. The assessment as harmless can be explained by the intention of selecting familiar and learned interaction patterns in the prototype concept. The hurdle of using the platform should thus be lowered. Overall, PQ was rated with an average value of 1.26 and a confidence of 0.49 for a first run, which is generally positive. The overall rating of HQ averages 1.04 with an even lower confidence of 0.39.

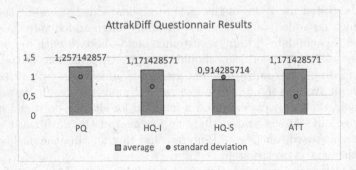

Fig. 3. Average values for the AttrakDiff dimensions: Pragmatic Quality, Hedonic Quality - Identity, Hedonic Quality - Stimulation, Attractiveness.

The results indicate potential for improvement in the design. The deficiencies identified based on the test results and statements of the subjects are as follows:

1. Learnability: Information about the features offered should be included for first-time users.
2. Labeling: Labels, legends, button positions may need to be redrawn/revised.

3. Sense of human connection: A way should be found to increase the interaction of human beings with other human beings within the OUP.

In conclusion, the results of the usability test and the evaluation of the AttrakDiff questionnaire provide valuable insights for the development of a user-centric urban data platform. The test outcomes revealed positive ratings for the tested functional groups, indicating their potential to add value for users. The feedback obtained through the thinking-aloud technique and the AttrakDiff questionnaire emphasized the importance of creating a sense of human connection within the platform. Users expressed their desire for the platform to reflect communities and facilitate interactions between individuals. This feedback highlights the need to incorporate features that promote social engagement and community-building. By addressing the identified areas for improvement and focusing on enhancing the platform's usability, aesthetics, and sense of human connection, we can lay a solid foundation for a future urban data platform that truly meets the needs and expectations of its users.

5   Conclusion and Future Work

Previous research has focused on the technical issues involved in designing OUP systems, but this work has laid the basics for designing OUPs that can actually be used well by citizens. The shortcomings identified can be examined more closely and improved in the design processes for future work. The results represent the passage of a first cycle in the UCD process and will continue to be optimized through repeated iterations. Future work may address whether the categorization of major functional groups can provide a basis for designing concrete evaluation criteria for an OUP. By analyzing existing OUPs and collecting covered functionalities, the development of an evaluation criterion could improve the design process for OUPs and thus provide the basis for formulating design templates for OUPs. An extension regarding the extension of various functionalities, such as the integration of social media-like aspects for the OUP to address the deficit of "humanity", could form the basis for an alternative interaction framework. In addition, research on the remaining focus groups, public service managers, researchers, and entrepreneurs remains relevant to optimize and bring together user experiences from all sides, especially because of the identified interdependencies between actors. Furthermore, the interaction framework can be extended with a digital twin. The changed and additional requirements for the Interaction Framework when 3D aspects of a digital twin or even augmented reality aspects are added, promise the development of new and creative user experiences.

References

1. Cheng, B., Longo, S., Cirillo, F., Bauer, M., Kovacs, E.: Building a big data platform for smart cities: experience and lessons from Santander. In: 2015 IEEE International Congress on Big Data, pp. 592–599 (2015). https://doi.org/10.1109/BigDataCongress.2015.91

2. Citykey App. https://citykey.app/. Accessed 07 Mar 2023
3. Cooper, A., Reimann, R., Cronin, D.: About Face 3 - The Essentials of Interaction Design. Wiley, Indianapolis (2017)
4. Referenzarchitekturmodell Offene Urbane Plattform (OUP) (2017). https://doi.org/10.31030/2780217. https://www.beuth.de/de/technische-regel/din-spec-91357/281077528
5. Duan, W., Nasiri, R., Karamizadeh, S.: Smart city concepts and dimensions. In: Proceedings of the 2019 7th International Conference on Information Technology: IoT and Smart City, pp. 488–492. ICIT 2019, Association for Computing Machinery, New York (2019). https://doi.org/10.1145/3377170.3377189
6. Helsinki 3D+. https://kartta.hel.fi/3d/#/legend. Accessed 07 Mar 2023
7. Osagie, E., Waqar, M., Adebayo, S., Stasiewicz, A., Porwol, L., Ojo, A.: Usability evaluation of an open data platform, pp. 495–504. dg.o 2017, Association for Computing Machinery, New York (2017). https://doi.org/10.1145/3085228.3085315
8. Sinnott, R.O., et al.: The urban data re-use and integration platform for Australia: design, realisation, and case studies. In: 2015 IEEE International Conference on Information Reuse and Integration, pp. 90–97 (2015). https://doi.org/10.1109/IRI.2015.24
9. Tcholtchev, N., Lämmel, P., Raabe, J.: Ein überblick urbaner Datenplattformen (2021). https://publica.fraunhofer.de/handle/publica/301009
10. Werkmeister, T.: Nutzerzentrierte interaction design patterns für international data space Ökosysteme. Ph.D. thesis, Ilmenau (2022). https://doi.org/10.22032/dbt.50711. https://www.db-thueringen.de/receive/dbt_mods_00050711

Machine Learning and Stochastic Methods

Optimisation of a Chemical Process by Using Machine Learning Algorithms with Surrogate Modeling

Ozge Keremer[1], Fadil Can Malay[1], Bilgin Deveci[2], Pinar Kirci[1(✉)], and Perin Unal[2]

[1] Bursa Uludag University, 16285 Bursa, Turkey
pinarkirci@uludag.edu.tr
[2] TEKNOPAR, 06000 Ankara, Turkey

Abstract. Process models are getting more detailed, thus computational costs are rising. For this reason, the main aim of process engineering is to provide effective and cost-efficient production processes. Computational methods are important for composing the field of process systems engineering. They are used in process design and simulation with the capability of modeling, prediction, and optimizing processes. Also, machine learning (ML) emerges for enhancing this capability with providing a solution by performing as surrogate models of complex relationships in processes. By this way, accurate and efficient process optimization is presented. In the paper, machine learning algorithms were used on data which is generated through the sampling of varied parts of an ethylene oxide (EO) process plant in Pyomo. The physical system being surrogate modeled is an ethylene oxide plug flow reactor. Also, it is evaluated for accuracy and speed of surrogate modeling for various ML algorithms and various sampling techniques which are random, stratified, latin hypercube.

Keywords: Machine Learning · Ethylene Oxide · Surrogate Modeling

1 Introduction

Optimization in chemical processes refers to the process of improving the efficiency and effectiveness of chemical processes by identifying and implementing changes that result in better process performance [14]. Optimization can involve a wide range of activities, including process design, process control, and process improvement. The goal of optimization is to maximize the yield, quality, and safety of chemical processes while minimizing the use of resources, energy, and time [14].

Chemical process optimization is a critical aspect of chemical engineering and is widely studied in academia and industry. There are numerous approaches to chemical process optimization, including mathematical modeling, simulation, experimental design, statistical analysis, and artificial intelligence-based techniques [14–16]. These techniques enable engineers to optimize chemical processes in a systematic and data-driven manner.

M. Younas et al. (Eds.): MobiWIS 2023, LNCS 13977, pp. 187–201, 2023.
https://doi.org/10.1007/978-3-031-39764-6_13

Some common optimization techniques used in chemical process optimization include; Mathematical modeling: Mathematical models are used to simulate chemical processes and optimize process parameters.

Statistical analysis: Statistical techniques are used to analyze data and identify patterns that can help optimize chemical processes.

Experimental design: Experimental design techniques are used to design experiments that can help to optimize chemical processes.

Artificial intelligence-based techniques: Artificial intelligence techniques, such as machine learning and neural networks, are used to optimize chemical processes [14–16].

Machine learning (ML) is a well-known and beneficial tool. Thus, it is utilized to optimize chemical processes. ML techniques are applied to diverse areas of process optimization in chemical engineering, such as process modeling, process control, and process optimization.

In chemical process optimization to be able to use ML, predictive models should be developed that can accurately predict process behavior and identify optimal process parameters [17, 18].

In chemical process optimization, to be able to use ML another way is to develop real-time process monitoring and control systems that can automatically adjust process parameters based on real-time data [17, 18].

Surrogate modeling is metamodeling or response surface modeling. It is utilized in science, engineering, and data analysis. Surrogate modeling is used to approximate a complex or difficult-to-evaluate function with a simpler or more efficient one.

Surrogate modeling is used to construct a mathematical model or a machine learning algorithm that will mimic the behavior of the original system or process, with a limited set of input-output data or simulation runs [1].

The paper is organized as follows: Sect. 2 presents a brief literature review about different types of surrogate modeling methods. Sections 3 and 4 describe optimization in the production process and surrogate modeling, respectively. In Sect. 5, an overview on machine learning in production process is given. Section 6 describes the presented project and utilized methods. The detailed experimental results are given in Sect. 7. The general conclusions are given in Sect. 8.

2 Literature Review

Various surrogate modeling methods are reviewed in [1], such as kriging, radial basis functions, and artificial neural networks, and provided examples of their applications in structural and multidisciplinary optimization. Also, the advantages and limitations of each method are discussed and recommendations are provided for selecting an appropriate surrogate modeling technique [1].

In [2], surrogate modeling techniques, optimization algorithms, and their combinations for solving complex optimization problems are reviewed. Also, the challenges and limitations of surrogate-assisted optimization are discussed, such as the need for expensive simulations and the difficulty in selecting appropriate surrogate modeling and optimization methods.

The performance of different surrogate modeling techniques, optimization algorithms, and their combinations on a set of benchmark problems are evaluated in the study. Besides, recommendations for selecting an appropriate surrogate-assisted optimization method are provided based on the problem characteristics and computational resources available in [3].

The paper [4] provides a comprehensive overview of surrogate modeling and its applications in engineering. Various methods of surrogate modeling are explored, including response surface methodology, kriging, and radial basis functions, and their advantages and limitations are discussed. Applications in engineering design optimization, uncertainty quantification, and reliability analysis are highlighted.

The paper [5] presents an approach to surrogate modeling called Bayesian optimization, which is applied to materials design optimization. Gaussian process regression is used to model the relationship between material properties and design parameters. And it shows that Bayesian optimization can find optimal materials design with fewer simulations than other optimization methods.

[6] presents an early example of surrogate modeling for simulation optimization, using Bayesian optimization algorithms. The effectiveness of surrogate modeling for optimizing a complex simulation model of a hydraulic press is demonstrated, reducing the number of simulations needed by a factor of 10.

[7] proposes a surrogate-assisted optimization approach for hydraulic fracturing treatments in oil and gas reservoirs. Kriging and support vector regression are used to construct surrogate models of hydraulic fracture simulations and showed that the approach can lead to significant reductions in the number of simulations needed for optimization.

The study provides a comprehensive review of surrogate modeling for computer-based engineering design optimization. Various methods of surrogate modeling are surveyed, including neural networks, kriging, and polynomial chaos expansions, and discussed their applications in different areas of engineering design [8].

The paper presents a surrogate modeling approach for optimization under uncertainty with expensive functions. A hybrid kriging and radial basis function model is used to construct surrogates of the objective function and uncertainty and showed that the approach can lead to significant reductions in the number of simulations needed for optimization [9].

The paper provides a comprehensive review of surrogate-assisted evolutionary algorithms, which combines surrogate modeling with evolutionary optimization. Various methods of surrogate modeling are surveyed, including Kriging, radial basis functions, and support vector regression, and discussed about their applications in different areas of optimization. The paper also highlights challenges and future directions for research in surrogate-assisted evolutionary algorithms [10].

3   Optimization in Production Process

Optimization in the production process refers to the systematic approach of maximizing the efficiency and effectiveness of a production system, by minimizing waste, reducing costs, increasing throughput, improving quality, and enhancing customer satisfaction.

The optimization of the production process is important in several areas and industries, such as:

1. Manufacturing: Optimization can be used to improve the efficiency and quality of manufacturing processes, such as assembly, machining, casting, or molding. This can result in reduced lead times, increased production rates, and lower production costs [5].
2. Supply Chain: Optimization can be used to improve the logistics and distribution of products, by reducing inventory, minimizing transportation costs, and improving delivery times. This can result in improved customer service and reduced supply chain costs [6].
3. Service Operations: Optimization can be used to improve the efficiency and quality of service operations, such as healthcare, hospitality, or banking. This can result in reduced waiting times, increased service capacity, and improved customer satisfaction [7].
4. Energy and Environment: Optimization can be used to reduce the energy consumption and environmental impact of production processes, by improving resource efficiency, minimizing waste generation, and reducing greenhouse gas emissions [8].

Optimization is necessary in all these areas because it can help organizations achieve their strategic objectives, such as increasing profits, improving quality, and enhancing customer satisfaction. Optimization can also help organizations to stay competitive in a rapidly changing market, by improving their agility, responsiveness, and innovation capabilities.

4   Surrogate Modeling

Surrogate modeling, also known as metamodeling or response surface modeling, is a technique used in engineering, science, and data analysis to approximate a complex, computationally expensive, or difficult-to-evaluate function with a simpler, cheaper, or more efficient one.

The idea behind surrogate modeling is to construct a mathematical model or a machine learning algorithm that can mimic the behavior of the original system or process, based on a limited set of input-output data or simulation runs. This surrogate model can then be used to predict the output for new input values or to perform sensitivity analysis, optimization, or uncertainty quantification.

Surrogate modeling can be applied to a wide range of problems in various fields, such as:

- Design optimization of engineering systems, such as aircraft wings, car frames, or electronic circuits, where the evaluation of each design requires expensive or time-consuming simulations or experiments [1].
- Calibration or validation of numerical models, such as climate models, fluid dynamics simulations, or financial models, where the true output is unknown or uncertain, and the surrogate model can provide a faster or more accurate estimate of the model error or bias [2].

- High-dimensional data analysis or machine learning, such as an image or speech recognition, where the surrogate model can capture the essential features or patterns of the data and reduce the computational or memory cost of the training or inference.

Overall, surrogate modeling is a powerful tool for approximating complex systems or functions with simpler ones, without sacrificing accuracy or reliability [3, 4].

4.1 Surrogate Modeling and Optimization

Surrogate modeling and optimization are closely related in the production process, as surrogate models can be used to efficiently optimize the production process by minimizing costs, maximizing throughput, and improving quality.

Surrogate modeling can be used to approximate complex, computationally expensive, or time-consuming functions that are involved in the production process. These functions can include the performance of machines, the behavior of materials, or the interactions between different components of the system. By building a surrogate model of these functions, the production process can be optimized more efficiently and effectively than by directly evaluating the original function [9, 10].

Optimization techniques, such as the design of experiments, response surface methodology, or evolutionary algorithms, can be used to find the optimal settings of the production process based on the surrogate model. These techniques can be used to minimize the number of experiments or simulations needed to find the optimal solution, thus reducing the time and cost required for optimization.

Surrogate modeling and optimization are used in various areas of the production process, including:

1. Manufacturing process optimization: Surrogate models can be used to optimize manufacturing processes such as machining, casting, or molding. This can lead to improved product quality, reduced lead times, and lower production costs.
2. Supply chain optimization: Surrogate models can be used to optimize logistics and distribution, such as reducing inventory, minimizing transportation costs, and improving delivery times. This can lead to improved customer service and reduced supply chain costs.
3. Process control optimization: Surrogate models can be used to optimize the control of production processes, such as temperature or pressure control. This can lead to improved process stability and reduced energy consumption.

Overall, the use of surrogate modeling and optimization in production process can lead to significant improvements in efficiency, quality, and cost-effectiveness, and can help organizations to stay competitive in the market [9, 10].

5 Machine Learning in Production Process

Machine learning has been increasingly used in the production process to improve efficiency, quality, and cost-effectiveness. Machine learning algorithms can analyze large amounts of data, identify patterns and anomalies, and make predictions or decisions based on that data [10].

Examples of machine learning applications in the production process:

1. Predictive maintenance: Machine learning can be used to predict when a machine or equipment is likely to fail, based on its usage and other parameters. This allows maintenance to be scheduled proactively, reducing downtime and improving reliability [11].
2. Quality control: Machine learning can be used to analyze data from sensors and cameras, and identify defects or anomalies in products. This allows defects to be detected and corrected earlier in the production process, reducing waste and improving quality [12].
3. Process optimization: Machine learning can be used to identify patterns in production data and optimize production processes to improve efficiency, reduce waste, and increase throughput [13].
4. Supply chain optimization: Machine learning can be used to optimize logistics and supply chain operations, such as predicting demand, optimizing inventory levels, and improving delivery times [13].

The use of machine learning in the production process has significant potential to improve efficiency, quality, and cost-effectiveness, and it is an area of active research and development.

5.1 Machine Learning in Optimization of Chemical Process

Machine learning (ML) is a powerful tool that can be used to optimize chemical processes. In chemical engineering, ML techniques can be applied to various aspects of process optimization, including process modeling, process control, and process optimization.

One way to use ML in chemical process optimization is to develop predictive models that can accurately predict process behavior and identify optimal process parameters [17, 18]. These models can be trained using historical data and can be used to identify optimal operating conditions for a given chemical process. For example, ML models can be used to predict the effect of different process variables, such as temperature, pressure, and flow rate, on process performance, and identify the optimal set of operating conditions that maximize the desired process output while minimizing waste [17, 18].

Another way to use ML in chemical process optimization is to develop real-time process monitoring and control systems that can automatically adjust process parameters based on real-time data. This approach is known as model predictive control (MPC) and involves using an ML model to predict future process behavior based on current process conditions. The MPC system can then use this prediction to adjust process parameters in real-time to ensure that the process remains within desired operating conditions.

The use of ML in chemical process optimization offers several benefits, including:

- Improved process efficiency: ML models can identify optimal process parameters that maximize process efficiency and reduce resource consumption.
- Increased process safety: Real-time process monitoring and control systems can identify and address potential safety hazards before they become serious.
- Reduced environmental impact: By optimizing process parameters and reducing waste, ML can help reduce the environmental impact of chemical processes.

- Faster product development: ML can help accelerate product development by predicting the behavior of new chemical formulations and identifying optimal manufacturing processes [17, 18].

Overall, the use of ML in chemical process optimization can help to improve the efficiency, safety, and sustainability of chemical processes, leading to significant benefits for both industry and society [19].

6 Proposed Approach and Methods

Linear regression, used in the study, is a statistical analysis method that allows one variable to be estimated from another by examining the relationship between two or more quantitative variables. In this analysis, the input and output data are distributed on a regression line and the relationship between the input and output in the system is determined [20, 21].

Decision tree, another method used in the study, is a supervised machine learning method that can be used in both classification and regression problems. A decision tree based on a root node usually consists of multiple nodes and branches decomposed from each node. The working principle of the decision tree starts from the root node. After the evaluation of each node, it is determined whether to move to the next layer, proceed to the leaf node, and the final decision is reached [22].

The decision tree approach is a method that can be used on large and complex data sets without the need for a complex quantitative framework. Decision tree models can be used to compress datasets into a more manageable number of categories or to determine how to divide significantly distorted information into a range. In this way, data analysis and decision-making processes become more understandable and applicable [23].

Another utilized method SVR is an adaptation of the latest statistical learning theory-based classification paradigm. The SVR follows the SRM principle, as opposed to the empirical risk minimization (ERM) approach that is employed in statistical machine learning methods and in training SVRs [24].

7 Computational Results and Discussion

7.1 Results Obtained by Using Random Forest, Gaussian Process Regression, and Deep Neural Networks

The R^2 test result refers to the R-squared value, which is a statistical measure of how well the regression model fits the data. R^2 reflects the ratio of the dependent variable explained by the independent variables.

Accuracy of surrogate modeling of an EO reactor for various machine learning algorithms, sampling techniques and the number of training points are given in Fig. 1a.

Speed of surrogate modeling of an EO reactor for various machine learning algorithms, sampling techniques and the number of training points are given in Fig. 1b.

Here, used machine learning algorithms are random forest regression (RF), Gaussian process regression (GP), and deep neural network (NN). Sampling techniques are random sampling (random), stratified sampling (strat), and latin hypercube sampling (lhs).

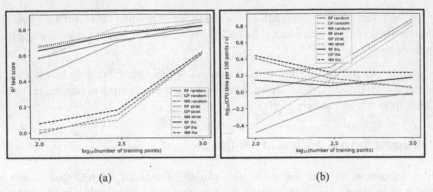

(a)   (b)

Fig. 1. a-Accuracy graph of RF-GP-NN. b-Speed graph of RF-GP-NN

The study [25] aimed to compare the accuracy and speed of different sampling techniques and supervised learning algorithms for surrogate modeling that replaces chemical models. In the study, supervised learning algorithms are trained on data generated through the sampling of many parts of an ethylene oxide (EO) process plant in Pyomo. Random forests, Gaussian processes, and neural networks are presented together with three different sampling techniques which are random, stratified, and latin hypercube.As a result, it is seen that the best results were obtained with Gaussian Process Regression in the basic study. In general, there was a differentiation in scores after 2.5 points. Another algorithm that provides close results as accuracy is seen as Random Forest.

7.2 Results Obtained by Using Decision Tree, Gaussian Process Regression, and Artificial Neural Networks

Another machine learning method examined in addition to the results of the study is Decision Tree. The reason for examining the algorithm is that it can work in harmony with one-dimensional regression problems.

When Fig. 2-a is examined, it is seen that the model created has very low learning values compared to Random Forest and Gaussian Process Regression, but it gives better results than Neural Networks in the data created with the LHS method.

Considering the CPU times, it is observed that it completes the work with more efficient results than other algorithms in terms of processing load time and complexity.

When Fig. 2-b is examined, the decision tree algorithm on CPU time consumed much lower CPU time between 2000 and 3000 points. The random sampling of the neural network, which is the closest among the algorithms used in the study, was able to give a result close to the decision tree. GP, on the other hand, seems to use more CPU than the two. However, GP produced more accurate results despite using more CPU time. As a result, it has been observed that although higher accuracy cannot be achieved with the decision tree, it can get better results with lower CPU time on a lower LHS than the Neural Network.

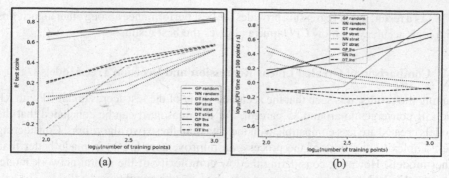

Fig. 2. a-Accuracy graph of DT-GP-NN. b-Speed graph of DT-GP-NN

7.3 Results Obtained by Using Decision Tree, Linear Regression, and Artificial Neural Networks

With the addition of the decision tree, the expected increase in accuracy value can not be obtained, but the complexity of the model is reduced. Afterwards, the linear regression model, which is another one-dimensional regression algorithm frequently used in the literature, is added and the test scores shown in Fig. 3 are obtained. For the model, it can be interpreted that the mse values decrease between 1000 and 3000 points and the accuracy values increase. If the machine learning methods used are compared within themselves; It is seen that linear regression gives better results between 1000 and 2500 points, but when the value of 3000 is reached, the results of some methods outperform LR. As a matter of fact, it can be interpreted that it is more adapted to the data than the decision tree except for the DT strat, and it gives data with less accuracy than the artificial neural networks except for the NN strat.

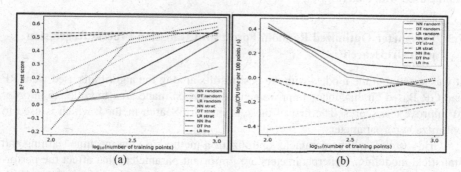

Fig. 3. a-Accuracy graph of DT-LR-NN. b-Speed graph of DT-LR-NN

When the results obtained with the addition of linear regression are examined over CPU time, it has a lower CPU time between 2000 and 3000 points. The decision tree used in the previous example seems to be the closest to the algorithms used in the study. Although it initially started with high CPU time on neural network strat sampling, it completed its operations at a lower CPU time compared to other algorithms used with

LHS. As a result, linear regression provides the best performance among other algorithms with high accuracy and low CPU time and gives the best results.

7.4 Comparison of Created Linear Regression and Decision Tree Models

Among the results, it is seen that the accuracy value of the test scores obtained with RF and GR converges to around 85 percent. For this reason, it can be concluded that the models created are less compatible with the data than these two algorithms. Considering the complexity and time of the process, an improvement has been made better than other models. However, considering the low complexity of the neural network model compared to NN, it can be commented that close results are obtained.

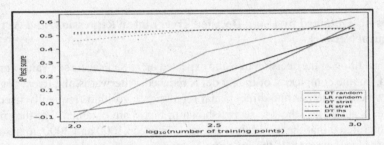

Fig. 4. Accuracy graph of DT-LR

As can be seen, the created decision tree model has better performance against linear regression. It is clear that the model created with the decision tree achieves an accuracy rate exceeding 60 percent at 3000 points and is a better machine learning method that can be used with data (Fig. 4).

7.5 Parameter Optimized Random Forest and Gaussian Process Regression with Gridsearch

It was stated that the models with the best results among the algorithms used were RF and GP. Based on this, many improvements have been made after the title 2.5 in order to improve test scores. The first of these is the GridSearch method, which is used to optimize hyperparameters.

GridSearch is a hyperparameter optimization method used in machine learning and statistical modeling. Hyperparameters are important parameters that affect the performance of a model and the combination of values that make up that performance. GridSearch tries to find the parameter combination that provides the best performance by trying different values of the hyperparameters for a given model.

It was observed that the accuracy value of the results obtained after the implementation of GridSearch increased slightly for all algorithms and sampling methods. In particular, quite good success has been achieved on randomly generated data. The GP model, which gave an accuracy value of over 80 percent before the hyperparameter

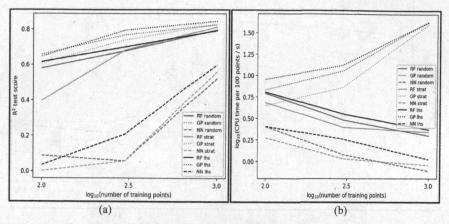

Fig. 5. a-GridSearch scoring result of RF and GP algorithms applied. b-CPU results of RF and GP algorithms implemented in GridSearch

optimization, exceeds 90 percent after GridSearch. It can be said that the increase in the accuracy values of the GP algorithm is also reflected in the increase in CPU usage.

Figure 5-b shows before and after GridSearch usage on CPU time. Between 2000 and 3000 points, GridSearch seems to have used lower CPU time than before it was implemented. In general, GridSearch consumes more CPU for both algorithms than before. As a result, cpu time increase is expected as GridSearch provides a parameter optimization. It is normal to have more CPU time here. On the other hand, since the accuracy values are more accurate, this CPU increase seems acceptable at these amounts.

7.6 Cross Validation for Gaussian Process Regression Model

Cross-validation is a method used to evaluate the performance of a machine learning model. It is preferred because it gives us an idea about the success of the generalization ability of the model and can be used to evaluate its adaptation to real-world problems, especially in the presence of limited data.

When cross validation is added, it is observed that the stratified sampling data on the GP give more negative results than the cross validation. However, when looking at other samples, it can be interpreted that although they starts with lower test results, they shows a smooth increase at the 3000 point (Fig. 6).

With the addition of cross validation, when the GP CPU graph is examined, it is seen that the CPU time normally increases compared to the state before it is added. It is observed that between 2000 and 3000 points, there is more CPU time than other algorithms.

As a result, we can see that cross validation increases the accuracy values for GP in general. However, the increase in these values also increases the CPU time value with the excess of the processes. As long as the CPU time values are at an acceptable level, more accurate results can be obtained by using cross validation for GP.

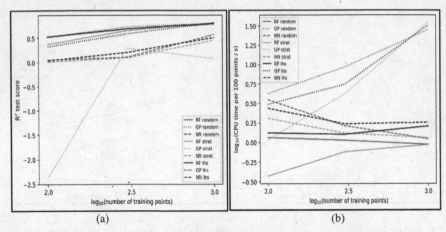

Fig. 6. a-Post cross validation GP test score graph. b-GP CPU score graph after cross validation

7.7 Cross Validation for Random Forest Model

When the cross validation process is performed on random forest, it is seen that the test scores are generally inconsistent. Accuracy values drop significantly and the range that can be obtained with data is stuck between 2000–3000 points. When looking at the CPU, it is seen that the data sampled with stratified starts at a higher value and gives results at the same values. The result obtained here is that the processing time generally remains the same (Fig. 7).

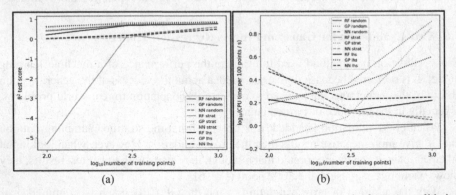

Fig. 7. a-RF test score graph after cross validation. b-RF CPU score graph after cross validation

7.8 Using the SVR Cross Validation Model

SVR (Support Vector Regression) is a version of the support vector machine algorithm adapted for regression problems. SVR is a machine learning model used to solve linear or nonlinear regression problems. When the model is studied and compared to the rest of the algorithm, it is concluded that it can not learn the data to a large extent.

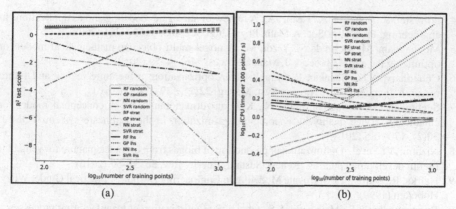

(a)   (b)

Fig. 8. The a-SVR cross validation accuracy rates. b-SVR cross validation CPU usage

When the CPU graph is examined with SVR cross validation, it is observed that an average result is obtained in general. CPU usage seems to be quite low in random and strat sampling results. It shows a better CPU time graph than other algorithms used in the study (Fig. 8).

As a result, SVR is an algorithm with a high margin of error for this data set, among other algorithms, as it does not give us accurate results in terms of accuracy, even if the CPU time remains at low values.

8 Conclusion

Providing efficient and cost-efficient production processes is the vital duty of process engineering. Because of the expensive computational costs of process models. Computational methods are utilized in process designs with machine learning to provide accurate and efficient process optimization.

In this study, the presented physical system being surrogate modeled is an ethylene oxide plug flow reactor. The accuracy and speed of surrogate modeling of an EO reactor for some ML algorithms and sampling techniques are examined and given as test scores and CPU times.

The focus of the paper is the usage of ML algorithms for surrogate modeling chemical processes with process simulation and optimization.

References

1. Forrester, S., Sobester, A., Keane, A.: Engineering design optimization using surrogate modelling: a comparative study. Proc. Roy. Soc. A Math. Phys. Eng. Sci. **463**, 3251–3269 (2007)
2. Sacks, J., Welch, W.J., Mitchell, T.J., Wynn, H.P.: Design and analysis of computer experiments. Stat. Sci. **4**, 409–423 (1989)
3. Regis, K.R., Shoemaker, C.A.: Constrained global optimization of expensive black box functions using radial basis functions. J. Glob. Optim. **31**, 153–171 (2005). https://doi.org/10.1007/s10898-004-0570-0

4. Forrester, A., Sobester, A., Keane, A.: A review of surrogate modeling and its applications in engineering. Proc. Roy. Soc. A Math. Phys. Eng. Sci. **463**, 3257–3281 (2008)
5. Moghaddam, M., Behzadi, S., Yazdi, M.: A novel multi-objective mathematical model for optimizing the casting process. J. Manuf. Process. **46**, 44–59 (2019)
6. Choudhary, A.K., Shankar, R.: Supply chain optimization: a literature review and future research directions. Int. J. Logist. Syst. Manag. **22**(2), 139–164 (2015)
7. Suebnukarn, S., Rungreunganun, N., Khunnawutmanotham, N.: A conceptual model for enhancing service quality by operational optimization in the healthcare system. TQM J. **30**(2), 170–185 (2018)
8. Nizami, A.S., et al.: Optimization of production of biogas from livestock manure for vehicular fuel in developing countries. Renew. Sustain. Energy Rev. **53**, 51–57 (2016)
9. Haftka, R., Gurdal, Z.: Surrogate Modeling in Engineering Design: A Practical Guide. Wiley, Hoboken (1999)
10. Bandyopadhyay, S., Mahapatra, S.S., Ghosh, S.: Optimization of manufacturing processes: a review. Int. J. Adv. Manuf. Technol. (2011)
11. Rajkumar, R., Lui, J.C.S.: Machine learning applications in manufacturing. Proc. IEEE (2018)
12. Chen, X., Chen, Y., Wang, Y.: Predictive maintenance in manufacturing industry: a review of recent developments. IEEE Access (2020)
13. Raut, N.K., Bodhe, S.H.: Quality control in manufacturing using machine learning techniques: a review. Int. J. Mech. Prod. Eng. Res. Dev. (2019)
14. Krishnan, R., Kumar, K.: Machine learning for production process optimization: a review. IEEE Trans. Semicond. Manuf. (2020)
15. Rangaiah, G.P., Srinivasan, R.: Optimization in Chemical Engineering. Wiley, Hoboken (2014)
16. Edgar, T.F., Himmelblau, D.M., Lasdon, L.S.: Optimization of Chemical Processes. McGraw Hill Education (2019)
17. Bonilla, L.F., Grossmann, I.E.: Handbook of Optimization in the Chemical Industry. Springer, Heidelberg (2019)
18. Sundaramoorthy, R., Saravanan, S.: Role of machine learning and artificial intelligence in chemical engineering. Artificial Intelligence and Machine Learning in Industry 4.0, pp. 263–285 (2020)
19. Mohan, S., Srinivasan, R.: Applications of machine learning in chemical engineering. Chem. Eng. Sci. **214**, 115462 (2020)
20. Mustapa, R.F., et al.: Educational building's energy consumption independent variables analysis using linear regression model: a comparative study. In: 2023 IEEE 3rd International Conference in Power Engineering Applications (ICPEA), Putrajaya, Malaysia, pp. 202–207. IEEE (2023)
21. Sidabutar, M.M., Firmansyah, G.: Comparison of linear regression, neural net, and arima methods for sales prediction of instrumentation and control products in PT. Sarana instrument. J. Res. Soc. Sci. Econ. Manag. **2**(08), 1694–1705 (2023)
22. Han, B., Zhang, S., Qin, L., Wang, X., Liu, Y., Li, Z.: Comparison of support vector machine, Gaussian process regression and decision tree models for energy consumption prediction of campus buildings. In: 8th International Conference on Hydraulic and Civil Engineering: Deep Space Intelligent Development and Utilization Forum (ICHCE), Xi'an, China, pp. 689–693 (2022)
23. Pallavi, M., Valsan, A.S., Thoufi, K.U.: Toxicity prediction in peptides and proteins using random forest, decision tree and logistic regression. In: International Conference on Futuristic Technologies (INCOFT), Belgaum, India, pp. 1–6 (2022)

24. Lahiri, S.K., Khalfe, N.: Process modeling and optimization of industrial ethylene oxide reactor by integrating support vector regression and genetic algorithm. Can. J. Chem. Eng. **87**, 118–128 (2009)
25. Huang, B.M.: Surrogate modelling for process simulation and optimisation. Master thesis, Department of Chemical Engineering and Biotechnology, University of Cambridge, 14 May 2021

Granular Traceability Between Requirements and Test Cases for Safety-Critical Software Systems

Mounia Elqortobi[1(✉)], Amine Rahj[1], and Jamal Bentahar[1,2]

[1] Concordia University, CIISE, Montreal, Canada
melqortobi@gmail.com, Jamal.bentahar@concordia.ca
[2] Khalifa University, EECS, Abu Dhabi, UAE

Abstract. Traceability is mandatory in developing safety-critical systems as pre-scribed by safety guidelines, such as DO-178C, and it is vital for avionics indus-tries. Testing is mandatory for requirement validation to ensure the safety and quality of a software product. Requirement traceability all along the development cycle is essential. Requirements' traceability and test generation fields have been studied extensively. This paper presents a granular traceability approach between low level requirements (LLRs) and test cases that is supported by a model-based test case generation. From LLR specifications we use model-to-model transfor-mation to obtain an extended finite state machine (EFSM) and its corresponding control flow graph (CFG) and data flow graphs (DFGs) that can support various granularity levels of traceability. The uniqueness of the proposed traceability app-roach is the creation of traceability elements at finer granularity during test case generation that satisfies MC/DC and Du path coverage criteria, and their retrieval for coverage analysis. The granularity level reached in this work corresponds to decision nodes, edges, predicates, and variables that are located on their source artifacts (CFG, DFG, EFSM). Several traceability techniques are used such as IDs and Links to create and retrieve traceability elements, coverage elements on mod-els, transformation records, and artifacts that ensure both the forward traceability of requirements by construction and backward traceability using graph exploration techniques.

Keywords: Requirement Traceability · Requirement Management · Forward Traceability · Backward Traceability · Test Case Generation · Test Case Traceability · Model-Based Traceability

1 Introduction

Despite considerable research efforts, requirement traceability remains a challenging problem in avionics software systems development. Requirements' coverage is required and conformity to the RTCA DO-178C standard [1] is mandatory. Avionics software must be certified before its integration into an airplane system. The certification process requires the creation of certification artifacts and their validation. All certification arti-facts are produced during the development life cycle. Testing is mandatory and should

M. Younas et al. (Eds.): MobiWIS 2023, LNCS 13977, pp. 202–220, 2023.
https://doi.org/10.1007/978-3-031-39764-6_14

satisfy the Modified Condition and Decision Coverage criterion (MC/DC). There is a need for bidirectional traceability between requirements' levels and test cases. Up to now, the development of avionics systems has relied on human intervention, which explains its high development cost. Engineers develop system specifications, extract high-level requirements (HLRs), refine them into LLRs, and then design, implement, and develop tests. According to the DO178C standard, the use of tools that support automation of the development process requires qualification before their integration and use within the development cycle. Avionics industries are investigating model-based development as a viable way of developing their systems, enhancing their safety and quality, and reducing their costs.

In this work, we present a test case generation process that supports requirements' traceability and describe a granular requirements' traceability approach that extends traceability between system specification and high-level requirements (HLRs), HLRs and low-level requirements (LLRs), and LLRs and test cases by creating the necessary traceability elements on an Extended Finite State Machine (EFSM) model and its corresponding data flow graph (DFG), and control flow graph CFG) during test cases generation. The test case generation technique must satisfy the MC/DC criterion that is mandated by the RTC DO178C [1]. This approach offers forward traceability by construction and supports backward traceability using graph exploration algorithms to collect traceability elements and artifacts. Traceability elements and artifacts are created using identification, links (ID), coverage elements, graph labeling techniques, complex data structure, repository, and databases.

This research work is part of an industrial project entitled CRIAQ/NSERC/ CMC & CS Canada AVIO 604 "Specification and Verification of Design Models for Certifiable Avionics Software". It addresses model-based development, model-based testing, and verification techniques for avionics software systems certification.

Next, we present the state of the art, describe the requirement traceability approach and how it is supported by our proposed test case generation with constraints solving.

2 Requirement Traceability State of the Art

Researchers have extensively studied requirement traceability [2–15]. Standardization organizations have established satisfiability criteria in several application domains. IEEE standard 830–1984 [2] states that: "A software requirements specification is traceable if (i) the origin of each of its requirements is clear and if (ii) it facilitates the referencing of each requirement in future development or enhancement documentation.". Gotel and Finkelstein [3, 4] express the concept in a more complete way: "Requirements traceability refers to the ability to describe and follow the life of a requirement, in both a forwards and backwards direction (i.e., from its origins, through its development and specification, to its subsequent deployment and use, and through all periods of on-going refinement and iteration in any of these phases.)". Francisco A. C. Pinheiro [5] wrote "Requirements traceability refers to the ability to define, capture, and follow the traces left by requirements on other elements of the software development environment and the traces left by those elements on requirements.".

Requirements traceability has been extensively studied and it is an established research domain The focus on requirements traceability has been primarily on the first part of the development cycle: requirements engineering that covers requirements' derivation from natural languages and semi-formal specification languages. The development of requirements engineering automation relies on meta models and models to specify traceability artifacts for certification. High-level languages such as UML [16, 17], SysML [18], and AADL [19] can be used for automatic model extraction if their compilers and interpreters are qualified.

Tools have been developed for the first part of the development cycle; surveys of existing tools can be found in [20, 21]. Some papers address traceability between requirements and use cases [10, 12–14, 23]. The existing techniques are either manual, such as requirements matrices, or based on specification languages transformation [11, 12, 21, 22]. To the best of our knowledge, there is no technique that offers low-level granularity to support bidirectional traceability and coverage assessment on models' feature elements.

Model-based testing has been the subject of extensive research, as shown in these surveys [24–26]. Substantial work has been done on generating test cases that satisfy the MC/DC criterion [27–31]. However, traceability related to the last part of the safety-critical software development process that contains test derivation to validate implementation codes and to assess the backward requirements traceability chain from test cases to requirements has received much less attention. The creation of traceability elements and certification artifacts to assess requirements' coverage at low-level granularity is not yet well studied. While test generation methods exist, they do not include the creation of traceability elements and coverage data that support bidirectional requirements traceability and the retrieval of traceability data.

Our approach to requirements traceability is focused on traceability artifact creation and retrieval at a low level of granularity. The granularity addressed is related to coverage elements for test case generation that handle test coverage criteria such as MC/DC, which is mandatory to fulfill the RTCA DO178C standard. The traceability relationship between HLRs, LLRs and test cases must be established and validated. The type of relations that exist between those artifacts can be a bijection, one too many or many too many. The bijection relation is the easiest, but it is not the most common relation. The other relations require handling lists of source artifacts and lists of target artifacts. Often, a qualification is given to a relation such as dependency relations between requirements. The extension of traceability relation to coverage elements during the creation of traceability data must support and propagate all modes of traceability and all types of relations.

The next subsection presents requirements traceability as described within the RTCA 178C [1], the requirements traceability approach and how it is supported by our test case generation with constraint solving.

2.1 Avionics Standards RTCA DO-178 B and C

The avionics industry has developed a set of standards to prevent catastrophic events related to their systems. The RTCA DO-178B standard provides guidance for producing software for airborne systems that perform their function with a level of confidence in safety that complies with airworthiness requirements [1, 2]. Indeed, the RTCA DO-178B defines objectives for software life cycle processes, activities, and data with a strong emphasis on verifying the satisfaction of High- and Low-Level Requirements (HLRs,

LLRs). Moreover, the complexity of airborne software has dramatically increased to the point where current validation techniques based only on testing are not sufficient [2, 3]. The increasing technical issues have led the avionics industry to introduce alternative means of validation and verification within a revised version, the DO-178C, and its supplements DO-331, DO-332 and DO-333 [1], the latter of which defines a formal method as "a formal model combined with a formal analysis.". The standards' requirements are listed below:

1. The executable code complies with the high-level requirements (HLRs).
2. The executable code complies with the low-level requirements (LLRs).
3. Test coverage of the high-level requirements (HLRs) is achieved.
4. Test coverage of the specifications (low-level requirements (LLRs)) is achieved.
5. Test coverage of the executable code is achieved.

Our proposed approach fits within the fourth item.

The defined Software Level by ARP4754, also known as the Item Development Assurance Levels (IDALs), are mentioned in the RTCA DO-178C [1] and are from a safety assessment process and hazard analysis that examines the effects of a failure condition in the system. The failure conditions are categorized by their effects on the aircraft, crew, and passengers and are listed below.

Catastrophic - Failure may cause deaths, usually with loss of the airplane.

Hazardous - Failure has a large negative impact on safety, performance, or reduces the ability of the crew to operate the aircraft due to physical distress or a higher workload or causes serious or fatal injuries among the passengers.

Major - Failure significantly reduces the safety margin or significantly increases crew workload. May result in passenger discomfort (or even minor injuries).

Minor - Failure slightly reduces the safety margin or slightly increases crew workload. Examples might include causing passenger inconvenience or a routine flight plan change.

No Effect - Failure has no impact on safety, aircraft operation, or crew workload.

Figure 1 illustrates the required tracing between certification artifacts, as noted in the RTCA DO-178C standard. Red-colored traces are required only for Level A, purple-colored traces are required for Levels A, B, and C, and green-colored traces are for Levels A, B, C, and D. Our work on test case generation and requirements is related to level A.

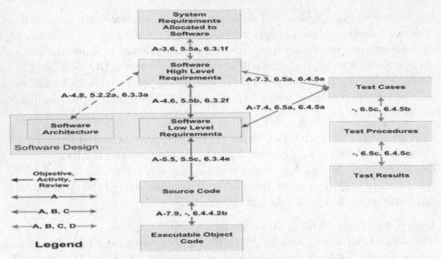

Fig. 1. RTCA Do-178C required traceability [1].

3 Proposed Traceability Approach

To collect traceability artifacts for software certification, the requirements traceability approach should have the following actions: trace element definition, identification, creation/recording, maintenance, retrieval, and utilization.

The proposed requirements traceability approach supports traceability links from the origin artifacts to requirement specification given as a UML profile document that represents the High-level Requirements or the target artifact. Direct transformation of specification languages can be used, down to Low level requirements (LLRs) from which we perform model extraction to obtain an EFSM behavior model. We use model-to-model transformation to obtain control flow graph (CFG) and data flow graphs (DFG) from an EFSM model. We determine coverage elements using graph features, use·labeling to create traceability elements, and we produce records through the generation of test cases (paths) for future use.

In this work, the focus is on the last leg of the requirements traceability chain. We address the low granularity of requirements traceability from HLRs as the origin artifact forwards to test cases as the target artifact, and backwards from the target to the source. We create traceability elements using labels, ID, links, locations on graphs, the recording and storage of traceability artifacts of requirements and test cases during their generation. We achieve forward traceability from LLRs to test cases by construction. However, backward traceability requires the use of graphic exploration algorithms to collect traceability artifacts and validate the traceability relationship with the test cases and LLRs. The other usage of traceability collection is coverage assessment of the MC/DC criterion. Figure 2 below depicts the entire traceability approach.

More specifically, the proposed traceability approach starts with high-level require-ments (HLRs) that are specified with UML. Abstract models such as EFSMs and CEF-SMs are extracted from UML specifications. They are models for low-level requirements (LLR) that can be used for automatic test case generation. In this work, we assume that

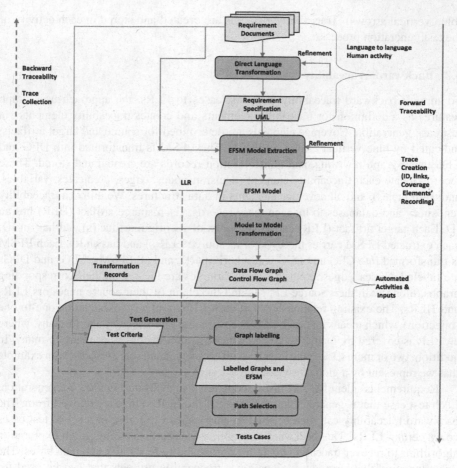

Fig. 2. Traceability methodology overview.

HLRs and LLRs have been specified and verified with industrial partners and research collaborators. The aim is to answer the traceability question using requirements specified as an EFSM and traceability elements defined to ensure bidirectional requirements traceability between LLRs and test cases.

Next, we present how forward and backward traceability are viewed in this approach.

3.1 Forward Traceability

In this approach, forward traceability from LLRs to their related test cases is obtained by construction. Here, test-case generation is guided by test coverage criterion, utilizing MC/DC criterion coverage and du path criteria and selecting paths using constraints-solving and exploration algorithms. MC/DC requirements are satisfied and validated during test case generation such that all the MC/DC requirements are met by construction. Figure 2 shows the forward traceability downstream in the test case generation approach (blue vertical arrows). Traceability elements are created and stored in each activity of the test generation process.

3.2 Backward Traceability

To support backward traceability from test cases to LLRs, the approach uses graph features as a definition for traceability elements and creates traceability elements via test case generation. Coverage elements are determined for source and target artifacts, indicated by blue vertical arrows on Fig. 2. The EFSM is transformed into DFG and CFG using graph rewriting, and transformation records are created and stored. These records locate each traceability element (decision nodes, edges, predicates, variables, and truth tables), and all coverage elements in data structures. We utilize a traceability repository and databases to manage these records. Each source artifact (HLR) has an ID. Each target artifact (LLR) carries the links of its origin artifact(s) and has an ID; each extracted EFSM carries the ID(s) of its source LLR(s) and has an ID. Each EFSM is transformed into CFG and DFG that inherit its ID, and all EFSMs, CFGs and DFGs are labeled. Nodes, edges, predicates, and variables are located on their corresponding graphs, along with their source EFSMs and the chain of their source ancestors LLRs and HLRs. The existing relationships between LLRs and test cases can be one-to one (bijection), which means that each LLR is covered by one test case, one-to-many, where an LLR is covered by many test cases (which is often the case), or many-to-many. In addition, two or more LLRs may interact with each other and share test cases, an example that we represent by a global test case.

Requirements' identifiers are also used to retrieve paths during test case generation. Each test case that is generated has the ID(s) of the LLR(s) they are derived from. The backward traceability can then be used to check that a test case or a set of test cases cover certain LLRs. This backward traceability can be done using graph exploration algorithms to recover traceability data from traceability repository and data bases. The documentation that is produced constitutes traceability artifacts that can be used for avionics software certification purposes.

In the following section we present an overview of our test case generation approach that offers traceability elements creation, forward traceability by construction and is complemented with backward traceability. Our approach offers an automatic and detailed traceability of coverage elements that distinguishes it from existing works.

4 Test Case Generation Methodology Overview

The proposed traceability approach is supported by model-based test case generation. It starts with the generation of local test cases based on an EFSM specification representing an LLR.

The main coverage criteria are the MC/DC (modified condition/decision coverage) and du-path. We assume that a truth table associated with each decision is given as an input and will be used for test case generation. To satisfy the MC/DC criterion in the code we need to satisfy the following four requirements:

1. Every decision in the program must be tested for all possible outcomes at least once;

2. Every condition in a decision within the program must be tested for all possible outcomes at least once;

3. Every condition in a decision must be shown to independently affect that decision's outcome. This requirement ensures that the effect of each condition is tested relative to the other conditions; and

4. Every exit and entry point in the program (or model) should be invoked at least once.

In this approach, the satisfaction of the MC/DC criterion applies to a model that is assumed to be close to the implementation abstract model, and the predicates are the same as those used in the implementation. In addition, the decisions are decomposed to a simple form.

The proposed traceability approach is supported by model-based test case generation. It starts with the generation of local test cases based on an EFSM specification representing LLRs. The test case generation uses graph rewriting as a means for model-to-model transformation to obtain a Data Flow Graph (DFG) and a control flow graph (CFG) of the EFSM. In the presence of interacting LLRs, we assume that each LLR is modeled as an EFSM, and that their interactions are modeled by the composition of EFSMs (CEFSM), from which we extract a communication graph that shows their relationships. The communication graph guides the generation of global test cases to reflect the interaction between LLRs. If a test case contains a node that belongs to a communication graph, it means that 2 LLRs are in a relationship. In our case, we use a test case generation algorithm that generates test cases that cover LLRs and satisfies the MC/DC that is mandatory by RTCA 178C. The details of test case generation can be found in [29–31].

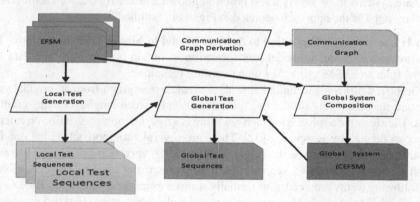

Fig. 3. Overall test case generation based on EFSMs [7–9].

Figure 3 shows a high-level overview of the test case generation methodology. The idea is to build on our previous test case generation technique [7–10] in which we defined traceability elements at a low level, and to which we add traceability elements creation, transformation records, identification, links, retrieval, and utilization for traceability analysis. The maintenance for this level of granularity means that the process must be completely re-done if the request change modifies the EFSM specification.

4.1 Traceability Elements' Creation

Traceability between requirements and test cases requires traceability elements' creation during the test case generation process. Traceability elements' creation is designed with Forward Traceability from LLRs to test cases and should show the coverage of LLRs by construction. Furthermore, the creation of traceability elements should also create traceability records to explore the labeled graphs and collect traceability elements for assessing Backward Traceability. The question is to determine which traceability elements are needed for the traceability creation processes. In our case, first of all, we need all the LLRs' IDs that propagate links to their corresponding HLRs, and all the chain of ancestors' artifacts. Next, we need all the models' traceability features (edges, nodes, predicates, and variables), and the coverage elements per type of graph (CFG, DFG) that are obtained by the model-to-model transformation and labeling processes. During the test generation process additional traceability elements are recorded to link each model's traceability elements to their LLRs, such as executable and non-executable paths.

To show traceability elements' creation within the process of test case generation, we need to clearly describe the test case generation process and thereby reveal the creation operations and what we obtain from the process. Figure 4 shows where traceability elements are created (in green).

4.2 Test Generation Process

For conciseness and for space concerns, the following is only an overview of the methodology, for more detail please refer to [29–31]. A test suite that is generated for avionics software systems must satisfy a test criterion known as the MC/DC for each decision. Five key steps of the approach depicted in Fig. 4 are outlined below.

Step 1: Use of Graph Rewriting to Achieve Model to Model Transformation. This is an automatic model-to-model transformation to obtain both control and data flow graphs from an EFSM using the graph rewriting technique.

Graph rewriting is a technique that helps create a new graph from an original graph using an algorithm. It is similar to a transformation between languages using grammar rules. The algebraic approach to graph rewriting is a rigorous approach based on category theory as defined by Rosenberg [32]. There are several sub-approaches; the one used in our approach is known as the single-pushout (SPO) approach [33]. In the literature, graph grammar is used as a synonym for a graph rewriting system. The definitions of the following terms are needed to formally transform models: Grammar, Rule Graph, State Graph, Match, Rule Morphism, Rules and Rule Application. Figure 5 provides an overview of the graph rewriting approach.

In our case, the grammar has been defined for the source and target models, as given in Table 1. For more details, please refer to our work in [29, 30] and Amine Rahj's thesis [31].

In this model transformation, both the source and target models are identified and linked to their source artifacts. During the process, traceability elements at the level of granularity of the graph, including those related to nodes, edges, predicates, and

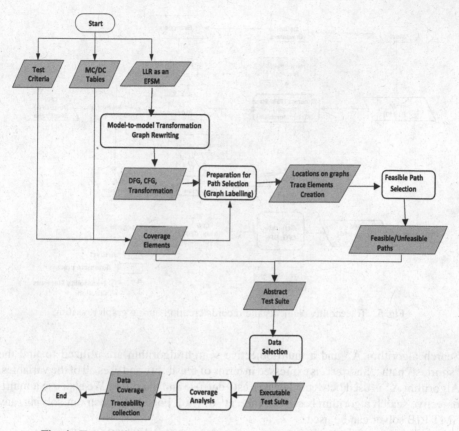

Fig. 4. Traceability elements creation and collection in EFSM test generation

variables, are identified and then records are created and stored in the database, as depicted in Figs. 4 and 5.

Step 2: Preparation for the Path. Figure 6 presents a flowchart of the graph labelling process. There are four types of information we need to locate on the graphs' elements. The MC/DC Tables (or Decisions) are affected by the graph element, the Rows, the Conditions, and the values of the Conditions. Thus, the final label depends upon each graph element. We start by labelling the decision points from the CFG with the MC/DC tables' IDs, as each MC/DC table is associated with one Decision (and thus with one predicate). Then for each table, we label the outgoing branches from the decision points with the row ID that matches the Decision outcome of that row. We also label the predicate edges from the DFG by means of transformation records. And finally, for each condition we label the d-use for all variables affecting that Condition on the DFG.

Step 3: Path Selection. The aim of this step is to select paths that have the potential to produce executable test cases and decide on their feasibility [34]. In Tool, we use jSMTLIB for parsing SMTLIB expressions and use the solvers with a test generation tool [35]. The following brief description shows the process of feasible path selection.

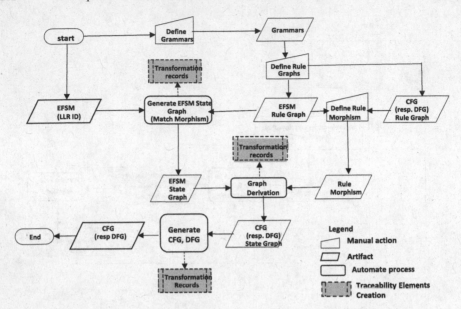

Fig. 5. Traceability elements and records creation during graph rewriting

Search algorithm A* and a multi-objective search algorithm are utilized to find the "shortest" path. "Shortest" is expressed in terms of feasibility and uses all of the variables. Algorithm A* is used between the "nearest" def-use and the p-use. We also use a multi-objective search algorithm based on Yano et Al. [36]. For SMT-constraint solving, any SMT-LIB solver can be used.

For this step, the following data is required: the Labelled DFG, the Transformation records, Heuristics, Temporal Logic, and Theory. A modification of the algorithm given in Amine Rahj's thesis [31] for traceability element creation is given below.

Precondition: MC/DC tables, labeled DFG
Labels applied during the previous steps
<T, R, C, Value of C> for def-uses
<T, R, P, Value of P> for p-uses
Where:
T: table
R: Row of MC/DC table
C: Condition
P: Predicate/ decision
For each table T in the set of MC/DC table
   For each (Row) R in T
      Find p-use in labeled <T, R, P, Value of P> in labeled DGF
        For each C in R find def-use with label <T, R, C, value of C>

Link p-use(C) and min-def-use(C)* with a def-clear-path**

Table 1. Grammars used in MC/DC-TGT

Grammar	Nodes/Arcs	Type	Attributes	Members	Member Type
EFSM	Nodes	State	Yes	Name	String
				ID	Integer
	Arcs	Transition	Yes	Input	SMTLib Expression expression
				Predicate	SMTLib Expression
				Computation Bloc	SMTLib Expression
Control Flow Graph	Nodes	Merge Point	Yes	ID	Integer
		Input Point	Yes	Input List	Enumeration
		Decision Point	Yes	Predicate	SMTlib Expression
		Computation Bloc	Yes	Computations	SMTlib Expression
	Arcs	Simple Edge	No	N/A	N/A
		Boolean Edge	Yes	Decision Value	Boolean
		Input Edge	Yes	Decision Value	Input Value
Data Flow Graph	Nodes	Computation Bloc	Yes	Computations	SMTlib Expression
	Arcs	Simple Edge	No	N/A	N/A
		Predicated Edge	Yes	Decision Value	SMTlib
		Input Edge	Yes	Decision Value	Input Value

Add feasible preamble and post-amble to form a complete path, and Create traceability elements.

(*) min-def-use(C) in the nearest of def-uses of the variables involved in C in term of "Approximation Level".

(**) If there is a c-use w.r.t. that particular variable, we ignore it for the MC/DC approach.

The def-clear path is constructed using a standard A* algorithm with feasibility as heuristic: $H(t) = + 1$ if the transition is feasible, $H(t) = + 100$ if not.

Link the other def-use(C) with min-def-use(C) and Create traceability elements.

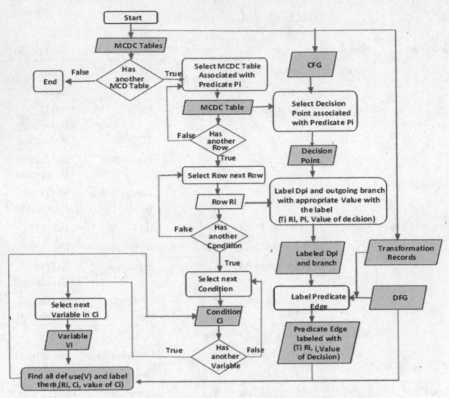

Fig. 6. Traceability elements creation during graph labeling

Algorithm 1: GenerateFeasiblePaths

Input: $labelled\_DFG, labelled\_CFG, MCDC\_Tables$
Output: $feasible\_paths, unfeasible\_paths$

$init(feasible\_paths, unfeasible\_paths)$
foreach $T_i \in MCDC\_Tables$ **do**
    foreach $p\_use_{labelled}(T_i, R_i, P_i, P_i.value) \in labelled\_DFG$ **do**
        $p\_use \leftarrow p\_use\_labelled(T_i, R_i, P_i, P_i.value)$
        foreach $Vertex_{labelled}(T_i, R_i, C_i, C_i.value) \in labelled\_DFG$ **do**
            $def\_use \leftarrow Vertex_{labelled}(T_i, R_i, C_i, C_i.value)$ **foreach**
            $varible \in C_i$ **do**
                $sub\_path \leftarrow def\_clear\_path(p_use, def\_use, variable)$
                $pathadd\_feasible\_preamble(subpath)$
                if $path.siFeasible()$ **then**
                    $feasible\_paths.add(path)$
                else
                    $unfeasible\_paths.add(path)$

All the obtained executable and nonexecutable paths are recorded and linked to their original artifacts.

Step 4: Data Selection. This step helps obtain feasible paths. For the sake of space, this step is not addressed here; it is described in [37].

Step 5: Coverage Analysis. Coverage analysis is important in test case generation and in backward traceability. Examples of its use include: (1) Requirements coverage validation from a given test case that was derived manually, to determine the covered LLRs' (2) trace coverage analysis obtained from a run of test cases on an implementation, and (3) trace failure analysis/diagnostics as shown in Fig. 7.

Automatic Test Results Analysis. Testing activity is a detection mechanism. To detect faults, the generated test cases (inputs) are applied to a system under test, and the obtained test results are analyzed to determine if the system being tested passes or fails. Test results analysis requires comparing the outputs of the system implementation, known as the actual outputs, and the expected outputs in order to detect faults. The result of test results analysis is called a verdict which falls within the set of (pass, fail, or inconclusive). The verdict is assigned by a judge or an oracle [38], which is often a human, that extracts the expected outputs from software artifacts and compares them with the actual outputs. Automatic oracles have some challenges, known as test oracle problems [38, 39]. The major problem behind the design and development of an oracle is related to the issues of controllability and observability in black-box testing, which are in turn related to the degree of software testability.

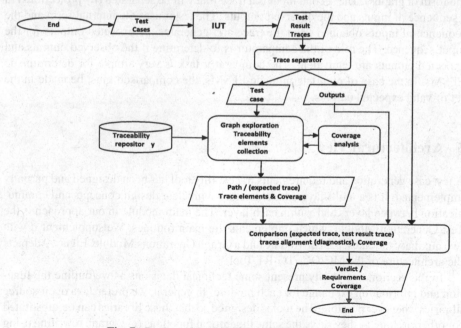

Fig. 7. Backward traceability and coverage analysis

The assumptions for this work are that the EFSM specification exists, and it is deterministic. It will be used to generate a specific test case from the inputs obtained from the trace. The inputs are given to the tester that will find the corresponding expected outputs and its associated verdict. The comparison between the expected and observed outputs can then be carried out as depicted in Figs. 7 and 8. The trace is a test result. It can also be obtained during the normal operation of a system.

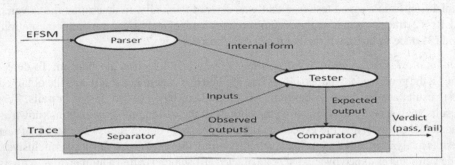

Fig. 8. Simple form of Test Results Analyzer

In this approach, the test results analyzer takes two inputs and delivers an output representing the verdict (pass or fail). The first input is an EFSM specification, which is parsed to obtain an internal form suitable for the test case generator (in our case it is in the form of graphs). The second input is a trace that will be separated (by projections) in a sequence of inputs and the observed outputs. The tester uses the internal form and the sequence of inputs obtained from the trace and generates the expected outputs for the input sequence. The role of the comparator is to determine if the observed outputs and expected outputs are equivalent. The comparator task is very simple for deterministic EFSMs. In the case of non-deterministic EFSMs, the comparison must be made in the set of valid expected outputs.

5   Architectural View

A test case generation and requirements traceability tool has been designed and partially implemented. It is a multi-layered architecture with clear design concepts and communication between layers and within each layer. The main module in our approach is the Test Generation Module, which implements the main routines. We supplement it with two auxiliary modules: a Data Module and a Graph Operations Module. Figure 9 depicts the architecture of the MC/DC -TG-RT Tool.

In this section, we briefly present some technical decisions as we outline the function and information exchange for each module. In general, we prefer Java open-source libraries whenever possible. The tool is designed so that those libraries can be substituted for others as long as they serve the same theoretical functions (e.g. graph rewriting using attributed grammar). The Graph Operations module is dedicated to frequently used, general-purposed graph operations. Its goal is to ensure the maintainability and reconfigurability of algorithms. The data module retrieves user inputs, constructs, manages data, and provides proxies to external libraries involved in creating and transforming the different graphs. Data Module is open to the rest of the MC/DC-TG-RT Tool in read-only mode.

The complexity of the data structures and algorithms involved in this approach reinforces the need to keep a detailed record of the results of the rule applications from the graph rewriting. These results are held in transformation records. Aside from being mandatory for V&V, they also simplify Steps 2 to 5. Recording the direct references to graph morphism images will make it possible to bypass search algorithms using object properties.

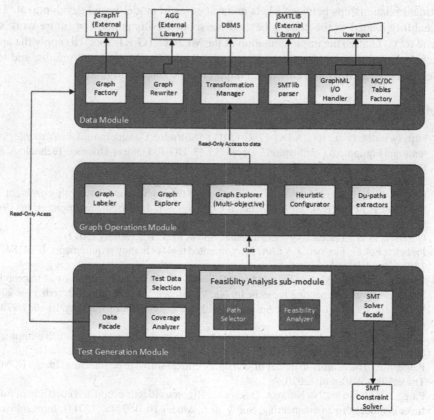

Fig. 9. MC/DC -TG-RT Tool architecture [29–31].

6 Conclusion and Future Work

In this paper, we presented a test case generation process that supports bidirectional traceability between low-level requirements and test cases. The proposed approach extends requirements traceability to a very low level of granularity that remains challenging in the field due to the amount of traceability elements to identify, create, store, and recover for analysis purposes. The coverage elements are defined on an extended finite state machine model and its corresponding graphs - obtained by model-to-model transformation using graph rewiring, their nodes, edges, predicates, and variables that may influence path execution. The creation of traceability elements is carried out during test case generation that should satisfy the MC/DC criterion. Forward requirements traceability is obtained by construction. As noted before, meeting the MC/DC criterion is mandatory in avionics industries, as specified in RTCDO178C. The test case generation method uses the constraints satisfaction technique as well as graph exploration algorithms to retrieve traceability elements during backward traceability or trace analysis for the purpose of post-failure diagnostics. To the best of our knowledge, our contribution represents the first technique that reaches this level of granularity in establishing traceability bidirectional relationships between LLRs and test cases in model-based development. The traceability related to the code is beyond the scope of this paper. For future work we intend to: (i) finalize the implementation of the MC/DC-TG-RT Tool' (ii) apply the approach to a sizable example with a chain of HLRs, LLRs, Models and graphs, and test cases' and (iii) address non-functional requirements' traceability.

References

1. http://www.rtca.org. RTCA/DO-178C (2011) "Software Considerations in Airborne Systems and Equipment Certification", December 13, DO-332 Object-Oriented Technology and Related Techniques Supplement to DO-178C and DO-278A, DO-331
2. IEEE Computer Society. ANSI/IEEE Standard 830-1984, 1984
3. Gotel, O.C.Z., Finkelstein, A.C.W.: An analysis of the requirements traceability problem. In: Proceedings of ICRE94, 1st International Conference on Requirements Engineering. 1994; Colorado Springs, Co; IEEE CS Press (1994)
4. Gotel, O., et al.: Traceability fundamentals. Softw. Syst. Traceability (2012)
5. Pinheiro, F.A.C., Goguen, J.A.: An object-oriented tool for tracing requirements. IEEE Softw. 13(2), 52–64 (1996)
6. Santiago, I., Vara, J.M., de Castro, M.V., Marcos, E.: Towards the effective use of traceability in model-driven engineering projects. In: Ng, W., Storey, V.C., Trujillo, J.C. (eds.) ER 2013. LNCS, vol. 8217, pp. 429–437. Springer, Heidelberg (2013). https://doi.org/10.1007/978-3-642-41924-9_35
7. Schwarz, H., Ebert, J., Winter, A.: Graph-based traceability: a comprehensive approach. Softw. Syst. Model. Springer (2010)
8. Paige, R.F.: Traceability in model-driven safety critical software engineering. In: 6th ECMFA Traceability Workshop (2010)
9. Paige, R.F., Drivalos, N., Kolovos, D.S., et al.: Rigorous identification and encoding of tracelinks in model-driven engineering. Softw. Syst. Model 10, 469–487 (2011). https://doi.org/10.1007/s10270-010-0158-8
10. Matthias, R., Hubner, M.: Traceability-driven model refinement for test case generation, engineering of computer-based systems. In: 2005. ECBS'05. 12th IEEE International Conference and Workshops on the. IEEE (2005)
11. Ramesh, B., Jarke, M.: Toward reference models for requirements traceability. IEEE Trans. Softw. Eng. 27(1), 58–93 (2011)
12. Krzysztof, W., Ahlberg, L., Persson, J.: On the delicate balance between RE and testing: experiences from a large company, requirements engineering and testing (RET). In: 2014 IEEE 1st International Workshop on. IEEE (2014)

13. Noack, T., Helke, S., Karbe, T.: Reuse-based test traceability: automatic linking of test cases and reusing requirements. Int. J. Adv. Softw. **7**(3/4) (2014)

14. Unterkalmsteiner, M., Feldt, R., Gorschek, T.: A taxonomy for requirements engineering and software test alignment. ACM Trans. Softw. Eng. Methodol. (TOSEM) **23**(2), 16 (2014)

15. Mustafa, N., Labiche, Y.: The need for traceability in heterogeneous systems: a systematic literature review. IEEE COMPSAC **1**(2017), 305–310 (2017)

16. Unified Modeling Language User Guide, The (2 ed.). Addison-Wesley. 2005. p. 496. ISBN 0321267974. , See the sample content, look for history

17. UML. Omg.org. Accessed 10 June 2023

18. SysML. omg.org. Accessed 10 June 2023

19. Architecture Analysis and Design Language, Software Engineering Institute, Carnegie-Mellon University, Pittsburgh, Pennsylvania, USA. Archived 2013-11-01 at the Wayback Machine

20. Tufail, H., Masood, M.F., Zeb, B., Azam, F., Anwar, M.W.: A systematic review of requirement traceability techniques and tools. In: 2017 2nd International Conference on System Reliability and Safety (ICSRS) (2017)

21. Kesserwan, N., Dssouli, R., Bentahar, J., Stepien, B., Labrèche, P.: From use case maps to executable test procedures: a scenario-based approach. Softw. Syst. Model. **18**(2), 1543–1570 (2017). https://doi.org/10.1007/s10270-017-0620-y

22. Kesserwan1, N., Al-Jaroodi, J.: Model-driven framework for requirement traceability. (IJACSA) Int. J. Adv. Comput. Sci. Appl. **12**(2) (2021)

23. Mustafa, N., Labiche, Y., Towey, D.: Traceability in systems engineering: an avionics case study. In: 2018 IEEE 42nd Annual Computer Software and Applications Conference (COMPSAC), Tokyo, Japan, pp. 818–823 (2018). https://doi.org/10.1109/COMPSAC.2018.10345

24. Dssouli, R., Saleh, K., Aboulhamid, E.M., En-Nouaary, A., Bourhfir, C.: Test development for communication protocols towards automation. Comput. Netw. **31**(17), 1835–1872 (1999)

25. Dssouli, R., Khoumsi, A., Elqortobi, M., Bentahar, J.: Testing the control-flow, data-flow and time aspects of communication systems, a survey. In: Book Chapter in Advances in Testing Communication Systems, Atif Memon, Ed. 1, vol. 17, pp. 95–155. Elsevier (2017). ISBN 978-0-12-812228-0

26. Yang, R., Chen, Z., Zhang, Z., Xu, B.: EFSM-based test case generation: sequence, data, and oracle. Int. J. Softw. Eng. Knowl. Eng. **25**(4), 633–667 (2015). (© World Scientific)

27. Wu, J., Yan, J., Zhang, J.: Automatic test data generation for unit testing to achieve MC/DC criterion. In: Proceedings of the IEEE Eighth International Conference on Software Security and Reliability (SERE), pp. 118–126, San Francisco, USA, June 2014

28. Elqortobi, M., El-Khouly, W., Rahj, A., Bentahar, J., Dssouli, R.: Verification and testing of safety-critical airborne systems: a model-based methodology. Comput. Sci. Inf. Syst. **17**(1), 271–292 (2020)

29. El Qortobi, M., Rahj, A., Bentahar, J., Dssouli, R.: Test generation tool for modified condition/decision coverage: model based Testing. In: SITA 2020: 38:1–38:6, Proceedings of ACM 2020 (2020). ISBN 978-1-4503-7733-1

30. Rahj, A., Elqortobi, M., Bentahar, J., Dssouli, R.: Test generation tool design for modified condition/decision coverage: model based approach. Int. J. Comput. Sci. Appl. Technomath. Res. Found. **18**(1), 1–25 (2021)

31. Rahj, A.: EFSM-based Test Suite Generation for MC/DC Compliant Systems: Tool Design, Master of Applied Science Thesis, Concordia University (2023)

32. Rozenberg, G.: Handbook of Graph Grammars and Computing by Graph Transformations, vol. 1–3. World Scientific Publishing (1997). ISBN 9810228848

33. Ehrig, H., et al.: Chapter 4. Algebraic approaches to graph transformation. Part II: single pushout approach and comparison with double pushout approach. In: Rozenberg, G. (ed.). Handbook of Graph Grammars and Computing by Graph Transformation. World Scientific, pp. 247–312. CiteSeerX (1997). 10.1.1.72.1644. ISBN 978-981-238-472-0

34. Kalaji, A.S., Hierons, R.M., Swift, S.: Generating feasible transition paths for testing from an extended finite state machine (EFSM). In: International Conference on Software Testing Verification and Validation, ICST, pp. 230–239 (2009)

35. Cok, D.R.: jSMTLIB: tutorial, validation and adapter tools for SMT-LIBv2. In: Bobaru, M., Havelund, K., Holzmann, G.J., Joshi, R. (eds.) NASA Formal Methods. NFM 2011. LNCS, vol. 6617, pp. 480–486. Springer, Berlin, Heidelberg (2011). https://doi.org/10.1007/978-3-642-20398-5_36

36. Yano, T., Martins, E., de Sousa, F.L.: MOST: a multi-objective search-based testing from EFSM. In: Proceedings of the 4th International Conference on Software Testing, Verification and Validation Workshops, IEEE Computer Society, Berlin, Germany, pp. 164–173 (2011)

37. Ting, S.: Automated coverage-driven test data generation using dynamic symbolic execution, Software Security and Reliability (SERE). In: 2014 Eighth International Conference on IEEE (2014)

38. Weyuker, E.J.: The oracle assumption of program testing. In: Proceedings of the 13th International Conference on System Sciences (ICSS), Honolulu, HI, pp. 44–49, January 1980

39. Barr, E.T., Harman, M., McMinn, P., Shahbaz, M., Yoo, S.: The oracle problem in software testing: a survey. IEEE Trans. Softw. Eng. **41**(5), 507–525 (2014). https://doi.org/10.1109/TSE.2014.2372785,November

Maximizing Signal to Interference Noise Ratio for Massive MIMO: A Stochastic Neurodynamic Approach

Siham Tassouli[✉] and Abdel Lisser

Université Paris Saclay, CNRS, CentraleSupelec, Laboratoire des Signaux
et Systèmes (L2S), 3, rue Joliot Curie, 91192 Gif sur Yvette Cedex, France
{siham.tassouli,abdel.lisser}@centralesupelec.fr

Abstract. In this paper, we consider the problem of maximizing the
worst user signal to interference noise ratio (SINR) for massive multiple input multiple output (MaMIMO). We reformulate the nonlinear
optimization model as a joint chance-constrained geometric program.
We derive then a deterministic equivalent for the obtained stochastic
problem. Based on the optimality conditions, we propose a neurodynamic approach for the optimization problem. We show that the proposal dynamical neural network is convergent and stable in the sense of
Lyapunov. Our numerical results indicate that our approach is robust
and outperforms a state-of-art convex approximation.

Keywords: Dynamical neural network · Geometric programming ·
Wireless networks · Joint chance constraints · Lyapunov Theory ·
Ordinary differential equations

1 Introduction

The Massive Multiple Input Multiple Output (MaMIMO) is an emerging technology for new communication systems and the Internet of Things (IoT). It is
based on the use of hundreds of antennas interfering with each other. It is one
of the candidate techniques for 5G and also a candidate to succeed 4G LTE and
LTE-A. The introduction of MaMIMO insured higher connectivity, the ability to
adapt to high density environments, reduced transmission latency for augmented
reality, energy efficiency meeting green communications guidelines and a better
quality of signal paths and security.

In recent years, MaMIMO resource allocation has been studied in several
works. Xuanhong et al. [1] investigate a joint resource allocation algorithm to
improve spectrum efficiency and throughput. Yin et al. [2] deal with the Mobility
Problem of Massive MIMO using Extended Prony's Method. Dikmen & Kulac [3]
examine power allocation algorithms for MIMO systems. Salah et al. [4] propose
an adaptive optimization technique focusing on maximizing Energy Efficiency
in adaptive massive MIMO networks.

M. Younas et al. (Eds.): MobiWIS 2023, LNCS 13977, pp. 221–234, 2023.
https://doi.org/10.1007/978-3-031-39764-6_15

In this paper, we propose a neurodynamic approach to solve a joint chance constrained nonlinear optimization model where the aim is to maximize the worst user SINR. Adasme et al. [5] propose a local search algorithm that allows obtaining feasible solutions for the problem of maximizing the worst user SINR for Massive MIMO. Mei & Zhang [6] derive a tractable lower bound of the average signal-to-interference-plus-noise ratio (SINR) at the receiver of each user, based on which two average-signal-to-average-interference-plus-noise ratio (ASAINR) balancing problems are formulated to maximize the minimum ASAINR among all users.

We reformulate our problem as a joint chance-constrained geometric optimization problem. Geometric programming was introduced by Duffin et al. [7] in 1967. Since then, geometric programming have been used to model and solve several optimization problems in several areas, i.e., aircraft design [8], communication systems [9], digital circuit optimization [10], information theory [11] ... . To solve optimization problems with joint chance constraints many works were conducted to give deterministic equivalents and study the optimality conditions. Cheng & Lisser propose a second-order cone programming approach for linear programs with joint probabilistic constraints. You et al. [12] use data-driven models to solve programs with joint chance constraints. Ono et al. [13] present a novel dynamic programming algorithm to approximate joint chance constraints.

The rest of the paper is organized as follows. In Sect. 2, we first give a brief description of the MaMIMO resource allocation problem we are studying. Then, we present a joint probabilistic geometric formulation of the problem of maximizing the worst user Signal to Interference Noise Ratio and we give the optimality conditions of the obtained problem. Based on the partial KKT system obtained in Sect. 2, we propose in Sect. 3 a neurodynamic approach to solve the initial problem. In Sect. 4, we conduct some numerical results in order to evaluate the performances of our approach.

2   Problem Formulation

We consider a single cell area, see Fig. 1, which is composed of a set of $\mathcal{U} = \{1, ..., K\}$ users. We assume that each user uses only one antenna to receive the data from the base station. The base station is equipped with T antennas. We aim to maximize the worst user SINR subject to some limits on the power assigned to each user. The SINR_i for user i can be expressed as follows [5].

$$\text{SINR}_i = \frac{p_i |g_i^H g_i|^2}{\sum_{j \in \mathcal{U}, j \neq i} p_j |g_i^H g_j|^2 + |\sigma_i|^2} \tag{1}$$

We formulate our optimization problem as follows

$$\max_{p \in \mathbb{R}_{++}^K} \min_{i \in \mathcal{U}} \frac{p_i |g_i^H g_i|^2}{\sum_{j \in \mathcal{U}, j \neq i} p_j |g_i^H g_j|^2 + |\sigma_i|^2}, \tag{2}$$

$$\text{s.t} \quad P_{min} \leq p_i \leq P_{max}, \forall i \in \mathcal{U}, \tag{3}$$

where p_i is the power to be assigned for each user $i \in \mathcal{U}$. $g_i \in \mathbb{C}^{T \times 1}$, $g_i^H \in \mathbb{C}^{1 \times T}$ and σ_i^2 are the beam domain channel vector associated to user $i \in \mathcal{U}$, its Hermitian transpose and Additive White Gaussian Noise (AWGN), respectively. We finally assume that the AWGN behaves according to an independent complex Gaussian distribution with zero mean and unit variance ($\sigma_i \sim \mathcal{CN}(0,1)$) while each entry in vectors g_i and g_i^H is a complex number that is assumed to behave as a quasi-static independent and identically distributed Rayleigh fading channel. P_{min} and P_{max} define the lower and the upper bounds for each power variable, respectively. Let $a_{ij} = |g_i^H g_j|^2 |g_i^H g_i|^{-2}$ and $b_i = |\sigma_i|^2 |g_i^H g_i|^{-2}$ and by introducing an additional variable w we rewrite (2)–(3) as

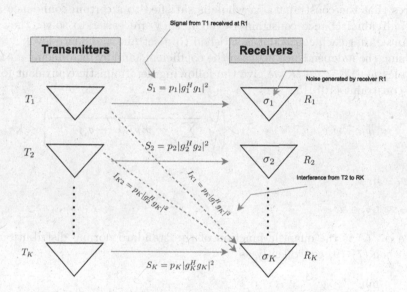

Fig. 1. Signal to Interference plus Noise Ratio, illustration.

$$\max_{p \in \mathbb{R}_{++}^K, w \in \mathbb{R}_{++}} w, \tag{4}$$

$$\text{s.t} \quad \sum_{j \in \mathcal{U}, j \neq i} a_{ij} p_j p_i^{-1} w + b_i p_i^{-1} w \leq 1, \forall i \in \mathcal{U}, \tag{5}$$

$$P_{min} \leq p_i \leq P_{max}, \forall i \in \mathcal{U}. \tag{6}$$

An equivalent minimization problem is given by

$$\min_{p \in \mathbb{R}_{++}^K, w \in \mathbb{R}_{++}} w^{-1}, \tag{7}$$

$$\text{s.t} \quad \sum_{j \in \mathcal{U}, j \neq i} a_{ij} p_j p_i^{-1} w + b_i p_i^{-1} w \leq 1, \forall i \in \mathcal{U}, \tag{8}$$

$$P_{min} \leq p_i \leq P_{max}, \forall i \in \mathcal{U}. \tag{9}$$

We consider the case where the coefficients a_{ij} and b_i are not completely known and normally distributed and independent, i.e., $a_{ij} \sim \mathcal{N}(\mu_{ij}, \sigma_{ij}^2)$ and $b_i \sim \mathcal{N}(\mu_i, \sigma_i^2)$. We then replace the deterministic constraint (8) with the following chance constraint [14]

$$\mathbb{P}\left\{\sum_{j \in \mathcal{U}, j \neq i} a_{ij} p_j p_i^{-1} w + b_i p_i^{-1} w \leq 1, \forall i \in \mathcal{U}\right\} \geq 1 - \epsilon. \qquad (10)$$

with $1 - \epsilon$, $0 < \epsilon \leq 0.5$, is a given confidence level. We use joint chance constraint instead of using individual constraints because the joint chance constraint ensures that the constraint as a whole is satisfied to a certain confidence level. The individual chance constraints even if they are easier to solve, they only guarantee that each constraint is satisfied to a certain confidence level.

Using the independence between the coefficients and by introducing auxiliary variables $y_i \in \mathbb{R}^+$, $i \in \mathcal{U}$, we give the following deterministic equivalent for the joint constraint (10) [15]

$$\sum_{j \in \mathcal{U}, j \neq i} \mu_{ij} p_j p_i^{-1} w + \mu_i p_i^{-1} w + \phi^{-1}(y_i) \left\{ \sqrt{\sum_{j \in \mathcal{U}, j \neq i} \sigma_{ij}^2 p_j^2 p_i^{-2} w^2 + \sigma_i^2 p_i^{-2} w^2} \right\} \leq 1, \forall i \in \mathcal{U},$$
$$(11)$$

$$\prod_{i \in \mathcal{U}} y_i \geq 1 - \epsilon, \qquad (12)$$

$$0 \leq y_i \leq 1, \forall i \in \mathcal{U}, \qquad (13)$$

where $\phi^{-1}(.)$ is the quantile function of the standard normal distribution. We write then (7)–(9) equivalently as

$$\min_{p \in \mathbb{R}_{++}^K, w \in \mathbb{R}_{++}} w^{-1},$$

$$\text{s.t} \quad \sum_{j \in \mathcal{U}, j \neq i} \mu_{ij} p_j p_i^{-1} w + \mu_i p_i^{-1} w +$$

$$\phi^{-1}(y_i) \left\{ \sqrt{\sum_{j \in \mathcal{U}, j \neq i} \sigma_{ij}^2 p_j^2 p_i^{-2} w^2 + \sigma_i^2 p_i^{-2} w^2} \right\} \leq 1, \forall i \in \mathcal{U},$$

$$1 - \epsilon - \prod_{i \in \mathcal{U}} y_i \leq 0, \qquad \text{(GP)}$$

$$- y_i \leq 0, y_i - 1 \leq 0, \forall i \in \mathcal{U},$$
$$P_{min} - p_i \leq 0, p_i - P_{max} \leq 0, \forall i \in \mathcal{U}.$$

The obtained equivalent deterministic problem (GP) is nonconvex, we apply then the logarithmic transformation $r_i = \log(p_i)$, $x_i = \log(y_i)$, $\forall i \in \mathcal{U}$ and $t = log(w)$ and obtain the following problem

$$\min \exp(-t), \tag{14}$$

$$\text{s.t} \sum_{j \in \mathcal{U}, j \neq i} \mu_{ij}\exp(r_j - r_i + t) + \mu_i\exp(t - r_i) \tag{15}$$

$$+\phi^{-1}(e^{x_i})\left\{\sqrt{\sum_{j \in \mathcal{U}, j \neq i} \sigma_{ij}^2\exp(2r_j - 2r_i + 2t) + \sigma_i^2\exp(2t - 2r_i)}\right\} \leq 1, \forall i \in \mathcal{U},$$

$$\log(1 - \epsilon) - \sum_{i \in \mathcal{U}} x_i \leq 0, \, x_i \leq 0, i \in \mathcal{U}, \tag{16}$$

$$\log(P_{min}) - r_i \leq 0, r_i - \log(P_{max}) \leq 0, \forall i \in \mathcal{U}. \tag{17}$$

Let $z = (r,t)^T$, for the sake of simplicity we write the optimization problem as

$$\min f(z), \tag{18}$$

$$\text{s.t} \ \ g_i(z,x) \leq 0, \forall i \in \mathcal{U}, \tag{19}$$

$$l(x) \leq 0, h_i(x) \leq 0, i \in \mathcal{U}, \tag{20}$$

$$v_i(z) \leq 0, w_i(z) \leq 0, \forall i \in \mathcal{U}. \tag{21}$$

where $f(z) = \exp(-t)$, $l(x) = \log(1-\epsilon) - \sum_{i \in \mathcal{U}} x_i$, $h_i(x) = x_i$, $v_i(z) = \log(P_{min}) - r_i$, $w_i(z) = r_i - \log(P_{max})$ and

$$g_i(z,x) = \sum_{j \in \mathcal{U}, j \neq i} \mu_{ij}\exp(r_j - r_i + t) + \mu_i\exp(t - r_i) + \phi^{-1}(e^{x_i}) \times$$

$$\left\{\sqrt{\sum_{j \in \mathcal{U}, j \neq i} \sigma_{ij}^2\exp(2r_j - 2r_i + 2t) + \sigma_i^2\exp(2t - 2r_i)}\right\} - 1$$

Lemma 1. *Problem (18)–(21) is biconvex on (z,x).*

Proof. The convexity on z is straightforward. We have $x \mapsto e^x$ is convex and $\phi^{-1}(.)$ is non decreasing, then $x \mapsto \phi^{-1}(e^x)$ is convex. (18)–(21) is then convex on x. The conclusion follows.

Definition 1. *Let $z^* \in \mathbb{R}^{K+1}$, $x^* \in \mathbb{R}^K$, $\alpha_i^{(1)}$, $\alpha_i^{(2)}$, β, γ_i, λ_i and ζ_i, $i \in \mathbb{U}$ such that*

$$\nabla_z f(z^*) + \sum_{i \in \mathcal{U}} \alpha_i^{(1)} \nabla_z g_i(z^*, x^*) + \sum_{i \in \mathcal{U}} \gamma_i \nabla_z v_i(z^*) + \sum_{i \in \mathcal{U}} \lambda_i \nabla_z w_i(z^*) = 0, \tag{22}$$

$$\beta \nabla_x l(x^*) + \sum_{i \in \mathcal{U}} \alpha_i^{(2)} \nabla_x g_i(z^*, x^*) + \sum_{i \in \mathcal{U}} \zeta_i \nabla_x h_i(x^*) = 0, \tag{23}$$

$$\alpha_i^{(1)} g_i(z^*, x^*) = 0, \gamma_i v_i(z^*) = 0, \lambda_i w_i(z^*) = 0, \alpha_i^{(1)} \geq 0, \gamma_i \geq 0, \lambda_i \geq 0, i \in \mathcal{U}, \tag{24}$$

$$\beta l(x^*) = 0, \alpha_i^{(2)} g_i(z^*, x^*) = 0, \zeta_i h_i(x^*) = 0, \beta \geq 0, \alpha_i^{(2)} \geq 0, \zeta_i \geq 0, i \in \mathcal{U}, \tag{25}$$

then (z^*, x^*) is called a partial KKT point of (GP).

The optimality conditions of problem (GP) are given in the following theorem

Theorem 1. *Let $z^* \in \mathbb{R}^{K+1}$, $x^* \in \mathbb{R}^K$, (z^*, x^*), if (z^*, x^*) is a partial KKT point of (GP) then (z^*, x^*) is a local optimum of (GP). Moreover, if $\alpha_i^{(1)} = \alpha_i^{(2)}$ then (z^*, x^*) is a KKT point of (GP).*

Remark 1. The main lines of the proof of Theorem 1 are given in [16].

3   Neurodynamic Approach

In this Section, we aim to construct a continuous-time dynamical system that converges to a KKT point of (GP). Therefore, we propose a dynamical neural network described by the following dynamical system

$$\frac{dz}{dt} = -(\nabla_z f(z) + \nabla_z g(z,x)^T (\alpha + g(z,x))_+ + \nabla_z v(z)^T (\gamma + v(z))_+ + \nabla_z w(z)^T (\lambda + w(z))_+), \tag{26}$$

$$\frac{dx}{dt} = -(\nabla_x l(x)^T (\beta + l(x))_+ + \nabla_x g(z,x)^T (\alpha + g(z,x))_+ + \nabla_x h(x)^T (\zeta + h(x))_+), \tag{27}$$

$$\frac{d\alpha}{dt} = (\alpha + g(z,x))_+ - \alpha, \tag{28}$$

$$\frac{d\gamma}{dt} = (\gamma + v(z))_+ - \gamma, \tag{29}$$

$$\frac{d\lambda}{dt} = (\lambda + w(z))_+ - \lambda, \tag{30}$$

$$\frac{d\beta}{dt} = (\beta + l(x))_+ - \beta, \tag{31}$$

$$\frac{d\zeta}{dt} = (\zeta + h(x))_+ - \zeta. \tag{32}$$

where $\alpha^{(1)} = (\alpha_1^{(1)}, ..., \alpha_K^{(1)})^T$, $\alpha^{(2)} = (\alpha_1^{(2)}, ..., \alpha_K^{(2)})^T$, $\gamma = (\gamma_1, ..., \gamma_K)^T$, $\lambda = (\lambda_1, ..., \lambda_K)^T$, $\zeta = (\zeta_1, ..., \zeta_K)^T$, $g = (g_1, ..., g_K)^T$, $v = (v_1, ..., v_K)^T$, $w = (w_1, ..., w_K)^T$ and $h = (h_1, ..., h_K)^T$ are time-continuous vectors. For convenience, let $y = (z, x, \alpha, \gamma, \lambda, \beta, \zeta)$ we write the dynamical system (26)–(32) shortly as

$$\frac{dy}{dt} = \eta(y) \tag{33}$$

$$y(t_0) = y_0, \tag{34}$$

where y_0 is a given initial point.

Now we study the stability and convergence properties for (26)–(32).

Theorem 2. *Let $y = (z, x, \alpha, \gamma, \lambda, \beta, \zeta)$ an equilibrium point of (26)–(32), then (z, x) is a KKT point of (GP). Furthermore, if (z, x) is a KKT point of (GP) then there exists $(\alpha, \gamma, \lambda, \beta, \zeta)$ such that $(z, x, \alpha, \gamma, \lambda, \beta, \zeta)$ is an equilibrium point of (26)–(32).*

Proof. Let $y = (z, x, \alpha, \gamma, \lambda, \beta, \zeta)$ an equilibrium point of (26)–(32), then $\frac{dz}{dt} = 0$, $\frac{dx}{dt} = 0$, $\frac{d\alpha}{dt} = 0$, $\frac{d\gamma}{dt} = 0$, $\frac{d\lambda}{dt} = 0$ $\frac{d\beta}{dt} = 0$ and $\frac{d\zeta}{dt} = 0$.

We have that $\frac{d\alpha}{dt} = 0 \iff (\alpha + g(z, x))_+ - \alpha \iff \{\alpha \geq 0,\ g(z, x) \leq 0$ and $\alpha^T g(z, x) = 0\}$,

Similarly, we have $\frac{d\gamma}{dt} = 0 \iff \{\gamma \geq 0,\ v(z) \leq 0$ and $\gamma^T v(z) = 0\}$ and $\frac{d\lambda}{dt} = 0 \iff \{\lambda \geq 0,\ w(z) \leq 0$ and $\lambda^T w(z) = 0\}$.

Furthermore, we have $\frac{dz}{dt} = 0 \iff -(\nabla_z f(z) + \nabla_z g(z, x)^T (\alpha + g(z, x))_+ + \nabla_z v(z)^T (\gamma + v(z))_+ + \nabla_z w(z)^T (\lambda + w(z))_+) = 0 \iff \nabla_z f(z^*) + \nabla_z g(z^*, x^*)^T \alpha + \nabla_z v(z^*)^T \gamma + \nabla_z w(z^*)^T \lambda = 0$. We obtain then, Eqs. (22) and (24) of the partial KKT system (22)–(25). Following the same steps we obtain Eqs. (23) and (25).
The controverse part of the theorem is straightforward.

Theorem 3. *For any initial point* $(z(t_0), x(t_0), \alpha(t_0), \gamma(t_0), \lambda(t_0), \beta(t_0), \zeta(t_0))$, *there exists an unique continuous solution* $(z(t), x(t), \alpha(t), \gamma(t), \lambda(t), \beta(t), \zeta(t))$ *for (26)–(32).*

Proof. Since $\nabla_z f(z)$, $\nabla_z g(z, x)$, $\nabla_x g(z, x)$, $\nabla_z v(z)$, $\nabla_z w(z)$, $\nabla_x l(x)$ and $\nabla_x h(x)$ are continuously differentiable on open sets, then all the second terms of the differential equations (26)–(32) are locally Lipschitz continuous. According to the local existence of ordinary differential equations also known as *Picard-Lindelöf Theorem*, the neural network (26)–(32) has a unique continuous solution $(z(t), x(t), \alpha(t), \gamma(t), \lambda(t), \beta(t), \zeta(t))$.

To prove the stability and convergence of the dynamical neural network (26)–(32), we first show the negative semidefiniteness of the Jacobian matrix $\nabla \eta(y)$ that we are going to use while defining the Lyapunov functions.

Theorem 4. *The Jacobian matrix* $\nabla \eta(y)$ *is negative semidefinite.*

Proof. Without loss of generality, we assume that $\beta + l(x) \geq 0$ and that there exists $0 \leq p, q, r, s \leq K$ such that
$$(\alpha + g)_+ = (\alpha_1 + g_1(z, x), \alpha_2 + g_2(z, x), \ldots, \alpha_p + g_p(z, x), \underbrace{0, \ldots, 0}_{K-p}),$$
$$(\gamma + v)_+ = (\gamma_1 + v_1(z), \gamma_2 + v_2(z), \ldots, \gamma_q + v_q(z), \underbrace{0, \ldots, 0}_{K-q}),$$
$$(\lambda + w)_+ = (\lambda_1 + w_1(z), \lambda_2 + w_2(z), \ldots, \lambda_r + w_r(z), \underbrace{0, \ldots, 0}_{K-r}),$$
$$(\zeta + h)_+ = (\zeta_1 + h_1(x), \zeta_2 + h_2(x), \ldots, \zeta_s + h_s(x), \underbrace{0, \ldots, 0}_{K-s}).$$

We represent the Jacobian matrix of η in the following form $\nabla\eta(y) =$

$$\begin{bmatrix} A_1 & A_2 & A_3 & A_4 & A_5 & 0 & 0 \\ B_1 & B_2 & B_3 & 0 & 0 & B_6 & B_7 \\ C_1 & C_2 & C_3 & 0 & 0 & 0 & 0 \\ D_1 & 0 & 0 & D_4 & 0 & 0 & 0 \\ E_1 & 0 & 0 & 0 & E_5 & 0 & 0 \\ 0 & F_2 & 0 & 0 & 0 & 0 & 0 \\ 0 & G_2 & 0 & 0 & 0 & 0 & G_7 \end{bmatrix}, \text{ where}$$

$$A_1 = -\left(\nabla_z^2 f(z) + \sum_{i=1}^{p}((\alpha_i + g_i)\nabla_z^2 g_i^p(z,x)) + \nabla_z g^p(z,x)^T \nabla_z g^p(z,x) \right.$$

$$\left. + \sum_{i=1}^{q}((\gamma_i + v_i)\nabla_z^2 v_i^q(z)) + \nabla_z v^q(z)^T \nabla_z v^q(z) + \sum_{i=1}^{r}((\lambda_i + w_i)\nabla_z^2 w_i^r(z)) \right.$$

$$\left. + \nabla_z w^r(z)^T \nabla_z w^r(z) \right),$$

$$A_2 = -\left(\sum_{i=1}^{p}((\alpha_i + g_i)\nabla_x \nabla_z g_i^p(z,x)) + \nabla_x g^p(z,x)^T \nabla_z g^p(z,x) \right),$$

$$A_3 = -\nabla_z g^p(z,x)^T, \qquad A_4 = -\nabla_z v^q(z)^T, \qquad A_5 = -\nabla_z w^r(z)^T,$$

$$B_1 = -\left(\sum_{i=1}^{p}(\alpha_i + g_i)\nabla_z \nabla_x g_i^p(z,x) + \nabla_z g^p(z,x)^T \nabla_x g^p(z,x) \right),$$

$$B_2 = -\left(\sum_{i=1}^{p}((\alpha_i + g_i)\nabla_x^2 g_i^p(z,x)) + \nabla_x g^p(z,x)^T \nabla_x g^p(z,x) + \nabla_x^2 l(x) \right.$$

$$\left. + \nabla_x l(x)^T \nabla_x l(x) + \sum_{i=1}^{s}((\zeta_i + h_i)\nabla_x^2 \zeta_i^s(x)) + \nabla_x h^s(x)^T \nabla_x h^s(x) \right),$$

$$B_6 = -\nabla_x l(x)^T, \qquad B_7 = -\nabla_x h^s(x)^T, \qquad C_1 = \nabla_z g^p(z,x),$$

$$C_2 = \nabla_x g^p(z,x), \quad C_3 = S_p = -\begin{bmatrix} O_{p\times p} & O_{p\times(K-p)} \\ O_{(K-p)\times p} & I_{(K-p)\times(K-p)} \end{bmatrix}, \quad D_1 = \nabla_z v^q(z),$$

$$D_4 = S_q = -\begin{bmatrix} O_{q\times q} & O_{q\times(K-q)} \\ O_{(K-q)\times q} & I_{(K-q)\times(K-q)} \end{bmatrix}, \ E_1 = \nabla_z w^r(z), \ E_5 = S_r = -\begin{bmatrix} O_{r\times r} & O_{r\times(K-r)} \\ O_{(K-r)\times r} & I_{(K-r)\times(K-r)} \end{bmatrix},$$

$$F_2 = \nabla_x l(x), \qquad G_2 = \nabla_x h^s(x), \qquad G_7 = S_s = -\begin{bmatrix} O_{s\times s} & O_{s\times(K-s)} \\ O_{(K-s)\times s} & I_{(K-s)\times(K-s)} \end{bmatrix}.$$

We rewrite then the Jacobian matrix $\nabla \eta$ as

$$\nabla \eta(y) = \begin{bmatrix} A_1 & A_2 & A_3 & A_4 & A_5 & 0 & 0 \\ A_2^T & B_2 & B_3 & 0 & 0 & B_6 & B_7 \\ -A_3^T & -B_3^T & S_p & 0 & 0 & 0 & 0 \\ -A_4^T & 0 & 0 & S_q & 0 & 0 & 0 \\ -A_5^T & 0 & 0 & 0 & S_r & 0 & 0 \\ 0 & -B_6^T & 0 & 0 & 0 & 0 & 0 \\ 0 & -B_7^T & 0 & 0 & 0 & 0 & S_s \end{bmatrix} = \left(\begin{array}{cc|c} A_1 & A_2 & \\ A_2^T & B_2 & \mathbb{B} \\ \hline & -\mathbb{B}^T & \mathbb{S} \end{array} \right),$$

where $\mathbb{B} = \begin{bmatrix} A_3 & A_4 & A_5 & 0 & 0 \\ B_2 & B_3 & 0 & 0 & B_6 & B_7 \end{bmatrix}$ and $\mathbb{S} = \begin{bmatrix} S_p & 0 & 0 & 0 & 0 \\ 0 & S_q & 0 & 0 & 0 \\ 0 & 0 & S_r & 0 & 0 \\ 0 & 0 & 0 & 0 & 0 \\ 0 & 0 & 0 & 0 & S_s \end{bmatrix}$. Since g is biconvex,

then $\nabla_z^2 g^p$ and $\nabla_x^2 g^p$ are positive semidefinite. Using the convexity of v, w, l, and h, we have that the matrices $\nabla_z^2 v$, $\nabla_z^2 w$, $\nabla_x^2 l$ and $\nabla_x^2 h$ are positive semidefinite. Furthermore, observe that for any square matrix M, we have that $M^T M$ is positive semidefinite. We conclude then that $\begin{bmatrix} A_1 & A_2 \\ A_2^T & B_2 \end{bmatrix}$ is negative semidefinite. It is clear that $\mathbb{S}$ is negative semidefinite, we have then $\nabla \eta$ is negative semidefinite.

The following definition and lemma are used later to prove the stability of the dynamical neural network (26)–(32).

Definition 2. *A mapping $F: \mathbb{R}^n \longrightarrow \mathbb{R}^n$ is said to be monotonic if*

$$(x - y)^T (F(x) - F(y)) \geq 0, \qquad \forall x, y \in \mathbb{R}^n$$

Lemma 2. *[17] A differentiable mapping $F: \mathbb{R}^n \longrightarrow \mathbb{R}^n$ is monotonic, if and only if the Jacobian matrix $\nabla F(x)$, $\forall x \in \mathbb{R}^n$, is positive semidefinite.*

Theorem 5. *The dynamical neural network (26)–(32) is stable in the sense of Lyapunov and converges to a KKT point of (GP).*

Proof. Let $\tilde{y}$ an equilibrium point of (26)–(32) and let V_1 the following Lyapunov function $V_1(y) = ||\eta(\tilde{y})|| + \frac{1}{2}||y - \tilde{y}||^2$.

We have $\frac{dV_1(y)}{dt} = \frac{d\eta(y)}{dt}^T \eta(y) + \eta(y)^T \frac{d\eta(y)}{dt} + (y - \tilde{y})^T \frac{dy}{dt}$. On the other hand, $\frac{d\eta}{dt} = \frac{d\eta}{dy} \frac{dy}{dt}$. We have then, $V_1(y) = \eta(y)^T (\nabla \eta(y)^T + \nabla \eta(y)) \eta(y) + (y - \tilde{y})^T \eta(y)$. Since $\nabla \eta$ is negative semidefinite, then $\eta(y)^T (\nabla \eta(y)^T + \nabla \eta(y)) \eta(y) \leq 0$. Moreover, by Lemma 2 we have $(y - \tilde{y}))^T \eta(y) \leq 0$. We conclude that $\frac{dV_1(y)}{dt} \leq 0$ and since V_1 is positive we have that the dynamical neural network (26)–(32) is stable in the sense of Lyapunov.

Observe that $\frac{1}{2}||y - \tilde{y}||^2 \leq V_1(y)$, then there exists a convergent subsequence $(y(t_k))_{k \geq 0}$ such that $\lim_{k \longrightarrow \infty} t_k = +\infty$ and $\lim_{k \longrightarrow \infty} y(t_k) = \hat{y}$ where $\hat{y}$ satisfies $\frac{dV_1(\hat{y})}{dt} = 0$.

We have by LaSalle's invariance principle that the neural network converges to the largest invariant set contained in S which is defined by $S = \{y(t)| \frac{dV_1(y)}{dt} = 0\}$.

Notice that $\frac{dy}{dt} = 0 \Leftrightarrow \frac{dV_1(y)}{dt}$, we have then that $\hat{y}$ is an equilibrium point of the dynamical system (26)–(32).

We introduce a second Lyapunov function defined as follows $V_2(y) = ||\eta(\tilde{y})|| + \frac{1}{2}||y - \hat{y}||^2$. Since V_2 is continuously differentiable, $\eta(\hat{z}) = 0$ and $\lim_{k \to \infty} y(t_k) = \hat{y}$ then $\lim_{t \to \infty} V_2(y(t)) = V_2(\hat{y}) = 0$. On the other hand, we have $\frac{dV_2(y)}{dt} \leq 0$ which leads to $\frac{1}{2}||y - \hat{y}||^2 \leq V_2(y)$. We conclude that $\lim_{t \to \infty} ||y - \hat{y}|| = 0$ and then $\lim_{t \to \infty} y(t) = \hat{y}$. We proved then, that the neural network (26)–(32) is convergent in the sense of Lyapunov to an equilibrium point $\hat{y} = (\hat{z}, \hat{x}, \hat{\alpha}, \hat{\gamma}, \hat{\lambda}, \hat{\beta}, \hat{\zeta})$ where $(\hat{z}, \hat{x})$ is a KKT point of problem (GP).

4   Numerical Experiments

In this Section, we conduct preliminary numerical results in order to evaluate the performances of our approach. For this purpose, all the numerical experiments were done using Python. To compute the partial derivatives and the jacobians, we use the package autograd. To generate the random instances, we use the package numpy.random. The ODEs of the recurrent dynamical neural networks are solved using the function solve_ivp of scipy.integrate library. We run our algorithms on Intel(R) Core(TM) i7-10610U CPU @ 1.80GHz. For the numerical experiments, we set $P_{min} = 0.1$, $P_{max} = 0.5$, $\epsilon = 0.1$, we generate the complex vectors $g_i \in \mathbb{C}^{T \times 1}$ and $g_i^H \in \mathbb{C}^{1 \times T}$ for each $i \in \mathcal{U}$ according to an independent complex Gaussian distribution function with zero mean and variance equal to one. Then, we multiply each of these vectors by a factor in the set $\{3.0, 4.0, 5.0, 7.0\}$. We generate the parameter σ_i for each $i \in \mathcal{U}$ according to an independent complex Gaussian distribution function with zero mean and variance equal to one. The variables a_{ij} and b_i are then computed as explained in Sect. 2. We assume that $\mu_{ij} = a_{ij}$, $\mu_i = b_i$ and we vary the values of σ_{ij} and σ_i in $\{0.1, 0.2, 0.3\}$. We compare our neural network with the state-of-the-art based convex approximations approach [18]. We only account for the quality of the solution and do not record the CPU time as current ODE solvers are time consuming.

4.1   Convergence Analysis

We first solve (GP) for $K = 5$ for different feasible initial point y_0, we observe the convergence process of the neural network for each case. We observe, see Fig. 2, that the neural network converges to the same final value for the different starting points.

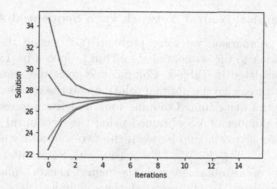

Fig. 2. Convergence of the neural network different starting points y_0.

4.2   Joint Constraints vs. Individual Constraints

In order to show the advantage of using joint constraints instead of individual constraints to deal with the uncertainty in constraints (8), We solve (GP) for different values of users, i.e., from $K = 2$ to $K = 20$ for both joint and individual chance constraints. We generate 100 instances of the stochastic variables a_{ij} and b_i and observe the number of times where the constraints (8) were not respected and we call them violated scenarios (VS for short). We recapitulate the obtained results in Table 1. Column one gives the number of users K, columns two and three give the optimal solution and the number of VS obtained using the individual constraints. Columns four and five represent the optimal solution and the number of VS obtained using the joint constraints. We observe that the number of VS while using individual constraint is larger than the number of VS while using the joint constraints. The difference in VS number becomes more important as the value of K increases. Using joint chance constraints ensures a better cover for the risk area.

Table 1. Individual constraints vs. Joint constraints for different values of K.

K	Individual constraints	VS	Joint constraints	VS
2	5.45	16	5.99	6
3	6.87	21	7.43	9
5	35.57	39	36.99	8
7	48.98	53	50.43	11
10	39.40	62	41.68	10
15	82.30	84	85.21	12
20	113.65	82	117.33	10

4.3   The Dynamical Neural Network vs. a Sequential Algorithm

For the sake of comparison we solve problem (GP) using the neurodynamic approach in addition to the sequential algorithm proposed in [18]. The obtained results are recapitulated in Table 2. Column one gives the number of users K, columns two and three give the optimal solution and the number of VS obtained using the sequential algorithm. Columns four and five represent the optimal solution and the number of VS obtained using the dynamical neural network. Finally, column six gives the gap between the two solutions which is computed as follows $GAP = \frac{(Solution_{SA} - Solution_{NN})}{Solution_{SA}} \times 100$, with $Solution_{NN}$ and $Solution_{SA}$ are the objective values obtained with the neural network and the sequential algorithm, respectively. We observe that the dynamical neural network gives better solutions compared to the sequential algorithm. Moreover, the number of violated scenarios for the solutions obtained using the neurodynamical approach is slightly fewer than this obtained using the sequential algorithm.

Table 2. Neural network vs. the sequential algorithm for different values of K.

K	Sequential Algorithm	VS	Neural Network	VS	GAP
2	5.40	12	5.10	6	5.88
3	25.77	10	25.61	8	0.62
5	28.97	11	28.88	9	0.31
7	68.79	10	68.56	8	0.33
10	70.81	21	69.68	14	1.62
15	84.43	7	84.39	6	0.04
20	117.37	13	117.33	10	0.03

Now we consider the case where $K = 5$ and we vary the value of ϵ in $[0.05, 0.4]$. We recapitulate the obtained results in Table 3. We observe that as ϵ increases the problem becomes less conservative. Moreover, we observe that the gap between the two approaches increases as ϵ increases as shown in Fig. 3 and the number of violated scenarios increases see Fig. 4. The difference in the number of violated scenarios becomes more significant as ϵ increases, hence the neurodynamical approach ensures a better robustness.

Table 3. Neural network vs. the sequential algorithm for different values of ϵ.

ϵ	Sequential Algorithm	VS	Neural Network	VS	GAP
0.05	30.23	4	29.89	2	1.13
0.1	29.47	15	29.07	9	1.37
0.15	28.96	22	28.53	11	1.50
0.2	28.56	32	28.10	19	1.63
0.3	27.87	54	27.40	26	1.71
0.4	27.30	63	26.81	34	1.82

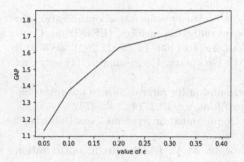

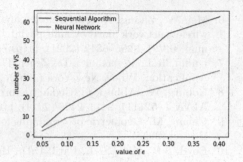

Fig. 3. Evolution of GAP function to ϵ.   **Fig. 4.** Evolution of VS function to ϵ.

5   Conclusion

This paper proposes a neurodynamic approach to maximize the worst user signal to interference noise ratio. We first give a geometric formulation for the maximization problem then we derive a stochastic formulation to deal with the uncertainty of wireless channels. Based on the partial KKT system of the obtained deterministic equivalent problem for the stochastic formulation, we propose a convergent dynamical system to solve the problem of maximizing the worst user signal to interference noise ratio. The dynamical neural network has the advantage of converging directly to a solution without using any convex approximation, unlike the state-of-art methods. In the numerical Section, we compare the performances of our neurodynamic approach to a sequential algorithm and show that our method gives better upper bounds for the optimal solution and covers better the risk area.

References

1. Lin, X., Xu, F., Fu, J., Wang, Y.: Resource allocation for TDD cell-free massive MIMO systems. Electronics **11**(12), 1914 (2022). https://doi.org/10.3390/electronics11121914. https://www.mdpi.com/2079-9292/11/12/1914
2. Yin, H., Wang, H., Liu, Y., Gesbert, D.: Dealing with the mobility problem of massive MIMO using extended Prony's method. In: ICC 2020–2020 IEEE International Conference on Communications (ICC), pp. 1–6 (2020). https://doi.org/10.1109/ICC40277.2020.9149225
3. Dikmen, O., Kulac, S.: Power allocation algorithms for massive MIMO system. Avrupa Bilim ve Teknoloji Dergisi (28), 444–452 (2021). https://doi.org/10.31590/ejosat.1005325
4. Salah, I., Mourad, M., Rahouma, K., Hussein, A.: Energy efficiency optimization in adaptive massive MIMO networks for 5G applications using genetic algorithm. Opt. Quant. Electron. **54**, 125 (2022). https://doi.org/10.1007/s11082-021-03507-5
5. Adasme, P., Soto, I., Juan, E.S., Seguel, F., Firoozabadi, A.D.: Maximizing signal to interference noise ratio for massive MIMO: a mathematical programming approach. In: 2020 South American Colloquium on Visible Light Communications (SACVC), pp. 1–6 (2020). https://doi.org/10.1109/SACVLC50805.2020.9129889

6. Mei, W., Zhang, R.: Performance analysis and user association optimization for wireless network aided by multiple intelligent reflecting surfaces. IEEE Trans. Commun. **69**(9), 6296–6312 (2021). https://doi.org/10.1109/TCOMM.2021.3087620
7. Duffin, R.J., Peterson, E.L., Zener, C.M.: Geometric Programming: Theory and Application. Wiley, New York (1967)
8. Hoburg, W., Abbeel, P.: Geometric programming for aircraft design optimization. AIAA J. **52**(11), 2414–2426 (2014). https://doi.org/10.2514/1.J052732
9. Chiang, M.: Geometric programming for Communication Systems. Now Publishers, Boston (2005)
10. Boyd, S.P., Kim, S.-J., Patil, D.D., Horowitz, M.A.: Digital circuit optimization via geometric programming. Oper. Res. **53**(6), 899–932 (2005). http://www.jstor.org/stable/25146929
11. Scott, C.H., Jefferson, T.R.: A generalisation of geometric programming with an application to information theory. Inf. Sci. **12**, 263–269 (1977)
12. You, B., Esche, E., Weigert, J., Repke, J.-U.: Joint chance constraint approach based on data-driven models for optimization under uncertainty applied to the williams-otto process. In: Türkay, M., Gani, R. (eds.) 31st European Symposium on Computer Aided Process Engineering, Volume 50 of Computer Aided Chemical Engineering, pp. 523 528. Elsevier (2021). https://doi.org/10.1016/B978-0-323-88506-5.50083-8. https://www.sciencedirect.com/science/article/pii/B9780323885065500838
13. Ono, M., Kuwata, Y., Balaram, J.: Joint chance-constrained dynamic programming. In: 2012 IEEE 51st IEEE Conference on Decision and Control (CDC), pp. 1915–1922 (2012). https://doi.org/10.1109/CDC.2012.6425906
14. Adasme, P., Lisser, A.: A stochastic geometric programming approach for power allocation in wireless networks. Wireless Netw. **29**, 2235–2250 (2023). https://doi.org/10.1007/s11276-023-03295-8
15. Tassouli, S., Lisser, A.: A neural network approach to solve geometric programs with joint probabilistic constraints. Math. Comput. Simul. **205**, 765–777 (2023). https://doi.org/10.1016/j.matcom.2022.10.025. https://www.sciencedirect.com/science/article/pii/S0378475422004384
16. Jiang, M., Meng, Z., Shen, R.: Partial exactness for the penalty function of biconvex programming. Entropy **23**(2), 132 (2021). https://doi.org/10.3390/e23020132. https://www.mdpi.com/1099-4300/23/2/132
17. Rockafellar, R.T., Wets, R.J.-B.: Variational Analysis. Springer, Heidelberg (1998). https://doi.org/10.1007/978-3-642-02431-3
18. Liu, J., Lisser, A., Chen, Z.: Stochastic geometric optimization with joint probabilistic constraints. Oper. Res. Lett. **44**(5), 687–691 (2016). https://doi.org/10.1016/j.orl.2016.08.002

Advanced Mobile Applications

Towards a Cash-on-Delivery System Based on Blockchain Technology for Developing Countries: A Case Study in Vietnam

Quy T. Lu[1]([envelope]), Ngan N. T. Kim[2], N. M. Triet[1], Huong H. Luong[1],
Hieu T. Nguyen[1], Phuc N. Trong[1], Khoa T. Dang[1], Khiem H. Gia[1],
Nguyen D. P. Trong[1], Loc V. C. Phu[1], Anh N. The[1], Huynh T. Nghia[1],
Bang L. Khanh[1], and Khanh H. Vo[1]([envelope])

[1] FPT University, Can Tho city, Vietnam
{quylt9,khanhvh}@fe.edu.vn
[2] FPT Polytecnic, Can Tho city, Vietnam

Abstract. Cargo transport patterns have played an extremely important role in the economic development of a region or a country. For developing countries, this model faces many risks affecting the interests of sellers and buyers. In Vietnam (i.e., the case study model in this study), traditional freight transport models are based on three methods, i.e., postal system, shipping company, or commercial platform electronic. However, the above models are all dependent on the shipping company (i.e., third party). If there is a conflict (e.g., loss of goods), it is difficult to determine who is responsible (i.e., seller, buyer, or carrier). Because of these risks, developing countries need to adopt a model of freight transport that ensures the interests of the parties involved (i.e., the seller and the buyer). In this article, we aim at a freight model that applies Blockchain technology and Smart contracts to eliminate risks from traditional models. The main contribution of this paper consists of three aspects: (a) proposes a model of cargo management and transportation based on Blockchain technology and Smart contract applied to Vietnam to replace the traditional shipping model; (b) implement the proposed model (i.e., proof-of-concept) on the Hyperledger Fabric platform; (c) evaluate the proposed model against the Hyperledger Caliper platform.

Keywords: Cargo transport patterns in Vietnam · Blockchain · Smart contracts · Hyperledger Fabric · Hyperledger Caliper

1 Introduction

The need to transport goods directly contributes to the development of the economy of a country (in particular) and the whole world (in general) [4]. Transportation needs are increasingly diverse from rudimentary transportation methods to methods that combine scientific and technical advances to interact with users (i.e., sellers, buyers) during transportation [13]. More and more companies specialize in shipping to optimize transit time as well as ensure during transportation of goods (e.g., Fedex, DHL, etc).

For developing countries, the need to transport goods is a challenge due to the lack of synchronization between the city and the countryside (specifically in Vietnam). In major cities (e.g., Ho Chi Minh City, Hanoi, Can Tho, Da Nang), the transportation process benefits from the development of public transport facilities, where transportation is more convenient. However, in other provinces (e.g., Ca Mau, Lao Cai), it is more difficult to transport goods due to infrastructure barriers. Specifically, in Vietnam there are three popular shipping models including the postal system, shipping companies and based on e-commerce channels (e.g., tiki, sendo, shopy, lazada).

Shipping is based on a postal system which means that provinces and cities have a hierarchical model of postal services from the province/city level to the district/town level[1]. In developing countries (i.e., Vietnam), this method is very popular due to its ease of use and convenience. People clearly specify the content of transportation and choose a mode of transportation (i.e., secure shipping or regular shipping). The fee of this model is the lowest compared to the other two models. We also investigated the postal system-based shipping and management process in two cities in the Mekong Delta, Can Tho City and Ben Tre Province, in November 2022. Specifically, the transportation process transfers based on the postal hierarchy presented in the Approach section of the paper. In the model of using shipping companies, the consignor (i.e., the seller) processes the goods to the consignee's address (i.e., the buyer). Shipping fees can be paid by the seller/buyer depending on the convention between the two parties. This process is considered more secure and safe during transportation than the traditional model. For the e-commerce platform-based approach, sellers post their products on these platforms and wait for the buyer to select the corresponding item. Shipping is supported by merchants or exchanges.

With transport processes incorporating today's advanced technologies (e.g., blockchain, smartcontract), state-of-the-art exploits the decentralized storage and transparency of data stored in distributed ledger. Some approaches are listed in the introduction in the related work section of the paper, such as localEthereum [3], OpenBazaar [11] based on Ethereum platform or models The proposed model is based on Hyperledger Fabric (e.g., [2,5,6,16]).

However, no case studies have been implemented for the Vietnamese environment in the above approaches. Specifically, our research problem is to take advantage of the available equipment of the decentralized electricity system. Specifically, this process is very suitable for extending Blockchain technology support in ensuring the transportation and distribution of goods. Sellers and buyers can be traced throughout the shipping process without having to update many modern equipments. Therefore, the main contribution of this paper includes three aspects: (a) proposing a model of management and transportation of goods based

---

[1] https://postofficepage.com/vietnam.

on Blockchain technology and Smart contract applied to Vietnam; (b) implement the proposed model (i.e., proof-of-concept) on the Hyperledger Fabric platform; (c) evaluate the proposed model against the Hyperledger Caliper platform.

The rest of the paper consists of 7 parts. After the introduction is the related work section, which presents state-of-the-art with the same research problem. The next two sections present our approach and the proposed model implementation (i.e., Sects. 3, 4). To demonstrate our effectiveness, Sect. 5 presents our evaluation steps in different scenarios before making comments in Sect. 6. The 7 section summarizes and outlines the next steps for development.

2   Related Work

In this section we summarize previous approaches to building a delivery system in developing countries. We divide into two main approaches: traditional delivery method and approach based on Blockchain technology.

2.1   Traditional Shipping Methods

The strengths and weaknesses in traditional freight systems are summarized below:

Shipping based on the postal system:

- Pros: No need to depend on smart devices (e.g., smartphones), meet in areas without Internet, support all user groups (including normal users - without the technology background), cheap shipping.
- Cons: Long waiting time, many risks in the transportation of goods, difficulty in tracing the status of the package during transportation.

Shipping based on courier company:

- Pros: Know the expected time to receive the goods, low risk, can retrieve the package status (i.e., location, status).
- Cons: high transportation fee, requires good public transport system (i.e., city), limited users.

Shipping goods based on e-commerce platforms:

- Pros: Take advantage of the equipment of the e-commerce platform to narrow the gap between sellers and buyers, know the expected time to receive the goods, low shipping fees, have many choices.
- Cons: Depends on 3rd party during transportation, easy to buy poor quality products.

Our proposed model is introduced in the next section (i.e., Approach section), which combines all the above advantages and addresses the disadvantages raised in the respective traditional approaches.

2.2   Delivery Method Based on Blockchain Technology

Delivery methods based on Blockchain technology can be classified into two groups: i) excluding the shipper and ii) promoting the role of the shipper.

For the first approach, Local Ethereum [3] (i.e., transaction support or DeFi Dapp) presented a blockchain and smart contract based approach in 2017. The transactions are completely secure using a single wallet address between the transfer and receipt of funds between the seller and the buyer. Similar development on the Ethereum platform, OpenBazaar proposes a connection channel between sellers and buyers paid with the digital currency ETH [11]. The main difference between OpenBazaar and Local Ethereum is that it involves three parties: the provider, the requestor, and the moderator (that is, a new controlling role). Specifically, instead of using predefined Smart Contracts (i.e., default). OpenBazaar supports defining Smart Contracts suitable for specific contexts. In addition, [1] exploited ETH-based trading to propose a COD/LOC mechanism - a new protocol to facilitate the transportation of products from the place of production to the consumer. The above approaches have not yet exploited the role of the carrier/shipping company. That is why they assume that the carrier is a trusted third party. This will be very risky when there is a conflict between the parties because the binding covers only two groups of seller and buyer and ignores the role of the carrier.

To address the above risk, a series of studies have been carried out to add the role of the carrier company to the system. For example, Son et al. [17] proposed a baseline model for shipping goods from sellers and buyers to replace the current CoD model. Specifically, the shipper plays the role of transiting goods from the seller to the buyer. However, this model has too many shortcomings related to shipping costs as well as the deposit for the package (i.e., in case the package is lost). To address this issue, Le et al. [9] has proposed a model that combines blockchain technology and smart contracts in shipping packages between sellers and buyers. The biggest difference between [9] and [17] is that a package deposit is required between the shopper and the shipper. During the transition, conflicting situations will be defined in the smart contract to decide who will be penalized. However, the disadvantage of this model is the limitation of the number of shippers during delivery. Specifically, each order is only identified by a fixed shipper. This is hardly applicable to the actual model. Therefore, Le et al. [10] has added a process to define smart contracts to expand the number of delivery shippers.

Besides, Duong et al. [2] propose a new approach based on the argument that trading sessions will last more than one section. Therefore, they propose a model based on Hyperledger Fabric that supports transactions with long confirmation times (i.e., between cities, and countries). Similarly, Son et al. [5] also propose a cross-platform model connecting many different markets, where sellers and buyers are not limited by payment tools between e-commerce platforms. Specifically, users can create an account at one e-commerce platform and make purchases at all other exchanges. In addition to solutions to support sellers and buyers in the process of exchanging goods, Ha et al. [6] have proposed a personal information protection model (i.e., seller and buyer) based on the access control model [7,15]. Specifically, sensitive information such as addresses and phone numbers can only be accessed by those with [23] permissions. This solution greatly helps in protecting the personal information of the seller and the buyer because this information is always available on other electronic exchanges (even those that do not play a role in the corresponding transaction). For cross-border transactions, Khoi et al. [12] have proposed a mechanism for transporting goods between countries that are not dependent on a trusted third party (i.e., bank) called Letter-of-Credit. This approach tries to work towards an open policy across countries (i.e., not constrained by the policies of a country, geographical region [14,24]).

However, the above approaches require an in-depth study to be carried out in Vietnam as well as to provide a model of freight transport for developing countries. In this article, we apply Blockchain technology and Smart Contract to replace the traditional shipping model in Vietnam (i.e., traditional post offices, courier companies, and e-commerce platforms). The next section presents detailed modeling and implementation steps among the three main user groups - seller, carrier, and buyer.

3   Approach

3.1   The Traditional Process of Transporting Goods

As presented in the Introduction and Related work sections, the article summarizes the traditional freight processes widely used in Vietnam (i.e., based on the postal system, based on shipping companies and e-commerce platforms).

Figure 1 shows the postal system-based shipping process (i.e., the steps for shipping are done sequentially from left to right). This model is applicable when delivering goods between provinces/cities (i.e., seller and buyer in two different cities). Specifically, the seller, after agreeing on the price and product with the buyer, will go to the nearest post office to send it to the buyer. The shipping and product costs are agreed between the seller and the buyer. The role of the post office is only to deliver the item to the address provided by the buyer. In Vietnam, post offices are divided into two levels (i.e., city/province - commune/district). Items are gathered at post offices in provinces before being shipped to other provinces. Here, the shippers (i.e., post office staff) receive the goods and transfer them to the recipient's address.

As for the shipping company mining model - a common example for this model is Cash-on-delivery. The role of the shipping company may include always

Fig. 1. The post-office case for transporting goods.

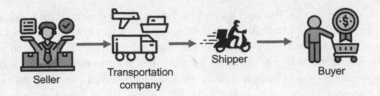

Fig. 2. The transportation company case for transporting goods.

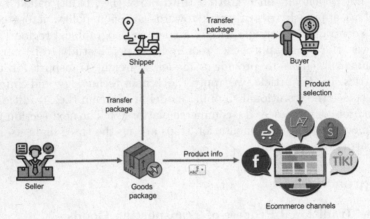

Fig. 3. The E-commerce channel case for transporting goods.

taking payment from the buyer. Figure 2 details the shipping process based on the shipping company. Specifically, the seller enters into a contract with the shipping company to deliver and receive money from the buyer. The company's shippers will deliver the goods to the required address.

Figure 3 shows the connection process between sellers and buyers through e-commerce platforms (e.g., Tiki, shoppe, Lazada, Sendo, etc.). Shipping companies are selected by default by the e-commerce platform or the seller. The main difference of this form compared to the other two forms is that the buyer knows the product information and related images. Buyers also have more choices.

In addition to the risks and limitations presented in the Introduction and Related work sections, these traditional models face a major disadvantage when the buyer wants to return the product due to a number of reasons (e.g., not meeting the customer's expectations). buyer, carrier's mistake). Specifically, shipping will be very time-consuming because the steps will be repeated like the shipping process. Moreover, traditional models still cannot provide a reputable service or increase interaction between sellers and buyers. In addition, solutions applied to Vietnam need to take into account the operating costs and technology background of users. To solve these limitations, we exploit this model, we exploit Blockchain technology and smart contracts to expand the freight system in Vietnam. In addition, Internet connection infrastructure is being developed by the

Vietnamese government for all 63 provinces[2], thus ensuring the updating of the goods' location during transportation. Based on the above analysis, we realize that the combination model of the current system with Blockchain technology and smart contract brings many benefits and solves the limitations of storage, data processing, transparency, and conflicts during transportation.

3.2 The Process of Transporting Goods Based on Blockchain Technology and Smart Contract

In this section we present the steps taken between the main actors in the system (i.e., the seller, the buyer, and the carrier)[3].

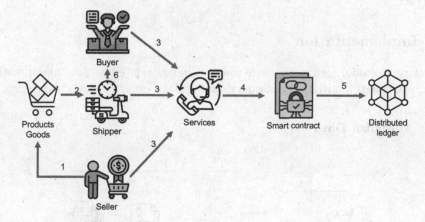

Fig. 4. The process of transporting goods based on blockchain technology and smart contract.

Figure 4 presents our proposal model based on blockchain technology and smart contract - the proposal system consists of six steps. We assume that the seller and the buyer have agreed on the delivery method as well as the price for the product. In this section, we design the system to move goods from seller to buyer. Specifically, step 1 presents the seller packing the product. Different from the model based on the traditional postal system (i.e., the seller sends the goods at the nearest post office), the seller is allowed to choose the corresponding shipping company (step 2). Step 3 presents the order confirmation process for each participating group. In it, the seller provides detailed information about the

---

[2] https://en.vietnamplus.vn/internet-infrastructure-to-get-strong-investment-this-year/221005.vnp.
[3] The role of Middleman, the originator of smart contracts, is not mentioned in this model. We assume that smart contracts accurately represent the requirements of the seller and the buyer. In addition, the handling of violations to determine the subject of compensation is also defined in smart contracts for each specific type of context.

product as well as a deposit to handle when there is a conflict. For shippers, their management company must pay a guarantee fee to avoid the case that the carrier loses or damages the goods during transportation. For the buyer, a deposit is required to resolve the conflict when the buyer does not want to pay the money. The above conventions are monitored through protocols designed on smart contracts and supported by pre-designed services in the system. Step 4 update the information to the smart contract to. The smart contract then updates the transactions to the distributed ledger and prepares for a new shipping process (step 5). Stakeholders can retrieve the package's location and estimated delivery time based on on-chain data updates. Finally, the buyer receives the goods and closes the transaction. Processes for handling conflicts or constraints when the buyer receives the goods are designed and executed automatically in the smart contract.

4   Implementation

Our reality model focuses on three main purposes related to data manipulation (i.e., wrapping) - initialization, query, and update - on the blockchain.

4.1   Initialize Data

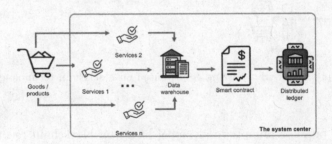

Fig. 5. Initialize data.

Figure 5 shows the steps to initialize the package data. These package types include information related to the sender (i.e., receiving address, weight, type of item), the recipient (i.e., receiving address, estimated time of receipt). In addition, the delivery and receipt of goods also requires a deposit of all three parties depending on the purpose and transactions between the parties to ensure automatic conflict resolution on the smart contract. In addition, information about which carrier belongs to which company, time, and place of delivery and receipt is also added to the metadata of the package. This is extremely important in cases where more than one shippers are involved in the shipment (i.e., the same or different shipping company). As for the storage process, services support concurrent storage (i.e., distributed processing as a peer-to-peer network) on a distributed ledger - supporting more than one user for concurrent storage reduce system latency. In general, the package data is organized as follows:[4]

```
goodsObject = {
"goodsID": goodsID,
"deliveryCompanyID": deliveryCompanyID,
"shipperID": shipperID,
"type": type of goods,
"buyerID": buyerID,
"sellerID": sellerID,
"quantity": quantity,
"unit": unit,
"packageID": packageID,
"addressReceived": received address,
"addressDelivery": delivery address,
"time": estimated delivery time,
"location": location,
"state": Null
};
```

Specifically, in addition to information for content extraction (i.e., place of origin, weight, item type, etc), we also store information regarding the status of the package at "addressReceived" (i.e., "state" - default value is Null). Specifically, "state" changes to 1 if the corresponding package has been received and shipped by the shipping company (i.e., "shipperID"); value 0 - pending (i.e., waiting for shipper to pick up). Also, "unit" stores the number of orders (e.g., 10) as well as which "packageID" they are assigned to. After receiving packages from the seller, the shipper checks them for compliance and waits for validation before syncing up the chain (i.e., temporary storage on the data warehouse). Then the pre-designed constraints in the Smart Contract are called through the API (i.e., name of function) to sync them up the chain. This inspection role is extremely important because they directly affect the shipping process of goods, as well as the premise for conflict resolution when any problems arise (e.g., damage to goods) goods, lost packages). The above information also contributes to conflict resolution (e.g., delivery delays). Definitions related to stakeholder deposit have been defined in our previous articles.

4.2   Data Query

Similar to the data initialization steps, the data query process also supports many simultaneous participants in the system for access (i.e., distributed model). Support services receive requests from shippers or sellers/buyers to access data

---

[4] The information related to the system participants is not listed in the article. Readers can refer to the group's previous studies at [2,5,16].

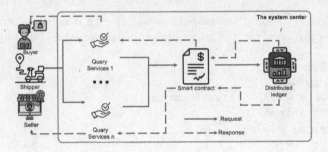

Fig. 6. Data query.

(i.e., respective packages). Depending on the query object we have different access purposes. Specifically, shippers query for the purpose of identifying consignee information and their addresses. In contrast, sellers/buyers view the status of their orders (i.e., after being delivered and received) as well as handle conflicts when something goes wrong. Figure 6 shows the steps to query the order data. These requests are sent as requests (i.e., pre-designed services as API calls) from the user to the smart contracts available in the system (i.e., name of function) before retrieving the data from the distributed ledger. All retrieval requests are also saved as query history for each individual or organization. For shipping processes that involve multiple discounts (i.e., multiple shippers deliver and receive the goods before reaching the buyer's address) package status updates are similarly generated between shippers (i.e., during or other shipping companies) and store them on a distributed ledger. In case the corresponding information is not found (e.g., wrong ID), the system will send a message not found results.

4.3   Data Updated

The data update routine is invoked only after verifying that the data exists on the thread (i.e., after executing the corresponding data query procedure). In this section, we assume that the search data exists on the string. Where none exists, the system sends the same message to the user (see Sect. 4.2 for details). Similar to the two processes of query and data initialization, we support update services in the form of APIs to receive requests from users before passing them to smart contract (i.e., name of function) for processing. The purpose of this process is to update the status of the package during transit as well as handle conflicts when something goes wrong. Figure 7 shows the process of updating order data. For package data (i.e., available) the update process includes only the transfer from the owner's address to the new address (i.e., new owner).

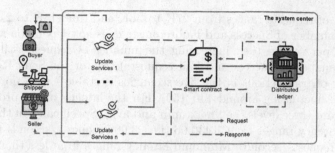

Fig. 7. Data updated.

5   Evaluation

Environment settings

Our model is deployed on Ubuntu 20.01 configuration, core i5 2.7Ghz, 8GB RAM. The proof-of-concept is implemented on the Hyperledger Fabric platform designed in docker containers. In this section, we measure the performance of chaincode in three scenarios (see Sect. 4 section), namely data initialization, querying and updating.

To evaluate the performance of the proposed model, we also define some metrics by exploiting Hyperledger Caliper[5]. Specifically, we analyze the following parameters: Success and Fail requests; Send Rate - transaction per second (TPS); Max, Min, and Average Latency(s); and Throughput (TPS). Our measurements are based on five scenarios (from 1,000 requests per second to 5,000 requests per second). The reason we stopped at 5,000 requests per second is because the number of Fail requests increases dramatically in the data update scenario (i.e., 5,000 requests/second).

5.1   Data Creation

The Table 1 presents the measurements across the five scenarios and the associated metrics. Specifically, for the number of requests for Success and Fail,

Table 1. Data creation of goods package.

Name	Success	Fail	Send Rate (TPS)	Max Latency (s)	Min Latency (s)	Avg Latency (s)	Throughput (TPS)
1,000 request	29,119	17,221	140.0	1,495.62	0.81	693.60	23.3
2,000 request	30,810	17,108	145.3	1,568.05	11.22	744.13	22.7
3,000 request	28,390	20,897	149.8	1,430.66	12.23	675.59	26.6
4,000 request	26,883	20,138	142.2	1,382.24	6.84	635.93	26.5
5,000 request	32,976	15,701	147.8	1,610.83	6.45	750.88	22.9

---

[5] https://www.hyperledger.org/use/caliper.

the number of requests ranges from 27K to 33K and from 15K to 21K, respectively. The number of Success and Fail requests does not depend on the number of requests per second (i.e., increasing the number of requests still does not affect the number of Success and Fail requests). As for the Send Rate (TPS), the number of transactions in the five scenarios is stable - with no discernible change (i.e., fluctuating around 140–150). For the latency of the proposed system, we record three levels (i.e., max, min and avg). Specifically, in the max scenario, the latency ranges from 1,430.66 (i.e., 3,000 requests/second) to 1,610.83 (i.e., 5,000 requests/second). Minimum latency ranges from less than 1 s (1,000 requests/second) to about 12 s (3,000 requests/second). The average latency of the whole system ranges from 635.93 to 750.88 s for each initialization request. Meanwhile, the throughput level fluctuates steadily between 22.7 and 26.6.

5.2 Data Query

To assess the responsiveness of the data retrieval request, we analyze the scenarios (i.e., 5 scenarios from 1,000 to 5,000 data retrieval requests per second). We initiate the retrieval request as dummy data (i.e., may not be compatible with data creation). For requests to access data that do not exist on-chain, the system returns a Fail request. In the first measurement regarding the number of requests successes and failures. We noticed a big difference between the number of successful requests (i.e., always above 106K) and the number of failed requests (i.e., less than 5K). Similar to the data creation scenario, Send Rate (TPS) and Throughput (TPS) are stable between 350 to 365 and 290 to 299, respectively. As for system latency, the maximum waiting time for data retrieval is 250 s (i.e., stable in all 5 measurement scenarios). Meanwhile, the minimum wait time for referrals is negligible (i.e., 0.01–0.02 s). Each request is answered on average in about 5 s pending retrieval (Table 2).

Table 2. Data query of goods package.

Name	Success	Fail	Send Rate (TPS)	Max Latency (s)	Min Latency (s)	Avg Latency (s)	Throughput (TPS)
1,000 request	106,268	4,260	354.0	252.36	0.01	4.92	290.20
2,000 request	107,040	4,253	356.5	251.90	0.01	5.23	292.80
3,000 request	107,984	4,578	360.7	252.04	0.01	5.30	296.80
4,000 request	107,717	4,554	359.8	251.98	0.01	5.30	296.00
5,000 request	109,553	3,854	363.6	251.68	0.02	5.15	299.90

5.3 Data Updated

As explained in the system settings, the reason the system only supports 5,000 requests per second is the spike in Fail requests in this measurement scenario. Specifically, the number of failed requests increased from 4,759 to 33,572 in the 5th scenario (i.e., about 6 times) - followed by the amount of Send Rate (TPS) increasing from 70.1 to 153.0 (2 times). This is different when compared to the two scenarios above - Send Rate (TPS) is stable. Minimum and average timeouts also spiked in the last two scenarios with changes from less than 1 s (i.e., 0.75) to 1,242.97 s (1.653x increase) and from 551.22 to 1,553.61 s (approximately 3-fold increase) - (see discussion to find out why). Meanwhile, Throughput (TPS) is still quite stable with a range of 9 to 13.4 TPS (Table 3).

Table 3. Data updated of goods package.

Name	Success	Fail	Send Rate (TPS)	Max Latency (s)	Min Latency (s)	Avg Latency (s)	Throughput (TPS)
1,000 request	19,034	3,561	60.9	1,300.20	0.59	491.22	10.5
2,000 request	19,991	4,421	66.9	1,404.62	5.48	543.80	10.5
3,000 request	18,885	3,481	59.9	1,290.87	0.53	479.67	10.6
4,000 request	20,659	4,759	70.1	1,542.62	0.75	551.22	9
5,000 request	16,657	33,572	153.0	2,360.13	1,242.97	1,553.61	13.4

6 Discussion

All of the above implementations (i.e., in the evaluation section) are deployed on our personal computers - configuration is limited. However, we found that the longest processing time in the case of a stable system (i.e., excluding system crashes - 5,000 updated requests/second) was 1,610.83 (i.e., 5,000) data creation requests/requests) approximately 26.8 min for an order creation request. This is acceptable in the real system (i.e., when the configuration of the machine is increased, the processing speed is increased). Also, there is a huge difference in the number of successful requests for data creation, data updated (lowest), and data query (highest). We use a data dummy when evaluating the system - generating data randomly and with no constraints between scenarios - so there is a high volume of failed requests when no data to update is found (i.e., each update has to go through a series of data in the system, increasing processing time).

In future work, we proceed to implement more complex methods/algorithms (i.e., encryption and decryption) as well as more complex data structures to observe the costs for the respective transactions. Deploying the proposed model in a real environment is also a possible approach (i.e., implementing the recommendation system on the FTM mainnet). In our current analysis, we have not considered issues related to the privacy policy of users (i.e., access control [15,16], dynamic policy [14,24]) - a possible approach would be implemented in upcoming research activities. Finally, infrastructure-based approaches (i.e., gRPC [8,20]; Microservices [18,21]; Dynamic transmission messages [22] and Brokerless [19]) can be integrated into the model of us to increase user interaction (i.e., API-call-based approach).

7   Conclusion

This paper presents research related to the improvement of the traditional freight transport model applied in Vietnam. Specifically, we propose a traditional freight model (i.e., the traditional postal system) that combines the constraints defined in the smart contract and the decentralized storage and transparency of the company blockchain technology. In this article, we have summarized three prominent traditional freight transport models in Vietnam as well as current approaches in the world. Thereby, we propose a freight model based on Blockchain technology and smart contract to solve the risks of the traditional model. Specifically, we implement the proposed model on the Hyperledger Fabric (i.e., proof-of-concept) platform. The evaluations related to three criteria (i.e., data initialization, data retrieval and data update) presented by us in the evaluation section based on the Hyperledger Caliper platform have demonstrated the feasibility of the model - proposal form. The pros and cons comments are listed in the discussion as well as possible expansion directions for the current system.

References

1. Two party contracts (2022). https://dappsforbeginners.wordpress.com/tutorials/two-party-contracts/
2. Duong-Trung, N., et al.: Multi-sessions mechanism for decentralized cash on delivery system. Int. J. Adv. Comput. Sci. Appl. **10**(9) (2020)
3. Ethereum: How our escrow smart contract works (2022). https://www.thenational.ae/business/technology/cash-on-delivery-the-biggest-obstacle-to-e-commerce-in-uae-and-region-1
4. Gwilliam, K.: Urban transport in developing countries. Transp. Rev. **23**(2), 197–216 (2003)
5. Ha, X.S., Le, H.T., Metoui, N., Duong-Trung, N.: DeM-CoD: novel access-control-based cash on delivery mechanism for decentralized marketplace. In: 2020 IEEE 19th International Conference on Trust, Security and Privacy in Computing and Communications (TrustCom), pp. 71–78. IEEE (2020)
6. Ha, X.S., Le, T.H., Phan, T.T., Nguyen, H.H.D., Vo, H.K., Duong-Trung, N.: Scrutinizing trust and transparency in cash on delivery systems. In: Wang, G., Chen, B., Li, W., Di Pietro, R., Yan, X., Han, H. (eds.) SpaCCS 2020. LNCS, vol. 12382, pp. 214–227. Springer, Cham (2021). https://doi.org/10.1007/978-3-030-68851-6_15
7. Hoang, N.M., Son, H.X.: A dynamic solution for fine-grained policy conflict resolution. In: Proceedings of the 3rd International Conference on Cryptography, Security and Privacy, pp. 116–120 (2019)
8. Lam, N.T.T., et al.: BMDD: a novel approach for IoT platform (broker-less and microservice architecture, decentralized identity, and dynamic transmission messages). Int. J. Adv. Comput. Sci. Appl. (2022)
9. Le, H.T., Le, N.T.T., Phien, N.N., Duong-Trung, N.: Introducing multi shippers mechanism for decentralized cash on delivery system. Int. J. Adv. Comput. Sci. Appl. **10**(6) (2019)
10. Le, N.T.T., et al.: Assuring non-fraudulent transactions in cash on delivery by introducing double smart contracts. Int. J. Adv. Comput. Sci. Appl. **10**(5), 677–684 (2019)

11. OpenBazaar: Truly decentralized, peer-to-peer ecommerce features (2022). https:// openbazaar.org/features/

12. Quoc, K.L., et al.: SSSB: an approach to insurance for cross-border exchange by using smart contracts. In: Awan, I., Younas, M., Poniszewska-Marańda, A. (eds.) MobiWIS 2022. LNCS, vol. 13475, pp. 179–192. Springer, Cham (2022). https:// doi.org/10.1007/978-3-031-14391-5_14

13. Sinha, D., Chowdhury, S.R.: Blockchain-based smart contract for international business-a framework. J. Glob. Oper. Strategic Sour. **14**, 224–260 (2021)

14. Son, H.X., Dang, T.K., Massacci, F.: REW-SMT: a new approach for rewriting XACML request with dynamic big data security policies. In: Wang, G., Atiquzzaman, M., Yan, Z., Choo, K.-K.R. (eds.) SpaCCS 2017. LNCS, vol. 10656, pp. 501–515. Springer, Cham (2017). https://doi.org/10.1007/978-3-319-72389-1_40

15. Son, H.X., Hoang, N.M.: A novel attribute-based access control system for fine-grained privacy protection. In: Proceedings of the 3rd International Conference on Cryptography, Security and Privacy, pp. 76–80 (2019)

16. Son, H.X., Nguyen, M.H., Vo, H.K., Nguyen, T.P.: Toward an privacy protection based on access control model in hybrid cloud for healthcare systems. In: Martínez Álvarez, F., Troncoso Lora, A., Sáez Muñoz, J.A., Quintián, H., Corchado, E. (eds.) CISIS/ICEUTE -2019. AISC, vol. 951, pp. 77–86. Springer, Cham (2020). https:// doi.org/10.1007/978-3-030-20005-3_8

17. Son, H.X., et al.: Towards a mechanism for protecting seller's interest of cash on delivery by using smart contract in hyperledger. Int. J. Adv. Comput. Sci. Appl. **10**(4), 45–50 (2019)

18. Thanh, L.N.T., et al.: IoHT-MBA: an internet of healthcare things (IoHT) platform based on microservice and brokerless architecture. Int. J. Adv. Comput. Sci. Appl. **12**(7) (2021). https://doi.org/10.14569/IJACSA.2021.0120768

19. Thanh, L.N.T., et al.: Sip-MBA: a secure IoT platform with brokerless and micro-service architecture. Int. J. Adv. Comput. Sci. Appl. (2021)

20. Thanh, L.N.T., et al.: Toward a security IoT platform with high rate transmission and low energy consumption. In: Gervasi, O., et al. (eds.) ICCSA 2021. LNCS, vol. 12949, pp. 647–662. Springer, Cham (2021). https://doi.org/10.1007/978-3-030-86653-2_47

21. Nguyen, T.T.L., et al.: Toward a unique IoT network via single sign-on protocol and message queue. In: Saeed, K., Dvorský, J. (eds.) CISIM 2021. LNCS, vol. 12883, pp. 270–284. Springer, Cham (2021). https://doi.org/10.1007/978-3-030-84340-3_22

22. Thanh, L.N.T., et al.: UIP2SOP: a unique IoT network applying single sign-on and message queue protocol. IJACSA **12**(6) (2021)

23. Thi, Q.N.T., Dang, T.K., Van, H.L., Son, H.X.: Using JSON to specify privacy preserving-enabled attribute-based access control policies. In: Wang, G., Atiquzzaman, M., Yan, Z., Choo, K.-K.R. (eds.) SpaCCS 2017. LNCS, vol. 10656, pp. 561–570. Springer, Cham (2017). https://doi.org/10.1007/978-3-319-72389-1_44

24. Xuan, S.H., et al.: Rew-XAC: an approach to rewriting request for elastic ABAC enforcement with dynamic policies. In: 2016 International Conference on Advanced Computing and Applications (ACOMP), pp. 25–31. IEEE (2016)

MITRE ATT and CK Threat Modelling Extensions for Mobile Threats

Thoai van Do[1], Van Thuan Do[2,3], Niels Jacot[3], Bernardo Flores[2], Boning Feng[2], and Thanh van Do[2(✉)]

[1] University of Oslo, Gaustadalléen 23B, 0373 Oslo, Norway
thoaivd@ifi.uio.no
[2] Oslo Metropolitan University, Pilestredet 35, 0167 Oslo, Norway
vt.do@wolffia.net, {bersan,boning.feng,thanh}@oslomet.no
[3] Wolffia AS, Haugerudveien, 40, 0673 Oslo, Norway
n.jacot@wolffia.net

Abstract. With the advent of 5G mobile networks enabling connectivity to billions of devices it is essential to model and analyze threat on mobile threats. To model sophisticated threats such as Advanced Persistent Threats (APT) the MITRE ATT&CK is one of the best threat modelling framework. Unfortunately, it does not address sufficiently mobile networks. This paper provides a brief description of the 5G mobile networks and the potential threats on it. The limitations of the MITRE ATT&CK for mobile networks are clarified before a description of the CONCORDIA Mobile Threat Modelling Framework (CMTMF) is given in details. The main part of the paper is the integration of the CMTMF in the MITRE ATT&CK.

Keywords: 5G mobile networks · 5G security · mobile threat analysis · mobile threat modelling · MITRE ATT&CK

1 Introduction

With the arrival of 5G offering a wide range of connectivity supporting various devices from data-hungry smartphones to primitive sensors and high precision devices requiring ultra-reliable and low latency connections, the number of connected devices has massively increased. According to Statista[1], "the number of Internet of Things (IoT) devices worldwide is forecast to almost triple from 9.7 billion in 2020 to more than 29 billion IoT devices in 2030". While these devices will provide useful and fancy applications and services which enrich the life of people they also bring with them new cyber security threats.

Indeed, the cyber threat landscape is dramatically changed due to the large and quickly expanding surface through billion devices and due to the huge amount of data generated by these devices. The traditional cyber security perimeter defense based on the

---

[1] https://www.statista.com/statistics/1183457/iot-connected-devices-worldwide/

M. Younas et al. (Eds.): MobiWIS 2023, LNCS 13977, pp. 252–263, 2023.
https://doi.org/10.1007/978-3-031-39764-6_17

filtering of incoming data for potential threats at entry points to the home network Perimeter is no longer sufficient. This calls for a new cyber security strategy namely Threat Intelligence and Threat Modelling which identify, analyze and provide mitigations to cyber threats.

Currently, the MITRE ATT&CK [1] is one of the most efficient threat modelling frameworks which provides solid fundaments for the description and analyses of cyber threats of enterprise networks and mobile devices. Unfortunately, it does address neither the 5G networks nor the mobile networks in general.

Indeed, as software mobile networks, 5G networks are not only subject to the same cyber threats as regular enterprise networks but are also exposed to the ones brought by its capability of providing connectivity to billions of IoT devices ranging from primitive sensors to advanced medical equipment requiring ultra-reliable and low-latency connections. Potential attackers to 5G networks have different behaviours, tactics and techniques that require extensions to the current MITRE ATT&CK framework. The Bhadra framework [2] is the first attempt to extend the MITRE ATT&CK framework for mobile networks which emphasizes the need for modelling threats in mobile networks but is unfortunately too simple and incompatible with the mainstream MITRE ATT&CK framework. The second proposal is the CONCORDIA Mobile Threat Modelling Framework (CMTMF) [3], which is a compatible combination of the enterprise, mobile and ICS (Industrial Control Systems) matrices of the MITRE ATT&CK framework. However, the work in CONCORDIA is still at early stage and lacks details about tactics and techniques. Most importantly, it is not yet integrated in the MITRE ATT&CK Framework. The work in this paper describes the integration of the CMTMF extension in the MITRE ATT&CK and enabling modeling of mobile threats in MITRE ATT&CK.

The paper starts with a brief introduction of the 5G mobile networks. Next, the threat modelling framework will be introduced followed by a concise description of the MITRE ATT&CK framework. The threats in the 5G networks are summarized before the CONCORDIA Mobile Threat Modelling Framework is explained. The main part of the paper is the description of the integration of the CMTMF in the MITRE ATT&CK. A description of a partial proof-of-concept implemented at the Secure 5G4IoT lab at the Oslo Metropolitan University is given to complete the paper which is concluded by some suggestions of further works.

2 Short Introduction of 5G Mobile Networks

Although as the 5th generation mobile network (5G does have the common characteristics of a mobile network it comes with fundamental differences with its predecessors 4G, 3G and 2G. Indeed, while earlier mobile networks are intended merely for mobile phones, the ultimate objective of 5G is to be able to support not only data-hungry smart phones but also Massive Machine Type Communication (mMTC) e.g. primitive IoT (Internet of Things) or sensors and also Ultra-Reliable Low Latency Communications (URLLC) necessary for autonomous driving, remote control in factories, remote surgery, etc. [4].

To be able to achieve its objectives 5G will make use of state-of-the art technology enablers like Cloud-Native, Software Defined Radio, Network Function Virtualization and Multi-Access Edge Computing (MEC) to realize its core concept called **Network slicing**.

The building blocks of the 2G, 3G and 4G mobile networks are network elements, physical entities which are built upon dedicated hardware computers running specific functional software and executing standardized communication protocols. Although mobile operators can reconfigure their networks by adding, moving or removing network resources to meet the demands, such a task could be tedious and time-consuming. The management and operation of traditional mobile networks although fully feasible are complicated and demanding a lot of resources.

The 5G mobile network differs radically from its predecessors because it is no longer composed of physical network elements but is made of virtual Network Functions (vNF) [6] as shown in Fig. 1. 5G is softwarised network that can also be cloudified i.e. its vNFs are moved from local servers to data centers in the cloud.

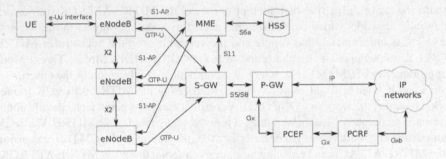

Fig. 1. The LTE Network Architecture (courtesy: YateBTS)

By instantiating and connecting a set of vNFs together using SDN (Software Define Networking), a virtual network can be dynamically created. Software-defined networking (SDN) technology is an approach to network management that enables dynamic, programmatically efficient network configuration in order to improve network performance and monitoring [6].

Such a virtual network constitutes the fundament of the concept of Network Slicing in 5G network. In fact, as stated in [7] "to realize network slicing, network slice logically consists of dedicated or shared network functions (NFs) of 5G SA network and resources by utilizing emerging technologies such as virtualization so as to provide required network capability".

3   Briefly About Threat Modelling Frameworks

Threat Modelling is the activity aiming at identifying, understanding and making simple descriptions or models of the potential threats and attack vectors that a system could be exposed for such that risk analyses, detection methods, countermeasures, and mitigation strategies can be developed. A threat modeling framework usually includes five components, namely threat intelligence, asset identification, mitigation capabilities, risk assessment and threat mapping, but may have different focuses [8] as follows:

- Asset-centric threat modelling frameworks focus on the assets of the target system
- Attack-centric threat modelling framework focus on the attackers and attacks
- System-centric threat modelling framework focus on target system

It will be shown later that the attack-centric approach is most appropriate for the threat modelling of mobile networks and the MITRE ATT&CK is selected as fundament for this work.

4   The MITRE ATT and CK

"MITRE's Adversarial Tactics, Techniques, and Common Knowledge (ATT&CK) is a curated knowledge base and model for cyber adversary behavior, reflecting the various phases of an adversary's attack lifecycle and the platforms they are known to target." [1].

Established in 2010, the Fort Meade Experiment (FMX) research facility allowed researchers to use MITRE's tools with the purpose of how to better detect threats [1]. The type of tests and activities done in that environment where always done under the assumption that a breach in their network or infrastructure has happened and the researchers were to document all the detected threats and come up with possible ways to impede a widespread effect or to protect the infrastructure from the tested exploits.

The MITRE ATT&CK includes a set of matrices which focus on different types of system such as Enterprise, Mobile, ICS (Industrial Control System), Cloud, etc.

The building blocks of MITRE ATT&CK framework consist of tactics and techniques.

Tactic explains the reason why an attacker performs a certain action [1]. An APT Advanced Persistent Threat (APT) can usually be modelled by a series of tactics.

Technique describes in details how an action is performed by an attacker. Multiple techniques can be grouped under the same tactic.

The Tactics and Techniques are classified in a set of matrices which focus on different types of system such as Enterprise, Mobile, ICS (Industrial Control System), Cloud, etc. and shall be used in the modelling of threats in these respective systems.

Last but not least the MITRE ATT&CK includes also procedures describing the implementation of tactics and techniques and mitigations when facing a specific threat.

5   Threats in 5G Mobile Networks

Although enhancements have been in 5G networks to strengthen security and privacy considerably compared to 4G networks the 5G new capabilities and features such as the support of a wider variety of devices and applications, virtualization and cloudification, interfacing with multiple vertical sectors, etc. introduced new threats to the 5G networks.

To have an overview of the threats to 5G networks, it is essential to identify all the entry points to the 5G network and thereafter to derive and analyze all the possible threats at these entry points. As shown in Fig. 2 these entry points are the following:

- Mobile devices

- Access network
- Core network
- External services and applications

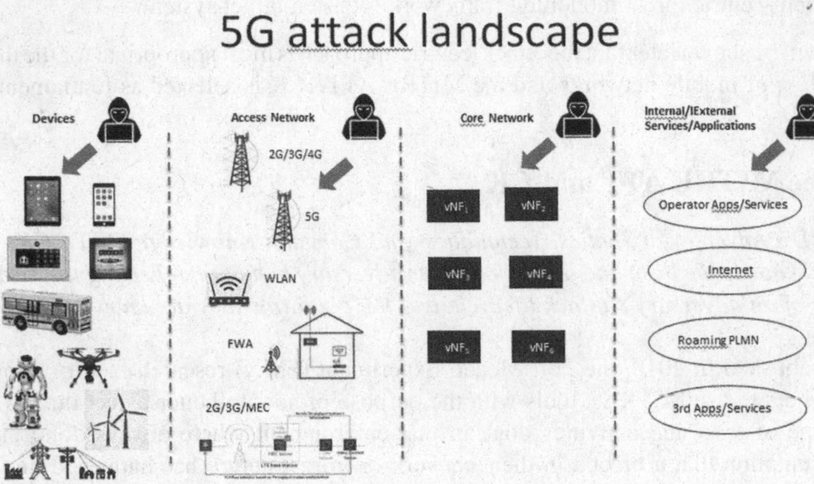

5G attack landscape

Fig. 2. Attack Entry Points to the 5G network

Let us now consider these entry points consecutively.

Mobile Devices

In the predecessor 4G, 3G and 2G networks, mobile devices are mostly smart phones that consist of two main components namely the Mobile Equipment (ME) and the Subscriber Identity Module (SIM). A smartphone can be fully identified by the mobile operator using the IMSI (International Mobile Subscriber Identity) and the IMEI (International Mobile Equipment Identity) and get granted access to the mobile network only after successful strong authentication. The landscape has been changed dramatically because 5G is supposed to support not only smartphones but an open range of devices ranging from primitive sensors to powerful supercomputers. Mobile operators do no longer have the knowledge of what kind of devices are operating in their networks because the authentication process only verifies that the device has a legitimate subscription i.e. IMSI, but cannot tell whether the device is benign and trustful or malicious and distrusting. A large number of infected devices can flood and take the mobile network down easily and so far there is no countermeasure to stop such a flooding attack because the devices are already inside the network. This is probably the biggest difference with the fixed networks which are protected by firewalls against unauthorized intrusions and only a limited number of trustful devices are allowed to penetrate the intranet.

If it is not possible to stop a flooding attack once it is started, the only solution may be to detect and prevent it before its initiation. For that, it is crucial to understand the behaviours of the devices and most importantly the techniques, tactics and knowledge of the potential attackers.

Access Network
The 5G Access Network is exposed to the same physical threats as its predecessors due to the common characteristic of an access network which is its huge geographical coverage making their protection quite challenging. Indeed, the base stations and antenna masts are scattered all around the country and are exposed to physical threats such as theft and vandalism. In addition, new threats are introduced with the new 5G capabilities and features such as local breakout allowing IP packets of roaming subscribers to be sent directly to the Internet from the visited network and MEC (Multi-Access Edge Computing). Direct interfacing with 3rd parties at the access network could be a vulnerability that can be exploited by attackers.

Core Network
The 5G Core Network is built up by software components and is hence as vulnerable as other software to cyber threats such as data confidentiality, data privacy, key security and encryption application level authentication [9]. Security measures have to be identified and designed meticulously to protect the Core Network. Although most operators tend to use private cloud instead of public multi-tenant cloud Virtualization and cloudification bring yet other challenges such as side-channel attacks, flooding attacks, hypervisor hijacking, malware injection, and virtual machine (VM) migration related attacks [9].

Interfacing with Applications and Services
In addition to the traditional interfaces with other mobile networks and interfaces with their own applications and services the 5G network had also interfaces with the Internet and third parties. Adequate perimeter defense such as firewalls, border control gateways secure gateways, etc. must be deployed to protect the mobile network while allowing legitimate traffic to flow normally.

6   The CONCORDIA Mobile Threat Modelling Framework (CMTMF)

Although the MITRE ATT&CK framework is quite efficient to model threats on enterprise networks, mobile devices, Industrial Control System), Cloud, etc. it is not sufficient to model mobile threats.

To illustrate this limitation let us consider the typical example of flood attacks by mobile devices.

This threat consists of two stages:

1. Stage 1 - Infection and hijacking of devices: occurs recursively on devices
2. Stage 2 - Flood attack on the mobile network: happens on the mobile network and will only be initiated when the number of infected devices has reached a certain threshold.

To model the flood attack on the mobile network it is not sufficient to use one matrix but two. First, the Mobile matrix should be used and then the Enterprise matrix. It is

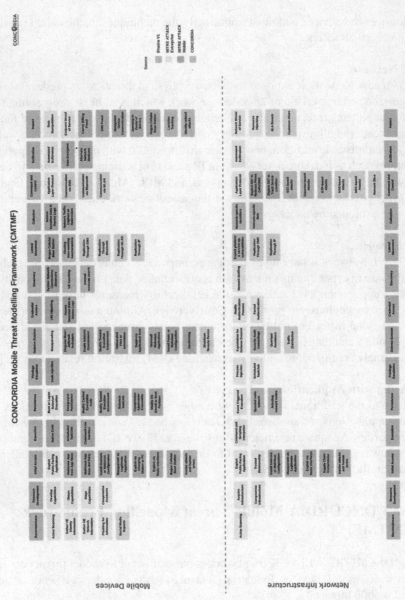

Fig. 3. The CONCORDIA Mobile Threat Modelling Framework (CMTMF)

not possible to link the two stages together. Further, when the flood attack is launched on the mobile network it is initiated repetitively on numerous devices. This technique should belong to the Enterprise matrix but its performance should belong to the Mobile matrix. Moreover, if the flood attack is launched on the control plane of the mobile network, there is currently no technique to describe it and new techniques specific for

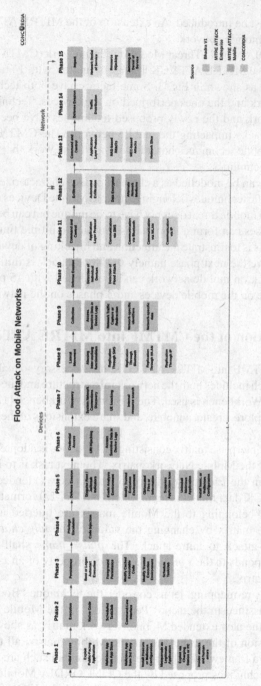

Fig. 4. The anatomy of Flood Attacks in Mobile Networks

mobile networks must be introduced. An extension of the MITRE ATT&CK is required to model threats on mobile network.

The CONCORDIA Mobile Threat Modelling Framework (CMTMF) is an extension which is aligned to the MITRE ATT&CK Enterprise matrix with 14 tactics from Reconnaissance to Impact as shown in Fig. 3. Some tactics have both techniques belonging to the mobile network and the ones performed on the devices. Techniques proposed by the Bhadra framework and the newly proposed techniques have been added to enable the modelling of attacks impacting the mobile network. The CMTMF has currently a few new specific mobile techniques but it is "living" framework that will be constantly updated with new techniques.

A mobile threat can be modelled as a chain of phases characterized by tactics which are realised by specific techniques belonging either to Mobile Devices or Network Infrastructure. A tactic in a mobile threat does not have to be unique but can be repeated multiple phases. Several phases can form a loop that is repeated multiple times before the next phase can begin. This is to illustrate the infection and hijacking of devices that is repeated multiple times before the next phase namely the flood attack is initiated. As shown in Fig. 4, a Flood attack on mobile network can be modelled with 15 phases in which 11 phases are repetitive on the mobile devices and 3 phases on the network infrastructure.

7   The Integration of the CMTMF into MITRE ATT&CK

To integrate the CMTMF into MITRE ATT&CK, it is necessary to make a new matrix for mobile domain which includes both the network infrastructure and the mobile device. For that, the ATT&CK Workbench is used. The ATT&CK Workbench [12] is an application allowing users to explore, create, annotate, and share extensions of the MITRE ATT&CK knowledge base.

The ATT&CK Enterprise matrix consisting of 14 tactics is adopted as the fundament as the fundament of the Mobile Network matrix. The next task is to include the Mobile matrix techniques in the Enterprise matrix to form a new extended Mobile Network matrix. The ATT&CK data model is represented in STIX 2.0 format.

The techniques belonging to the Mobile matrix are queried and mapped to the enlarged Enterprise matrix by changing the value of the *kill_chain_phases* property from mitre-mobile-attack to mitre-attack. The *phase_name* shall correspond to the phase_name corresponds to the *x_mitre_shortname* property of an *x-mitre-tactic* object in the Enterprise matrix.

To illustrate this re-mapping, let us consider the technique "Boot or Logon Initialization Scripts" classified in the tactic "Persistence" in the Mobile matrix which is in now re-mapped to the new extended Mobile Network matrix as shown in Fig. 5.

After the inclusion of the techniques of the Mobile matrix, all the techniques proposed by the Bhadra framework [2] for the mobile domain such are also included. Last but not least, the techniques proposed by the CONCORDIA Mobile Threat Modelling Framework (CMTMF) are included. To illustrate the task the JSON STIX description of the proposed *"NAS-based attacks"* technique associated to the tactic *"command-and-control"*. Attacks on the Non-Access Stratum (NAS) [11] on the mobile network are typical threats that may happen only on the 5G mobile networks.

```
{
        "modified": "2023-03-16T18:26:46.043Z",
        "name": "Boot or Logon Initialization Scripts",
        "description": "Adversaries may use scripts automat ically executed at boot or lo-
gon initialization to establish persistence. Initialization scr    ipts are part of the underlying
operating system and are not accessible to the user unless the    device has been rooted or
jailbroken. ",
        "kill_chain_phases": [
          {
            "kill_chain_name": "mitre-mobile-attack",
            "phase_name": "persistence"
          }
        ],
        ::::::::::
    },
```

Fig. 5. Mapping technique to the new extended Mobile Network matrix

It is worth noting that the inclusion of techniques to the Mobile Network matrix is continuous work in progress and new techniques will be added once they are identified.

To describe an Advanced Persistent Threat (APT) like the flood attack on the mobile network, the ATT&CK Navigator [12] is used. The ATT&CK Navigator is a web-based tool for annotating and exploring ATT&CK matrices. It can be used to visualize defensive coverage, red/blue team planning, the frequency of detected techniques, and more. For the description of an APT attack we propose to create a new layer and to select the tactics and techniques that may be used in this attack (Figs. 6 and 7).

```
          "x_mitre_deprecated": false,
          "x_mitre_detection": "",
          "x_mitre_domains": [
            "enterprise-attack"
          ],
          "x_mitre_is_subtechnique": false,
          "x_mitre_platforms": [
            "Android",
            "iOS",
          ],
          "x_mitre_version": "1.0",
          "x_mitre_data_sources": [
            ""Network Traffic: NAS Traffic Flow""
          ],
          "type": "attack-pattern",
          "id": "attack-pattern--02c5abff-30bf-4703-ab92-1f6072fae939",
          "created": "2023-03-23T19:55:25.546Z",
          "created_by_ref": "identity--c78cb6e5-0c4b-4611-8297-d1b8b55e40b5",
          "revoked": false,
          "external_references": [
            {
              "source_name": "mitre-attack",
              "url": "https://xxx/T3001",
              "external_id": "T3001"
            }
```

Fig. 6. JSON STIX description of NAS-based attacks technique (Part 1)

```
          "modified": "2023-05-04T18:06:40.829Z",
          "name": "NAS-based attacks",
          "description": "By infecting and hijacking mobile phones and IoT devices adversaries may
order them to perform simultaneously Non-Access Stratum (NAS) procedure [3GPP TS 24.501  5G;.
System architecture for the 5G System (5GS) -   3GPP TS 29.518 5G System, Access and Mobility
Management Services] such as Authentication request, UE configuration update, Registration, etc.
and hence overloading the control plane of the 5G core network.  All the subscriber's access will be
blocked resulting to a Denial of Service. In a worst scenario, the 5G Core Access and Mobility Man-
agement Function (AMF) may crash and the whole 5G Core will collapse",
          "kill_chain_phases": [
            {
              "kill_chain_name": "mitre-attack",
              "phase_name": "command-and-control""
            }
          ],
          "x_mitre_contributors": [
            "Thoai van Do",
            "Bernardo Flores",
            "Thuan Do van",
            "Boning Feng",
            "Niels Jacot",
            "Thanh van Do"
          ],
```

Fig. 7. JSON STIX description of NAS-based attacks technique (Part 2)

8 Conclusion

In this paper we have demonstrated the urgent need to model and analyze the cyber threats in the mobile network which did not yet receive sufficient attention due to the misunderstanding about the mobile network. Although 5G mobile networks are softwarised and cloudified the mobile architecture differs considerably from the fixed IP networks and multiple mobile protocols are different and specific to the mobile networks. The MITRE ATT&CK is a very powerful cyber threat modelling framework but is unfortunately not sufficient for the modelling and analyses of threats on the mobile network. This paper describes the continuation of work in the EU CONCORDIA project that proposes an extension to the MITRE ATT&CK called the CONCORDIA Mobile Threat Modelling Framework (CMTMF). Indeed, the integration of the CMTMF is carried out and although is not yet completed with all the techniques, its feasibility is demonstrated. For further works, more threats on the mobile networks will be modelled and analyzed and more techniques will be added.

References

1. Strom, B.E., Miller, D.P., Nickels, K.C., Pennington, A.G., Thomas, C.B.: MITRE-ATT&CK: Design-and-Philosophy (2018). https://www.MITRE.org/publications/technical-papers/MITRE-attack-design-and-philosophy
2. Rao, S.P., Holtmanns, S., Aura, T.: Threat modelling framework for mobile communication systems (2020). http://arxiv.org/abs/2005.05110
3. Santos, B., et al.: Threat modelling for 5G networks. In: 2022 International Wireless Communications and Mobile Computing (IWCMC). The Printing House; Dubrovnik, Croatia (2022). ISBN: 9781665467490
4. 5G America: Becoming 5G advanced: the 3GPP 2025 Roadmap (2022)
5. 5GPP: 5G PPP Architecture Working Group - View on 5G Architecture, Version 1.0 (2016)
6. Hakiri, A., Gokhale, A., Berthou, P., Schmidt, D., Gayraud, T.: Software-defined networking: challenges and research opportunities for future internet. Comput. Netw. **75**, 453–471 (2014). https://doi.org/10.1016/j.comnet.2014.10.015
7. GSMA: E2E Network Slicing Architecture - Version 1.0 (2021)
8. Nweke, L., Wolthusen, S.: A review of asset-centric threat modelling approaches. Int. J. Adv. Comput. Sci. Appl. **11**, 1–6 (2020). https://doi.org/10.14569/IJACSA.2020.0110201
9. GSA (Global mobile Suppliers Association): 5G Security Primer: A GSA White Paper (2019)
10. Ahmad, I., Kumar, T., Liyanage, M., Okwuibe, J., Ylianttila, M., Gurtov, A.: Overview of 5G security challenges and solutions. IEEE Commun. Stan. Mag. **2**, 36–43 (2018)
11. ETSI: 5G; Non-Access-Stratum (NAS) protocol for 5G System (5GS); Stage 3 (3GPP TS 24.501 version 16.5.1 Release 16) - ETSI TS 124 501 V16.5.1 (2020)
12. MITRE ATT&CK® Workbench. https://attack.mitre.org/resources/working-with-attack/. MITRE ATT&CK® Navigator. https://mitre-attack.github.io/attack-navigator/

Virtual Career Advisor System

Tracey John[1], Dwaine Clarke[1(✉)] ⓘ, Daniel Coore[2], Fabian Monrose[3], and John McHugh[4]

[1] University of the West Indies, Bridgetown, Barbados
tjohn@hummingbirdresearchgroup.net, declarke@declarke.net
[2] University of the West Indies, Kingston, Jamaica
daniel.coore@uwimona.edu.jm
[3] Georgia Institute of Technology, Atlanta, GA, USA
fabian@ece.gatech.edu
[4] University of South Florida, Tampa, FL, USA
mchugh@cs.unc.edu

Abstract. The Dolphin system is a novel virtual career advisor system that implements artificial neural networks trained on student data to provide students with career advice. The Dolphin system consists of two advisors: an Experiences-to-Careers advisor and a Careers-to-Experiences advisor. Each advisor uses an artificial neural network. The Experiences-to-Careers advisor takes as input a student's course experience ratings and returns as output a career ranking. The Careers-to-Experiences advisor takes as input a student's career ranking and returns as output course experience ratings. We present the design, implementation and evaluation of the Dolphin system.

Keywords: Artificial neural network · Artificial neural network model · Back-propagation learning algorithm · Career advisor system · Machine learning

1 Introduction

A student at a university is typically assigned an advisor who is a faculty member that the student can contact to receive advice on which careers would be the best fit for the set of courses the student has taken or may be interested in taking and receive advice on which courses would be the best fit for the careers the student may be interested in pursuing. Unfortunately, in a department where the student to faculty ratio is very high, an advisor may not be able to devote as much time to each of his advisees as the advisor or advisee would like.

At a university, student grades are under the authority of the university's registrar office. The university may not give access to student grades or allow student grades to be used to develop a virtual advisor system because of security and privacy concerns.

The Dolphin system [4] is a novel virtual career advisor system that implements artificial neural networks trained on student data to provide students with career advice. The Dolphin system introduces a novel computational system to career advisement. The Dolphin system consists of two advisors: an Experiences-to-Careers advisor and a Careers-to-Experiences advisor. Each advisor uses an artificial neural network (ANN). The Experiences-to-Careers advisor takes as input a student's course experience ratings and returns as output a career ranking. The Careers-to-Experiences advisor takes as input a student's career ranking and returns as output course experience ratings. The main objective of the Dolphin system is to introduce a highly-available career advisor with which a student can receive satisfactory career advice. We present the design, implementation and evaluation of the Dolphin system.

Importantly, the student data that the Dolphin system uses, a student's course experience ratings and career ranking, is different from the student's grades. For example, a student may earn an A in a course but not enjoy the course. The Dolphin system uses student data that a university does not typically collect to provide students with career advice.

We use ANNs for the Dolphin system as an ANN uses patterns the ANN has learned in the data to predict the output for new input [5]. As we detail in Sect. 4.3, in our implementation of the Dolphin system, we train, validate and test the ANN models on a computer different from the computer which runs the server with the Dolphin system's user interface. After we train, validate and test the ANN models on one computer, we then copy the models to a different computer which runs the server with the Dolphin system's user interface to deploy the models. The Dolphin system's user interface uses these models to return career advice to student queries. The student data is not stored on, and does not need to be accessed by, the computer which runs the server with the Dolphin system's user interface. The Dolphin system provides career advice without the student data being stored on the computer which runs the server with the Dolphin system's user interface.

The main contributions of this paper include:

1. A novel virtual career advisor system, the Dolphin system, that implements artificial neural networks (ANNs) trained on student data to provide students with career advice. The Dolphin system introduces a novel computational system to career advisement.
2. Our design of the Dolphin system including the data that we use for the Dolphin system and our design of each advisor's artificial neural network.
3. Results showing that the majority of students who used the Dolphin system to receive career advice indicated that they were satisfied with the career advice they received from the Dolphin system.
4. Results showing that the majority of students who used the Dolphin system to receive career advice indicated that they prefer to use the Dolphin system along with a human advisor. Of these students, a common reason for the students' choice is that the Dolphin system provides a perspective different from that of a human advisor.

The paper is organized as follows. Section 2 describes related work. Section 3 details the data we use to train, validate and test the Dolphin system's ANNs.

Section 4 details the ANNs we use in the Dolphin system. Section 5 presents the Dolphin system's user interface. Section 6 presents results from students who used the Dolphin system to receive career advice. Section 7 concludes the paper.

2   Related Work

John and Clarke [4] introduce the Dolphin system and the Dolphin system's Experiences-to-Careers advisor. In this paper, we extend this work with the Dolphin system's Careers-to-Experiences advisor. This paper presents an updated design of the Dolphin system, including an updated design of the Dolphin system's Experiences-to-Careers advisor. This paper also presents an implementation of the Dolphin system that uses more recent software, TensorFlow [7], to implement each advisor's artificial neural network. With this implementation, this paper also presents the results of evaluating each advisor's artificial neural network and the results of students who used the Dolphin system to receive career advice.

MASACAD (Multi-Agent System for ACademic ADvising) [3] incorporates an artificial neural network to offer university Computer Science students academic advice using a representation of students' grades as part of the input to the artificial neural network. Whereas the MASACAD system used an artificial neural network to determine academic advice for a student, the Dolphin system uses artificial neural networks to determine career advice for a student. Importantly, the Dolphin system does not use student grades because a university may not give access to student grades or allow student grades to be used to develop a virtual advisor system because of security and privacy concerns. The Dolphin system uses student data that a university does not typically collect to provide students with career advice. Also, the Dolphin system consists of an Experiences-to-Careers advisor which takes as input a student's course experience ratings and returns as output a career ranking and a Careers-to-Experiences advisor which takes as input a student's career ranking and returns as output course experience ratings. We believe that the design of the Dolphin system is novel.

3   Data

3.1   Data to Train, Validate and Test the Dolphin System's ANNs

We conducted this research among Computer Science students. The Computer Science degree program at the university at which we conducted this research is a three-year program with first-year, second-year and third-year courses. Also, students are generally in their first year, second year or final (third) year in the Computer Science degree program. The university's academic calendar consists of two semesters, the first semester (Semester I) and the second semester (Semester II). We note that we believe that the Dolphin system's design can also be applied to degree programs other than the degree program we used for this research and universities other than the university at which we conducted this research.

We use an anonymous, paper survey to survey students for data to train, validate and test the Dolphin system's ANNs. For this survey, students were recruited via email and from second-semester third-year Computer Science courses with large enrollments.

We survey a set of students to each indicate the courses the student has taken or is taking and rate each of the courses the student has taken/is taking with the student's course experience rating according to the student's level of enjoyment of the course with (5) as the highest rating and (1) as the lowest rating. These ratings form the student's course experience ratings.

We identify a list of popular Computer Science careers based on the courses the university offers and the employment opportunities available to students: Computer Programmer/Software Engineer, Network Engineer, System Administrator, University Faculty Member and Web Developer. We also survey the set of students to each rank these careers in the order in which the student is most interested with (5) for the career in which the student is most interested and (1) for the career in which the student is least interested (careers are listed in alphabetical order). Each career must have a unique rank, i.e., the student must select 5 for a career exactly once, select 4 for a career exactly once, etc. This ranking forms the student's career ranking.

With reference to a student's course experience ratings, in the data for the ANNs, if a student did not take a course, we use zero as the course experience rating for this student's course. ANNs use numerical values as inputs. The more students that have rated a course, the more data we have for the course and the more data for the course the ANNs can use during training, validation and testing. The Careers-to-Experiences advisor returns as output course experience ratings (cf. Sect. 4.2). With using zero if a student did not take a course, when the Careers-to-Experiences advisor is deployed, courses which many students rate highly tend to be rated more highly than courses for which there is less data or students give lower ratings.

With reference to a student's career ranking, we note that, instead of a career ranking, we could have surveyed a student for career ratings where a student rates each career with a rating. However, using a career ranking as the Experiences-to-Careers advisor's output and course experience ratings as the Careers-to-Experiences advisor's output allows us to have some comparison of using a ranking versus using ratings when we evaluate the Dolphin system.

The students on which we conducted this survey are typically in their final semester (second semester of the final year) in the Computer Science degree program. Thus, the Dolphin system uses data typically from students in their final semester in the degree program to provide students at all stages in the degree program with career advice. Furthermore, using data typically from students in their final semester in the degree program helps to reduce the number of unrated courses in the data we use to train, validate and test the ANNs.

3.2 Sets

We split the set of students we surveyed in Sect. 3.1 randomly into three subsets: a training set, a validation set and a test set. For each of the Experiences-to-Careers advisor and the Careers-to-Experiences advisor, the training set is used to train configurations of the advisor's ANN, the validation set is used to select a configuration of the advisor's ANN and the test set is used to evaluate the performance of the selected ANN configuration.

Importantly, because the validation set is used to select a configuration of the advisor's ANN, we use approximately 25% of the students for the validation set to help ensure that the validation set is representative of the students in our survey. The test set is the same size as the validation set. Thus, the training set is approximately 50% of the students and the validation set and test set are each approximately 25% of the students. As the validation and test sets are the same size, the set of students is split randomly into the three subsets, then one of the sets of approximately 25% of the students is selected as the validation set with the other set of approximately 25% of the students then selected as the test set.

3.3 Implementation

Let n_E be the number of courses. Let n_C be the number of careers. In our current version of the Dolphin system, the number of courses $(n_E) = 26$ and the number of careers $(n_C) = 5$. For each of the students we surveyed in Sect. 3.1, we record the survey that the student submits as a vector consisting of 31 elements. The first 26 elements of this vector are the student's course experience ratings. The final 5 elements of this vector are the student's career ranking.

Let n_V be the number of students in the validation set. Let n_T be the number of students in the test set. We surveyed a set of 110 students for data to train, validate and test the Dolphin system's ANNs (cf. Sect. 3.1). We then split this set of students randomly into a training set, a validation set and a test set as described in Sect. 3.2. Thus, the number of students in the training set = 54, the number of students in the validation set $(n_V) = 28$ and the number of students in the test set $(n_T) = 28$. Correspondingly, the total number of vectors recording the data from the students we surveyed in Sect. 3.1 = 110, the number of vectors in the training set = 54, the number of vectors in the validation set $(n_V) = 28$ and the number of vectors in the test set $(n_T) = 28$.

4 Artificial Neural Networks

4.1 Experiences-to-Careers Advisor ANN

The Experiences-to-Careers advisor takes as input a student's course experience ratings and returns as output a career ranking. As stated in Sect. 3.3, the number of courses $(n_E) = 26$ and the number of careers $(n_C) = 5$. In this section, we describe the design of the Experiences-to-Careers advisor.

Course	COMP1105	COMP1115	COMP1125	COMP1130	COMP2105	COMP2115	COMP2125	...	COMP3930
Course Experience Rating	3	4	4	3	5	0	0	...	5

Fig. 1. An example of the representation of course experience ratings.

Career	Computer Programmer/ Software Engineer	Network Engineer	System Administrator	University Faculty Member	Web Developer
Rank	5	3	1	2	4

Fig. 2. An example of the representation of a career ranking.

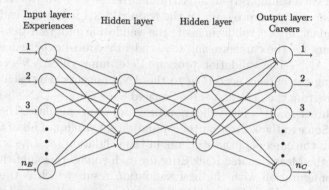

Fig. 3. Experiences-to-Careers advisor's ANN in the Dolphin system.

Figure 1 presents an example of the representation of a student's course experience ratings that is used as input to the Experiences-to-Careers advisor's ANN during training, validation, testing and deployment. In the example in Fig. 1, the student highly enjoyed/enjoys the course COMP2105 and did not take the course COMP2115. Section 3.3 presents the vectors recording the data from the students we surveyed in Sect. 3.1. As presented in Sect. 3.3, the first n_E elements in each of these vectors are the student's course experience ratings.

Figure 2 presents an example of the representation of a career ranking that is used as the Experiences-to-Careers advisor's output. In the example in Fig. 2, Computer Programmer/Software Engineer is ranked highest and System Administrator is ranked lowest. Section 3.3 presents the vectors recording the data from the students we surveyed in Sect. 3.1. As presented in Sect. 3.3, the final n_C elements in each of these vectors are the student's career ranking.

Figure 3 illustrates the ANN that we configure for the Experiences-to-Careers advisor in the Dolphin system. The Experiences-to-Careers advisor's ANN's input layer, Experiences, is a single layer with n_E nodes. For the Experiences-to-Careers advisor, we use an ANN with two hidden layers with each hidden layer having the same number of nodes. The Experiences-to-Careers advisor's ANN's output layer, Careers, is a single layer with n_C nodes. The ANN is a feed-forward artificial neural network using the back-propagation learning algorithm [5] with full connectivity between the layers.

We use configurations with different settings for the number of nodes in each hidden layer, the learning rate, and the number of epochs used during training for the ANN. During training, the learning rate determines the rate at which the ANN's weights are changed and an epoch is an iteration of the ANN through all of the students in the training set.

We use supervised learning. For each configuration of the number of nodes in each hidden layer, the learning rate, and the number of epochs used during training, we train the ANN using the training set with the input as the training set's students' course experience ratings and the output as the corresponding career rankings. For each configuration, after training the ANN with the configuration, we then run a validation program on the trained ANN using the validation set. For each student in the validation set, the validation program determines the ANN's outputs for the careers using the student's course experience ratings as input to the ANN. The validation program determines the ANN's career ranking by ranking the careers according to the ANN outputs. For each career, the validation program then calculates the Squared Rank Error = (ANN's career rank - student's career rank)^2. The validation program then calculates the configuration's Mean Squared Rank Error on the validation set = sum of all of the Squared Rank Errors of the careers of the students in the validation set$/(n_C \times n_V)$. After determining the Mean Squared Rank Error for each configuration of the ANN, we select the configuration with the best validation result which is the configuration with the lowest Mean Squared Rank Error. Thus, we select the configuration whose career rankings most closely match the validation set's students' career rankings when the validation set's students' course experience ratings are used as inputs to the ANN. We denote the ANN with this configuration as ANN_{EC}.

After ANN training and validation, we then run a test program on ANN_{EC} using the test set to evaluate the performance of ANN_{EC}. The test program calculates the Mean Squared Rank Error on the test set = sum of all of the Squared Rank Errors of the careers of the students in the test set$/(n_C \times n_T)$.

When deployed, the Dolphin system's Experiences-to-Careers advisor uses its ANN_{EC} to take as input a student's course experience ratings and return as output ANN_{EC}'s outputs for the careers. The Experiences-to-Careers advisor determines ANN_{EC}'s career ranking by ranking the careers according to ANN_{EC}'s outputs. The Experiences-to-Careers advisor outputs ANN_{EC}'s career ranking.

4.2   Careers-to-Experiences Advisor ANN

The Careers-to-Experiences advisor takes as input a student's career ranking and returns as output course experience ratings. As stated in Sect. 3.3, the number of courses $(n_E) = 26$ and the number of careers $(n_C) = 5$. In this section, we describe the design of the Careers-to-Experiences advisor.

Figure 2 presents an example of the representation of a student's career ranking that is used as the Careers-to-Experiences advisor's ANN's input during training, validation, testing and deployment. Figure 1 presents an example of the representation of course experience ratings that is used as the Careers-to-Experiences advisor's output.

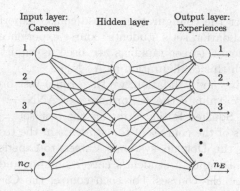

Fig. 4. Careers-to-Experiences advisor's ANN in the Dolphin system.

Figure 4 illustrates the ANN that we configure for the Careers-to-Experiences advisor in the Dolphin system. The Careers-to-Experiences advisor's ANN's input layer, Careers, is a single layer with n_C nodes. For the Careers-to-Experiences advisor, as the number of nodes in the Careers-to-Experiences advisor's ANN's input layer, n_C, is small, we use an ANN with one hidden layer. The Careers-to-Experiences advisor's ANN's output layer, Experiences, is a single layer with n_E nodes. Similar to the Experiences-to-Careers advisor's ANN, the Careers-to-Experiences advisor's ANN is a feed-forward artificial neural network using the back-propagation learning algorithm with full connectivity between the layers.

We use configurations with different settings for the number of nodes in the hidden layer, the learning rate, and the number of epochs used during training for the ANN. As described in Sect. 4.1, during training, the learning rate determines the rate at which the ANN's weights are changed and an epoch is an iteration of the ANN through all of the students in the training set.

We use supervised learning. For each configuration of the number of nodes in the hidden layer, the learning rate, and the number of epochs used during training, we train the ANN using the training set with the input as the training set's students' career rankings and the output as the corresponding course experience ratings. For each configuration, after training the ANN with the configuration, we then run a validation program on the trained ANN using the validation set. For each student in the validation set, the validation program determines the ANN's outputs for the courses using the student's career ranking as input to the ANN. For each course, the validation program calculates the ANN's course experience rating by rounding the ANN's output to the nearest integer. For each course, the validation program then calculates the Squared Rating Error = (ANN's course experience rating - student's course experience rating)^2. The validation program then calculates the configuration's Mean Squared Rating Error on the validation set = sum of all of the Squared Rating Errors of the courses of the students in the validation set$/(n_E \times n_V)$. After determining the Mean Squared Rating Error for each configuration of the ANN, we select the configuration with the best validation result which is the configuration with the lowest Mean Squared Rating

Error. Thus, we select the configuration whose course experience ratings most closely match the validation set's students' course experience ratings when the validation set's students' career rankings are used as inputs to the ANN. We denote the ANN with this configuration as ANN_{CE}.

After ANN training and validation, we then run a test program on ANN_{CE} using the test set to evaluate the performance of ANN_{CE}. The test program calculates the Mean Squared Rating Error on the test set = sum of all of the Squared Rating Errors of the courses of the students in the test set$/(n_E \times n_T)$.

When deployed, the Dolphin system's Careers-to-Experiences advisor uses its ANN_{CE} to take as input a student's career ranking and return as output ANN_{CE}'s outputs for the courses. For each course, the Careers-to-Experiences advisor calculates ANN_{CE}'s course experience rating by rounding ANN_{CE}'s output to the nearest integer. The Careers-to-Experiences advisor outputs ANN_{CE}'s course experience ratings.

4.3 Implementation

We use TensorFlow [7] to implement the ANNs in the Dolphin system. Using TensorFlow, each ANN is implemented using a DNNRegressor deep neural network model. Each DNNRegressor model uses the rectified linear unit (ReLU) activation function and loss reduction as the scalar sum of weighted losses.

We train, validate and test the DNNRegressor models on a computer different from the computer which runs the server with the Dolphin system's user interface. After we train, validate and test each DNNRegressor model on one computer, we then copy the model to a different computer which runs the server with the Dolphin system's user interface to deploy the model. The Dolphin system's user interface uses these models to return career advice to student queries. The data from the students we surveyed in Sect. 3.1 is not stored on, and does not need to be accessed by, the computer which runs the server with the Dolphin system's user interface. The Dolphin system provides career advice without the data from the students we surveyed in Sect. 3.1 being stored on the computer which runs the server with the Dolphin system's user interface.

4.4 Experiences-to-Careers Advisor ANN Results

For ANN training and validation for the Experiences-to-Careers advisor (cf. Sect. 4.1), we use configurations with the following settings for the number of nodes in each hidden layer, the learning rate, and the number of epochs used during training:

- number of nodes in each hidden layer: 2, 3, 4, 5, 10, 15, 20, 25, 30.
- learning rate: 0.01, 0.1, 0.5, 1.0.
- number of epochs used during training: 1, 500, 1000, 1500, 2000, 2500, 3000, 3500, 4000, 4500, 5000.

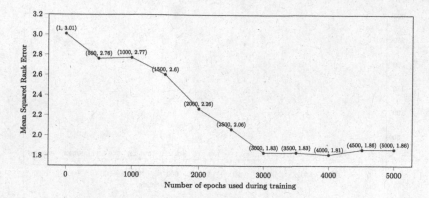

Fig. 5. Mean Squared Rank Error computed by the validation program on the validation set for the ANN configured with the number of nodes in each hidden layer = 3 and the learning rate = 0.1 for the different values of the number of epochs used to train the ANN in the Experiences-to-Careers advisor.

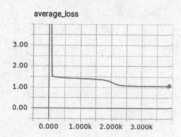

Fig. 6. Average loss during the training of the Experiences-to-Careers advisor's ANN_{EC} on the training set as presented by TensorFlow's TensorBoard.

When the ANN is configured with the number of nodes in each hidden layer = 3, the learning rate = 0.1, and the number of epochs used during training = 4000, the validation program calculates the best (lowest) validation result on the validation set with Mean Squared Rank Error = 1.81. Thus, we use this configuration as ANN_{EC}'s configuration. We note that Fig. 3 presents an image of the ANN with this configuration.

Figure 5 presents the Mean Squared Rank Error computed by the validation program on the validation set for the ANN configured with the number of nodes in each hidden layer = 3 and the learning rate = 0.1 for the different values of the number of epochs used to train the ANN in the Experiences-to-Careers advisor. As shown in Fig. 5, the Mean Squared Rank Error is at its lowest value at the number of epochs used during training = 4000, then the ANN overfits when the larger numbers of epochs are used to train the ANN.

For the configuration we use for ANN_{EC}, Fig. 6 presents the average loss during the training of ANN_{EC} on the training set as presented by TensorFlow's TensorBoard [6]. As shown in Fig. 6, during the training of ANN_{EC} on the training set, the average loss decreases and then remains relatively steady.

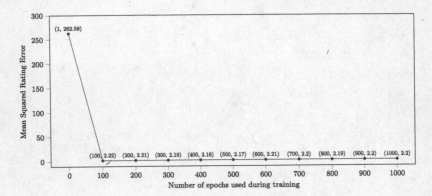

Fig. 7. Mean Squared Rating Error computed by the validation program on the validation set for the ANN configured with the number of nodes in the hidden layer = 4 and the learning rate = 1 for the different values of the number of epochs used to train the ANN in the Careers-to-Experiences advisor.

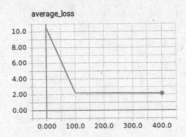

Fig. 8. Average loss during the training of the Careers-to-Experiences advisor's ANN_{CE} on the training set as presented by TensorFlow's TensorBoard.

With reference to ANN testing (cf. Sect. 4.1), when we ran the test program on ANN_{EC} using the test set to evaluate the performance of ANN_{EC}, the result was Mean Squared Rank Error = 2.49. As described in Sect. 4.1, the test set is not used in ANN training and validation.

4.5 Careers-to-Experiences Advisor ANN Results

For ANN training and validation for the Careers-to-Experiences advisor (cf. Sect. 4.2), we use configurations with the following settings for the number of nodes in the hidden layer, the learning rate, and the number of epochs used during training:

- number of nodes in the hidden layer: 2, 3, 4, 5, 10, 15, 20, 25, 30.
- learning rate: 0.01, 0.1, 0.5, 1.0.
- number of epochs used during training: 1, 100, 200, 300, 400, 500, 600, 700, 800, 900, 1000.

When the ANN is configured with the number of nodes in the hidden layer = 4, the learning rate = 1, and the number of epochs used during training = 500, the validation program calculates the best (lowest) validation result on the validation set with Mean Squared Rating Error = 2.17. Thus, we use this configuration as ANN_{CE}'s configuration. We note that Fig. 4 presents an image of the ANN with this configuration.

Figure 7 presents the Mean Squared Rating Error computed by the validation program on the validation set for the ANN configured with the number of nodes in the hidden layer = 4 and the learning rate = 1 for the different values of the number of epochs used to train the ANN in the Careers-to-Experiences advisor. As shown in Fig. 7, the Mean Squared Rating Error is at its lowest value at the number of epochs used during training = 500, then the ANN overfits when the larger numbers of epochs are used to train the ANN.

For the configuration we use for ANN_{CE}, Fig. 8 presents the average loss during the training of ANN_{CE} on the training set as presented by TensorFlow's TensorBoard [6]. As shown in Fig. 8, during the training of ANN_{CE} on the training set, the average loss decreases and then remains relatively steady.

With reference to ANN testing (cf. Sect. 4.2), when we ran the test program on ANN_{CE} using the test set to evaluate the performance of ANN_{CE}, the result was Mean Squared Rating Error = 2.33. As described in Sect. 4.2, the test set is not used in ANN training and validation.

5   User Interface

The Dolphin system's user interface is a web interface. In the current version of the system, a user does not use a user account with the Dolphin system. This allows a user to use the Dolphin system to receive career advice without needing to register or login with a user account. The previous version of the Dolphin system [4] used user accounts which can be protected with passwords, or other methods of access control [1,2], or other methods of authentication such as multi-factor authentication. The Dolphin system processes the course experience ratings and career rankings entered by users in memory and does not store this data on disk. The Dolphin system does not use HTTP cookies. A user's web client and the web server with the Dolphin system's web interface communicate with each other using the Transport Layer Security (TLS) protocol, which provides server authentication and confidentiality and data integrity of traffic between the client and server.

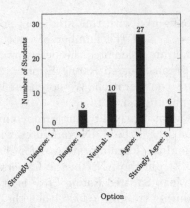

Fig. 9. Bar graph showing, for each option, the number of students who circled the number associated with the option that corresponds to the student's level of agreement with the statement: I am satisfied with the overall career advice I received from the Dolphin system.

	Number of Students	Percentage of Students
a. I prefer the Dolphin system over a human advisor.	5	10%
b. I prefer a human advisor over the Dolphin system.	9	19%
c. I prefer the Dolphin system along with a human advisor.	34	71%
	Total = 48 students	

Fig. 10. Statistics for the results on the Dolphin system versus a human advisor.

6   Student Results

We use an anonymous, paper survey to survey a set of 48 students to gather their feedback on the Dolphin system after they used the Dolphin system to receive career advice. We conducted this survey on students typically in their second and final years in the Computer Science degree program. For this survey, students were recruited via email and from second and third-year Computer Science courses with large enrollments. None of the students on which we conducted this survey are among the students whose data we use to train, validate and test the Dolphin system's ANNs. In this section, we present the results of this survey.

We asked students to circle the number that corresponds to the student's level of agreement with the following statement on system advice: I am satisfied with the overall career advice I received from the Dolphin system. Students were presented with five options for which they were to circle one option. Figure 9 presents a bar graph with each option and, for each option, the number of students who circled the number associated with the option.

We asked students to compare the Dolphin system with a human advisor. Students were presented with three statements from which they were asked to circle one statement. Figure 10 presents a table with each statement and, for each statement, the statistics for the statement. We also asked students to explain the reason for the student's choice. Of the students who circled statement a, common reasons for the students' choice were that the Dolphin system gives satisfactory results, students have received unsatisfactory advice from human advisors and the Dolphin system is convenient. Of the students who circled statement b, common reasons for the students' choice were that a human advisor would be able to give more insight about the advice that the human advisor recommends and a human advisor would be able to listen to and respond to a student's queries. Of the students who circled statement c, common reasons for the students' choice were that the Dolphin system provides a perspective different from that of a human advisor and students prefer to receive advice from both advisors.

The Dolphin system introduces a novel computational system that increases the number of avenues from which a student can receive career advice. In Fig. 9, the majority of students (33 students (69%)) circled numbers 4 or 5 indicating that they were satisfied with the career advice they received from the Dolphin system. In Fig. 10, the majority of students (34 students (71%)) circled statement c indicating that they prefer to use the Dolphin system along with a human advisor. Of the 71% of the students who indicated that they prefer to use the Dolphin system along with a human advisor, a common reason for the students' choice is that the Dolphin system provides a perspective different from that of a human advisor. We believe that the results presented in Figs. 9 and 10 validate our design of the Dolphin system.

7   Conclusion

Future work includes introducing virtual career advisor systems that use techniques different from ANNs to determine career advice. We have presented the design, implementation and evaluation of the Dolphin system.

References

1. Clarke, D.: Design and implementation of a public key-based group collaboration system. Comput. Commun. **34**(3), 407–422 (2011)
2. Clarke, D.: Hybrid certificate closure-chain discovery public key system. Int. J. Comput. Sci. Eng. **9**(4), 312–324 (2014). https://doi.org/10.1504/IJCSE.2014.060714
3. Hamdi, M.S.: MASACAD: a multi-agent approach to information customization for the purpose of academic advising of students. Appl. Soft Comput. **7**(3), 746–771 (2007)
4. John, T., Clarke, D.: Virtual career advisor system with an artificial neural network. In: Benferhat, S., Tabia, K., Ali, M. (eds.) IEA/AIE 2017. LNCS (LNAI), vol. 10350, pp. 227–234. Springer, Cham (2017). https://doi.org/10.1007/978-3-319-60042-0_26
5. Russell, S., Norvig, P.: Artificial Intelligence: A Modern Approach. Pearson, Boston (2020)
6. TensorBoard. https://www.tensorflow.org/tensorboard/
7. TensorFlow. https://www.tensorflow.org/

Correction to: Interactive Behavior Change Model (IBCM 8.0): Theory and Ontology

Brian Cugelman[(⊠)] 🆔 and Agnis Stibe 🆔

Correction to:
Chapter "Interactive Behavior Change Model (IBCM 8.0):
Theory and Ontology" in: M. Younas et al. (Eds.):
Mobile Web and Intelligent Information Systems, LNCS 13977,
https://doi.org/10.1007/978-3-031-39764-6_10

In an older version of this paper, the placement of two sections 3.5 and 3.6 was presented incorrectly. This was corrected.

The updated original version of this chapter can be found at
https://doi.org/10.1007/978-3-031-39764-6_10

Author Index

M. Younas et al. (Eds.): MobiWIS 2023, LNCS 13977, pp. 279–280, 2023.
https://doi.org/10.1007/978-3-031-39764-6

Printed in the United States
by Baker & Taylor Publisher Services